Evangelical Lutheran Synod of East Pennsylvania

History of the Evangelical Lutheran Synod of East Pennsylvania

1842-1892

Evangelical Lutheran Synod of East Pennsylvania

History of the Evangelical Lutheran Synod of East Pennsylvania
1842-1892

ISBN/EAN: 9783337064433

Printed in Europe, USA, Canada, Australia, Japan

Cover: Foto ©ninafisch / pixelio.de

More available books at **www.hansebooks.com**

REV. PROF. CHARLES A. HAY, D. D.
Born February 11, 1821   Died June 26, 1893.

HISTORY

OF THE

Evangelical Lutheran Synod

OF

EAST PENNSYLVANIA,

WITH

BRIEF SKETCHES OF ITS CONGREGATIONS.

PUBLISHED BY THE SYNOD IN COMMEMORATION OF
ITS SEMI-CENTENNIAL ANNIVERSARY.

1842-1892.

PHILADELPHIA:
LUTHERAN PUBLICATION SOCIETY.

Built upon the foundation of the apostles and prophets, Jesus Christ himself being the chief Corner-stone.—*Ephesians* ii. 20.

CONTENTS.

		PAGE
I.	Preface	5
II.	Programme of Semi-Centennial Celebration (including Brief Historical Notes, Order of Exercises, and Jubilee Poem)	7
III.	Historical Sketch of the Synod	15
IV.	Table of Synodical Meetings and Officers	47
V.	Sketches of Congregations	49
VI.	Statistical Table, Showing the Progress of Synod by Decades	323
VII.	Parochial Reports for the Year Ending September, 1892.	324
VIII.	Register of Pastors	338
IX.	Index of Churches and Pastoral Charges	369
X.	Constitution of Synod, as Amended September, 1892	373

ILLUSTRATIONS.

	PAGE
1. Portrait of Prof. Charles A. Hay, D. D. ....Frontispiece	
2. Engraving of the Hill Union Church, near Annville, Pa.	58
3. Engraving of the First Evangelical Lutheran Church and Parsonage, Annville, Pa.	61
4. Engraving of St. Paul's Evangelical Lutheran Church, Allentown, Pa.	79
5. Engraving of Zion's Evangelical Lutheran Church, Manheim, Pa....	111
6. Engraving of St. Matthew's Evangelical Lutheran Church, Philadelphia, Pa.	142
7. Engraving of St. Matthew's Evangelical Lutheran Church, Reading, Pa.	160
8. Engraving of the English Evangelical Lutheran Church and Parsonage, Pottsville, Pa.	172
9. Engraving of St. Peter's Ev. Lutheran Church, Riegelsville, Pa.......	187
10. Engraving of Zion Evangelical Lutheran Church, Lykens, Pa.......	196
11. Engraving of St. John's Evangelical Lutheran Church, Lancaster, Pa.	206
12. Engraving of Seventh Street Evangelical Lutheran Church, Lebanon, Pa.	208
13. Engraving of St. James' Evangelical Lutheran Church and Parsonage, Ashland, Pa.	216
14. Engraving of St. Matthew's Evangelical Lutheran Church and Parsonage, Schuylkill Haven, Pa.	221
15. Engraving of Messiah Evangelical Lutheran Church, Philadelphia, Pa.	239
16. Engraving of St. Paul's Evangelical Lutheran Church, Easton, Pa...	250
17. Engraving of Calvary Evangelical Lutheran Church, West Philadelphia, Pa.	259
18. Engraving of St. Stephen's Evangelical Lutheran Church, Lancaster, Pa.	261
19. Engraving of St. Peter's Evangelical Lutheran Church, Easton, Pa...	263
20. Engraving of St. John's Evangelical Lutheran Church, Steelton, Pa...	267
21. Engraving of Bethany Ev. Lutheran Church, Philadelphia, Pa......	280
22. Engraving of Bethlehem Evangelical Lutheran Church, Harrisburg, Pa.	285
23. Engraving of Immanuel Evangelical Lutheran Church, Norwood, Pa.	288
24. Engraving of St. Matthew's Ev. Lutheran Chapel, Allentown, Pa....	292
25. Engraving of Trinity Evangelical Lutheran Church, Coatesville, Pa. .	300
26. Engraving of Ebenezer Evangelical Lutheran Church, Berbice, British Guiana, S. A.	313

(4)

PREFACE.

In addition to the Historical Address delivered at the celebration of the semi-centennial anniversary of the Synod, it has been thought best, in the exercise of the liberty given the committee by Synod, to publish a brief sketch of every congregation now in our connection, and also a few general tables illustrating the progress and present condition of the Synod, concluding with the amended form of constitution and by-laws, as adopted at the late convention in Lancaster.

The separate sketches, prepared by the respective pastors or under their direction, display great diversity in compass and style. The incompleteness of old records is lamented by many of the writers, and their entire loss by others. The committee, having free access to the invaluable treasures of the Lutheran Historical Society at Gettysburg, Pa., has endeavored, by the use of these and by direct correspondence, to supply as far as possible the more essential details inaccessible to local authorities. The final proof of the sketches, thus amended, has in every case been submitted to the accredited authors for approval.

The record of events closes with the completion of the various manuscripts within the period intervening between the session of Synod in September and the close of the year 1892. The present rapid development of our churches is constantly furnishing new items of interest, and many such have been offered to the committee as this work has been passing through the press; but justice to all has compelled the rigid exclusion of additional material. It is earnestly hoped that pastors and church councils are preserving full and accurate accounts of these events for the future historian.

The illustrations embodied are such as were furnished by the respective congregations in response to request of the committee, as published in the church papers and included in circular letter addressed to each pastor. It is matter for regret that not all our pastorates have availed themselves of the opportunity thus afforded.

The Clerical Register was formed by a careful collation of the manuscripts presented, and embodies also in condensed form the results of further investigation and correspondence. It is believed that it will be found generally accurate.

Many pastors, in forwarding their manuscripts, have taken occasion to express their gratitude to the Synod for instituting the work of investigation. It appears to have awakened a deeper interest in the local churches, and stimulated pastors and people to greater effort to maintain and improve the precious heritage received from the fathers. May the publication of our little volume tend to cultivate this spirit, and thus promote the prosperity of Zion.

The death of the Synodical Historian having occurred just as our work was passing through the press, it has been thought fitting to present to the reader, on the second page, a life-like portraiture of the familiar countenance. No one felt a keener interest in the welfare of our Synod than did Dr. Hay, and his sudden departure is most widely deplored. The memory of his gentle spirit, his unfailing enthusiasm and his simple faith will long linger as an inspiration, and his influence will still be felt at our annual gatherings.

HENRY S. BONER,
CHAS. E. HAY,
M. COOVER,
Committee.

1842. 1892.

JUBILEE CELEBRATION

OF THE

Evangelical Lutheran Synod

OF

EAST PENNSYLVANIA,

HELD IN

ST. JOHN'S CHURCH,

(REV B. F. ALLEMAN, D. D., PASTOR.)

LANCASTER, PA.,

THURSDAY EVENING, SEPTEMBER 22, 1892.

LUTHERAN PUBLICATION HOUSE PRINT.

The
Evangelical
Lutheran Synod of
East Pennsylvania is one of
the twenty-six District Synods now
constituting the General Synod. Its congregations are found in 13 counties in the southeastern
part of the State; and in these counties there exist also numerous
congregations connected with the Synod of Pennsylvania. In all, there
are 8 Synods within the bounds of this State, besides scattered congregations
belonging to other Synods. The Minutes of 1891 report, for the Synod
of East Pennsylvania, 85 Ministers, 117 Congregations, 14
Preaching Stations, and 18,766 Communing Members.
The entire Lutheran Church in this country contains now, approximately, 5,200 Ministers, 9,000 Congregations,
and 1,200,000 Com-
muning Mem-
bers.

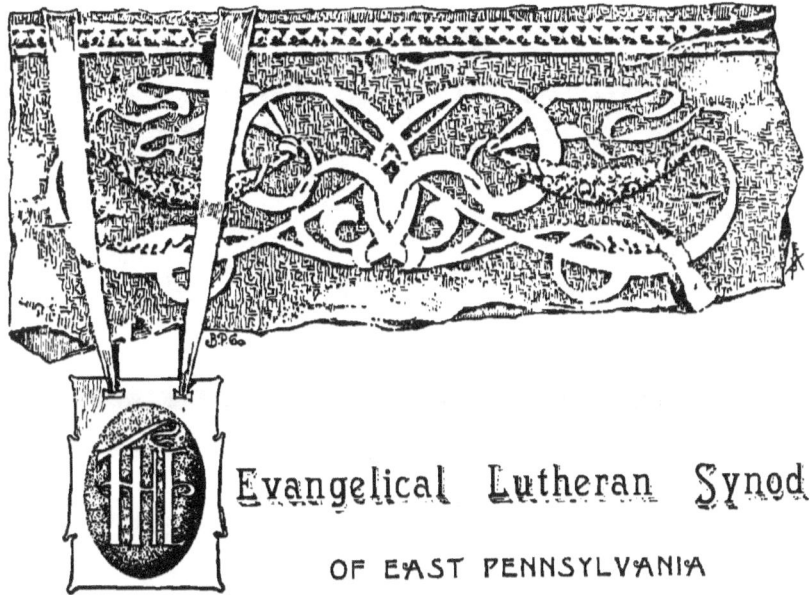

Evangelical Lutheran Synod
OF EAST PENNSYLVANIA

was formally organized, and the name adopted, in the lecture-room of Trinity Church, Lancaster, May 3d, 1842.

There were present on that day, and participating in the movement, nine ministers and two laymen, who had retired for the purpose from the Synod of Pennsylvania, then in session at that Church.

The first annual meeting was held in St. Peter's Church, Pikeland, Chester County—where the President, Rev. Frederick Ruthrauff, was the pastor—beginning October 15th, 1842, within a few days of fifty years ago. At that session the Constitution was framed.

In the meantime, a quarter of a century ago, the organizing of the Susquehanna Synod cut off a large part of this Synod's territory. That Synod now presents a statistical showing, in the number of ministers, etc., equal to half that of this body.

The places and dates of all the annual meetings, together with the names of officers, are printed from year to year, in tabular form, in the Synodical Minutes.

PRESIDING OFFICER.   Rev. M. SHEELEIGH, D.D.

ORGAN VOLUNTARY—ANTHEM: "Before Jehovah's Awful Throne."
Dr. Madan.

INVOCATION,   :   By Rev. J. H. MENGES.

HYMN: No. 33 in Book of Worship—"Thee We Adore, Eternal Lord."

READING OF SCRIPTURE: Psalm xlvi., and 1 Corinthians, iii.
By the President of the Synod.

PRAYER,   :   By Rev. D. M. Gilbert, D. D.

ANTHEM: "How Beautiful Upon the Mountains."   *L. O. Emerson.*

HISTORICAL ADDRESS,   By Rev. Prof. C. A. HAY, D. D.

ANTHEM: Thanksgiving,   *Novello.*

HISTORICAL REMINISCENCES,   :   By Rev. W. M. BAUM, D. D.,
    Rev. L. E. ALBERT, D. D., Rev. E. S. HENRY.

FIVE-MINUTE VOLUNTARY ADDRESSES.

ANTHEM: "I Will Sing of the Mercies of the Lord."   *A. J. Abbey.*

PRAYER,   :   :   By Rev. S. A. HOLMAN, D. D.

DOXOLOGY: "Praise God, from Whom All Blessings Flow."

BENEDICTION,   :   Rev. W. L. HEISLER.

POEM:
SYNODICAL JUBILEE.

BY REV. MATTHIAS SHEELEIGH, D. D.

JOHN IV. 38.—"Other men labored, and ye are entered into their labors."—*The Saviour.*
I CORINTHIANS iii. 10.—"I have laid the foundation, and another buildeth thereon. But let every man take heed how he buildeth thereupon."—*St. Paul.*

As roll the planets in their spheres,
We note the signs of circling years,
That, measured out, 'neath God's decree,
Extend from birth to Jubilee.

Yet not in skyey space alone,
But here as well, in earthly zone,
Within His Church's light and grace,
The doings of the Lord we trace.

At length, full fifty years have sped
Since hopefully were fathers led,
In wisdom sought above their own,
To lay in faith a corner-stone.

To-day, as from this holy place
Is viewed our Synod's goodly base,
'Tis ours, as in the years agone,
To heed how we should build thereon.

Here long may their successors build,
With faith and zeal from heaven filled,
While fathers in their glory bend,
Watching this temple fair extend!

As now in praise we bow us down
For mercies that our being crown,
Honored those early men, and true,
Who "builded better than they knew."

Could those for Christ who labored here
Ring out with ours their praises clear,
To-day how would they tell abroad
Of work performed for man and God!

Like some cathedral early planned,
A joy and wonder through the land,
And on whose height shall future eyes
With shoutings hail the capstone rise,—

So, on our Synod, good and blest,
Long may God's benediction rest,
While gladdened eyes from many a home
View rising wall and rounding dome.

When all our work on earth is o'er,
With faithful fathers, gone before,
"Not unto us," may we exclaim,
"But glory to Thy holy Name!"

"Hitherto hath the Lord helped us."—1 Samuel vii. 12.
"The Lord doth build up Jerusalem."—Psalm cxlvii. 2.

HISTORICAL SKETCH.

BY REV. PROF. CHARLES A. HAY, D. D.

At the meeting of the East Pennsylvania Synod held in 1891 at Middletown, Pa., the President, Rev. W. H. Dunbar, in his official report, called attention to the fact that we were on the eve of the semi-centennial year of our existence as a Synod, and suggested that "it might be a matter of wisdom, as well as of interest, to take some steps looking to a permanent record of events in the history of our Synod and its congregations." He also suggested to Synod "the propriety of the appointment of a Synodical Historian for this purpose."

The Synod subsequently approved of this suggestion and resolved to celebrate the semi-centennial anniversary at the next meeting of Synod and to appoint such a Historian, "who shall prepare a history of the Synod, and so far as possible brief histories of its congregations, the history of Synod to be read at the semi-centennial anniversary, and all this historical matter to be afterwards published and then preserved in the archives of Synod."

Having been appointed by the Synod as its Historian, I have carefully examined the published minutes of its proceedings, and other accessible publications throwing light upon its history, and herewith present a brief sketch of its origin and of some of the features of its subsequent development and efficiency.

At the meeting of the Pennsylvania Ministerium held in Lancaster, May 22 to 26, 1842, a memorial was presented by a number of ministers and laymen, members of the Synod, who had on the day before held a meeting and discussed the propriety "of forming a new Synod in the Eastern district of Pennsylvania." This memorial reads as follows:

"*To the Reverend Synod of Pennsylvania, &c.*,

DEAR BRETHREN:—We, the undersigned, members of Pennsylvania Synod, and brethren within its bounds, respectfully present the following memorial:

1. We earnestly ask you forthwith to take measures for the amicable division of the Pennsylvania Synod. Our reasons for this are the following:

(*a*) Harmony of views and feelings is essential to the success of all associations, but especially of all Christian associations, in which that spirit of love which is the very life of religion must necessarily suffer if this be wanting. But this harmony has long been wanting among us, and the occurrences of every year seem to make the prospect of its restoration still worse. We believe that a separation of the conflicting elements among us would, by preventing collision, remove the evil. One cause of this may have been the next reason which we would urge as a ground of division, viz.:

(*b*) The largeness of our present synodical body. It is natural that a diversity of sentiment should prevail where so many men, differently educated, are brought into so close connection with each other. In addition to this, many of our smaller pastoral districts, and all of our country congregations, are deprived of the pleasure and profit of synodical meetings, by their being unable to entertain so many members as our Synod contains.

(*c*) Difference of language is another difficulty that now clogs our synodical proceedings. Many of our churches are unable to participate in our meetings, from their ignorance of the language in which our deliberations are conducted. Synod having declared its determination to abide by the use of one language, there seems an obvious call for the organization of a body that will admit the indiscriminate use of the German and English.

(*d*) A difference of views in regard to the General Synod and its institutions is another cause of difficulty for which this would be a remedy.

(e) The new or revised constitution threatens to exclude a number of us, and to prevent others from entering the Synod, who can never pledge ourselves to some of its principles by subscribing it in the manner which it requires.

It is not necessary that we should go into detailed argument upon the various points to which we object, but we may simply state, that we are unwilling to subscribe any such system of church government. We cannot bind ourselves to the constant use of any liturgy, and especially of one which we have never seen, or had sufficient opportunity to examine; and, finally, we cannot submit to the distinctions made between our American and Foreign ministers and institutions, in favor of the latter.

2. We ask that this division be made upon the principles of Christian freedom, and that each minister and church of the Pennsylvania Synod be left at perfect liberty to select the synodical body with which they will associate themselves.

3. Whilst we claim a fair proportion of all the funds and legacies belonging to Synod, we desire also to co-operate in the Foreign Mission established by Synod.

4. We desire to establish the most fraternal relations, and maintain mutual good will between the two bodies thus created. And we pray that the blessing of the Great Head of the Church may rest upon us all, and prosper all our plans for the advancement of his cause and glory.

All which is respectfully submitted, with a request for immediate action, by your brethren in Christ.

F. RUTHRAUFF,
J. RUTHRAUFF,
W. M. REYNOLDS,
S. D. FINCKEL,
G. HEILIG,
F. R. ANSPACH,
T. STORK,
D. KOHLER,
J. WILLOX,
J. VOGELBACH,
J. L. FREDERICK,
G. HARTMAN,
— HADDON.

The minutes of that meeting of the Pennsylvania Synod state that "The committee on the memorial reported that it was not expedient to divide the Synod, and that the memorialists be requested to consider more maturely the subject of separation and be entreated to remain in connection with the Pennsylvania Synod. After an animated discussion of this report, in which many of the brethren participated, the Synod finally resolved that we can in no wise consent to a division of this body; but, should any brethren consider it desirable to separate from us, an honorable dismission shall be given them as individuals, if they so request."

From the published minutes of the East Pennsylvania Synod we learn that "The memorialists, being unsuccessful in their efforts to secure an amicable division of the Synod, then withdrew to the Lutheran lecture-room. The following brethren were present: Rev. Messrs. F. Ruthrauff, J. Ruthrauff, W. M. Reynolds, G. Heilig, F. R. Anspach, J. Willox, T. Stork, J. Vogelbach, W. Laitzle and the lay delegates, J. L. Frederick and G. Hartman. Rev. F. Ruthrauff was appointed Chairman and T. Stork Secretary. Opened with prayer by the Chairman. On motion

Resolved, That we organize ourselves into a Synod, to be called *The Evangelical Lutheran Synod of East Pennsylvania;* and adopt for the present the constitution of the General Synod, with such alterations as may from time to time be necessary."

Another meeting was held on the following day, when "the members spent some time in familiar colloquy upon the subject of new measures. After a free and full interchange of sentiment, in which there seemed to be essential unanimity, it was deemed advisable that public expression should be given to the views entertained by this Synod, in order to define our position on a subject so liable to misconstruction. It was, therefore, on motion of T. Stork,

Resolved, That, whilst we disapprove of all disorderly and fanatical proceedings in religious worship, and in protracted efforts for the salvation of souls, we cordially commend the most decisive and energetic measures for the conversion of sinners and edification of the Church, adhering strictly to the admonition of the apostle, that 'all things be done decently and in order.'"

The first regular meeting of the Synod was held in St. Peter's church, Chester county, where it assembled on the 15th of September, 1842. At this meeting the Synod numbered twelve pastors, with twenty-four congregations; it resolved to connect itself with the General Synod; adopted the Liturgy then published by the Pennsylvania Synod; approved a proposed device for a synodical seal, viz., an eye fixed upon an open Bible, surrounded by the words, "*The Bible our Creed—God our Judge*," and it appointed a delegate to represent it at the next meeting of the Pennsylvania Synod.

The second annual meeting was held in St. Matthew's church, Philadelphia, October 21, 1843, when, at the calling of the roll, every member was present, numbering eighteen ministers after admitting Rev. Messrs. J. P. Schindel, G. Diehl, D. F. Finckel, Daniel Miller, John McCron and Eli Swartz. Fourteen lay delegates were present. Delegates were received from several synods connected with the General Synod, viz., Hartwick, Maryland and West Pennsylvania.

Among the topics of special interest to a student of the history of our Synod is, first of all, *its Relation to the German Ministerium of Pennsylvania and Adjacent States and Territories, now commonly known as the Pennsylvania Synod*. This Synod originated, as has been already shown, in the secession from the Pennsylvania Synod by a few of the regular members of that body, for reasons assigned in the memorial already cited, and it gave practical proof of its desire to maintain friendly relations with the Pennsylvania Synod by sending to it in 1843 as an accredited delegate one of its most active members, the Rev. Theophilus Stork. At the next meeting of this Synod Rev. Stork reported as follows: "In obedience to appointment I attended the last meeting of the Pennsylvania Synod, held in St. Paul's church, Philadelphia, as the delegate of this body. The appointment of a delegate at this time was not simply a matter of ecclesiastical courtesy, but was designed, if possible, to conciliate the adverse elements of the two Synods, and establish fraternal relations. We felt that, both bodies being professedly Lutheran, and occupying a field embracing essentially the same geographical limits, it was exceedingly desirable that we should maintain towards each other the most amicable relations, believing that, notwithstanding our differences of opinion on some points, we might still as Christians, under the harmonizing influence of love, live together as brethren, "as fellow-citizens with the saints, and of the household of God."

"With such views and feelings I was little prepared even to apprehend the actual result of my mission."

"The first session of Synod was opened on Monday morning, the 12th of June. When the delegates from other Synods were called upon to present their credentials, I arose and stated that I had been appointed a delegate from the East Pennsylvania Synod to the Pennsylvania Synod, and laid a certificate from the President attesting my commission, together with the printed minutes, upon the table. Dr. Miller, from Reading, immediately arose, and, after some preliminary remarks explanatory of the ground he was about to assume, offered the following resolution, which, after some discussion, was adopted:

"'*Resolved*, That we cannot recognize brother Stork as a delegate, nor that body as a Synod, until it formally recall by a resolution the accusations made against this body.'

"I was so taken by surprise that, in the excitement of the

moment, I did not realize the position in which we were placed, and said nothing. After returning home and reflecting on the transactions of the morning, I felt dissatisfied under a conviction that I had not discharged my duty as the representative of the East Pennsylvania Synod. I, therefore, returned in the afternoon session, and obtained permission to address the Synod. I assured them that we desired to maintain the most friendly relations and correspondence with them. And I further assured them that, if we had injured them by unjust charges, we were ready to make any reasonable concession, and to recant every charge not founded in fact; and finally, I begged them to specify the charges by which they felt themselves so aggrieved as to exclude us from their fraternal regard. I asked this, that the Church might understand the real position of the two Synods, and that our body might be prepared for intelligent action at its next session.

"After an animated discussion they passed the following resolution in answer to my inquiry:

"'*Resolved*, That the accusations of the Synod of East Pennsylvania are contained in *that circular*, and in all their after proceedings harmonizing therewith.' * * * etc."

The Synod of East Pennsylvania expressed its entire satisfaction with the course pursued by its delegate, and, on motion of Prof. Reynolds, it was

"*Resolved*, That we have heard with regret our delegate's statement of the failure of his mission to the Pennsylvania Synod; and that we are still desirous of establishing friendly relations with that body. In reply to the resolutions passed by them relative to our body, we can merely say, that they suggest no means of removing the difficulties existing between us, as we are not aware that we have, in any of our proceedings, said or sanctioned anything that can be considered unchristian or unjust to the Pennsylvania Synod. As soon, however, as aught that might be so construed is pointed out to us, we shall be ready to recall the offensive word or act, whichever it may be, so far as in our power; or to give such explanations as comport with truth and propriety. Meanwhile any further overtures for friendly correspondence will naturally come from the Pennsylvania Synod—though in the meantime we shall endeavor to 'keep the unity of the Spirit in the bond of peace.'"

For several years after this the proceedings of the Synod of East Pennsylvania were not printed in pamphlet form, and the official protocol of the meetings in 1844, '45 and '46, we regret to say, cannot now be found: but from an abstract of the minutes of 1845 (when the Synod met in Lebanon), published by the Secretary in the *Lutheran Observer*, we learn that in that year Rev. Mr. Ernst, of the Pennsylvania Synod, was received as an advisory member by our Synod, in proof of the friendly feeling on the part of this Synod towards the Pennsylvania Ministerium.

In *1847*, also, at the session in Germantown, Rev. S. K. Probst, of the Pennsylvania Synod, was introduced and received as an advisory member.

In *1849*, when at Reading, the East Pennsylvania Synod

"*Resolved*, That we sincerely rejoice in the approximation to a more perfect union of the Church, manifested in the action of the Pennsylvania Synod relative to a professorship in our Theological Seminary at Gettysburg; and that we most cordially approve of the action of the *Board of Directors* in the election of Rev. C. R. Demme, D. D., in accordance with the desire of the *Pennsylvania Synod*, and that we should be highly gratified with his acceptance of the same."

At the session of the East Pennsylvania Synod in *1850*, at Easton, four members of the Pennsylvania Synod (C. W. Schaeffer, Jeremiah Schindel, J. W. Richards and C. A. Hay), anxious to bring about, if possible, a better state of feeling between the two bodies, presented a memorial on that subject, which was referred to a large committee, who reported *unanimously* as follows:

"The committee to whom was referred a memorial from four

members of the Synod of Pennsylvania, on the subject of the estrangement between that body and ourselves, beg leave to report :

"'That they examined the various documents put into their hands bearing on this subject. Your committee rejoice at the prospect of establishing more friendly relations with the Synod of Pennsylvania; and whereas, those four brethren in their memorial inform us that the Synod of Pennsylvania holds this body responsible for a certain anonymous *circular*, containing charges against the Synod of Pennsylvania, so understood by that body, viz.: with a design on the part of said Synod to introduce into their connection, by a constitutional partiality, ministers from Germany who are rationalistic, unevangelical or infidel in their sentiments, and immoral in their conduct, and to do injustice to brethren born and educated in this country; and whereas, we desire to do justice to ourselves and to the Synod of Pennsylvania, therefore:

"*Resolved*, That we deeply regret the estrangement that has so long separated us from the brethren of the Synod of Pennsylvania.

"*Resolved*, That we earnestly desire a more fraternal connection with that body, and would rejoice to open a correspondence with them.

"*Resolved*, That we never did hold ourselves responsible for the '*circular*' to which there is reference in a resolution of the Pennsylvania Synod held in Philadelphia in 1843, and in the memorial of those four members addressed to us; and we do not now acknowledge that document as an expression of our sentiments, but, on the contrary, most heartily disavow the offensive sentiments of the 'Circular' pointed out in the memorial of the four brethren, and regret any action that may have arisen from misconception."

"Respectfully submitted, G. Diehl,
F. Ruthrauff,
J. McCron,
R. Weiser,
J. A. Brown,
J. Winecoff,
T. Stork,
A. Wieting."

After an animated discussion, the report was unanimously

adopted. The Synod thereupon appointed the *Rev. Messrs. T. Stork, F. Ruthrauff and G. Diehl* to meet the Synod of Pennsylvania at its next convention, in Allentown, to establish friendly relations and to open a correspondence with that body. At that meeting of the Pennsylvania Synod that committee was most kindly received, and the Pennsylvania Synod unanimously adopted the following resolutions:

"1. That this Synod cordially responds to the sentiments on the subject of Christian fellowship expressed by the brethren of the East Pennsylvania Synod.

"2. That we fraternally recognize them as a Synod of the Evangelical Lutheran Church, and cordially receive their representatives in our midst.

"3. That Synod, from this time forth, appoint a delegate to represent this body in the Synod of East Pennsylvania upon the same terms as we are represented in the sister Synods generally."

The *East Pennsylvania Synod*, when the above-named committee (Stork, Ruthrauff and Diehl) had reported at Danville in 1851,

"*Resolved*, That we have heard, with the greatest pleasure, from the Committee appointed by Synod to represent this body before the *Pennsylvania Synod*, of their cordial reception and successful mission; and that we most fondly hope, earnestly desire and fervently pray that the fraternal relations thus established may be perpetuated."

"At this meeting Rev. W. J. Eyer appeared as the delegate from the Synod of Pennsylvania, with assurances of the fraternal feelings and good wishes of the body he had the honor to represent. He met with a hearty welcome and was invited to take his seat among us."

At the meeting of the East Pennsylvania Synod in 1852 the committee entrusted with the minutes of the Pennsylvania Synod of the same year report as follows:

"Your Committee rejoice that this Synod have passed a series of resolutions indicative of a speedy re-union of that body with the General Synod. To these resolutions we are led, say they, through the conviction that *we all agree in the essential, fundamental doctrines of our beloved Mother Church*, and that we are therefore prepared for an outward union, from which we can expect a rich blessing."

Having thus accomplished the long-desired reconciliation between these Synods, occupying the territory between the Delaware and Susquehanna rivers, those members of the old Pennsylvania Synod who were yearning for its return to the General Synod now bent their energies in this direction, and their efforts were crowned with success in the spring of 1853, when, at its meeting of that year in Reading, it determined to re-unite with the General Synod, which it had helped to organize in 1820, and from which it had been so long separated.

This having now been accomplished, and these two Synods being now harmoniously associated in the same general body, there seemed to be no good reason why they should not actually coalesce, instead of separately spreading over this mesopotamian territory, and, after thus combining all their parishes, peaceably divide the territory between them. Accordingly, a proposition of that kind was made to the Synod of *East Pennsylvania*, at the meeting in 1853, by a member of the Pennsylvania Synod, which was placed in the hands of a committee, whose report, after considerable discussion, and after the offering of various amendments, which were rejected, was adopted in its original form as follows :

"The committee on Document 13 would respectfully report, that said document is a communication from Rev. Charles Hay, suggesting to this Synod the desirableness of taking some initiatory steps towards securing a geographical division of the two Synods (Pennsylvania Synod and East Pennsylvania Synod) occupying principally the same ground. In reference to this paper, your Committee would say :

"1. That they are not able to understand the geographical

chart of Brother Hay, which he has submitted to our inspection, and consequently they are not prepared to pronounce upon its practicability.

"2. Your Committee are of opinion, without any reference to the specific form of division suggested in this paper, that such a geographical division is wholly unfeasible.

"3. Besides, we can see no valid reason for such a division. We should rather seek a still greater assimilation of spirit, 'endeavoring to keep the unity of the Spirit in the bond of peace,' realizing 'how good and how pleasant it is for brethren to dwell together in unity.'"

"4. As this communication is not official, we do not know that it demands any further attention.

T. STORK,
J. WINECOFF,
D. STECK."

Notwithstanding this rebuff, the agitation of this subject in both these Synods was not allowed to subside, but both were prevailed upon to appoint committees instructed to give the matter a careful investigation.

These committees met in Philadelphia (at Lindsay & Blakiston's Book Store), in 1855, agreeing heartily to endorse the proposed plan of fusion and subsequent geographical division. The Chairman of the joint committee, Rev. Benjamin Keller, accordingly presented our report to the Pennsylvania Synod in Lancaster in 1856, recommending a special meeting of the East Pennsylvania Synod in Philadelphia in 1857, when the Pennsylvania Synod should be in session there, and the holding of a joint meeting of both Synods at that time in order to discuss the question of union and subsequent division into two or three Synods. To the surprise and mortification of many who were present (members of other Synods connected with the General Synod), decided opposition to this report was made by some of the most influential members of the Synod of Pennsylvania. Dr. Demme remarked: "Ich bin dagegen: der Geist in der Ost-Pennsylvanischen Synode ist ein anderer!" Dr. Mann remarked: "Ich bin auch dagegen; der Apfel ist noch nicht reif; sonst fällt er von selbst vom Baume." Mr. Yeager, of Hamburg, Pa., vehemently asserted: "Ich bin auch dagegen; dann wird alles Englisch!" Then Dr. C. W. Schaeffer expressed his regret that such a spirit was manifested, but he said it was evident that it would be unwise to press the matter now, as the Synod was not yet prepared to take definite action in regard to it. It was on his motion that the Synod resolved: "That we are not yet prepared to take definite action in this matter."

The reports of the Presidents of both these Synods about this time called attention to unpleasant inter-synodical disagreements and interferences on the part of the pastors and congregations, and a joint committeee was appointed by both the Synods " to draft such rules in reference to congregational action as may secure fraternal love and harmony." In the minutes of the East Pennsylvania Synod of 1857, we read that "The two committees met and, after a very full and friendly interchange of opinions, concluded that no such rules as would effectually remedy existing evils could be drafted, and that some degree of confusion, with occasional unpleasant influences or collisions, is unavoidable, so long as the two Synods continue to occupy in common the same ground." Whereupon the committee submitted the following proposition:

"*Resolved*, That a committee of — ministers and laymen be appointed by this Synod, to confer with a like one from the Synod of Pennsylvania, on the union of the two Synods, and such a geographical division of the field as may secure the object aimed at and the best interests of the Church."

"After much discussion, a motion was made to amend the resolution by *deferring action in the matter till next year*, which amendment was adopted by the following vote: Yeas, 26; nays, 14."

At a subsequent stage of the proceedings it was

"*Resolved*, That in our action upon the above report we have by no means desired to convey to our brethren of the Synod of Pennsylvania, the impression that we disapprove of the end contemplated in the report, but simply to avoid the appearance of importunately pressing the matter upon their attention; and we hereby pledge ourselves cordially to respond to any intimation on their part of a readiness to enter into preliminary arrangements for effecting so desirable a result. This was adopted by a *unanimous* vote."

In our synodical minutes of 1858 we find a committee reporting upon the minutes of the Pennsylvania Synod of the same year as follows:

"In these minutes cognizance is taken of the unfortunate interferences which, owing in part to the fact that both Synods occupy substantially the same territory, have too often occurred between some of the members of both bodies. This is an evil of long and loud complaint on both sides, and one which, with the best intentions and the most generous as well as most vigorous efforts, has not been entirely removed.

"The action of the *Pennsylvania Synod* on this subject is very decided, not only rebuking any of its members guilty of violating its 'Ministerial Ordnung' in this particular, but declaring also to strike their names from their ministerial roll. This *action*, however, is made dependent on a full concurrence of like action by our Synod.

"Your Committee is not prepared, *ex animo et ex corde*, to recommend to this Synod the unqualified endorsement of this principle. The main idea is certainly commendable, and meets our hearty approval, and should be sought by every member of this body religiously to be carried out. Yet there are conceivable circumstances, the like of which have not unfrequently occurred in the past history of this Synod, where, prompted by love of the Church, as well as a regard for the welfare and retention of her membership, there may be more virtue in the breach than in the observance of this principle. It is particularly charged upon our delegate to the *Synod of Pennsylvania* to explain to them more fully our understanding of this action. [Signed, A. C. Wedekind, John R. Willox and Joseph Stulb.]"

The report was amended and adopted as above.

In the minutes of our Synod of 1859 we find the report of the *Joint Committee of Conference on Inter-Synodical Relations,* as follows :

"*Resolved,* 1. As a general rule, we adopt the principle of non-intervention in the charges belonging to our respective Synods.

"2. In cases of difficulty and dissatisfaction arising in any charge, it will be the duty of said charge, or part of a charge, first to bring the difficulty, cause of complaint, etc., before the Conference or Synod to which it belongs, and if the difficulty be not adjusted to the satisfaction of those complaining, and it have its origin in consequence of inter-synodical relations, that then the President of each of the Synods appoint a committee of three to confer together in reference to the matter, and they be instructed to pursue such a course in its adjustment as they conscientiously believe will promote the best interests of the Church.

"3. That similar committees shall be appointed in cases where charges are to be formed from congregations belonging to both Synods.

"4. That the action of these joint committees be submitted to each Synod for concurrence and confirmation. [Signed, S. K. Probst, C. J. Ehrehart, G. J. Martz, E. S. Henry and E. W. Hutter.]"

Item 1 was adopted.

Items 2, 3 and 4 were stricken out, and the following was passed :

"*Resolved,* That under existing circumstances, we believe it to be impossible to devise any system of rules that will be adequate to meet the exceptional cases referred to in the above report."

In 1861 the committee of the East Pennsylvania Synod on the minutes of the Pennsylvania Synod calls attention to "the very kind and Christian spirit of the paragraph having reference to the efforts of this Synod (*i. e.* the Synod of Pennsylvania), in healing the differences between the two bodies."

In 1862 the President of the East Pennsylvania Synod, Rev. Dr. Seiss (who subsequently joined the Pennsylvania Synod), stated in his official report: "It was the remark of your retiring President [C. A. Hay] last year, that the principal part of his official correspondence had been of an unpleasant character, originating in the rivalry of contending factions in some of our churches, and in some of those in the Synod of Pennsylvania. I regret equally with him that my own experience in this respect corresponds, to a large extent, to his, and from the same causes." After describing some of these inter-synodical difficulties, he adds: "From this the Synod will learn how unfortunate the relations are between these two bodies. And the ever-recurring annoyances of this kind which the Synod and its presiding officers are compelled to endure from year to year, to say nothing of the wrongs and mischiefs involved, ought by this time to satisfy all that the period has come when decisive measures should be taken to bring them to an end. The Synod of Pennsylvania is evidently willing and anxious to come to some understanding on the subject, and to adopt any reasonable and feasible arrangements for this purpose to which we may agree, having herself several times moved in the matter, and also recently made certain acknowledgments and retractions which ought to go far to persuade us to meet them in a fraternal and conciliatory spirit." He proposed " the creation of a Board or Committee of Reference or Arbitration, with full powers, etc. * * and that every brother found guilty of improper interference, who will not promptly submit to the decision of this Committee or Board, be at once suspended from exercising the functions of his ministry."

The committee to whom this report was referred (of which the Rev. Dr. Greenwald was Chairman), approved of the plan recommended by the President, but adds: "We are persuaded, however, that *there is a better way, to which the Synods must come at last.* We therefore propose, and earnestly recommend, that the two Synods existing on the same territory should unite, and then divide the territory into two or more Synods, having distinct geographical boundaries." Dr. Greenwald had been our delegate to the Pennsylvania Synod that year, and in his report said, among other things: "The existence of two Synods on the same territory is contrary to the rule of the General Synod. * * The existence of the East Pennsylvania Synod *has been a blessing to the Church in eastern Pennsylvania,* and the Head of the Church has given it great prosperity. Many of the large and influential English churches in our cities and large towns, and elsewhere, would perhaps not exist if the East Pennsylvania Synod had not been organized; and perhaps no other form was possible at the time than that which it has. Still it is true, that before its organization there was but one Synod on the territory, and that there are now two is owing to its subsequent organization. Our Synod ought to make the first advance toward a change. As the irregular synodical relations originated with us, we ought to inaugurate measures that may bring order out of the present disorder. * * *The reasons for the existence of an English Synod on the territory of the German Synod no longer exist.* The importance of giving greater encouragement and more extensive development to the English interests of the church in eastern Pennsylvania, was *the principal motive that led to the organization of the East Pennsylvania Synod.* At that time the Pennsylvania Synod was exclusively a German body, etc. * * So long as the two Synods exist on the same territory, there will be unhappy collisions. Constituted as human nature is, these are unavoidable. * * There is a feasible remedy. * * There are in our Synodical territory the most distinct and natural boundaries for the formation of two or more Synods, etc."

After much discussion, on motion of Rev. L. E. Albert, it was

"*Resolved,* That a committee of five be appointed by this Synod, to meet a similar committee from the Synod of Pennsylvania, to whom shall be entrusted for final settlement the matters under dispute between the two Synods ; and that this committee be also a committee of conference, to take into consideration the union of these Synods, and report at the next meeting of our Synod."

From the minutes of 1863 we learn that the committees of the two Synods met in Reading in January of that year, failing, indeed, to adjust the inter-synodical difficulties entrusted to them, but finding far less diversity of opinion than had been supposed to exist in regard to the "far more important question committed to their consideration." Concerning this the following resolutions were adopted :

"1. *Resolved,* That in the judgment of this joint committee the union of the Synod of Pennsylvania and the Synod of East Pennsylvania, at the earliest period deemed practicable by the two Synods, is in the highest degree advisable.

"2. *Resolved,* That we request both Synods, at their next sessions, to take into consideration whether such union cannot be consummated at once.

"3. *Resolved,* That, whilst we do not venture to recommend any specific plan for such union, we would submit for the examination of the Synods the following papers presented at the meeting of this conference, viz.: Plan submitted by Rev. E. Greenwald, D. D., of the Synod of East Pennsylvania, and the Plan submitted by Rev. G. F. Krotel, of the Pennsylvania Synod."

The former of these proposed the formation of two Synods, separated by the Schuylkill river, the eastern one to retain the old name and the western one to have the name of the East Pennsylvania Synod. The other plan proposed a complete and permanent fusion of the two Synods, to bear the name of "The United Synod of the German Evangelical Lutheran Ministerium of Pennsylvania and of the Evangelical Lutheran Synod of East Pennsylvania."

The Pennsylvania Synod, at its meeting in June, 1863, fully discussed this subject and adopted the following resolutions:

"*Whereas*, The various embarrassments arising from the occupation of one and the same territory by the Synod of East Pennsylvania and our Synod are more and more felt; and

"*Whereas*, We all, as Christians, church-members and ministers, acknowledge the duty of promoting peace and good-will among all men, especially among members of the same household of faith; therefore,

"1. *Resolved*, That in the opinion of this Synod a union between the Synod of East Pennsylvania and our Synod is eminently desirable.

"2. *Resolved*, That we, on our part, adopt the following positions as the basis upon which any plan of union that might be presented must be constructed:

(*a*) The position taken by our Synod, and officially expressed in the Order of Ordination, and in the Constitution for Congregations, recommended by the Synod, with regard to the doctrines and usages of the Evangelical Lutheran Church, shall remain undisturbed.

(*b*) The full and equal rights due and secured to the two languages used by ministers and people in Eastern Pennsylvania shall not be interfered with.

(*c*) The liberal and tolerant construction and application of the aforesaid principles, which have hitherto characterized the mutual intercourse of the members of this body, shall be strictly maintained.

(*d*) The legal obligations and chartered rights of this Synod, and of the congregations connected with it, shall not be in any wise affected or restricted, unless with the full consent of all the parties concerned.

(*e*) The name of this Synod shall not be sunk in any designation by which any proposed union of the two Synods shall be known.

"3. *Resolved*, That these resolutions be respectfully laid before the Synod of East Pennsylvania, at its next meeting, by our delegates to that body."

In 1863 our President reports on this subject: "This joint committee assembled in Rev. Keller's church in Reading * * but left the inter-synodical difficulties where it found them. * * The Synod of Pennsylvania has had this very question under serious, protracted and earnest discussion, etc. It behooves this body to meet the action of the Pennsylvania Synod in the same candid, frank and fraternal spirit that characterized theirs. The olive-branch is sincerely offered; shall it be as sincerely accepted?" Our delegate to the Synod of Pennsylvania (Rev. Dr. Valentine) reported that when this subject was under discussion at the Pennsylvania Synod he had felt it his duty to express to the Synod of Pennsylvania the opinion that it was the desire of this body to unite with that *on terms including an immediate division of the territory into two Synods with geographical boundaries*, but that a simple fusion into one Synod would be of doubtful acceptableness, etc. And our committee of conference, in their report in 1863, recommend the following resolutions for adoption by the Synod:

"1. *Resolved*, That in our inmost hearts we reciprocate the feeling of fraternal love, and the desire for closer unity and more amicable co-operation involved in the action of the venerable mother Synod, and that in the opinion of this Synod a union of these two Synods, by a fusion into one, or on the basis of a geographical arrangement, is eminently desirable.

"2. *Resolved*, That in the opinion of this Synod the best way to accomplish this eminently desirable result would be for the two Synods to meet in convention for the purpose of fraternal consultation and for final action, should they see fit, at a time and place fixed by a joint committee appointed by the officers of both Synods.

"3. *Resolved*, That in such joint convention, at the call of any three members of either Synod, any resolution shall require for its adoption a majority of each Synod.

"4. *Resolved*, That we heartily accede to the positions laid down by the Pennsylvania Synod, under the twenty-second resolution of their last session, and that we, on our part, adopt the following positions, as the basis upon which any plan of union that may be presented must be constructed."

[Reiteration of the Pennsylvania Synod's *resolutions, etc.* (see page 33) under *a, b, c, d, e.*] "The name of this Synod shall not be sunk in the issue of this effort to reorganize the Lutheran elements upon the territory of East Pennsylvania."

"5. *Resolved*, That whilst the recent action of the Synod of Pennsylvania seems to indicate a preference for an actual union of both Synods, and whilst we decidedly prefer a geographical division of the territory now jointly occupied by them, we think it nevertheless more prudent that neither Synod should in advance insist upon its preferences in this respect, but that both should enter the proposed convention prepared to adopt and carry out any arrangement that the united wisdom of the ministers and lay delegates there assembled may determine upon.

"6. *Resolved*, That a committee of three clergymen and three laymen be appointed at the present meeting of this Synod, to act in conjunction with a similar committee which we ardently hope our mother Synod will appoint, to make all necessary preparations for such a joint convention, and to announce the time and place of meeting. [Signed, C. P. Krauth, C. A. Hay, G. Parson, C. A. Kugler, J. G. L. Schindel.]"

The Secretary adds: "Dr. Krauth, at his own request, was permitted to sign his name to the report, as thus amended."

The minutes of the Pennsylvania Synod for 1864 contained the report of that Synod's part of the joint committee appointed to make the needful arrangements for a general convention of the two Synods to consider the subject of synodical union. It is as follows: "Your committee have the honor to report that they met in conference with the committee of the Synod of East Pennsylvania, Rev. Dr. Seiss serving as the Chairman, and gave their serious consideration to the subject laid before them, but they were unable to arrive at any satisfactory result, and adjourned to meet again at the call of the Chairman. Respectfully submitted, by W. J. Mann, Chairman."

The minutes state that "The above report was adopted, and the discussion of the subject continued until the hour for adjournment arrived, when its further consideration was postponed until a later period during the meeting. Inasmuch as the Synod afterwards determined to hold a special meeting in July, it was concluded that this subject should be further considered at that time. The following preamble and resolutions were adopted at that special meeting in July, 1864 :

"WHEREAS, The Synod of East Pennsylvania appointed a committee to confer with a similar committee from this body, to consider the terms upon which a union of the two Synods, or a geographical division of the territory occupied by them, could be effected ; and

"WHEREAS, The President of this body, prior to the last stated meeting of the Synod of Pennsylvania, appointed such a Committee of Conference ; and

"WHEREAS, These Committees, upon conferring together, found it impossible to accomplish anything further than to resolve to postpone the further consideration of the matter until after the meeting of this Synod to be held in Pottstown ; and

"WHEREAS, The pressure of business at Pottstown and at this special meeting has rendered a consideration of this momentous business out of the question ; therefore, be it

Resolved, That this Synod has not changed its position in regard to this matter, and still, in good faith, presents the same terms of union."

"*Resolved*, That we request the Joint Committee of Conference to resume their deliberations as soon as possible."

Then followed the retiring of the Pennsylvania Synod's delegates from the General Synod at York, and the President of the East Pennsylvania Synod (Dr. Fink), in his official report in 1864, remarks : " From the action of the Synod of Pennsylvania and Adjacent States on this subject, both at its regular and special meetings, as I learned it from observation and its published reports, I am inclined to think that further action on the part of this Synod, looking to a union of the two bodies, would be at once dishonorable and useless. The whole matter having been treated most cavalierly by the one party, I take the liberty most respectfully and earnestly to recommend to this body that the further consideration of the proposed union of the Synod of Pennsylvania and the Synod of East Pennsylvania be held in abeyance, until the older Synod, by its action, will make it possible for this Synod to further entertain the subject, and at the same time maintain its honor and self-respect." * * "Our relations to others who bear the same name, and occupy the same territory with ourselves, have always been peculiar, but never so *very* peculiar as now. Harmony and fellowship cannot subsist between two Synods, unless they treat each other with decent respect, argue their differences candidly and temperately, and pursue towards each other an open, fair and friendly line of conduct. We have, especially of late years, manifested in every possible way a spirit of conciliation, forbearance and concession, which has not always been met with the same spirit. We have sought peace, fellowship and union. In these we have not been successful to the full measure of our desire. Our duty to ourselves and to our Divine Master will permit us to yield no more, to concede no more, but peremptorily enjoins upon us to plant ourselves more firmly than ever upon the great principles and purposes which led to the formation of the Synod of East Pennsylvania. Believing that the territory we occupy belongs of right to King Jesus, and that we have a well-authenticated commission to possess and cultivate it for him, we should enter upon our mission with new zeal and redoubled energy. No one can occupy a middle ground any longer; he that is not for us is against us. Our Synod has a work to do. May the Lord give her wisdom and strength to do it well, and then, and not until then, will the Evangelical Lutheran Church in Eastern Pennsylvania become, what God designed her to be everywhere—a living power for good—a very ark of salvation for redeemed sinners!"

In *1865* the Standing Committee of Conference reported that no communication had been received by them from the Synod of Pennsylvania, and "the Committee was hereupon discharged."

In 1866 [after Fort Wayne!] a committee on the "Papers of the Pennsylvania Synod" reported as follows:

"The Committee No. 2, to whom has been referred the 'Fraternal Address' issued by a committee of the Synod of Pennsylvania, with accompanying letter of Rev. G. F. Krotel, D. D., as Chairman of that committee, submitting the Address to this body, respectfully report:

"I. That the Address has been prepared and published in accordance with a resolution of the Synod of Pennsylvania, adopted at Lancaster, after its secession from the General Synod, to invite 'All Evangelical Lutheran Synods, Ministers and Congregations in the United States and Canadas, which confess the Unaltered Augsburg Confession, to unite with them in a convention for the purpose of forming a Union of Lutheran Synods.'

"II. That this Address, under the plea of love, peace, fraternity and unity, assails the General Synod, and passes it under utter condemnation, as unworthy of confidence or support, and asks us to unite in their proposed effort to organize another General Union, to accomplish the objects which, it is alleged, the General Synod has failed to secure.

"Your Committee propose the following as the judgment and testimony of this Synod in this matter:

"*Resolved*, 1. That this Synod respectfully, but with emphasis, declines to take the desired, or any, part in the proposed movement, and solemnly declares that in its view and conviction, it is unjustifiable, schismatic, and fraught with sad consequences to the unity and welfare of our Lutheran Zion, and ought to be discountenanced by all who love its peace and desire its prosperity.

"*Resolved*, 2. That we testify our undiminished confidence in the General Synod, and pledge, against all its opposers and defamers, our continued endeavors to promote its influence and power, already realized as rich in blessings to our beloved Church.

"*Resolved*, 3. That we appoint a committee of five, whose duty it shall be to act in conjunction with a committee already appointed by the Synod of West Pennsylvania, to issue and circulate a Fraternal Appeal to the Church, in order to counteract the effort made to alienate the churches and synods of the General Synod from that body, and unite them in this intended new organization.

"*Resolved*, 4. That we earnestly entreat the Synod of Pennsylvania to desist from the movement they propose in their Address, as replete with the most unhappy results of discord, strife and division to the Church, and injury to the cause of Christ.

                        "M. VALENTINE,
                         E. S. JOHNSTON,
                         A. R. HORNE,
                         J. F. McLAIN."

Adopted.

In *1867* the Pennsylvania Synod refused to receive our delegate to that body and sent to our Synod a communication on that subject. The Committee to whom this was referred reported that it was "a certified copy of the action taken by the German Evangelical Lutheran Ministerium of Pennsylvania, in refusing to receive the delegate to that body appointed by this Synod at its last session, and in refusing to 'continue cordial relations and brotherly communion' with this Synod.

"The grounds upon which the Ministerium bases this action are: *First*,—the opinion expressed by our Synod at its last meeting, in regard to the character and probable influence of the Address issued by said Ministerium, inviting 'All Evangelical Lutheran Synods, Ministers and Congregations in the United States and Canadas, which confess the Unaltered Augsburg Confession, to unite with them in a convention for the purpose of forming a Union of Lutheran Synods,' and, *Secondly*,—The 'Fraternal Appeal' issued conjointly by this Synod and that of West Pennsylvania, 'in order to counteract the effort made to alienate the

Churches and Synods of the General Synod from that body, and unite them in this new organization.'

"The Ministerium, after rejecting our delegate and sundering the bonds of fraternal intercourse between itself and the Synods of West and East Pennsylvania, 'respectfully requests these Synods to review the principles of their action, so that it may be ascertained whether they may not be able in this emergency to pursue some course which, by the blessing of the Lord, may be in like manner just to us [the Ministerium] and honorable to themselves.'

"In reply to which the Committee propose the adoption of the following preamble and resolutions :

"*Whereas*, We are thoroughly convinced that our judgment of the character and tendency of the aforesaid Address of the Ministerium of Pennsylvania was correct at the time it was delivered ; and

"*Whereas*, Subsequent events have furnished unmistakable and lamentable evidence that those who issued it are fully resolved to run the plowshare of division and disorganization, if possible, through all our synods and congregations ; therefore,

"*Resolved*, That we see no cause for modifying the judgment aforesaid, or for regretting the affectionate warning addressed by us to our churches ; further,

"*Resolved*, That, as the Ministerium of Pennsylvania has seen fit to sunder the bonds of union between us, no just and honorable course remains for us to pursue but to accept the issue thus forced upon us, and stand upon the defensive—maintaining a consistent adherence to the faith and principles we have long professed and practised, and praying that those who have assumed this hostile attitude may, sooner or later, acknowledge their error and approach us with such proofs of their sorrow for the harm they have done, that we may be able, consistently with self-respect and a due regard for ecclesiastical order, and for the real welfare of our beloved Zion, once more to extend to them the hand of synodical fellowship. S. SENTMAN,
CHARLES A. HAY,
CHARLES KUGLER."

Regretting that I could not with greater brevity present a sufficiently accurate account of the relations originally existing and subsequently developed between the Pennsylvania Synod and our own, I now hasten to make a very few statements concerning the attitude sustained by our Synod toward some of the leading issues that have interested our churches since our organization.

SECESSION OF THE SUSQUEHANNA CONFERENCE.

This Conference, composed of the ministers and churches in the northern part of the territory occupied by this Synod, was from the time of its organization distinguished for its zeal and active efficiency in all manner of church work. In 1867 it petitioned to be dismissed from our body for the purpose of organizing an independent Synod in that part of the State. The Synod "affectionately, yet most earnestly, requested those brethren to withdraw their application for the present," but, as they urged their plea with increasing earnestness, the Synod reluctantly granted their request. In 1871 the East Pennsylvania Synod "kindly and affectionately invited the Susquehanna Synod to return to this body;" to which the Susquehanna brethren responded in 1872:

Resolved, That we reciprocate the regard of the Synod of East Pennsylvania, but do not think that the time has yet arrived when it would be advisable for us to seek a re-union with it."

THE MINISTERIUM QUESTION.

In 1870 the East Pennsylvania Synod appointed a committee to report a year later on the propriety of dispensing in future with all ministerial sessions, *i. e.*, meetings composed of ministers alone, some of the clerical brethren holding the opinion that the lay representatives of the churches should be allowed to take part in all ecclesiastical business. This matter was subsequently referred to the General Synod, which, at its meeting in Baltimore in 1875, adopted a form of Constitution for District Synods, in which provision is made in Article VIII. for the holding of meetings by ministers alone, by such Synods as may desire to continue the custom long prevalent in our country ; but it specifies also in Article VIII., Section 14, that *"in all cases where District Synods have not made provision for a Ministerium, all the powers and duties prescribed in this article shall devolve on the Synod."*

LICENSURE.

This Synod has been much exercised on the subject of the induction of men into the holy office of the ministry. At its meeting in Hughesville, in 1856, it declined "to make any change in our method of inducting men into the ministerial office"; *i. e.*, it determined to continue licensing them by a vote of the Ministerium to perform all ministerial acts. The Synod thus, at that time, still entrusted the ministers alone with the responsibility of deciding who should be admitted to the holy office ; that is, it regarded them as constituting a strictly self-perpetuating order of men. During the progress of the meeting at Lancaster, in 1892, however, at which time the above account of its past history was presented, the Synodical Constitution was carefully revised, and it was materially improved in this respect, by the adoption of the principle that *the Synod* is to decide upon the final ordination of applicants, thus entitling the lay element of the body to take part in deciding who shall become a minister.

BENEFICIARY EDUCATION.

The East Pennsylvania Synod has always taken a deep interest in this cause. It has aided several hundred young men in their preparation for the ministry. It had *eighteen* on its funds at the time of the withdrawal of the Susquehanna Conference, and it faithfully met its obligation to them, despite the loss of the supplies it had before received from the churches that had thus seceded. It expended during that year for this cause $3,625.29.

It is, of all the Synods, most punctual in the payment, at regular intervals during the year, of its voluntarily assumed dues to the students. The young men gratefully appreciate this treatment on the part of the Synod, as it practically adds much to the value of what is advanced to them. They are in the habit of calling it the *Banner Synod*.

PASTORS' FUND.

There is quite a history connected with the relation of our Synod to this department of church work. The Synod has always disapproved of the mutual-beneficial principle in the matter of relief for disabled or superannuated ministers, their widows and orphans; and it has always acted on the principle that the duty of caring for such cases rested upon the whole Church and not upon the clergy alone. Accordingly, it has habitually appealed to the churches to contribute annually for this purpose; and the biennial reports of the trustees of the General Synod's Pastors' Fund prove that this Synod has often given more for this purpose than all the other Synods combined.

THE LUTHERAN PUBLICATION BOARD

had its origin, practically, in this Synod. The original proposition for the establishment of a Translation and Publication Society came from what was then the Susquehanna Conference, and the committee appointed by the Synod to report upon it, whilst regarding its immediate establishment as inexpedient and unnecessary, yet proposed the calling of a convention "to consider the propriety of establishing some organization by which the mind of the Church can be more especially awakened on this subject." Such a convention was held in Germantown in 1855, concerning which a committee consisting of Messrs. Hutter, Stork and Albert reported to our Synod at Lebanon in that year, that "it was attended by a number of clergymen and laymen belonging to this and other Synods; that at this convention the initiatory steps were taken for the organization of such a society, etc.;" and the Synod

"*Resolved*, That, regarding this Society as the offspring of this Synod, begun and prosecuted under its auspices, we cherish a parental interest in its welfare and success, and will rejoice in any evidence we may perceive of its advancement and growth to a more mature and vigorous degree of Christian usefulness."

This institution, at first a beneficiary of the Church, barely kept alive by the contributions of our people, has steadily grown (under the gratuitous and skilful management of its wise directors and under its present energetic and efficient Superintendent, Henry S. Boner), until it has become a liberal contributor to all the leading benevolent operations of the Church. In its report to the last General Synod its financial strength is given as $100,000.

EMMAUS AND TRESSLER ORPHANS' HOMES.

In these institutions, also, the East Pennsylvania Synod has always shown a deep interest. It acted in harmony with the Pennsylvania Ministerium and the West Pennsylvania Synod many years ago in urging the trustees of the *Fry Estate at Middletown* to make a direct application of the revenues of that estate to the purposes intended by the founder of the Emmaus Orphans' Home, and it now has the satisfaction of beholding the salutary effects of its efforts in the enlarged and beneficent operations of that institution.

One of the oldest and still living ministers of Synod, Rev. P. Willard, through whose agency the Tressler property was purchased and soldiers' orphans secured, was for many years the active and efficient Superintendent of the *Tressler Orphans' Home;* and it is mainly owing to his self-denying and laborious exertions that that institution for many years bore the well-earned reputation of being the most admirably conducted Soldier's Orphans'

Home in the State of Pennsylvania. Now that the policy of the State authorities has made it necessary for the soldiers' orphans to be concentrated in a few institutions especially intended for them, our Church-orphans have become entirely dependent upon the charitable gifts of our own people, and we may confidently trust that there will be no lack of sympathy or of benevolent effort for them on the part of our Synod.

WOMEN'S HOME AND FOREIGN MISSIONARY SOCIETIES.

This Synod cordially responded to the action of the General Synod at its session in Carthage, Ill., in 1877, recommending the establishment of separate missionary societies by the women of our churches. Fifty-five of such associations exist upon our territory, banded together in a "Synodical Woman's Home and Foreign Missionary Society," the proceedings of the annual meetings of which will hereafter be regularly printed in connection with our minutes.

HISTORIES OF THE CHURCHES.

In the minutes of 1854 we find a committee reporting upon the proceedings of the Susquehanna Conference, which it highly eulogizes, as "being animated by a spirit of activity and enterprise, which makes it an example well worthy of the imitation of all similar bodies, not only in our own Synod, but in the whole Church." Among other praiseworthy doings of that Conference it enumerates "a plan which the brethren have devised for preserving the history of our Church, the main feature of which is, that each pastor within the bounds of Conference prepare a concise and faithful history of the church or churches under his care, for preservation in the library of the Historical Society of our Church at Gettysburg." The Synod cordially approved of this plan, and earnestly recommended to all its pastors the prompt preparation of such sketches. Some of the brethren cheerfully heeded this recommendation, and these sketches, in print or in manuscript, are now carefully preserved in the library of the Lutheran Historical Society. It is earnestly desired and hoped that this semi-centennial year of our existence as a Synod will not be suffered to pass by without witnessing the fulfilment of the request, reiterated by our Synod at its last session, viz., that all our ministerial brethren prepare brief histories of their churches for permanent preservation in the library of our Historical Society.

SYNODICAL MEETINGS AND OFFICERS.

The Evangelical Lutheran Synod of East Pennsylvania was organized at Lancaster, Pa., May 2, 1842. Its founders were Rev. Messrs. F. Ruthrauff, J. Ruthrauff, W. M. Reynolds, D. D., G. Heilig, F. R. Anspach, D. D., J. Willox, T. Stork, D. D., J. T. Vogelbach, W. G. Laitzle, and Mr. J. L. Frederick and Gen. G. Hartman. The Synod was incorporated by an act of the Legislature, approved February 11, 1847.

No.	Year	Place	President	Secretary	Treasurer
1	1842	Pikeland	Rev. F. Ruthrauff	Rev. T. Stork, D. D.	Rev. F. R. Anspach, D. D.
2	1843	Philadelphia	Rev. J. P. Schindel	Rev. T. Stork, D. D.	Rev. F. R. Anspach, D. D.
3	1844	Reading	Rev. J. P. Schindel	Rev. J. L. Schock, D. D.	Rev. J. Ruthrauff.
4	1845	Lebanon	Rev. J. P. Schindel	Rev. J. L. Schock, D. D.	Rev. J. Ruthrauff.
5	1846	Milton	Rev. J. Ruthrauff	Rev. G. Diehl, D. D.	Rev. A. Wieting.
6	1847	Germantown	Rev. J. Ruthrauff	Rev. G. Diehl, D. D.	Rev. A. Wieting.
7	1848	Selinsgrove	Rev. J. Ruthrauff	Rev. G. Diehl, D. D.	Rev. A. Wieting.
8	1849	Reading	Rev. T. Stork, D. D.	Rev. J. McCron, D. D.	Rev. W. F. Eyster.
9	1850	Easton	Rev. T. Stork, D. D.	Rev. J. McCron, D. D.	Rev. W. F. Eyster.
10	1851	Danville	Rev. T. Stork, D. D.	Rev. J. Winecoff	Rev. P. Willard.
11	1852	Pottsville	Rev. J. A. Brown, D. D.	Rev. J. J. Reimensnyder	Rev. A. C. Wedekind, D. D.
12	1853	Philadelphia	Rev. J. A. Brown, D. D.	Rev. J. J. Reimensnyder	Rev. A. C. Wedekind, D. D.
13	1854	Lewisburg	Rev. J. A. Brown, D. D.	Rev. B. Sadtler, D. D.	Rev. A. C. Wedekind, D. D.
14	1855	Lebanon	Rev. G. Parson, D. D.	Rev. B. Sadtler, D. D.	Rev. E. W. Hutter, D. D.
15	1856	Hughesville	Rev. G. Parson, D. D.	Rev. D. Steck, D. D.	Rev. E. W. Hutter, D. D.
16	1857	Lancaster	Rev. G. Parson, D. D.	Rev. D. Steck, D. D.	Rev. E. W. Hutter, D. D.
17	1858	Bloomsburg	Rev. E. W. Hutter, D. D.	Rev. C. J. Ehrehart	Rev. R. A. Fink, D. D.
18	1859	Harrisburg	Rev. D. Steck, D. D.	Rev. R. A. Fink, D. D.	Rev. E. S. Henry.
19	1860	Sunbury	Rev. C. A. Hay, D. D.	Rev. S. Domer, D. D.	Rev. E. Greenwald, D. D.
20	1861	Germantown	Rev. J. A. Seiss, D. D.	Rev. M. Sheeleigh, D. D.	Rev. L. E. Albert, D. D.
21	1862	Reading	Rev. A. C. Wedekind, D. D.	Rev. T. T. Titus	Rev. M. Valentine, D. D.
22	1863	Milton	Rev. R. A. Fink, D. D.	Rev. L. E. Albert, D. D.	Rev. C. J. Ehrehart.

EAST PENNSYLVANIA SYNOD.

No.	Year	Place	President	Secretary	Treasurer
23	1864	Lehanon	Rev. L. E. Albert, D. D.	Rev. J. R. Dimm, D. D.	Rev. S. Sentman.
24	1865	Easton	Rev. E. Greenwald, D. D.	Rev. E. W. Hutter, D. D.	Rev. A. C. Wedekind, D. D.
25	1866	Danville	Rev. S. Sentman	Rev. J. H. Heck	Rev. G. Parson, D. D.
26	1867	Pottsville	Rev. M. Valentine, D. D.	Rev. H. C. Shindle	Rev. M. Rhodes, D. D.
27	1868	Lancaster	Rev. G. F. Stelling, D. D.	Rev. H. C. Shindle	Rev. M. Rhodes, D. D.
28	1869	Lebanon	Rev. P. Rizer	Rev. S. A. Holman, D. D.	Rev. P. Raby.
29	1870	Harrisburg	Rev. J. R. Dimm, D. D.	Rev. S. A. Holman, D. D.	Rev. P. Raby.
30	1871	Philadelphia	Rev. M. Sheeleigh, D. D.	Rev. S. A. Holman, D. D.	Rev. P. Raby.
31	1872	Easton	Rev. S. A. Holman, D. D.	Rev. S. Henry	Rev. L. E. Albert, D. D.
32	1873	Germantown	Rev. B. C. Suesserott	Rev. S. Henry	Rev. L. E. Albert, D. D.
33	1874	Pottsville	Rev. C. A. Hay, D. D.	Rev. S. Henry	Rev. L. E. Albert, D. D.
34	1875	Reading	Rev. E. S. Henry	Rev. J. F. Reinmund, D. D.	Rev. W. M. Baum, D. D.
35	1876	Columbia	Rev. S. Henry	Rev. J. F. Reinmund, D. D.	Rev. W. M. Baum, D. D.
36	1877	Lebanon	Rev. Joel Swartz, D. D.	Rev. W. H. Dunbar, D. D.	Rev. W. M. Baum, D. D.
37	1878	Philadelphia	Rev. Joel Swartz, D. D.	Rev. W. H. Dunbar, D. D.	Rev. L. E. Albert, D. D.
38	1879	Harrisburg	Rev. W. M. Baum, D. D.	Rev. W. H. Dunbar, D. D.	Rev. L. E. Albert, D. D.
39	1880	Allentown	Rev. W. M. Baum, D. D.	Rev. J. A. Singmaster	Rev. L. E. Albert, D. D.
40	1881	Lancaster	Rev. W. M. Baum, D. D.	Rev. J. A. Singmaster	Rev. E. Huber, D. D.
41	1882	Pottsville	Rev. T. C. Billheimer, D. D.	Rev. G. C. Henry	Rev. E. Huber, D. D.
42	1883	Germantown	Rev. T. C. Billheimer, D. D.	Rev. P. C. Croll	Rev. E. Huber, D. D.
43	1884	Easton	Rev. T. C. Billheimer, D. D.	Rev. P. C. Croll	Rev. L. E. Albert, D. D.
44	1885	Ashland	Rev. E. Huber, D. D.	Rev. P. S. Hooper	Rev. L. E. Albert, D. D.
45	1886	Reading	Rev. E. Huber, D. D.	Rev. J. A. Hackenberg	Rev. L. E. Albert, D. D.
46	1887	Lebanon	Rev. E. Huber, D. D.	Rev. J. A. Hackenberg	Rev. W. M. Baum, D. D.
47	1888	Philadelphia	Rev. W. H. Dunbar, D. D.	Rev. J. A. Hackenberg	Rev. W. M. Baum, D. D.
48	1889	Steelton	Rev. W. H. Dunbar, D. D.	Rev. Chas. E. Hay	Rev. W. M. Baum, D. D.
49	1890	Columbia	Rev. W. H. Dunbar, D. D.	Rev. Chas. E. Hay	Rev. D. M. Gilbert, D. D.
50	1891	Middletown	Rev. R. W. Hufford, D. D.	Rev. Chas. E. Hay	Rev. D. M. Gilbert, D. D.
51	1892	Lancaster	Rev. R. W. Hufford, D. D.	Rev. W. H. Lewars	Rev. D. M. Gilbert, D. D.

Note.—The officers are credited in the above table with titles received up to the date of this publication, although the latter were in many cases not borne during the terms of service indicated.

SKETCHES OF CONGREGATIONS.

I. FRIESBURG (COHANSEY) CHURCH, SALEM COUNTY, N. J.

BY REV. S. J. MCDOWELL.

The history of the Friesburg Lutheran Church dates back to 1726. Some time during that year, Rev. Peter Tranberg, a Swedish pastor, began to serve a small body of Lutherans that settled in and about the district now known as Friesburg. In the year 1732 a young man, Jacob M. Miller by name, who had come to this country with the Rev. John Christian Schultze, settled among the little band of Lutherans, and apparently infused new life into it. With his coming increased activity arises, and things are brought into a better shape. The "little Lutheran congregation" so "long a time in existence," now becomes strong enough to build for itself a church. In 1739 this is undertaken and completed. It was a frame structure, and stood until replaced by one of brick in 1768.

Rev. Tranberg also served two other congregations with the one at Friesburg; one at Raccoon, eighteen miles from Friesburg, and the other at Pennsneck, both along the Delaware river. He continued dividing his time between these three places until he removed to Wilmington, Del., in 1740. After that, he supplied the Friesburg people for three more years. He was relieved of this congregation by Pastor Gabriel Näsmann, in October, 1743. The latter held services for them once a month from Wicaco, Philadelphia. It was always on a week-day, and usually on a Monday. He preached in both the English and German languages for them.

In 1745 they were without a pastor, and applied for one to the

German ministers of Philadelphia. In April of that year they visited Pastor Brunnholtz, who promised that the pastors of Philadelphia would visit them at least once or twice a year to look after their spiritual interests. In the meantime they were to have a school-master sent them, who was to see to the proper education of their children, and read a sermon for them every Sunday. Jacob Löser was at once sent to attend to this part of the agreement. He carried with him a copy of Francke's Postille, from which he read a sermon every Lord's day. It was his duty to catechise the children and prepare them for confirmation when the Philadelphia pastor should arrive to perform all marriage ceremonies, baptize the children and hold communion. This arrangement lasted more than half a century.

Several of these visits from the Philadelphia pastors receive special mention in the Hallesche Nachrichten. Brunnholtz visited them in 1749, and again in 1752, at which time he promised them, if possible, to see to it that they should be visited more frequently. In 1760 Pastor Handschuh visited them, accompanied by part of his own church council of Philadelphia, for the purpose of holding communion. It was on the 24th day of June, and a large congregation had gathered for worship—some coming more than thirty miles through all the summer heat. On this occasion twelve children were baptized, and one hundred and twenty communed. After Pastor Brunnholtz died Pastor Handschuh was too busy to find any time for Friesburg, and they were without a single visit from a regularly ordained minister for two years.

In 1760 Pastor Henry Melchior Mühlenberg spent a week with them. At this time one hundred and twenty-five communed. It was from the 8th to the 14th of June, and he lodged with Mr. Jacob Fries, from whom the place has taken its name. The house in which Mühlenberg then lodged is still standing. It is now occupied by a member of the congregation, and our young people of the Christian Endeavor Society will hold their next social in the very room where that venerable pioneer of Lutheranism in America spent the summer evenings one hundred and thirty-two years ago.

In 1763 he again visited the congregation, bringing with him his wife and daughter. At this time he visited the now aged

Jacob M. Miller, who, having infused new life into the little band in its infancy, continued a zealous member of the congregation until his death.

The above arrangement of supplies from the Philadelphia ministers continued with more or less interruption until 1800. In that year the school-master of the congregation was licensed to preach for them. His connection with them as pastor was, however, of short duration. He was succeeded by Rev. Wm. Baetes, one of Dr. Helmuth's theological students, 1808–1810. Then followed Rev. C. F. Cruse, 1819–1824, who subsequently entered the Episcopal Church in New York State. During his pastorate the congregation had dwindled down to forty-three communicant members. From 1833–35 Rev. Mark Harpel served them; from 1835–37 Rev. W. M. Reynolds, who translated Acrelius' "History of New Sweden," &c. He was followed by Rev. Jacob C. Duy, 1837–39. In 1839 Rev. Edw. Town served them a short while; from 1842–51 Rev. John R. Willox; from April 1852 to October 1854, Rev. A. L. Bridgeman; from 1855–57 Rev. Ferdinand Berkemeyer; from 1858–66 Rev. J. N. Unruh. Rev. Unruh found the congregation very small and disheartened. Under his care it again revived and became very strong. He was followed by Rev. Sylvander Curtis; then by Rev. J. W. Lake from 1871–74; from 1874–79 by Rev. P. M. Rightmyer; from 1879–81 by Rev. W. P. Evans. He was followed by Rev. A. W. Lentz, 1882–86, and he in 1887 by Rev. J. E. Dietterich, now pastor of the newly organized mission at Bridgeton, New Jersey.

The congregation belonged to the Ministerium of Pennsylvania from the organization of that body until 1842. Then Pastor Willox left the Ministerium, and took the congregation with him into the newly organized East Pennsylvania Synod. With this Synod it remained until the New Jersey Synod was formed. When that was merged into the New York and New Jersey Synod, the congregation became a member of the latter body. It was brought back into the East Pennsylvania Synod again by Rev. Dietterich in May, 1891. Its present pastor is Rev. S. J. McDowell, of the Class of 1892 of the Theological Seminary at Gettysburg.

The congregation is in a good condition, having a membership of two hundred, with a Sunday-school of about two hundred and fifty members, and a Y. P. S. C. E., numbering about ninety members. The congregation supports a pastor, and has preaching twice each Lord's Day, and a midweek prayer meeting. The value of the church property is estimated at $10,000.

May God's blessing rest upon this ancient land-mark, and ever assist it in securing and supporting faithful men to administer in it the divinely-appointed means of grace. That it may close its history with pastors as pious and zealous in the cause of Christ as were the devoted fathers who cared for it in its infancy, is our sincere prayer.

II. SCHAFFERSTOWN CHARGE: BRICKERVILLE, LANCASTER CO.; SCHAEFFERSTOWN, LEBANON CO.

BY REV. M. FERNSLER.

1. ST. JOHN'S, BRICKERVILLE.

The old Warwick church, with which the present St. John's congregation claims historic identity, was organized by Rev. John Caspar Stoever, in the year 1730. Thirty-six names of male members appear on the records. Rev. Stoever served until 1743. Then records are silent until 1770. In the year 1743 the Penns, John, Thomas and Richard, issued a patent for thirty-five acres of land, in trust, for the use of this church forever.

From 1770 to 1773, the Rev. H. M. Mühlenberg was pastor. Rev. Dr. Helmuth served from the spring of 1774 to May, 1775; Rev. Schwarback, of Virginia, from May, 1775, to some time in 1776. Rev. Helmuth again served until some time in 1777, when Rev. Stoever, now aged, again took charge, "preaching as much as he could, being sickly," until 1779. In this year, "on Good Friday, May 13, he administered the communion to the children newly confirmed, and in the afternoon of that day died." Rev. J. D. Schroeder took charge in 1780, and left in 1781. Aug. 12, 1806, the corner-stone of the present brick church building was laid, the Revs. Emanuel Schultze and John Plitt officiating. On October 25, 1807, it was dedicated; Revs. Schultze, Dr. H. M.

Mühlenberg, and Dr. George Lochman, of Lebanon, were present on the occasion. Rev. Schultze had been pastor for some years. He preached his last sermon on November 20, 1808, and March 11, 1809, he died. About this time the Schaefferstown Lutheran church united with that at Brickerville, and they jointly elected the Rev. Wm. Baetes, of Philadelphia, who took charge July 8, 1810. In June, 1814, Rev. Baetes moved into the newly-built brick parsonage, now standing near the Brickerville brick church. In 1815 the old school-house belonging to this church was rebuilt. After serving for twenty-six years, Rev. Baetes preached his farewell sermon on August 14, 1836. The "honorable" Charles Philip Miller, of Milton, Pa., having been called, moved into the parsonage September 25, 1836, and served as pastor until November 28, 1841. The churches "Swamp, Kisselberger, Weisecher and Manheim, united with Brickerville" in forming a pastoral charge, and called Rev. Christopher G. Frederick, who moved into the Brickerville parsonage July 29, 1842, preaching his first sermon as pastor August 7, 1842. He resigned and left in 1849. Rev. T. T. Jeager served as pastor from 1850 to 1852; Rev. Charles Rees from 1854 to 1856.

The following facts are gathered from the "paper books." The Rev. M. Harpel was called as pastor and took charge in 1859. He served until 1870, when he resigned. When the Synod of Pennsylvania withdrew from the General Synod, Mr. Harpel preferred not to go with them. At the meeting of the East Pennsylvania Synod, in 1867, he appeared with George W. Steinmetz, Esq., as delegate-elect, and with a formal application signed by many of the members of the congregation, including eleven of the church-council. Both Mr. Harpel and the congregation were cordially received by that body. A suit brought by disaffected parties for the possession of the church property in 1868 was lost.

Rev. S. S. Engel was called as pastor, and served from the spring of 1870 until 1874. On May 23, 1874, Rev. W. S. Porr was elected as pastor, serving until January, 1875. when he moved to Lancaster, continuing his services in the congregation. however, until June 27, 1875. A committee, consisting of Revs. D. P. Rosenmiller, G. J. Martz and W. I. Cutter, appointed by the

Lebanon Conference of the East Pennsylvania Synod, now supplied the pulpit until December 20, 1875, when Rev. Cutter moved into the parsonage as the regular pastor-elect.

Already in August, 1875, the desire of some members "once again to hear a man from the Old Synod" having been granted, Rev. Thomas Jeager preached in the church. He at once made a further appointment, and the vacant alternate Sundays were from this time utilized by various ministers of the Pennsylvania Ministerium, until at a meeting called by them January 14, 1876, but neither announced nor sanctioned by the acting pastor, Rev. Cutter, and his adherents, a resolution was passed to sever the connection of the congregation with the East Pennsylvania Synod. Both parties continued to use the church building.

A bill of complaint was entered in the Lancaster Court, January 26, 1876, praying that an injunction be issued, restraining the party adhering to the Ministerium from entering the church. The master's decision, adverse to the granting of such injunction, was sustained by the Court.

In September, 1878, the East Pennsylvania Synod, in re-districting pastorates, united the Brickerville and Schaefferstown churches to constitute a pastoral charge. Rev. M. Fernsler, having been called, entered the parsonage October 28, 1878, and preached his opening sermon in the church on Sunday, November 10, 1878. He was installed as pastor, January 19, 1879, by Revs. W. S. Porr and J. Peter, a committee appointed for that purpose by the President of the East Pennsylvania Synod.

A suit for ejectment having been brought by the other party, June 4, 1879, the case was tried in December, 1881, and September, 1883, the jury in each case failing to find a verdict. The third trial, in September, 1884, was decided in favor of the plaintiffs, but this judgment was reversed by the Supreme Court, and a new trial ordered. The case was tried for the fourth time in February, 1886, resulting again in favor of the plaintiffs, the verdict being finally confirmed by the Supreme Court, October 4, 1886.

This decision appears to have rested upon the recognition of the meeting held on January 14, 1876, and the opinion that the members who, with Rev. Cutter, refused to participate in that meeting, really thereby seceded and forfeited their rights in the congregation. The defendants, upon the other hand, have always contended that the meeting in question was irregular, and its recognition by the courts the result of a failure to give due weight to some established principles of Lutheran Church polity.

Upon learning the final issue of the case, Rev. Mr. Asay, pastor of the "James Coleman Memorial Church," on the Elizabeth Farms, appeared at the Lutheran parsonage with full authority, and invited the Lutheran people to come and hold their services in said Memorial Church. This Christian offer was gratefully accepted, and regular services there held until the new house ot worship, forty by sixty feet, erected in sight of the old church building, was finished. The latter was dedicated August 7, 1889, Dr. E. Huber and Revs. W. H. Lewars and C. H. Asay assisting the pastor. A membership of one hundred and sixty, with their pastor, entered the beautiful new church with their hearts full of gratitude and praise to God. In November following forty-seven more members were added. Many have since then died or removed. Still others live at such a distance that they are unable to attend services, and are hence not included in the number (one hundred and fifty-two) reported at the last meeting of Synod. Thousands of dollars were spent by these people during the long and wearisome litigations. In consequence, there is still some debt resting on the new house of worship, but this is being reduced. The outlook is fair, services are well attended, and harmony prevails.

2. SCHAEFFERSTOWN.

The Lutheran church at this place was erected in 1765, the steeple being built two years later. In 1819 considerable repairing was done inside and some alterations made. The church was repainted about twenty years ago. In 1884 it was again remodeled, at a cost of $6,100. The steeple was taken down from the west and put up at the east end. The west gable wall was removed, and sixteen feet added to the length of the building. The interior was entirely renewed. Opposite the pulpit stands a pipe organ said to be over one hundred years old. Close to the church building is a small Sunday-school and prayer house, controlled by separate trustees. This is really at present an encumbrance, as it prevents the erection by the congregation of a suitable building for the Sunday-school.

The congregation worshiping in this ancient temple was organized some time before the erection of the building. There exists a glimpse of burial records as far back as 1720. It appears that pastoral functions were exercised at one period by C. F. Mühlenberg, M. D. Rev. Emanuel Schultze was apparently the first regular minister who officiated in the church. Whether he served the congregation which was styled the "Heidelberg Gemeinde" (so called from the ancient name of the town) existing prior to the organization of this church, we have no means of ascertaining. His pastorate extended from 1765 until 1809. Our oldest citizens remember him as continuing to labor when quite aged and infirm. The next pastor, serving with great earnestness from about 1810 until 1836, was Rev. Wm. Baetes. The third pastor, from 1837 until 1849, was Rev. Jonathan Ruthrauff, who was fervent and undaunted in his preaching. Rev. J. M. Deitzler served faithfully from 1850 until 1865, when the pastorate of Rev. U. Graves, lasting about one year, followed. On April 11, 1866, Rev. M. Fernsler was unanimously elected pastor, with the understanding that the church alone should thenceforth constitute a pastoral charge. The Synod failing to sanction the division of the charge, Rev. Fernsler declined the call. Rev. G. J. Martz was elected August 21, 1867, and served until November 1, 1878. Rev. M. Feinsler, the present pastor, preached his introductory sermon, December 1, 1878.

Very interesting centennial services were held in 1865, during which addresses and sermons were delivered by Revs. E. Huber, of Hummelstown, Daniel Schindler, of Lebanon, J. M. Deitzler, of Annville, E. S. Henry, of Pine Grove, and U. Graves, the pastor. Many of the facts contained in the above have been gleaned from a historical sketch prepared by a committee for that occasion.

Since the days of Rev. Ruthrauff, meetings for prayer and mutual exhortation have been maintained, resulting in great good. The charter of the congregation, obtained in 1855, gives the rights of membership to all persons admitted who shall contribute annually a sum not less than fifty cents towards the current expenses. In the light of this provision, the membership is about four hundred and fifty. Amid many discouragements, the pastor and his faithful helpers are laboring on in hope.

STATIONS ABSORBED— RICHLAND AND TEMPLEMAN.

Richland is a small town, two miles east of Myerstown, along the Philadelphia and Reading railroad. At this place a small congregation was organized twenty-five years ago by Rev. G. J. Martz. A small house of worship, still there, was erected jointly by the Lutherans, Reformed and Tunkers or German Baptists, each party being entitled to hold services every third Sunday. When the present pastor of Schaefferstown charge commenced his services here, there were about a dozen members. He for some years continued to hold services regularly every three weeks. Finding, however, no material available to build up with without robbing others, and the membership growing less by death and removal, the few good members were transferred to Schaefferstown church, and no services have been held there by the present pastor during the last year; a number of the people there belong to churches within a few miles.

Templeman Chapel is a small Sunday-school house, erected by the community, one mile east of Cornwall, in the spring of 1887. Provision was made in the charter that the Lutherans of the General Synod and the Reformed could hold services there alternately. A number of Lutheran members having moved there from the Schaefferstown and Brickerville churches, it was supposed best to organize and commence services. The pastor of Schaefferstown promised to preach in the afternoon every four weeks.

An organization was effected in May, 1887, with twenty-two members, and regular services were held every four weeks. A few were added, but the number in a few years so decreased by death and by removals, that for about a year or so no services have been held there on the Lutheran side. Within a short distance there is a regular General Council church, with a fine house of worship, and supplied every two weeks with preaching by a regular pastor from Lebanon. There are still a few members remaining at Templeman (now Rexmont) and their desire is that services should again be held there.

III. ANNVILLE CHARGE, LEBANON CO.—HILL AND ANNVILLE.

BY REV. W. H. LEWARS.

1. HILL CHURCH (BERG KIRCHE).

This church is located in what is now North Annville township, Lebanon county, Pa., about two and one-half miles northwest of the city of Lebanon, and is the mother of all the Lutheran churches in this vicinity.

It has from the beginning to the present been a union church, in which the Lutheran and Reformed congregations have worship.

BERG KIRCHE.

The first edifice was erected in 1733. The material consisted of roughly hewn logs. These also served as seats, quite in contrast with the modern pew. For many years there were no stoves in the building.

During the winter months a fire was built on the outside with logs, of which there was an abundance, around which the people gathered awaiting the arrival of the minister.

When, finally, stoves were introduced, considerable and serious difficulties arose in the congregations.

Some idea of the primitive history of this church can be gained from the following:

Rev. George Lochman, D. D., in speaking of churches in Lebanon county in 1812, says: "Unter diesen ist die Berg Kirche Gemeine, die aelteste. Schon im Jahr 1733 ist sie gessammalet worden, zu einer Zeit da die Indianer noch haefige Einfaelle in die Gegend machten und mordeten."

He further states that people often took their guns with them to church to defend themselves against the savages.

During divine services, men with loaded muskets were placed at the doors as sentinels. According to the first records kept, it was called "the Church on the Quittapahilla."

Its Lutheran pastors have been—1733–1779, extending over 46 years, John Caspar Stöver; 1779–1794, a pastorate of 15 years, Frederick Theodore Melsheimer; 1794–1815, a pastorate of 21 years, George Lochman; 1815–1836, a pastorate of 21 years, William G. Ernst. In 1836 Rev. Jonathan Ruthrauff became the pastor, continuing to serve about 13 years.

In 1850 A. C. Wedekind made the first entry in a Record commenced by him. He made the last entry September 18th, 1853, presumably serving the congregation in connection with Lebanon (Zion) about three years. He was followed by J. M. Deitzler, about 1856, Christian A. Fetzer, 1860–1863, and George P. Weaver, 1863–1864.

Rev. J. M. Deitzler, who followed, made his first entry April 16, 1865, and continued to serve the congregation until the spring of 1890, his pastorate extending over twenty-five years.

On April 15, 1890, the present pastor, Rev. W. H. Lewars, entered the field.

The first pastor and his wife are buried in the "graveyard" adjoining the church. The spot where their bodies repose is marked by two roughly hewn sandstones. The workmanship is crude; but an attempt was made by loving hands to embellish them with art in the shape of a figure representing a cherub. With great labor and patience the following inscription was obtained—the peculiar use, as well as want, of capitals will be noticed by the reader, as well as discrepancies in orthography, etc.

Heir Ruhet in seinem erlöser entschlaffen Johan Casper Stöver erster Evangel Luthericher prediger in pensilvanien, ist geboren in Der under paflz* D. 21 Dec 1707 er zeigte mit seiner Ehe Frau

* Pfalz.

Maria Catharine 11 kinder 4 sein in die ewigkeit voran gegangen, er starb D 13 May 1779 seines alters 71 y 4 mon 3 wo u 2 Tag.

The present building, which is the second, is of brick, and was erected in 1837.

A very quaint old Record, bound in rawhide, having entries of baptisms, deaths, etc., as early as 1734, is in the possession of the present pastor.

A German Bible printed at Halle in 1793, and bought by the congregation in 1798 for 16 shillings and 6 pence, is still in use in conducting the altar service.

A communion cup bearing date of 1745 is also in possession of the congregation.

There is an endowment of eleven hundred dollars upon this church for the benefit of the Lutheran congregation.

2. First Lutheran Church, Annville.

In 1804 members of the Lutheran congregation worshiping in the Hill Church (Berg Kirche), who lived at and near Annville, concluded to organize a church at home, and, accordingly, in conjunction with members of the Reformed denomination, erected a fine stone church building upon a lot donated by Martin Ulrich and Adam Reugel.

The two congregations worshiped in this edifice until 1871, when for various reasons a separation was deemed advisable, whereupon the Reformed organization purchased the interest of the Lutherans in the property for three thousand dollars, and the latter erected a building, which is now occupied by the above-named congregation.

The corner-stone was laid in 1872. At the time when the separation between the Lutherans and the Reformed took place, a division also occurred among the Lutherans, the difficulty having arisen from a difference of opinion in regard to what were then known as "new measures." That portion of the congregation antagonistic to what they regarded extreme practices withdrew, and organized St. Paul's church (General Council).

The names of the pastors who have served this congregation since 1804 are: Revs. George Lochman, 1804-1815; William G. Ernst, 1815-1849; G. F. Krotel, 1849-1853; H. S. Miller,

1854-1859 (?); Wm. S. Porr, 1859-1860; C. A. Fetzer, 1860-1863; Geo. P. Weaver, 1863-1864; J. M. Deitzler, 1865-1890; and W. H. Lewars, 1890 to the present.

The church edifice cost ten thousand dollars, and is built of limestone. The lot upon which it stands was donated to the congregation by John D. Biever, who paid about one-half the cost of the building. He also erected a two-story brick "sexton's house" on a lot adjoining the church, and bought a two-story

FIRST EVANGELICAL LUTHERAN CHURCH, ANNVILLE, PA.

brick house about one-half square from the church and donated it as a parsonage. He subsequently determined to build a parsonage on a lot adjoining the church, on the side opposite the "sexton's house," but died before this was accomplished. His widow, Mrs. Rebecca Biever, afterwards carried out his intentions, in the erection of a substantial and commodious brick parsonage.

He also placed an endowment upon the church to the amount of three thousand dollars. This amount was supplemented by his widow to the extent of two thousand one hundred dollars, she having made the church her residuary legatee. The total interest-bearing fund is $5,100. In addition to this, a permanent fund of one thousand dollars was placed upon the cemetery, the amount coming from the same estate.

It is but due to say, that the commendable generosity here recorded grew out of a life-long Christian character. The piety of Mr. Biever was acknowledged by all who knew him. He assumed a directing and sustaining influence in the church for half a century, and for forty-nine years was the Superintendent of the Sunday-school.

The congregation was served for almost a quarter of a century by Rev. J. M. Deitzler, during which time the church and other buildings were erected. The present pastor, Rev. W. H. Lewars, entered the field in April, 1890.

IV. SPRINGTOWN CHARGE, BUCKS CO.—SPRINGFIELD, DURHAM, SPRINGTOWN.

BY REV. O. H. MELCHOR.

The churches constituting the present "Springtown Charge" were for many years a part of the "Kintersville charge," in connection with the congregations of Nockamixon and Lower Tinicum. The pastoral records of all these congregations indicate that from the dates of organization, respectively, they were all served, with rare exceptions, by the same pastors until the year 1879.

1. TRINITY, SPRINGFIELD.

The oldest of the five, Trinity congregation of Springfield, was organized about 1751, and for twelve years was served by supplies or missionaries.

In 1763 John Michael Enderlein became pastor. He was followed by Rev. Augustus Herman Schmidt. Rev. Peter Ahl became pastor in 1789, and served until 1797. Rev. John Conrad Jeager was pastor from 1797 to 1801; Rev. John Paul Ferdinand Kramer, from 1801 to 1803; Rev. John Nicholas Mensch, from

1803 to 1823; Rev. Henry S. Miller, from 1823 to 1838; Rev. C. F. Welden, from 1838 to 1842; Rev. C. P. Miller, from October, 1842, to September, 1865; Rev. W. S. Emery, from December, 1865, to July, 1879, at which time the present pastor took charge.

Tradition claims that a log church was built about 1751, and that it was also used as a school-house. Be that as it may, beyond the memory of the oldest inhabitant a school-house has stood under the shadow of the church. The first stone edifice was erected in 1763. This was replaced by another in 1816, and the present one was built in 1872.

2. DURHAM.

Prior to 1812 there were three church organizations in Durham township. The earliest account of any religious services is dated 1728, and these were held in a school-house connected with the Durham Iron Works. The first organization was an English Presbyterian one in 1742, at the Iron Works. Later, there was an influx of Germans, and a German Presbyterian church (merged, finally, into the German Reformed) was organized in 1790, which worshiped in a barn. At a still later period, services were held in another school-house by German Lutherans and German Reformed.

There is no record of the organization of a German Lutheran congregation; but on the 8th of August, 1812, these three bodies united and purchased an acre of ground, in the township of Durham, near the Iron Works, and appointed trustees to erect a house for the worship of God, to be known as "Durham Union church," for the joint use of the English Presbyterians, the German Reformed and the Lutherans. In 1876 Presbyterian services were finally abandoned, and the church property now is owned jointly by the Reformed and Lutherans.

The church edifice of 1812 was replaced by a handsome stone building in 1857, which was remodeled in 1889, presenting a handsome interior, while without it is "beautiful for situation, the joy of the whole earth."

From 1812 there are data for a history of the congregation. Rev. John Nicholas Mensch was at this time the pastor, serving from 1811 to 1823, preaching also at Springfield and Lower Tinicum. He was succeeded by the following:

Revs. Henry S. Miller, 1823-1838; C. F. Welden, 1838-1842; C. P. Miller, 1842-1865; W. S. Emery, 1865-1879; O. H. Melchor, July 1, 1879 to the present time.

The records show that down to 1879 all of these pastors also served the congregations of Tinicum and Springfield.

3. CHRIST'S, SPRINGTOWN.

This was a point for occasional preaching as early as 1860, but it did not become a regular station until 1871. It is in reality a child of the Springfield church. The corner-stone for a union church was laid on May 18, 1872. This church was for the joint use of the Lutherans, Reformed, Presbyterians and Mennonites, and is known as "Christ's Church, of Springtown." A Lutheran congregation was regularly organized on April 6, 1874, by Rev. W. S. Emery, pastor.

In the spring of 1879, the Kintnersville charge, by the recommendation of Conference, divided, Tinicum and Nockamixon forming one charge, and Durham, Springfield and Springtown the other. The latter at once extended a unanimous call to the present pastor, who accepted, and took charge July 1, 1879.

The pastor being a member of the East Pennsylvania Synod, and the congregations being a part of the Ministerium of Pennsylvania, the congregations voted, with but three negative ballots at Durham and two at Springfield, to sever connection with the Ministerium and to unite with the East Pennsylvania Synod. This vote was taken at Durham in August, 1879, and at Springfield the following year. Springtown unanimously followed Durham and Springfield. From this time on, the history of these congregations is written in the reports of the East Pennsylvania Synod.

All the churches of this charge are still owned jointly by the Lutherans and Reformed, and services are held in both the English and the German languages. The German is, however, rapidly dying out in the Durham congregation, and Springfield, during the present pastorate, has introduced English services at stated intervals. In this congregation *Pennsylvania German* is spoken exclusively. The church buildings are comparatively new and all are free of debt, Durham and Springfield having handsome pipe organs.

V. KINTNERSVILLE CHARGE, BUCKS CO.—NOCKA-MIXON AND UPPER TINICUM.

BY REV. S. S. DIEHL.

1. NOCKAMIXON.

The Lutheran congregation of Nockamixon was organized about the year A. D. *1752*. The first church was on the hill north of the village of Ferndale. In 1812 the Lutheran and Reformed congregations united in fellowship. The corner-stone of the first *Union* church was laid on Easter Monday, April 19, 1813. The corner-stone of the present structure was laid July 3, 1875. The church seems to have been served for some years by supplies. The regular pastors were as follows:

Revs. John Michael Enderlein, 1766; Jacob S. Miller, 1773; Peter Ahl, 1789; Augustus Herman Schmidt, 1798; John Paul Ferdinand Kramer, 1801; John Nicholas Mensch, 1803; Henry S. Miller, 1823; C. F. Welden, 1838; C. P. Miller, 1842; W. S. Emery, 1865; O. H. Melchor, 1880; S. S. Diehl, 1892.

In February, 1880, the congregation decided by a vote of 69 to 25 to sever its connection with the Pennsylvania Synod of the General Council, and to connect with the East Pennsylvania Synod of the General Synod. Immediately after this decision, Rev. O. H. Melchor, a member of the congregation, was elected pastor. The congregation then joined the pastoral charge of Rev. Melchor, consisting of Durham, Springfield and Springtown. Of this charge the congregation was a part till January, 1892, when the charge of Rev. Melchor was divided and Nockamixon, of Rev. Melchor's charge, and Upper Tinicum, of Rev. Fleck's charge, formed a new charge, electing Rev. Samuel S. Diehl, of the Gettysburg Seminary, as the first pastor. Several of the members of this congregation are now pastors in Lutheran churches, namely, Rev. Wilson Selner, of Luthersburg, Clearfield Co., Rev. O. H. Melchor, of Springtown, Bucks Co., Rev. D. R. Becker, of Palmyra, Pa.

2. UPPER TINICUM.

The Upper Tinicum Lutheran congregation was organized by

Rev. John R. Willox, Lutheran pastor at Riegelsville, who held occasional services in the school-houses of the vicinity. As a result there was a general desire for a house of worship in the neighborhood. The corner-stone of the new church was laid on Whitsunday, 1851, and the dedication occurred in the autumn of the same year. This church was always served in connection with Rieglesville. The pastors serving the congregation were as follows :

Revs. J. R. Willox, 1851 ; C. L. Keedy, 1862 ; Nathan Jeager, 1863 ; Theophilus Heilig, 1864 ; D. T. Koser, 1877 ; C. L. Fleck, 1887 ; S. S. Diehl, 1892.

In January, 1892, the congregation decided to join with Nockamixon church of Rev. Melchor's charge and thus form a new pastorate.

VI. WHITEMARSH CHARGE, MONTGOMERY COUNTY —WHITEMARSH AND UPPER DUBLIN.

BY REV. MATTHIAS SHEELEIGH, D. D.

1. WHITEMARSH.

This church is located thirteen miles north of the centre of Philadelphia, two miles above the corporate limits of the city. The North Pennsylvania Railroad runs one mile east of the church. The Barren Hill church is four miles to the west. In the county there are twenty-six Lutheran churches ; five being in connection with the East Pennsylvania Synod, and twenty-one with the Pennsylvania Synod.

The region is highly picturesque. From an eminence in the vicinity twenty-two places of worship are counted. The imaginary "marsh" is nowhere visible, either on lowland or highland. In this vicinity, Gen. Washington rested his army for seven weeks, in 1777, after the battle of Germantown, and before retiring to Valley Forge.

According to a declining custom, the church edifice and cemetery are owned conjointly and equally with a German Reformed congregation. "The Union Church" is the familiar designation in the community. June 14, 1817, is the date of the first formal meeting for organizing—now 75 years ago.

Those present were identified with congregations of the two denominations named, at Germantown, six to seven miles southward. Rev. Caspar Wack, Reformed, presided, and Jacob Gilbert, Lutheran, served as secretary. At a later meeting, January 24, 1818, presided over by Rev. John C. Baker, Lutheran, it was reported that Philip Sellers had presented the lot on which the church now stands; to which adjoining ground was directly purchased. The cost of the edifice and furnishing amounted to $3,409.20.

An Act of Incorporation was secured, approved by Governor Joseph Hiester on March 30, 1818. The corporate title reads, "The Trustees of the Union Church of Whitemarsh."

A meeting was held at the Union school-house of Whitemarsh, October 18, 1818, to elect officers for the respective congregations. The names of those chosen at this first election are Jacob Gilbert, Christian Grafley, Henry Daub, William Egbert, Peter Shull, Daniel Gilbert and John Trexler, on the Lutheran side; and Henry Scheetz, John Haney, John Miller, Jacob Kibler, William Bitting, Henry Scheetz, Jr., and Jacob Wentz, for the Reformed side.

In 1830, the names of officers were the following: Lutheran—Christopher Grafley, Daniel Nace, John Dutill, Jacob Ettinger, John Katz, Samuel Dewees, Samuel Felty, and John Dager; Reformed—Henry Scheetz, John Haney, Abraham Zimmerman, John Y. Henk, George Streevy, Henry Scheetz, Jr., John Kehr, and Francis Kehr.

Turning to the records of 1840, the following new names appear among the Lutheran officers: Daniel Bickle, William Egbert, Henry Harner, Samuel Evans, John Dager, William Shugard, and Bernard Bisbing. In 1850, still other new names appear in the Council: Daniel Slifer, John Kuhler, Abraham Slifer, John Sorber and — Neiman.

The present Lutheran Council consists of the following: Trustees—Samuel Van Winkle, and Charles C. Slifer; Elders—George D. Heist, Mahlon F. Scheetz and Samuel Yeakle; Deacons—Belding B. Slifer, William S. Kerper, and Frank S. Harner.

The church edifice is of stone. It was erected in 1818; was remodeled and extended in 1861; and again, in 1882, underwent a general renovation and improvement. Extensive shedding was built in 1848, at a cost of $347.83. In 1876, the cemetery was enlarged by the purchase of five acres of adjoining ground, for $2,000.00.

From the beginning to the present, the Lutheran pastors have been the following: Rev. John C. Baker, 1818 to 1828; Rev. Benjamin Keller, 1829 to 1835; Rev. C. W. Schaeffer, 1835 to 1841; Rev. Frederick R. Anspach, 1841 to 1850; Rev. William H. Smith, 1850 to 1852; Rev. Prof. Henry Haverstick and Rev. Luther E. Albert, supplied about three months in 1852; Rev. William M. Baum, 1852 to 1854; Rev. David Swope, 1855 to 1856. The last named was the first pastor settled in the place; the church having previously been served, successively, by pastors of St. Michael's of Germantown, and St. Peter's of Barren Hill. This was also the beginning of the pastoral charge as now constituted, *i. e.*, the Whitemarsh and Upper Dublin congregations. Then followed Rev. Benjamin C. Suesserott, 1856 to 1857; Rev. Lewis Hippee, 1857 to 1859; Rev. Edward J. Koons, 1860 to 1862; Rev. George Sill, 1863 to 1869; and Rev. Matthias Sheeleigh, D. D., April 27th, 1869, to the present.

There now remain two hundred and twenty names of living members in the Lutheran church-book. This congregation has never owned the needful convenience of a parsonage. The present pastor and family now live in their own house in the village of Fort Washington, being about half way between the churches, which are four miles apart. Within the last ten years this congregation has realized at least five bequests of several hundred dollars each. The ladies have for years been active in a local Home Missionary Society, in which both money and labor have been cheerfully given to needy churches, missionaries and orphans.

Three ministers have gone out from the membership of the Union church: two Lutherans—Rev. William W. Bowers and Rev. William Tryday; and one Reformed—Rev. William Sorber. These brethren have all been called hence, after doing good service for the Master. They died respectively in 1873, 1876 and

1878, at the early ages of 48, 55 and 53 years. The body of the first named is buried here.

About sixty years ago the Sunday-school was begun. Among its earlier superintendents were William Tryday and William W. Bowers, named as having become ministers. The school has generally been well attended. More good might, however, be hoped for if a special room for the school were provided, separate from the audience chamber. There are now reported as being in the school 13 teachers and 130 scholars enrolled.

So far as the writer can learn, Lord's Day evening services were never regularly held before his own pastorship. The call, in answer to which he came to the pulpit, specifies only one service in two weeks for this congregation. Of his own free will he chose to afford evening preaching; and now, after nearly a quarter of a century, it would not be willingly dispensed with in either of the "Union" congregations.

In early years some of the church services were conducted in the German language; but probably no regular German service has been thought necessary during the last 45 or 50 years, inasmuch as the German is now scarcely known as a living tongue within ten or twelve miles, looking northward.

We trust that spirituality is growing in the congregations of this charge. Within the last twenty years the grace of giving has also much increased. To the general call, beyond the local or home work, the response is returned with a noticeable readiness.

2. Upper Dublin.

This church is about four miles north from that of Whitemarsh. It also bears the name of a township. The neighborhood designation, not yet extinct, is "Puff's Church," after Valentine Puff, who was an adjoining land-holder, and a member of the original congregation. · Unlike the other church, this is wholly Lutheran. Good roads, some of which are turnpikes, connect the two places and cross the parochial field in different directions.

The present congregation is of comparatively recent origin, although the inheritor of its site from a much earlier organization. That was purchased in the year 1753 by several Lutherans for a church, school-house and burial-ground. It lies a mile east of the new borough of Ambler, at the junction of the Butler turnpike and Susquehanna street. The latter highway runs southeast towards a point on the Delaware river above Philadelphia, projected in colonial times, with a view of making direct communication with the Susquehanna river, a hundred miles distant. But the road comes suddenly to an end a half mile north-west of the church.

Numerous Germans having early settled in the vicinity, Rev. John Frederick Handschuh, then pastor at Germantown, ten miles southward, organized a congregation in 1753 or 1754, and continued services there until 1757. It is possible that he preached at this point a year or two previous. A church and school-house were erected. The church was a log structure, and the school-house was referred to as being "roomy."

Dr. Henry M. Mühlenberg, then in Philadelphia, preached there several times, and in the Halle Reports refers to the congregation, under date of June 18, 1754. Dr. Mühlenberg, who had the general oversight for several years, sent his student, William Kurtz, to serve this people for about a year, from 1757 to 1758. Rev. John Helfrich Schaum then supplied the place from New Hanover, 1758 to 1762; Rev. Henry M. Mühlenberg, then served as pastor, 1762 to June, 1763; Rev. Nicholas Kurtz, of Germantown, 1763 to 1764; Rev. John Ludwig Voigt, of Germantown, 1764 to 1765; Rev. Jacob Van Buskerk, of North Wales, 1765 to 1769; Rev. John Frederick Schmidt, 1769 to 1785; Rev. Anthony Hecht, of Tohickon and North Wales, 1785; Rev. Jacob Van Buskerk again, 1785 to 1795; Rev. Henry A. Geissenhainer, 1797 to 1801; Rev. Frederick D. Schaeffer, of Germantown, 1801 to 1810. About 1810, or soon after, the gospel ministrations ceased, the people having become scattered to other points, and few being left who appreciated the German language. In process of time, the church edifice decayed and disappeared.

A generation later, steps were taken which resulted in the restoration of divine service and the organization of the present congregation. Chiefly through the efforts of the Hon. John B. Sterigere—then a prominent attorney at Norristown, and formerly a Congressman and a State Senator, whose kindred repose here—

a charter was procured from the Legislature in 1852, making conditional provision for a Lutheran congregation at the old burial-ground, where his body also now rests. Previous to this, in 1835, a resident, Conrad Emig, had left by will six hundred and sixty-four dollars to secure protection to this cemetery.

Religious services were resumed in 1852, in the public school-house opposite, and conducted with some degree of regularity until a church was built. In this work of initiating service, Rev. Wm. M. Baum, of Barren Hill, took part. In 1855, when Rev. David Swope came to Whitemarsh, the pastoral duties devolved on him, as the congregations were now united as one pastorate, a relation still existing.

The present comfortable house of worship, built of stone, with basement for Sunday-school, was begun in 1857. The corner-stone was laid October 15 of that year, and the dedicatory services were held July 18, 1858. The pastors, since the retirement of Rev. Mr. Swope in 1856, have been the same as at Whitemarsh.

Commodious shedding, 200 feet in length, was built in 1867. In 1885, a small farm of 16 acres, immediately adjoining the early church property, was purchased. Five acres have been converted into a cemetery, known as Rose Hill Cemetery, making one of the most beautiful burial places. Many are now procuring lots. Our people in the city find this a very desirable and accessible place for the laying of their departed to rest.

Later, the church edifice was neatly painted and otherwise renovated. At the same time, changes were made for removing the choir from the gallery to an angle near the pulpit, on the floor of the main audience room.

At this date of writing, ninety-six persons are counted on the church-book as members entitled to communion.

The church council is at present as follows:
Trustees—Charles Houpt, Edwin H. Faust, Theodore Fleck; Elders—John M. Rex, Frederick Pfitzenmeyer, Peter Weaver; Deacons—Alvin B. Faust, Rudolph Dilthey, Thomas S. Gillin.

Among former members and officers may be named John B. Rittenhouse, Daniel Rynear, William Webster, Daniel Gilbert, Henry Houpt, Adam W. Fleck, John Kuhler, Jacob Smith, Alvin

D. Faust, Jacob W. Lenhart, William Beck, Charles Dilthey, James Doran, and others.

The Sunday-school was organized September 30, 1858. It has generally been zealously conducted, and has produced effective results. In 1883, its 25th anniversary was celebrated with great interest, when a history of the school was written by Mrs. Dr. Hannah E. Wilson. The following have been superintendents: William Webster, Alvin D. Faust, Jacob W. Lenhart, Thomas S. Gillin, James Doran, and Samuel A. Faust.

A helpful Ladies' Aid Society has been maintained in the church for several years past. On the decease of a late member of the congregation, the example of a handsome bequest to her church came to light.

In both congregations, catechisation has been steadily maintained as a preparation for full membership.

Within these congregations, there are taken thirty copies of the Lutheran Observer, two hundred copies of the Lutheran Sunday-School Herald, twenty-five copies of the Augsburg Teacher, etc.

At the pleasant village of Fort Washington, half-way between the two churches of this charge, a very promising Sunday-School was commenced in a Hall, December 21, 1890. It bears the designation Lutheran, and is under the superintendency of Mr. Howard S. Jones, formerly of Philadelphia. The school is not organically connected with the parish, but it is expected to secure, at an early day, the consent of the two congregations to the organizing of a church.

VII. ZION'S CHURCH, HUMMELSTOWN, DAUPHIN CO.

BY REV. H. G. SNYDER.

There is no account, in the existing records of the church, of the organization of this congregation, but fortunately we can fix the date very closely from an old deed, bearing date June 24, 1756. On that day Frederick and Rosina Hummel granted two lots of ground to the congregation. That it was regularly organized prior to that date, is evident from the fact that the deed mentions a "*church erected on a part of said lots,*" and the conveyance is made to "Theophilus England, then pastor," and the "representatives" of the congregation, Andrew Schrötle, Frederick Forster, Leonard Witmeyer, and Daniel Wunderlich. The centennial " History of Dauphin County," claimed to be "a safe reference," is perhaps correct in the statement that the Lutheran church had "begun an enterprise in Hummelstown as early as 1753."

PASTORS.

Theophilus Engelland was pastor in 1756. The next name that appears (only in the auditing of accounts) is that of Michael Enderlein, first mentioned in 1771, and running until 1778. William Kurtz was pastor from 1781–1795. Then occurs an interval when the congregation "was without divine service and religious instruction"; and there was great rejoicing and prosperity, when, in 1804, John Frederick Ernst came among them. He was succeeded in 1807 by John Paul Ferdinand Kramer. John Henry Vanhoff followed on June 23, 1811. Here the congregation was probably without a pastor again for several years, or supplied from some other place. C. R. Demme took charge in June, 1819. On October 6, 1822, he was succeeded by Peter Scheurer. Henry G. Stecher became pastor December 5, 1830, and continued for 24 years, when he was compelled to resign on account of the infirmities of age. George Haines was his successor, October 27, 1854. J. F. Probst followed November 1, 1856. A. S. Link was elected to succeed him on December 1, 1858, and remained until April 27, 1861. The next pastor was E. Huber, June 15, 1861. Peter Rizer was elected to fill the vacancy caused by Rev. Huber's resignation, October 27, 1866, and served until January 1, 1873. P. S. Mack succeeded him on June 2, 1873. Then followed in order, J. H. Leeser, July 1, 1877, to April 1, 1885; I. B. Crist, June 1, 1885, to January 1, 1890; H. G. Snyder, June 1, 1890, to the present time.

CONNECTION WITH OTHER CHURCHES.

There is no mention of any connection with other churches until the pastorate of Henry G. Stecher at Hummelstown, Shoop's, Sand Hill and Union Deposit. Shoop's church separated from the charge about 1850, the other three remaining longer. Since 1873 Hummelstown has supported its own pastor.

CHURCH PROPERTY.

The first church was a log structure, said to have been completed May 16, 1766. Having become too small, it was replaced, in 1815, by a beautiful blue limestone building. After the new church was built, the old one was used as a school-house, but, owing to the carelessness of the teacher, it was destroyed by fire in December, 1817. This second building was enlarged and remodeled in 1855, at a cost of over $4,000, the church being converted into an audience room above and a Sunday-school room below. Drs. Krotel and Hay preached the dedication sermons. The Sunday-school rooms were again remodeled and the church renovated at a cost of $306.35, and re-opened for divine service May 25.

On June 18, 1891, the congregation decided to erect a new church. Plans and specifications were secured from J. A. Dempwolf, architect, York, Pa., and the work was begun in October. The corner-stone was laid November 29, Dr. McKnight preaching the sermon. The entire building is of Hummelstown brownstone, contains main auditorium, Sunday-school, infant class, Bible class and library rooms all on one floor, main auditorium carpeted throughout, cathedral glass windows, heated with steam and lighted by electricity. It will be dedicated January 22, 1893.

Prior to 1857, the pastors lived either in their own or in rented homes, but in this year a handsome, commodious brick parsonage was erected on the lot of ground owned by the congregation, on Main street. This was removed in October, 1891, to the rear of the same lot, fronting on Rosina street, in order to make room for the new church building, which now occupies one of the most eligible sites in the town.

ORGANIZATIONS AND BRANCHES OF CHURCH WORK.

The church council consists of the pastor, who is *ex officio* chairman, three trustees, four elders and four deacons. The congregation is divided into three districts, with representation in the council in proportion to size. Council meets quarterly in regular session, but very frequently for special work.

The Sunday-school existed as far back as 1830, but it was a union school, conducted in the German language, on the order of the week-day school. It met with violent opposition, the country members strongly objecting to its being held in the church, on which account it was disbanded after a few years. It was reorganized in a school-house in 1837. In 1842 it was again taken into the church and conducted in a more modern way.

The remodeling of the church in 1855 created the desire and furnished the opportunity for a distinctively Lutheran school, which was accordingly organized. Henry L. Hummel was its first superintendent, and continued in office until 1872. His successors and their terms were as follows: Frank C. Earnest, from 1872–1874; Geo. I. Hummel, 1874–1875; Dr. Jacob Shope, 1875–1880; H. J. Hummel, 1880–1882; Dr. Charles H. Clark, 1882–1888; C. P. Haehnlen, 1888–1892; and L. W. Ebersole, the present incumbent. It has an Officers' and Teachers' Association, which holds monthly meetings for business and discussion of Sunday-school work, and a weekly teachers' Bible class, conducted by the pastor.

The Ladies' Aid Society was organized in 1875, and pledged to work "for the good of the church at home and abroad." In January, 1881, the "Woman's Home and Foreign Missionary Society" was organized. In 1882 it reported 45 active and 5 honorary members, and contributed $25. In the course of time the society was disbanded, but on September 18, 1889, it was reorganized with its original title and object.

On September 5, 1890, a Society of Christian Endeavor was organized, and now numbers 40 active and 22 associate members. The society contributes $25 annually to Foreign Missions, raised by the "two cents a week" plan.

So far as the writer has been able to learn, but one minister has gone out from this congregation, the Rev. John A. Earnest, D. D.

The congregation now numbers about 200 communicant members, and is well organized and equipped for efficient service.

VIII. UNION DEPOSIT CHARGE, DAUPHIN CO.—SAND HILL, SANDY HOLLOW, UNION DEPOSIT, HOERNERSTOWN.

BY REV. J. M. DEITZLER, ASSISTED BY REV. W. H. LEWARS AND REV. A. WIETING.

1. Sand Hill Church.

As early as 1756, this congregation possessed a house of worship, known as the "Berg Kirche," in Derry township. It stood upon the Sand Hills, two miles southeast of Hummelstown, near the present location of the brownstone quarries. It was surrounded by a fine grove of chestnut and oak trees, on an unfrequented public road, and stood until 1875, a period of one hundred and nineteen years. The present building is of red sandstone, with a small belfry. The old communion-set, presented by Ulrich Hubscher and Wendel Poh, has been in use for one hundred and seventeen years. Articles of incorporation were drawn in 1891, the following being trustees at that time: Jacob Books, Michael Hall, John Bender, John Walty, John Fuhrman, Anthony Beersley, Philip Beersley, Henry States, Thomas Smith.

Eleven persons communed at Easter in 1812. There are now thirty-five communicant members. The congregation owns some fifteen acres of land adjoining the church, and a good sexton's house.

The church was generally served by the pastors who ministered at Hummelstown, until the formation, in 1873, of the Union Deposit charge, with which it has since been connected.

2. Sandy Hollow Church.

In the year 1844, Mr. John Diller, a tanner, residing at Sandy Hollow, extended an invitation to Rev. A. Wieting, of Middletown, to preach in the school-house at the former place. The invitation was accepted, and services conducted every two weeks for two years, beginning with August, 1844. In 1846 a neat little church, 35x50 feet, was erected, the location being on the Jonestown road, nine miles east of Harrisburg, in West Hanover township. After holding a protracted meeting in the new building, the pastor organized a congregation with 33 members. After preaching for about eight years longer, Rev. Wieting was succeeded by Rev. Wm. G. Laitzle, who served as supply from 1852–1854. The succeeding pastors have been: G. J. Martz, 1855–1868; H. D. Kutz, 1869–1871; E. Daron, 1872–1875; E. S. Brownmiller, 1875–1881; G. J. Martz, 1882–1883; A. K. Zimmerman, 1885–1887; J. A. Danner, 1887; J. M. Deitzler, 1890 to the present time.

A new tin roof was put upon the building last year, and the interior neatly papered and carpeted. The congregation now numbers about forty members.

3. St. John's Church, Union Deposit.

This is a union church. Its constitution was adopted November 29, 1847, and is signed by the following persons representing the Lutheran congregation: Geo. Keplinger, David Ramler, Conrad Wagner, Jacob Hocker, David Berst. The corner-stone was laid in the same year. The congregation has been served by the following pastors: Lewis G. Eggers, 1847–1852; Wm. G. Laitzle, 1852–1854; George Haines, 1854–1856; A. S. Link, 1858–1861; Eli Huber, 1861–1866; Peter Rizer, 1866–1873. Up to this time the congregation was a part of the Hummelstown pastorate. Since then, the following pastors have served: E. S. Brownmiller, 1874–1881; Geo. J. Martz, (supply) 1882–1883; A. K. Zimmerman, 1885–1887. After the resignation of the last-named pastor, the charge was served for a brief period by Rev. John A. Danner, who was conditionally received into the East Pennsylvania Synod from the Reformed Church, but has since gone back to his first love. Rev. J. M. Deitzler became pastor in June, 1890. The congregation is now, after a long period of discouragement, in a hopeful condition, numbering 63 communicant members.

4. St. John's Church, Hoernerstown.

This congregation, organized in August, 1891, was admitted to Synod at its session in September of the same year, and added to the Union Deposit Charge. It has a substantial and energetic membership, forty in number, a fine new church, and a growing Sunday-school.

IX. ST. PAUL'S CHURCH, ALLENTOWN.

BY REV. J. A. SINGMASTER.

The oldest Lutheran congregation in the vicinity of Allentown, and probably in Lehigh county, is known as the Salzburg (Salisbury) church. Its first edifice, presumably of logs, was built as early as 1741.

In 1762 Allentown, then called Northampton, is said to have been laid out by James Allen. In the same year the Lutherans and Reformed erected a building of l gs to serve as a church and probably also as a school-house. This building stood in the rear of the lot where Zion's Reformed church now stands.

The first Lutheran pastor was John Joseph Roth, who had been a Roman Catholic Studiosus and was from Siegen in Germany. In December, 1761, pastor Roth was in charge of the Indian field and Old Goschenhoppen congregation. December 8th he visited Mühlenberg and stated that he had tendered his resignation at Indianfield and accepted charge of Upper Milford, and desired to be received into the Ministerium. At the meeting of the Ministerium June 28, 1762, at Philadelphia, delegates from Indianfield appeared, bringing with them their pastor Roth, and applied for his examination in order to his being received into the Ministerium. He was examined as to doctrine, earnestly admonished, and asked to await a future decision as to his admission into the Ministerium after a fuller acquaintance. The decision was received by him with tears and deep emotion. December 15, 1762, Upper Milford wrote to Mühlenberg that they desired to have Mr. Roth as their pastor; that he now for some time had preached to them, that they had knowledge of his doctrine and life, and that they desired him to unite with the Ministerium. In his answer dated January 3, 1763, Mühlenberg urges them to unite with the little congregation at the School-house, and as Upper Saucon had become vacant by the removal of Friederici

ST. PAUL'S EVANGELICAL LUTHERAN CHURCH, ALLENTOWN, PA.

beyond the Blue Mountains, they should unite and make provision for the support of a pastor, who should reside among them.

So John Joseph Roth became pastor of the Upper Milford, Saucon and Allentown Congregations, retaining also Indianfield.

At the meeting of the Ministerium in Philadelphia, October 16, 1763, delegates were present from Saucon and Indianfield. It is said that none came from Allentown and Upper Milford through fear of attacks by the Indians. A letter was read from Upper Milford, commending Mr. Roth for his purity of life and his zeal in official duty, and one from the inhabitants of Allenstown in Hamton county, who desire that Mr. Roth may be recognized and approved as their pastor. The question of receiving Diaconus Roth into full membership with the Ministerium was carefully considered, Monday, October 17, 1763; the delegates were examined as to the desire of the congregations, to which they testified. He was then received, after needful admonition, into full membership, each minister giving him his hand and hearty wish for God's blessings upon him. This is the first mention of Allentown and its Lutheran congregration by name in the Hallesche Nachrichten, in October, 1763.

Unfortunately, the services of Roth as pastor did not continue long, as he died, and was buried May 13, 1764, at Upper Saucon church.

From 1764, after the death of pastor Roth, until the close of 1769, the four congregations of the charge to which Allentown belonged were vacant and dependent on occasional visits from neighboring clergymen.

In 1769, towards the close of the year, these congregations, with the addition of Macungie, obtained the services of Rev. Jacob Van Buskerk, the great-grandfather of the present pastor. Dr. Van Buskerk was born at Hackensack, N. J., in 1739. At the age of twenty he became a member of Mühlenberg's family in order to be prepared for the ministry. He became Mühlenberg's assistant, was ordained in 1763, and became pastor of the above-named churches in 1769. He remained pastor until 1778. He served the Macungie church, with a short intermission, until near his decease, which occurred in 1801 at Upper Dublin, where his remains lie buried.

In 1773 the Reformed withdrew from the union church, having built a church of their own. The Lutherans occupied the log church until 1794.

After the resignation of Rev. Van Buskerk, the congregation was apparently without a pastor for several years.

In the Protocol of the Ministerium for 1781, Allentown has become connected with Dry Lands, Irish Settlement and Indianland. These congregations then applied to the Synod for a pastor. The answer was that the Ministerium regrets the want of pastors and requests neighboring pastors to visit them as often as possible, preaching and administering the sacraments, and advises the congregations to select lay-readers capable of conducting the kinderlehre and leading the singing.

In 1783 John Christian Leps attended the meeting of the Ministerium as pastor at Allentown, and the place is mentioned as giving name to a pastorate. It is probable therefore that he resided here. Mr. Leps was a native of Denmark, and had resided in the Danish West India islands. He arrived in Philadelphia in 1773. He was a man of scholarly attainments, and was engaged by Dr. Kunze as teacher of a Seminary which he endeavored to establish. The Seminary failed, and Mr. Leps was ordained upon a call from Loonenburg, now Athens, New York, and in July, 1774, he removed thither. In 1778 he was still in New York, but longed to return to Pennsylvania. It is not known how long he remained at Allentown—not over seven years at most.

In one of the venerable church records occurs the name of Rev. Carl Christoph Goetz, "a native of Worms." His first entry bears the date of November, 1785; the last June 8, 1788. This is all that is known of him.

In the list of ministers present at the Synod in 1793 is the name of Joseph Wichterman, among the licensed candidates: his residence is given as Allen township. The congregations of each charge are given, and he has charge of Allentown and the church in Hanover township, with 123 communicants. He was received into the Ministerium in 1791, upon an application from Bedminster, New Jersey. He left Allentown at the time of the meeting of the Synod.

In 1793 George Frederick Ellisen, a candidate from Germany,

was examined and licensed as a candidate to have charge of Upper Milford, Upper Saucon, Salisbury and Allentown. In 1795 Steiner's church is added to this charge. In 1796 his name was on the roll but he was not at Synod; in 1797 it disappears from the roll, and his license, not having been renewed, expired.

In 1794, during the pastorate of Licentiate Ellisen, the old log church was abandoned and the erection of a larger stone structure begun on the site of the present St. Paul's. From the accounts kept by the treasurer, Leonard Nagle, we glean the following interesting particulars. For the first time the record is made in English and that quite readable. The trustees were John Horn, John Roth, Peter Hartz and Henry Shantz. The corner-stone was laid June 24, 1794. The consecration took place September 4, 1795. The cost was nearly 1300 pounds sterling. Building was expensive at that time. Day laborers received from five to six shillings a day. Pine boards were $22 per thousand feet. Nails cost 11 pence (22 cents) per pound. About $230 were expended for this item alone. "The old church was sold to Valentine Fatzinger at vendue for 17 pounds." The treasurer credits himself with six shillings and nine pence "for Rum at Raising"!! £99 were collected toward the new church by Philip Klotz and Andrew Young, at Philadelphia. The indebtedness in March, 1797, was about £300.

In the year 1800 Rev. John Conrad Jaeger became pastor of St. Paul's. His charge consisted of Christ church, Hanover, where he lived, Dry Lands, Friedens in Saucon, and Allentown.

In each of his four churches Mr. Jaeger preached once in four weeks on Sunday morning, and while he was pastor there was never any service at night in Allentown. The salary paid Mr. Jaeger by the Allentown church was $100. Mr. Jaeger retained charge of these four churches until 1831, but his son, Joshua, was licensed to preach in 1827, and assisted his father in his whole charge until 1831, when the father resigned charge of Allentown and Friedens church, of which his son became pastor.

Allentown in 1830 was a town of 1500 inhabitants, but the opening of navigation on the Lehigh and the supply of water to the town gave a fresh impulse to its growth, and it was felt by pastors and congregation that there must be a resident pastor and more frequent services. When, therefore, Rev. Joshua Jaeger was elected as pastor, he settled in town, and soon offered to preach every other Sunday morning. His call only required services once in four weeks and offered $100 as salary. His proposal was accepted and the salary increased to $150. In 1832, however, the father died and the son was elected in the other two churches; he could, therefore, no longer preach oftener than once in four weeks in the morning, but he proposed to preach on two Sunday evenings in each four weeks. This arrangement was made and remained unaltered throughout the whole time of his ministry, and the salary, $175, also remained unaltered.

In 1834 a Sunday-school was established by members of the Lutheran and Reformed congregations. In its establishment Mr. Jaeger took a very active part, going around from house to house, and urging his members to send their children. The school met in the Lutheran church until the completion of the Reformed church, in the erection of which a room was provided for the school, when, in 1839, the school was removed to its new quarters. In September, 1856, the school separated, each organizing anew in their respective churches.

The rapid growth of the town made it apparent to Mr. Jaeger that St. Paul's must have a pastor for itself and one who could preach in English as well as in German. Therefore, on Easter, April 11, 1852, at the close of the morning service, he presented his resignation, to take effect immediately.

Upon the resignation of Rev. Jaeger, the congregation, by the advice of the Synod, called two pastors, one for the German portion, the other for the English. The former secured the services of Rev. Jacob Vogelbach; the latter those of Rev. Beale M. Schmucker. They both came in October, 1852. Rev. Vogelbach took charge also of the congregations which nearly a century before had been connected with Allentown. Hence he could preach only every other Sunday morning, but oftener at night, at St. Paul's. The English pastor thus occupied the pulpit at about half the regular services. "The contrast however between the audiences was very great," says Schmucker in an "Historical Discourse" delivered at the twenty-fifth anniversary of St. John's. "The earnestness and pulpit power of Mr. Vogelbach, then in the vigor of his best days, attracted crowded audiences. The English audiences were very small." But the work grew, so that early in 1854 measures were taken for the erection of a church, the corner-stone of which was laid June 25. The consecration of the new St. John's English Lutheran church took place May 6, 1855.

While St. John's was in process of erection, plans for building a new St. Paul's were maturing. By the 21st of May, 1854, a committee reported that $7100 had been subscribed. The final service was held in the old church on Easter, 1855. The name St. Paul's was adopted for the new church May 27, 1855, the former name having been "the German Evangelical Lutheran church." The cost of the edifice was about $15,000. It was consecrated September 21, 1856, Drs. Mann and Hutter of Philadelphia, the Moravian bishop Wolle, of Bethlehem, and Rev. Dubs, of the Reformed Church, assisting the pastor, Rev. Vogelbach. The latter terminated a popular and successful pastorate in February, 1857. His salary had been $300 from St. Paul's.

Immediately after the resignation of Mr. Vogelbach, the congregation determined to separate from the country churches and, for the first time in its history, support a pastor alone. Rev. A. T. Geissenhainer became pastor at a salary of $800, in the spring of 1857, and terminated his pastorate in August, 1858.

Rev. Wm. G. Mennig, of Pottsville, was elected as the next pastor in January, 1859, at a stipulated salary of $600, which, however, was raised after some years to $1000. He took charge in February. His preaching produced a deep spiritual impression, resulting in a genuine revival of religion. The "revival meetings," however, did not receive the endorsement of a considerable number of the members, who stigmatized these special services as "new measures." The minority, moreover, secured the unwarranted interference of the Ministerium of Pennsylvania. This in due time induced the pastor and the church to sever their connection with that body, and to unite with the Synod of East Pennsylvania, the latter in 1872, the former in the year following.

But they were not suffered to go in peace. Their opponents instituted legal proceedings for the possession of the property, chiefly on the ground that the East Pennsylvania Synod was not truly Lutheran. In a bitter, long, expensive and now classic trial, St. Paul's, the East Pennsylvania Synod and the General Synod were completely vindicated by favorable decisions in the local and in the Supreme Court of the State. The losers immediately (in 1875) organized St. Michael's church, which is now large and prosperous.

During Mr. Mennig's pastorate previous to 1873, the congregation had attained a membership of about 750. He reported 400 when he united with the East Pennsylvania Synod. Advancing years and the need of English services prompted him to resign in the Spring of 1877, after a pastorate of eighteen years. He remained a member of St. Paul's until his decease, frequently supplying its pulpit and that of other churches. He died July 15, 1887.

The action of a congregational meeting in October, 1877, authorizing the use of English in the Sunday evening service, marks another era in the history of St. Paul's. The use of German at the morning and English at the evening service still continues, to the satisfaction of all concerned. The Sunday-school, however, has become English, excepting a large German Bible-class.

Rev. Charles E. Hay began a successful pastorate on December 1, 1877. The membership increased from 400 to 608; and the Sunday-school numbered 660 according to the pastor's last synodical report, in 1889. Various new societies were established and benevolence stimulated. A debt of $4200 was paid during the early years. In 1884 a splendid new pipe organ was purchased at a cost of $3000. In 1889 a commodious parsonage was erected, costing, together with the lot, about $5000. Nearly $42,000 were contributed for all purposes during the twelve years of his pastorate. On February 10, 1890, he resigned, and, with the coöperation of 133 members who withdrew from St. Paul's, founded St. Matthew's Lutheran church. Quite a large number of scholars from the Sunday-school also accompanied them.

The present pastor, Rev. J. A. Singmaster, took charge May 1, 1890. St. Paul's again manifested its recuperative power in recovering from the depletion of its ranks. Beginning with 366 members, it has increased to over 450. The Sunday-school numbers 600. In less than three years, almost $13,000 have been raised for all purposes. The principal improvements made consist of the entire remodeling of the Sunday-school rooms, the introduction of steam heating into the church, and the laying of a new sidewalk; all of which cost nearly $2,000. The parsonage debt has also been canceled. The outlook is promising.

The property of the congregation consists of St. Paul's church, an imposing two-story brick edifice of gothic architecture. It is surmounted by a steeple 190 feet in height, containing a tower-clock and two bells, the larger of which is noted for the sweetness and strength of its tone. The auditorium contains galleries on three sides and seats over 800 people. The lower story is devoted to the Sunday-school and is divided into four rooms, separated by sliding partitions. About a square south of the church, on South Eighth street, stands the parsonage, a fine ten-room house with modern conveniences.

During the last forty years four new congregations have gone forth from St. Paul's. Two others have been founded in the city, making seven Lutheran churches in Allentown. Probably a third of the population is Lutheran. Two of the churches use the English language exclusively in their services; the rest both English and German.

In the preparation of this sketch the writer has availed himself of Dr. Schmucker's "Historical Discourse," which traces the history of St. Paul's with more or less accuracy as far as 1855.

X. HAMILTON CHARGE, MONROE CO.—HAMILTON, ST. MARK'S, TANNERSVILLE, ST. JOHN'S, BRODHEADSVILLE, MT. ETON.

BY REV. R. H. CLARE.

1. CHRIST'S CHURCH, HAMILTON TOWNSHIP.

The history of the Lutheran and Reformed congregations, now worshiping in Christ's Union church, Hamilton township, Monroe county, according to the old German records on hand, dates back to 1768, although, judging from the large number of communicants then already gathered, it would appear that the Lutheran congregation must have existed long before this. A baptismal record is on hand bearing date of 1763, in the handwriting of the Rev. J. A. Friedricus (Friederici). A communion record of the same year contains the name of the mother of the child of the above record. From this and other evidences on hand it would appear that an effort was made as early at least as 1763 (we may assume much earlier) to organize the Lutherans into a congregation in this section of Monroe (then Northampton) county. The first evidences of a permanent organization do not appear till 1768. That year finds thirty-seven names enrolled as communicants, and the following year seventy-three, of whom fifteen were catechumens.

In 1775 this congregation, as well as its sister of the Reformed denomination, had assumed fair proportions, and in that year three acres of land were secured to build thereon "a church and school house and for a burial place." One acre of this land was presented by Philip Bossard, of the Reformed church, one acre by George Hartlieb, a member of the Lutheran church, and one acre was purchased by the congregations. A log church and school house were erected the same year, and prosperity seems to have attended their projects. The relations between the two congregations seem to have been harmonious, and there was a steady growth of membership and also an accumulation of wealth. In 1820 the congregations owned several hundred acres of land, which was sold, the proceeds being devoted to the erection of a new church.

Plans were completed in 1829, when the congregation erected their new edifice. This new church, a large stone structure, was dedicated November 6 and 7, 1830, by the pastors, the Rev. J. B. Gross, of the Lutheran church, and the Rev. H. L. Hoffeditz, of the Reformed church. The church cost $3,690.91.

The Lutheran congregation was chartered by the State in 1816, and owns a parsonage and sixteen acres of land near the church. The present parsonage was built in 1837, and extensively repaired in 1883.

The Hamilton church is properly called the "mother church" in this county, no less than six congregations in different parts of the county having been organized by those who at one time were members of this congregation.

The present membership is two hundred and forty.

The following is a list of the pastors who have served this congregation from its organization till the present time:

Revs. J. A. Friederici, 1763–1790; Frank Niemyer, 1790–1803; Chas. F. Endress, 1803–1805; C. Diehl, 1805–1810; J. Colson, 1810–1812; P. Rupert, 1812–1818; H. Kurtz, 1818–1823; P. Rupert (second term), 1823–1828; J. B. Gross, 1828–41; Geo. Heilig, 1841–1857; S. S. Kline, 1858–1860; H. Seifert, 1860–1869; J. R. Focht, 1869–1874; Geo. Roths, 1874–1882; R. H. Clare, 1882–1892; Cyrus E. Held, 1892.

2. St. Mark's Church, Jackson Township.

St. Mark's Lutheran and Reformed church is located in Jackson township. The Lutheran congregation was organized about 1830, and the Rev. Joseph B. Gross was its first pastor. He was followed in regular succession by the pastors of the Hamilton charge, interrupted only by the brief pastorate of Rev. A. Rumpf, in 1857–8.

In 1851 Peter Woodling donated the land, and the new church was built. The present number of Lutheran communicants is sixty-five.

3. St. Paul's, Tannersville.

St. Paul's Evangelical Lutheran church of Tannersville was erected in 1834 upon land deeded to a board of trustees elected by the "inhabitants of Tannersville," and the building and grounds were to be used for church purposes forever. The Lutheran and Reformed congregations conjointly erected the building, and no other denominations have ever worshiped in it. The Lutheran congregation was organized some time previous, and had been worshiping in a school-house. Rev. Joseph Gross was its first pastor, and ministered to the congregation until 1836. He was in turn succeeded by the following clergymen: Rev. George Heilig, who remained ten years, Rev. Jacob Rumpf, one year, Rev. S. S. Kline, Rev. Henry Seifert, Rev. Joseph B. Focht.

During the pastorate of the Rev. J. B. Focht the congregation severed its connection with the Hamilton charge and united with a charge under the General Council. The cause of this separation was the "new measures" introduced by the pastor of the Hamilton charge. From 1869 to 1883 this congregation remained in connection with the Ministerium of Pennsylvania, being served by Rev. J. H. Fritz as supply for the six months preceding Easter, 1873, and by Rev. A. M. Strauss from 1875 to 1883.

During the pastorate of Rev. R. H. Clare at Hamilton, this congregation again united with the Hamilton charge of the Synod of East Pennsylvania of the General Synod. Rev. R. H. Clare was pastor from 1883 till July, 1892, when Rev. Cyrus E. Held became pastor of the Hamilton charge, which includes this congregation. The church is a "union church," and the Reformed and Lutheran denominations worship in it upon alternate Sabbaths. The present number of Lutheran communicants is one hundred and twenty-five.

4. St. John's, Bartonsville—Hamilton Charge.

St. John's Evangelical Lutheran church is located about one mile south of Bartonsville. The congregation was organized about 1841, and the Rev. George Heilig was its first pastor. The church building was erected upon ground deeded to the Lutheran and United Presbyterian congregations. The latter body, however, never worshiped regularly in the church which was shortly after erected, and principally by Lutherans. The Lutheran congregation has had continuous worship in the church erected about 1841, and has since its organization maintained its connection with the East Pennsylvania Synod of the General Synod.

The church building having become too small for the use of the congregation and very much out of repair, ground was broken in the spring of 1892 for a new church building. The corner-stone of the new edifice was laid June 5, 1892, by Rev. R. H. Clare, according to the usage of the Lutheran church, and it is hoped that the new church will be ready for dedication before the close of 1892. This congregation has since its organization been regularly served by the pastors of the Hamilton charge. The present membership of this congregation is one hundred and forty.

5. Brodheadsville Church.

During the pastorate of Rev. Henry Seifert in the Hamilton church, a Lutheran congregation was organized at Brodheadsville. Through the efforts of C. D. Brodhead, the sum of sixteen hundred dollars was raised in 1860, and a union church was built for the use of the Lutheran and Reformed denominations. Rev. Henry Seifert served this congregation (organized in 1860) with great acceptance till 1869, since which time it has been regularly ministered to by the pastors of the Hamilton charge. The present Lutheran membership is one hundred and thirty. The estimated value of the church property of the two congregations is $3,800.

Located about one mile from the church is "Fairview Academy," under Lutheran control. This academy was planned and built in the spring and summer of 1881, by Prof. (now Rev.) George G. Kunkle. The first session opened with sixty students. Prof. T. H. Serfass at present has charge of the institution, which is doing a good work for our church, several of its graduates having entered the Lutheran ministry.

6. Mount Eton Church.

This church is located in Ross township, Monroe county, Pa., and is the joint property of the Lutheran and Reformed denominations. The Lutheran congregation was organized in 1884 by the Rev. R. H. Clare, then pastor of the Hamilton Charge. Rev. Clare served this congregation from 1884 to 1892. The Rev. Cyrus E. Held took charge July 1, 1892. The present membership is about sixty. The church property owned by the congregation is worth $5,000.

XI. ST. PAUL'S CHURCH, ARDMORE, MONTGOMERY CO.

BY REV. M. COOVER.

In a country home in Lower Merion, on the 17th day of October, 1765, three male infants received the sacrament of holy baptism. From this recorded ministerial act dates the history of St.

Paul's Lutheran church of Ardmore. Who performed this sacred rite and ministered in spiritual things to the small community of Christian believers, no record tells us. No church building sheltered the worshipers. In some house on or very near the present cemetery grounds was heard the German choral and the story of the gospel told to listening Christians of the Lutheran faith in the language of their beloved Reformer. The only information which can be secured concerning the first acts of this organized band of earnest Christians has its source in a recorded purchase of land with a dwelling house to be used for a place of public worship and a plot for the burial of their dead.

At sheriff's sale, September 3, 1765, sixty-six and three-fourths acres of land were purchased by Mr. John Hughes, and sold in the following month to a committee of six men to furnish a location for a church. By agreement on the part of the committee, the dwelling house located upon this purchased property was to be used for an Evangelical Lutheran Church "as long as the sun and moon endure," and six acres of the tract were to be reserved for a cemetery. Should the congregation become able by sale of the remaining land or by contributions to build a church, the dwelling house was again to be used as a place of residence. The congregation however failed to pay for the tract, and in 1769 the committee of purchasers sold it to Stephen Goodman, who in turn conveyed 133 perches to a committee of four trustees, himself being one of the number. This property was to remain " in trust for the religious society of people called Lutherans, of Merion and adjacent townships, for the purpose of erecting thereon one or more churches, or places of religious worship, and as a place for interring the members of the Lutheran congregation, or such persons as they may direct." An organization was no doubt effected in the year 1765, which authorized the committee to make the purchase of land in view of erecting a church ; and the dwelling located on this property served as a place of worship from October, 1765, until 1769, when the first church, a humble log building, was erected. There is no history of the dedicatory service, nor of officiating clergy. From the time of its organization until 1830 the congregation was supplied with spiritual ministrations chiefly by ministers of the Germantown pastorate.

The first recorded public services are indicated simply by a memorandum of collections and infant baptisms. From this we learn that there was preaching on Thursday, Christmas-day, 1766, and also on the following Sabbath. The first stated communion was administered September 22, 1767, to forty-three communicants. Services of similar nature were no doubt held previous to this, but no record was kept. The officiating clergyman at the dedication of the first church building, 1769 or 1770, was probably Rev. Mr. Van Buskerk of the Germantown pastorate, or his successor, the Rev. John Frederick Schmidt. Succeeding the ministration of these in the Merion pastorate were Revs. Henry Miller and John Weinland. During the services of the latter in the year 1787, the same in which the revered Henry Melchior Mühlenberg passed to his final rest, the stone school-house was built which now serves for chapel and vault in the cemetery. The church, in an interesting debit account with the builders, in addition to obligations for hauling stone and sand, shows itself debtor " to Christopher Tomiller for one day's digging foundation and quart of rum, 5 shillings and 9 pence." In those good old days the workmen wanted to be in good *spirits* while engaged in such sacred duties.

In 1790 Rev. Frederick D. Schaeffer, D. D., began his work in Germantown, continuing in the pastorate for 22 years. During his associated work in Lower Merion, the second church was dedicated in the summer of 1800. The old log church was torn away and a stone building was erected in conjunction with the school-house built 13 years before. During the last 12 years of Dr. Schaeffer's ministry in Germantown there were no regular services nor sacramental ministrations in the Lower Merion pastorate. A transition of language from German to English was taking place, which made demands for English preaching which could not be supplied. Until the year 1799 the meagre church record was written in German, and for twelve subsequent years the record is partly in the German and partly in the English language, until the latter became the prevailing tongue.

From 1810 to 1828 there was no pastor. The pulpit was filled occasionally by Rev. J. C. Baker, who succeeded Dr. Schaeffer, and also by ministers of other denominations. The recorded names are : Rev. Casper Wach, Rev. Dr. Runkel, of the German Reformed church, Dr. Ely, Presbyterian, of Philadelphia, who sent as pulpit supplies several students receiving theological instruction under him, Rev. Wm. Bishop, Presbyterian, and Rev. H. G. Jones, D. D., of the Lower Merion Baptist church, who served from 1826 to 1828. Mr. Chas. Kugler then invited Rev. B. Keller, of Germantown, to minister here, and together with Rev. C. P. Krauth, D. D., from St. Matthew's, Philadelphia, and Rev. C. F. Schaeffer, then a student under his father, the pastorate was supplied from 1828 to 1830. In 1830 Rev. Jeremiah Harpel came, the first regular pastor, officiating at the same time in Cohansey and living in Francisville. During his ministry the third church building was erected, a stone edifice of humble proportions on the site of the old building. The corner-stone was laid May 14, 1833, at which service the church received its name, St. Paul's. Drs. Mayer, Krauth, Demme, and Rev. B. Keller were present, together with the pastor. On Nov. 24 of the same year, the church was dedicated, the sermon being preached by Rev. Mr. Wolle of the Moravian church.

Rev. J. Harpel resigned in 1834, having served four years. Succeeding him were Mark Harpel, his brother, serving for a few months, Charles Barnitz, the first pastor residing in this pastorate and serving four and one-half years, and Edward Town, two and one-half years.

From 1842 to 1844 there was no settled pastor. During this period Rev. S. D. Finckel, of Germantown, preached occasionally. In April, 1844, the property of the church was increased by a purchase of several acres of land, which together with a former small purchase gave the congregation a possession of four and one-quarter acres.

In the autumn of 1844 Rev. Nathan H. Cornell became pastor, serving four years ; and following in order were : Rev. Wm. H. Smith, two years, Rev. Prof. H. H. Haverstick, six months, and Rev. W. D. Roedel, four years, from 1851 to 1855. In Mr. Roedel's ministry the parsonage was built, a substantial house still occupying its position on the grounds of the cemetery. It is no longer used as a parsonage, but is rented by the congregation, the location being somewhat distant from the present church building. After the resignation of Rev. Mr. Roedel, Rev. Mr. Haverstick again became a supply for six months, until a call was extended to Rev. T. T. Titus, who ministered from 1856 to 1861. An interesting and comprehensive history of the church from its founding till the year 1860 was written by Mr. Titus and published for the pleasure of his parishioners.

Succeeding Mr. Titus were Rev. J. H. Heck, ministering seven and one-half years, and Rev. H. J. Watkins, five years, 1869-74. In 1873 preparations were made for the fourth church building. A lot on Lancaster Avenue was presented by Mr. Charles Kugler, a pillar and trustee of the church, and gladly accepted by the congregation as a location for a new house of worship. Rev. Mr. Watkins resigned the charge before the church was completed, and was succeeded by Rev. W. H. Steck, who entered upon his pastoral work in March, 1874. The new church was dedicated September 5, 1874, Rev. F. W. Conrad, D. D., LL. D., preaching the dedicatory sermon. The church is built of stone, with the audience room on the second floor, the first floor being used for lecture-room, Sunday-school services and library. Recent improvements have fitted the building with steam-heating apparatus, new upholstery and carpetings. Two preaching services are held every Sunday. A weekly prayer-meeting and an active Sunday-school organization add to the efficiency of church work. The pastoral aids in the congregation are a Mite Society, Woman's Home and Foreign Missionary Society, and a Young People's Luther Alliance; and special mission aid is given by a large membership to the Mission Society of the Philadelphia Conference.

In 1883, Dr. Anna S. Kugler, a member of this congregation, became a medical missionary on our mission territory in India. After five years of service and a three years' furlough, she again sailed for India in August, 1891. Rev. Mr. Steck resigned his pastorate March, 1890, and was succeeded in July of the same year by Rev. M. Coover, who accepted a call after the completion of his studies in the Seminary at Gettysburg.

In 1889 the trustees of the church made a purchase of five additional acres, extending westward from the old cemetery grounds, to furnish a larger space for sepulture. On this elevated spot are the grassy mounds and moss-covered markers of departed Christians sleeping the years away. The village church bell, in sounding distance, tolls the hours of prayer and Sabbath days over resting Revolutionary heroes, colonial Christians, and ancient fathers with sleeping families at their side: over forms whose ardent souls loved and worshiped on the spot where now they sleep their last and quiet sleep. And still the ministry continues, from wondering babe at baptismal font to slumbering pilgrim borne to his last and undisturbed repose.

XII. ST. PETER'S CHURCH, BARREN HILL (LAFAYETTE HILL), MONTGOMERY COUNTY.

BY REV. A. H. F. FISCHER.

The early settlers at Barren Hill and vicinity were Germans, some of whom were connected with the Lutheran church at Germantown, six miles distant. Owing to disturbances in that congregation during the years 1753–5, some Lutheran and German Reformed families bought an acre and thirty-five perches of land for the erection of a school-house and for a place of burial. The purpose of the purchase is thus stated in the deed, dated March 14, 1758: "For the use of a church, a school-house and burying ground, to be erected on the hereby granted lot of land for the only proper use and behoof of the Dutch Protestants, their heirs and successors forever, and for no other use." Both parties united in building the school-house, which was used not only for school purposes, but occasionally for public services held by Lutheran pastors and Rev. Michael Schlatter, of the Reformed church. To this new enterprise several elders, formerly of Germantown, attached themselves. The school-house soon became too small, and in 1759 Christopher Raben (Robins), of Whitemarsh, and Wighard Müller and Christopher Jacobi, of Germantown, informed Rev. H. M. Mühlenberg that they intended to erect at Barren Hill a church, which was to be under Synod, and in connection with the Philadelphia congregation. Mühlenberg was thus recognized because he had rendered great assistance in the erection of the school-house, an acknowledgment of which is thus recorded in the Minutes: "Our collectors having, in his name and with his letters of recommendation, raised contributions to defray the expenses of the school-house, and having, after these were paid, also, by means of his written petitions, collected money in Philadelphia and in the provinces of New Jersey and New York for the building of St. Peter's church, he himself having, at the same time, as far as it was possible for himself and fellow laborers, served us in the preaching of the gospel."

In the building of the church the Reformed had no share. The ground and school-house were transferred to Revs. Richard Peters, Charles Magnus Wrangel, D. D., Provost of the Swedish Lutheran churches in Pennsylvania and New Jersey, H. M. Mühlenberg and Henry Keppele, Sr., of Philadelphia, John Koplin, of Providence, Valentine Miller, Ludwig Kolb and Matthias Sommer, members of the church in Whitemarsh, as trustees. The first school teacher was Michael Seely, who afterwards became blind. In 1765 Conrad Bischoff was teacher, and in 1768 John George Kühn. H. M. Mühlenberg laid the corner-stone of the church in 1761, but it was not completed until several years later. It was a substantial stone edifice, with galleries on three of its sides, and a steeple, surmounted by a cock, a reminder, doubtless, of the one that figured in the history of the denial of the disciple after whom the church was named. It remained standing until 1849. The history of its building is a story of struggle, prayers and tears. They were burdened with debt. C. Raben endeavored to reduce the debt by means of a lottery—a means often used in those times to raise funds for houses of worship. Fifty pounds were thus secured. The noble Henry Keppele, of Philadelphia, gave his bond for three hundred pounds. After the difficulty at Germantown had been settled and that congregation was again united with Synod, a number of members who assisted Barren Hill returned to their old home, and thus the difficulties at St. Peter's increased.

On March 13, 1765, C. Raben, who had assumed much of the debt, declared that if he were not extricated from his embarrassing condition, he would sell the church to "*any sect, even to the Papists.*" In this crisis, Keppele, Wrangel and Mühlenberg each obligated himself for one-third of the debt. Mühlenberg addressed Ziegenhagen at London, Francke at Halle, and others, in behalf of the needy church. A collection in the Anglican church for a non-conformist congregation was not allowed in England, but the Archbishop of Canterbury sent twenty guineas out of his private means. In 1766 a Reformed creditor threatened that, unless his loan of one hundred pounds with interest were paid, he would bring the matter to court. Under these circumstances, Mühlenberg had a transfer of the property made to St. Michael's, of Philadelphia, so as to afford a legal protection. He attempted to use his wife's patrimony to liquidate the debt, which she sensibly prevented.

In 1768 ninety pounds' worth of the widely celebrated Halle medicines came to Mühlenberg as a contribution to Zion's church at Philadelphia and Barren Hill, to be equally divided. August 4, 1768, Dr. Ziegenhagen, chaplain to the king of England, authorized Mühlenberg to draw on him for five hundred pounds sterling. But what principally enabled the securities to meet their obligations was a bequest of thirteen thousand gulden ($5,200) from the Count of Roedelsheim, in Germany, to the German Lutheran congregations of Pennsylvania, three thousand of which ($1,200) were expressly given to the church at Barren Hill. The joy of the struggling church can be imagined better than described.

The first election of which we possess a record (though an older record is mentioned as having surreptitiously disappeared) was held April 1, 1766, when Henry Katz, John Bauer, Andrew Koeth and Philip Lehr were chosen elders, and William Hiltner and John Fischer deacons. In June, 1769, Rev. John Frederick Schmidt accepted the charge of the Germantown congregation, and preached occasionally at Barren Hill, in which church service had been previously held every other Sunday by the Germantown and Philadelphia ministers during the time of Pastors John Nicholas Kurtz, 1763-1764, John Ludwig Voigt, 1764-1765, Jacob Van Buskirk, 1766-1769, and Christopher Emanuel Schultze, 1765-1769. Through the war, and for several years after its close, Rev. H. M. Mühlenberg, as also his son, Rev. H. E. Mühlenberg, of St. Michael's, Philadelphia, officiated here, followed by the Revs. Daniel Schroeder, 1776-1782(?), and John Frederick Weinland, 1786 to 1789, of the Germantown congregation, whose several labors helped to keep the congregation together.

During the Revolution the church received considerable injury, having been by turns occupied by the contending armies, and used as a battery and stable. Rev. H. M. Mühlenberg, in his journal, under date of November 4, 1777, says that "it was used as a stable for horses by a portion of the American army encamped in the vicinity," and further mentions that a short time previous the British army had been here and taken from the people their horses, oxen, cows, sheep and hogs. Lafayette used the church as a point of observation during his brief stay on the Hill, in the middle of May, 1778, and came near being captured by General Grant with a strong detachment of the British army.

The next pastor, Rev. Frederick D. Schaeffer, has left the following interesting account of the condition of affairs at this time: " In the year 1790 I was called to the congregation of St. Peter's as its regularly ordained minister, and found the church and school in such a lamentable condition as to be commiserated. Only a few heads of families remained; the greater number of children had already been sent to English schools, and an English schoolmaster had been appointed to teach without my knowledge. The church building was in a deplorable condition, like a neglected or disordered house, the rude walls, windows and frames broken and shattered, and the roof appeared also ready to fall in." As the church was injured during the war, the congregation applied to the Assembly, who passed an act, April 13, 1807, authorizing them to hold a lottery to meet the expense. For want of unanimity this was not carried out, and a committee of seven members was appointed in 1809, through whom the buildings and surrounding property were repaired, and the church re-dedicated January 7, 1810, in the presence of a large assembly. After a pastorate of over twenty-two years Mr. Schaeffer resigned, preaching his farewell sermon August 23, 1812.

Rev. John C. Baker followed, and remained until 1828. During his ministry the German language was entirely dispensed with and the English substituted. Rev. Benjamin Keller commenced his labors in February, and remained until 1835. He was followed by Rev. C. W. Schaeffer, under whom the parsonage, costing nearly $900, was built. Rev. F. R. Anspach became pastor January 1st, 1841, and remained until 1850. He held the last communion in the old church April 8, 1849, when the present fine edifice was erected, at a cost of $6,471.46. Under his services the church was greatly strengthened. Rev. W. H. Smith succeeded him in 1850, and resigned May 10, 1852. In November, 1852, Rev. W. M. Baum accepted, served till May, 1858, and was followed by Rev. S. Sentman, who resigned April, 1862. In his ministry the centennial celebration of the church was observed with appropriate ceremonies. Rev. C. L. Keedy was the next pastor, 1862 to 1865, followed by Rev. J. Q. Waters, whom Rev. J. R. Dimm succeeded in 1867. Rev. T. C. Pritchard took charge September 1, 1871, and remained until July, 1883. His successor was Rev. J. Q. McAtee, who resigned November, 1888. February 1, 1889, the present pastor, Rev. A. H. Frank Fischer, took charge. The church at present numbers about 240 members, is free of debt, is surrounded by about eight acres of cemetery, inclosed by an iron railing and wall. In addition to a good parsonage, with an acre of ground, the church owns another excellent property. Though one of the first churches in Pennsylvania, she is still bringing forth fruit in old age. Her later sons in the ministry, Revs. W. S. Freas, D. D., M. S. Cressman and F. W. Staley, are doing noble work for the Master. Her history, though at times dark, is most inspiring. Her list of servants contains many who stand high in the annals of American Lutheranism. That her growth may be commensurate with that of the great city on whose border she has stood for more than a century and a quarter, is the prayer of all her faithful children.

XIII. ST. PETER'S CHURCH, MIDDLETOWN, DAUPHIN COUNTY.

BY MR. S. L. YETTER.

St. Peter's is the oldest Lutheran church in Dauphin County, with the exception of the "Hill" church in Derry township. Lot No. 135, upon which the old church edifice now stands, was deeded September 18, 1764, by George Fisher and Hannah, his wife, to Peter Woltz, George Frey and Dieterick Schoball, of Lower Paxton township, Lancaster county (now Swatara township, Dauphin county), Province of Pennsylvania, for the sum of seven shillings and six pence, with additional rental of one grain of wheat per annum, payable each consecutive first of May. The deed was acknowledged before Justice John Allison, and attested by Joseph Greenwood and Henry Renick. It is written on parchment, is in a good state of preservation, and is recorded at Lancaster, in Deed Book M, page 365. It bears the old colonial seal of Lancaster county. In the same year a petition was sent to King George III. through John Penn, Lieut. Governor of the Province, praying for the privilege of erecting a church, and for the privilege of collecting funds for the same purpose, which was granted by license, bearing date September 28, 1764, to Christian Roth and David Ettele, to raise by subscription twelve hundred pounds in the space of three years. This document bears the autograph of John Penn, and is countersigned by Joseph Shippen, his secretary. There are no papers to show how much of this money was raised. It would appear from the reading of this document that the members were poor. In fact, David Ettele, one of the Committee, walked as far as Philadelphia on his collecting tour. Many of the members were driven from their homes by the hostile Indians who roamed the surrounding forests, and who for years had been desolating this frontier with tomahawk, scalping knife and torch.

The church was built in 1767. The corner-stone was laid by Justice James Bird, in presence of the Rev. T. Engelland, the first pastor, N. Hornell, Conrad Bucher, and the church wardens and elders, Jno. C. Roth, Jno. Metzgar, Geo. Philip Shage, Gottlieb D. Ettla and Jacob King, together with the Building Committee. There were placed in the corner-stone a German Bible, printed at Halle in 1763; the shorter catechism of Martin Luther, printed at Philadelphia in 1764; three wafers, a half-pint bottle of wine, together with some money in Pennsylvania currency.

The building was constructed in old red sandstone, and was two stories high, with a gallery on three sides and a stairway leading from each door to the gallery. The windows were small, as were the panes of glass in them. The first floor was of bricks that were nine inches square. The pews were narrow, with high, straight backs. The pulpit was a sort of martin-box on an enlarged scale, supported by a post eight or ten feet high, and reached by a narrow winding stair; over it, like a huge extinguisher, hung a sounding-board. There was no provision for heating, but sixty years later stoves were introduced. They were looked upon by the oldest members as a dangerous innovation. The first stoves were capable of receiving into their interiors sticks of wood four feet in length. The membership of "St. Peter's Kirche" numbered sixty-six old and sixty-three young persons. In August, 1793, George Frey and Jacob King, acting for the congregation, purchased lot No. 134 for £3, and a yearly rental of one grain of wheat. By mistake the deed was made to Frey and King, but their executors afterwards conveyed a deed to the congregation, bearing date October 7, 1807.

On the 10th of March, 1807, application was made by the congregation to the Supreme Court and Attorney-General for a charter of incorporation. On the 21st of the same month Gov. Thomas McKean issued a warrant to Timothy Matlack, Master of Rolls, to issue the charter prayed for by the petitioners. In 1813 the steeple was built, for which purpose the sum of $1211.35 was subscribed by one hundred and ninety-three persons.

In 1826 Jane Hannegan sold lot No. 133 to the congregation.

In 1830 the brick floor was replaced by a wooden one; the straight-backed pews gave way to more comfortable ones; a new pulpit was erected, with steps on either side and a recess underneath where the pastor could retire to prepare himself for his duties, and a number of other changes were made.

In 1835 the lecture-room was built.

In 1855 the parsonage on High street was erected.

On September 4, 1867, the church celebrated its centennial anniversary, at which were present many distinguished clergymen and persons prominent in the State. On this occasion one hundred grains of wheat, enclosed in a silken bag, were sent, as a full satisfaction of one clause of the original deed, to Hon. Robert J. Fisher, of York, Pa., the oldest of the living legal heirs of George Fisher, who sold the church lot to the congregation. The Lutheran ministers present on this occasion were Rev. A. H. Lochman, D. D., Rev. Peter Sahm, Rev. S. D. Finckel, D. D., Rev. Prof. C.

J. Ehrehart, Rev. G. J. Martz, Rev. G. W. Hemperly, Rev. W. H. Steck, Rev. J. B. Anthony, Rev. W. M. Baum, D. D., Rev. Peter Raby, Rev. F. A. Barnitz, Rev. C. Reimensnyder and Rev. J. B. Keller.

The pastors of the church from 1767 to 1867 were the Revs. J. T. Engelland, 1767–1773; T. F. Illig, 1773–1778; J. Kurtz, 1788–1793; P. Pentz, 1793–1795; H. Miller, 1795–1803; J. D. Peterson, 1803–1812; F. C. Schaeffer, 1812–1815; G. Lochman, 1815–1826; A. H. Lochman, 1826–1830; J. H. Van Hoff, 1830–1834; P. Sahm, 1834–1837; S. D. Finckel, 1837–1840; J. Vogelbach, 1844–1847; L. Gerhart, 1847–1848; W. M. Baum, 1848–1852; B. Sadtler, 1853-1856; C. J. Ehrehart, 1856–1865, and P. Raby, 1865–1872.

In 1872 Rev. J. W. Finkbiner was installed as pastor. During his administration it was found that the old building was becoming inadequate to accommodate the increasing membership, and that it was inconveniently located. Town lots Nos. 149 and 150 were secured from the Frey Estate at a yearly rental of $15.00 each.

At a congregational meeting, March 7, 1876, it was resolved to erect a new church edifice. Plans were adopted June 11, 1877, the corner-stone was laid Sept. 6 of the same year, and the church was dedicated Feb. 2, 1878. It is of the Gothic style of architecture, containing an auditorium on the amphitheatre plan, a Sunday-school room with an annex separated by a glass partition from the infant department, and a library room. The pews in the auditorium are constructed of chestnut, ash and poplar. From the vestibule to the front, the floor has a gradual slope. The pulpit, altar and railing are of the same material as the pews. There are three large memorial windows, size 12 by 20 feet; the one in the east being in memory of Jno. Croll (who was Superintendent of the Sabbath-school for fifty years), by his daughters; the south window in memory of Margaritta Cameron, wife of Simon Cameron; the north window in memory of Sophia Young, by her son James Young. The structure cost $19,000.00. The architect was S. B. Valk, of New York.

In 1883 Rev. Finkbiner resigned the pastorate, and in 1884, Rev. H. C. Holloway was elected, who served the congregation until 1889.

In 1890 the present pastor, Rev. F. W. Staley, was elected. At his installation, Rev. B. F. Alleman, D. D., delivered the address to the pastor, and Rev. W. H. Dunbar the sermon to the congregation. In the summer of 1890 the Sunday-school room was enlarged at a cost of over $3,000.00. In 1891 a large pipe-organ was built and placed in the church by Messrs. Midmer and Son, of Brooklyn, at a cost of $3,500.00. This organ is one of the best, has an excellent tone, and adds greatly to the appearance of the church. About November, 1891, Col. James Young had the walls of the auditorium very handsomely frescoed. In September, 1891, for the first time in the history of this congregation, the East Pennsylvania Synod convened in this church. In the spring of 1892 the parsonage on High Street was sold. A few months later the Trustees of the church purchased for $6,000.00 the handsome and commodious residence of Mr. J. H. Baxtresser on Spring Street, scarcely a block from the church. This house has all the modern conveniences, reflecting a great deal of credit upon the members, and giving a comfortable home to their pastor. The property belonging to the congregation is valued at $35,000.00.

Early in the present century this church seems to have awakened to the necessity of imparting religious instruction to the young. A Sunday-school was organized in 1819. It was probably a crude affair. The children were taught to read the Bible in German and English. The first superintendent and teacher was a Mr. Sneath; in 1823 he was succeeded by Mr. Jno. Croll. In 1873 Mr. Croll was succeeded by Mr. Geo. A. Lauman, and in 1889 Mr. I. O. Nissley, the present superintendent, succeeded Mr. Lauman. The school now numbers over 600. The membership of the church has more than doubled itself since Rev. Staley became its pastor. Considerable interest and enthusiasm is manifested by the younger members in church work, and the present outlook is most encouraging. The indications are that old St. Peter's will march abreast with her sister churches, and will gladly do her part in the evangelization of the world.

XIV. ST. JAMES' LUTHERAN CHURCH, GREENWICH, WARREN CO., N. J.

BY REV. T. C. PRITCHARD.

The early history of this venerable foundation and Christian church stretches over two centuries. It goes back to the date of those who fled from the horrors of the "Thirty Years' War" and sought an asylum in the New World. The original settlers were German, and brought with them their religion and religious institutions. Before the erection of the church, religious exercises were conducted regularly in their households, holding in their isolation from the great world to the Lutheran faith. The schoolmaster, then as now, was abroad in the land. When Johann Berger arrived in Sopatcong, he assumed the additional functions of pastor to the scattered community. He had never been ordained, but was deemed competent to officiate as reader and expounder of the Scriptures. He read to the assembled families one of Dr. Luther's sermons or house-postils. But desiring to enjoy more fully the privileges of the church, they sent to Germany for clerical supplies. In the "Hallesche Nachrichten" it is stated that in the year 1760 letters were received from Lutherans living in "Greenwich township" and "Anweel or Anwill township," asking for the preaching of the gospel.

In the same work, of a later date, the statement is again made, that letters or messages were received from the Lutheran congregation of "Greenwich an den Blauen Bergen," showing that the church was in existence as an organization previous to 1762.

The first church erected was called St. John's. It was a union church, Lutheran and German Reformed. This was in 1769. This date, too, marks the beginning of preaching by stated pastors. The German Reformed congregation, by death, removals and other causes, became extinct, and the Lutherans acquired sole possession of the property. A complete re-organization followed. They changed the name to St. James', and affiliated with St. Michael's church in Philadelphia. The tenets of the new organization, formally declared, were the Unaltered Augsburg Confession, and through more than a century of existence it has clung steadfastly to this profession of faith.

In 1790 another and more commodious church was erected. It was built of stone, and was a great improvement upon the first.

In 1834 the present large and beautiful edifice was erected. It is built of brick and in the most substantial manner. Thus, during one hundred and some thirty years, three houses of worship have been used by this congregation in the service of God and the culture of Christianity. During all these years, the organization has had an existence which, without a break, has come up to to-day full of vitality and power for good.

We now naturally turn to the list of those who during this period were shepherds of the flock. Our church record begins A. D. 1769. From 1770–1773, Peter Mühlenberg; 1773–1777, Christian Streit; 1777–1781, Rev. Braas; 1781–1790, John Frederick Ernst; 1792–———, John Conrad Jeager; 1812–1815, Christian Endress; 1815–1837, J. P. Hecht; 1837–1847, Daniel Miller; 1847–1851, John McCron; 1851–1865, J. K. Plitt; 1865–1868, M. H. Richards; 1868–1880, S. Henry; 1880–1883, F. T. Hoover; 1883–the present, T. C. Pritchard.

The churches at Riegelsville, Stewartsville and Phillipsburg have been at times parts of this charge. At present St. James constitutes the field. But one minister has gone out of this fold —Rev. W. A. Shipman, the pastor of the Lutheran church of Johnstown, Pa.

XV. ST. JOHN'S CHURCH, MAYTOWN, LANCASTER CO.

BY REV. W. H. HARDING.

The Evangelical Lutheran Church of this place was founded upon the Augsburg Confession in the year 1770. The congregation began its worship of God in a little old log church at the corner of the old town cemetery. Services were continued here until the year 1804, when the stone church in which the congregation worships to-day was erected.

The first pastor of this early people was the Rev. Michael Enderlein, who served them from 1770 to 1778. The number of those who surrounded the Table of the Lord on their first communion-day, in 1770, was twenty-eight. This appears to be about the number of the members comprising the organization; for we find that at the two communions held in 1771 there were respectively twenty-four and twenty-eight communicants. A brief time after organization, a number of persons gave gifts to the congregation. Frederick Swartz gave a communion cup, Jacob Wolf a baptismal bowl, and Mr. Hofin a collection bag and bell. It appears that the bag was funnel-shaped, fastened at the end of a long pole, and at the end of the bag was a little bell, which would jingle as it was passed in and out of the pews. The preaching seems to have been all in German for a number of years after organization. The following places seem to have been connected in the charge, viz.: Maytown, Elizabethtown, Mt. Joy and Marietta.

Rev. J. Frederick Ellery was pastor from 1778 to 1784; Rev. Frederick Theodore Melshheimer, from 1784 to 1801.

Rev. John Frederick Ernst, coming from Cooperstown, N. Y., preached his first sermon November 28, 1802. During his ministrations the congregation were enabled to quit their old log sanctuary and erect for themselves a very pretty two-story stone church, in which we worship at the present time. The cornerstone of this was laid April 21, 1804. The communicant membership at that time was nineteen.

Rev. J. P. F. Kramer took charge November 2, 1806, and continued until 1812. Rev. Kramer came from Paxton township, Dauphin Co., Pa.

Rev. Wm. Gotthold Ernst served from March 22, 1812, to 1815.

Rev. John Jacob Strein came December 31, 1815, and served until 1825. The communicant membership in the year 1816 was forty-five; in 1825 it was seventy. From this year until December, 1828, we can find no record of any pastor's care over the church.

Rev. Frederick Ruthrauff took charge December, 1828, and closed his relations as pastor April 29, 1832.

Rev. Peter Sahm took charge June 30, 1833, serving until 1837.

Rev. L. Gerhardt took charge November 4, 1838, and continued his service until October 24, 1847. It was during this pastorate that the St. Luke's congregation of Bainbridge became connected with this charge.

In the year 1839 St. Luke's, of Bainbridge, in connection with the German Reformed congregation, purchased their church property from Mr. Henry Haldeman, and continued to be a union church until September, 1891, when the half-interest held by the Reformed people was purchased from them.

During the ministry of Rev. Gerhardt, Rev. M. J. Alleman, now pastor at York, Pa., left St. John's congregation to take up his studies at Gettysburg for the gospel ministry.

The Rev. Wm. Gerhardt (brother of Rev. L. Gerhardt), came to the charge November 4, 1847, and left November 17, 1850.

Rev. Jacob B. Crist came March 1, 1852, resigning in 1855.

It appears that after the departure of Rev. Crist, Rev. M. Sondhaus came; but as to date of his coming or departure nothing definite is known.

Rev. W. G. Laitzle came June 1, 1855.

The preaching points at this time seem to have been the following: Elizabethtown, Bainbridge, Mt. Joy, Centreville, and Maytown. Up to this date, the German preaching had been growing less and less from year to year, and when Rev. Laitzle closed his work with the charge (1862), it seems that the German went with him without any serious objections from the congregations.

Rev. B. F. Apple came August 8, 1862, remaining until near the close of 1864. He was followed by Rev. J. W. Early, during whose administration much that is of interest to the pastorate was brought to pass, as is recorded in the minutes of the Bainbridge congregation, from which we quote:

"BAINBRIDGE, *August* 19, 1867.

"The Church Council met, pursuant to call, at the house of S. Hackenberger. The members present were J. S. Horst, S. Hackenberger and Geo. Hackenberger, Elders; C. Gamberling and John Fahs, Trustees. By unanimous vote, Geo. Hackenberger was chosen chairman. He stated the object of the meeting to be for the purpose of appointing a Committee to consult with the Maytown Church Council on next Saturday at Maytown, concerning the change of pastor, our separation from the Elizabethtown charge, and the forming of a new charge to consist of this place and Maytown, and also whether we will or will not accept the offer of the Pennsylvania Synod, in a letter sent to Maytown, all agreeable to recommendation of our present pastor, Rev. J. W. Early.

"The President then appointed S. Hackenberger, John Fahs, and Geo. Hackenberger, the Committee to consult with Maytown Council. G. W. HACKENBERGER,
"*Secretary of Church Council.*"

The report which this Committee returned after meeting the Maytown Council, is as follows:

"We met the Council of the church in Maytown on Saturday, August 24, 1867, according to your instruction. By a unanimous vote it was agreed to separate our churches from the Elizabethtown charge, and to form a new pastoral district to be composed of Maytown and Bainbridge. We took no final action on the offer of the Committee of the Pennsylvania Synod, because a majority of the Joint Committee believed that, as Maytown has no other constitution than that of the General Synod as recorded in its English hymn-book, and as Bainbridge is constitutionally a General Synod church, it is best to refer the whole matter to a congregational vote, the majority to decide whether we remain General Synod churches or connect ourselves with the Pennsylvania Synod and alter our constitutions. It was believed, however, by a majority of the Committee, that the interests of our churches can best be attended to by uniting with some Synod connected with the General Synod. * * *

"Agreeably to the constitution, an election was published August 25, to be held in two weeks, to see whether we shall join the Pennsylvania Synod or seek connection with a Synod connected with the General Synod.

"S. HACKENBERGER,
"JOHN FAHS."

The only members of the Maytown Council present at this joint meeting of whom we are able to learn at this late date, were Harry H. Johnstin and John Hays.

"LUTH. CHURCH, BAINBRIDGE, *September 8,* 1867.
"This being the day appointed for a vote to be taken * * * The minutes of the previous meeting of the Committee were read and adopted. The report of the Maytown Committee was now read, after which remarks were made by several members, after which the vote was taken, which resulted as follows:

"For the Pennsylvania Synod, 5.
"For the East Pennsylvania Synod, 13.

* * * * * *

"G. W. HACKENBERGER,
"*Secretary of Church Council.*"

After this final separation of Maytown and Bainbridge from the

Elizabethtown charge, Rev. J. W. Early's labors with these two congregations came to an end.

Rev. F. T. Hoover came May 24, 1868, and served as the first pastor to this newly-formed pastorate in its connection with the East Pennsylvania Synod, remaining until 1870.

Rev. D. Stock began his ministerial duties with the charge April 1, 1871, continuing until 1873.

Rev. G. P. Weaver labored here from May 2, 1873, until 1875.

Rev. J. V. Eckert from October 1, 1876, until 1880.

Rev. M. H. Stine came April 1, 1880. During his ministry here the Maytown congregation received a handsome gift in the form of a beautiful church parsonage. This was granted to the St. John's Lutheran church March 8, 1891, by the Hon. Simon Cameron. The deed declares that it is given " In testimony of the love and affection borne by him for the memory of his deceased wife, Margaretta Brua Cameron, who was an exemplary member of the Lutheran Church." Rev. Stine ended his labors here July 1, 1882.

Rev. J. Houseman came December 1, 1882; Rev. C. M. Aurand, March 30, 1884; Rev. A. H. Shertz preached his introductory sermon November 7, 1885, and closed his pastoral relations with this people July 27, 1890.

Rev. W. H. Harding accepted the formal call extended April 10, 1891, but did not assume full pastoral care until July 1, after his seminary course at Gettysburg was completed.

During the months of September and October, 1891, the church council of Bainbridge entered into negotiations with the Reformed church for the purchasing of the half-interest in the church property held by them. The price was agreed upon, and the property was paid for in full April 25, 1892.

In the winter months of 1891 and 1892 the repair of St. John's church and steeple was begun, and finally completed at an expense of $197. In the fall of 1892 the parsonage was remodeled at a cost of about $350.

The amount of the pastor's salary is $500 and the use of the parsonage. The present societies of the churches are the following:

A prayer meeting and a Ladies' Aid Society at each church;

at Maytown, a Woman's Home and Foreign Missionary Society, and the Young People's Society of Christian Endeavor.

The Sunday-schools in both churches are in excellent order, numbering about 200 at Maytown and 135 at Bainbridge. The present membership at St. John's, of Maytown, is 139, and at St. Luke's, of Brainbridge, 105.

XVI. ZION'S CHURCH, MANHEIM, LANCASTER CO.

BY J. H. SIELING, M. D., ASSISTED BY JOHN M. ENSMINGER, ESQ.

The history of this ancient church is quite interesting. Unfortunately much of it is unwritten, and not a little had to be gleaned from the recollections of the oldest members and friends of the present congregation. Fragmentary dottings found here and there, added, developed a history of which the present pastor and people feel justly proud.

In 1761 Nicholas Merrett, of Warwick township (now Penn), deeded a small tract of land two miles southeast of Manheim (now owned by David and Mary Conrad) for the consideration of one silver shilling, to Heinrich Hans, Ludwig Becker, Peter Erman, Christian Gyger and Martin Spickler, councilmen, for the purpose of erecting a Lutheran church thereon. Here was built a small log edifice with a ground floor, which stood till 1770, when a firebrand, said to have been brought from a neighbor's dwelling, razed this first artificial temple of the wilderness to the ground, just as the pastor (name not now known) appeared upon the scene to deliver his Sabbath morning's discourse from its sacred desk.

During these years (1760 to 1770) Baron Henry Wm. Stiegel, the founder of the town of Manheim, Sabbath after Sabbath gathered his workmen from the glass factory and others together in a chapel which he had set apart in his palatial residence on the northeast corner of Market Square, and in the German language exhorted them in the doctrines of the Lutheran faith.

The church was founded A. D. 1770 out of the remains of the conflagration and the gatherings of the noble hearted Christian Baron. It was not, however, until the following year, 1771, that a thorough organization was effected. Rev. F. A. C. Mühlenberg, of the Borough of Lancaster, was elected pastor, and he wrote the constitution and by-laws in German. He said, "We will bring order out of disorder."

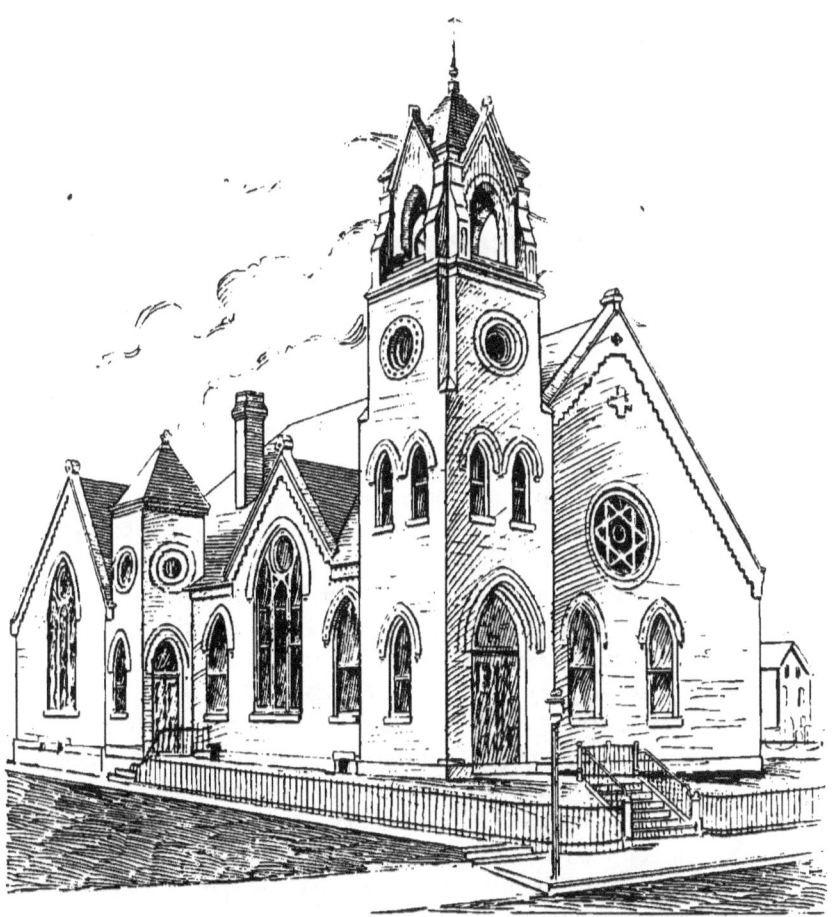

ZION'S EVANGELICAL LUTHERAN CHURCH, MANHEIM, PA.

On the 4th day of December, A. D. 1772, Baron Stiegel deeded a beautiful lot of ground in the centre of this most beautiful town, Manheim, fashioned and shaped by his own hand after the town in his native country and given the identical name, for the consideration of five shillings and the rent of a *red rose* annually for ground-rent in the month of June forever, if lawfully demanded. The romantic rental was only twice demanded by him. The trustees named in this indenture are Peter Erman, Henry Wherley and Henry Martzall.

A log church was erected thereon, with three-sides gallery and a candlestick pulpit. The floor was made of brick, and the walls were chinked and daubed. Near the close of the eighteenth century, Ulrich Keyser said in German that he wanted to be buried with "Gesang und Klang" (singing and tolling). Consequently he bought a 500 pound metal bell and placed it in the belfry. It was rung for his obsequies in 1804. About 1820 the walls were plastered and a wooden floor put in.

The following pastors served this congregation (a few dates lost): Revs. F. A. C. Mühlenberg, D. D., 1771–1778; John D. Schroeder, 1778–1782: Fred. Theodore Melsheimer, 1783–1789; John David Young, 1789–1790; John Fred. Ernst, 1802–1805. Rev. Ernst died heart-broken, and lies buried in the yard of the church he so faithfully served. He was beloved by all the people who knew him; but, for delivering a patriotic Fourth of July oration at the Big Spring near town, the church council locked the door of the church against his entering it to perform its solemn rites. This so mortally worried him that he took sick immediately and never recovered, dying with a broken heart the following October 24, 1805. Rev. Henry Scriba, 1807; Wm. Baetes, 1810–1828(?); Frederick Ruthrauff, 1828(?)–1832; Peter Sahm, 1833–1835; C. P. Miller, 1836–1841; Christopher G. Frederick, 1842–1849; John H. Menges (who introduced evening service with tallow dips for lights) 1849–June 23, 1851; Chas. Rees, 1854–1856; George Haines, 1857–1858.

The church was rebuilt in 1858 after the fashion of the day, *i. e.*, a one-story brick structure of somewhat Grecian architecture, with a low pulpit and a gallery at the opposite end over the vestibule. The corner-stone was laid May 19, 1857, at which the pastor was assisted by Revs. Wm. Baetes and J. H. Menges. The church was dedicated September 26 and 27, of the same year. An eight hundred and fifty pound bell was placed in the tower by the congregation. Revs. D. P. Rosenmiller served in 1858; Jos. R. Focht, 1864–1868.

SUNDAY-SCHOOL ORGANIZED.

In 1867 the Lutheran members of "The Manheim Union Sunday-school" concluded that it was their duty, for the interests of the church and the Master's cause, to erect an enduring monument in the form of a Sabbath Home for the children of the Lutheran and other families of and around Manheim. On the 10th day of November, the first session was held. Mr. Geo. D. Miller was elected Superintendent. For the first few years an old melodeon furnished the instrumental part of the music, afterward a double bank chapel-organ took its place and was used in school and church service. This was the first organ in a Manheim church. The first quarter of a century of the school has just been celebrated. The four Superintendents were all present —Mr. Miller, 14 years; Peter Keath, 1 year; D. E. Shimp, 1 year; Ezra Reist, 9 years. Dr. Sieling is the fifth and present Superintendent, the first in the second quarter century.

Rev. Kaempfer served 1868–1869; J. C. Barnitz (Supply) 1869–1870; Jacob Peter, 1871–1890; John H. Menges, June 19, 1891–the present.

Under this pastorate the church has been rebuilt. The corner-stone was laid, August 16, 1891, the pastor being assisted by Dr. E. Huber. The church was dedicated April 24, 1892, the pastor being assisted by Rev. R. W. Hufford, D. D., President of East Pennsylvania Synod, Revs. M. Fernsler and I. W. Bobst. The present structure, in the eastern end of the church yard, is built of brick, of Gothic architecture, with a beautiful base course of sandstone. It is 92 feet long and 55 feet wide, divided into six apartments, viz.: auditorium, Sunday-school, primary class and library rooms, and two vestibules. The rooms are divided by Wilson's rolling partitions. After these are raised, all the apartments are thrown into one. All the walls are frescoed on the inside. The building is heated throughout by steam and lighted by gas. There is an organ in each room. The auditorium is graced by an excellent pipe organ made by Samuel Bohler, of Reading, at a cost of $2,500.00. The building throughout is of modern finish and finely equipped. The tower is 80 feet high, and is surmounted by a weather-vane. The bell was donated by Dr. J. H. Sieling's Bible Class, and weighs 2850 lbs. (E flat). The windows are all stained glass, and were donated by individuals. A large Red Rose was placed in the circular window in the pulpit recess. The rose is surmounted by the inscription, "Baron Henry Wm. Stiegel," and supported by the name of "Rev. J. H. Menges." The building was erected at a cost of $13,000.00. On the day of dedication the remaining unprovided debt of $5,000.00 was assumed by individuals. It is proposed by the Stiegel Castle, No. 166, K. G. E., to erect a memorial fountain on the beautiful lawn in front of the church.

The present value of the church property is about $20,000. The membership is about 180. The Sunday-school numbers 285. The church council consists of: Elders, Ezra Reist and Dr. J. H. Sieling ; Trustees, Jno. M. Ensminger, D. E. Shimp and Chas. W. Sheeler ; Deacons, N. W. Long, John F. Devert, John M. Ressler and John K. Bemesderfer ; Pastor, Rev. John H. Menges, in the sixty-ninth year of his age. In April of 1891 this congregation was left alone in the "Manheim Charge." "The Hill church" and "Petersburg" withdrew to form "the East Petersburg Charge." The services are principally English, one German sermon being delivered every other Sunday morning. Every Sunday morning and evening there are services. A very interesting Young People's Society of Christian Endeavor was organized August, 1892, which has done great good and promises to be the means of saving many souls.

XVII. PIKELAND CHARGE, CHESTER CO.—ST. PETER'S, PIKELAND ; CENTENNIAL, KIMBERTON.

BY REV. J. A. HACKENBERG.

1. St. Peter's Church, Pikeland.

For the first forty years the records of this congregation were kept in the books of Zion church, as the same pastor served both. These records have unfortunately been lost. Hence we must look to tradition for most of the facts during that period. The first religious meetings were held in private houses as early as 1751. During the period from that to 1770 reports show that Rev. Henry Melchior Mühlenberg visited this community and preached from house to house. Authentic records begin in 1771. It was on May 16 of that year that Michael König (descendants now King) and Henry Hipple each sold to Peter Hartman, George Emerie, Conrad Miller and Adam Moses, trustees, a small lot of land to be the location of a church and burial ground. Michael König sold one acre and eight perches for twenty shillings, and Henry Hipple forty-five perches for five shillings.

On this ground the congregation built and dedicated in 1772 a log church capable of accommodating five hundred people. This fact Mühlenberg reported to the church in Germany. Regular services were now held by the pastor of Zion's church, with which it was connected as a pastorate. The preaching services were exclusively in German until the term of Rev. Jacob Wampole (1827-1836) when an occasional service was held in English. The English became from necessity more and more frequent, until the term of Rev. John McCron (1844), when the German was entirely discontinued. The congregation was incorporated by the Legislature of Pennsylvania in 1779 as St. Peter's German Evangelical Lutheran church. From this point we are able to trace the succession of pastors down to the present.

SUCCESSION OF PASTORS.

The regular pastors after Mühlenberg were: Revs. Ludwig Voigt, 1779-1790-3 (nominally pastor to 1800); J. F. Weinland, 1790-1800; Fred. Plitt, 1804-1807 (?); J. Rowenauch, 1807 (?)-1811 (?); Fred. Jasinsky, 1811-1815; F. W. Geissenhainer, Jr., 1817-1827; F. W. Geissenhainer, Sr., (serving with his son), 1818-1823; Jacob Wampole, 1827-1836; Frederick Ruthrauff, 1836-1843; John McCron, 1844-1847; Daniel Miller, 1847-1849; Peter Raby, 1849-1858; Samuel Aughey, 1858-1859; Cornelius Reimensynder, 1859-1863; N. H. Cornell, 1863-1874; S. S. Palmer, 1874-1875; J. F. Hartman, 1876-1880; J. R. Dimm, 1880-1882; J. A. Hackenberg, 1882 to the present.

SUCCESSION OF CHURCH BUILDINGS.

The log church erected in 1772 was used as a house of worship for forty years. Up to this time the church was exclusively Lutheran. But now a new church must be built, and the Lutheran people entered into an arrangement with the few German Reformed families living in the neighborhood to build a Union church. The corner-stone was laid August 13, 1811, and the church dedicated October 4, 1812, under the name of St. Peter's. The cost was $2,836.45½. This building was used alternately each Sunday by the Lutheran and Reformed for twenty-two years, when, during the ministry of Rev. Jacob Wampole, it was destroyed, with its splendid pipe-organ and other valuable contents, by an incendiary fire, on the 20th of January, 1835.

On April 24, 1835, the corner-stone of a new church was laid. The church was dedicated April 12, 1836. This church was used and owned conjointly by the Lutherans and Reformed, as the previous one had been, until 1889, when the Lutherans, feeling the need of a church of their own, under the ministry of Rev. J. A. Hackenberg, moved for a separation. This was accomplished by a public sale of the old building; the German Reformed becoming the purchasers. The Lutherans at once set to work to build a church, and having secured a lot on the opposite side of the road, laid the corner-stone of the present beautiful church August 27, 1889. The pastor was assisted on the occasion by Rev. M. S. Cressman, of Lionville. The church was dedicated free of debt on May 7, 1890; the dedication sermon being preached by Rev. J. H. Menges, of Philadelphia. Cost, about $7,000. The present prosperous condition of the congregation attests the wisdom of the separation.

OTHER CHURCHES GROWING OUT OF ST. PETER'S.

This church has been the mother of several congregations, among which are St. Matthew's Lutheran church, of West Vincent, and St. Paul's, of Lionville, now constituting the Lionville charge, both large and vigorous churches. Another is St. Peter's of the General Council, a stone's throw from our own. This church withdrew from the old or original organization in 1840 on account of "new" or "revival" measures introduced into the church by Rev. F. Ruthrauff. They built their church in 1843.

The fourth congregation formed from this is the Central Lutheran church of Phœnixville, organized in 1876 by Rev. S. S. Palmer, on retiring as pastor of St. Peter's. The fifth church growing out of St. Peter's is the Centennial Lutheran church, of Kimberton.

Those who have been called into the Lutheran ministry from the membership of St. Peter's are: Revs. P. Sheeder, M. Sheeleigh, Alex. McLaughlin, Jacob Friday, Ezekiel Auld and M. E. McLinn.

One fact in the history of this congregation is worthy of special mention in this connection. The first annual meeting of the East Pennsylvania Synod, after its organization in the basement of "Old Trinity," Lancaster, was held in this church. One of the only two lay delegates present when the new English Synod was organized was Gen. George Hartman, delegate from this church, accompanying the pastor, Rev. F. Ruthrauff. He invited the new ecclesiastical body to meet in this church in its first annual convention, and it met here October 15–18, 1842.

PARSONAGES.

This congregation owned a parsonage at West Pikeland, about two miles from the church, for nearly fifty years, but on account of changes in the pastoral territory its location was found to be disadvantageous for the pastor, and it was sold and the present one built at Kimberton in 1884.

2. CENTENNIAL CHURCH, KIMBERTON.

The Centennial Lutheran Church, of Kimberton, was organized in 1876 by Rev. J. F. Hartman. The first church council was composed of the following:

Elders—Isaac R. Root, Josiah Schultz and Geo. H. Detterline; Deacons—John R. Holman, Benjamin March and Peter R. Raby; Trustees—David P. Thomas, Jacob Beaver and C. F. Bush.

They purchased a Quaker meeting-house and fitted it up for a place of worship, dedicating it in 1877. During the summer of 1884, under the ministry of Rev. J. A. Hackenberg, the building was beautifully frescoed and otherwise improved. This church has been since its organization connected with St. Peter's in forming the Pikeland charge.

In compiling the above, valuable assistance has been received from an anniversary sermon by Rev. J. R. Dimm, D. D.

XVIII. PINE GROVE CHARGE, SCHUYLKILL CO.—JACOB'S, SALEM'S, ST. PETER'S AND ST. JOHN'S.

BY REV. E. S. HENRY.

1. JACOB'S CHURCH.

This congregation was organized in the year 1780. It stands two miles west of Pine Grove. The first church was erected in 1780. The second building was put up in 1833. This house of worship was renovated a few years ago. The congregation owns half the parsonage, is free of debt, and has a few hundred dollars in its treasury. Rev. William Kurtz was pastor from its organization to 1798, followed by Revs. Andrew Schultze, 1798 to 1802; John Knoske, 1802 to 1811; George Mennig, 1811 to 1833; William G. Mennig, 1834 to 1839; A. B. Gockelen, 1839 to 1845; B. Sadtler, 1845 to 1849; E. Breidenbaugh, 1849 to 1852; Elias S. Henry, just ordained by the Synod of East Pennsylvania, at Pottsville, took charge September 21, 1852, and after forty years is still the pastor. The congregation is composed of Pennsylvania Germans. The greater part of the services are in the German language. There has been some English preaching for several years past in the congregation. This church was established long before the town of Pine Grove was commenced. The two Lutheran congregations there took quite a number of the members away who formerly held to Jacob's church. But there yet remain over two hundred. This congregation has services every other Sunday. There are several Sunday-schools kept up the whole year. There is communion twice a year. The present church council are Samuel Stein, Trustee; Oliver Mease, George Emerich, John D. Felty, Levi Felty, Elders; M. Robinson Hughes and William Aungst, Deacons. The Rev. J. B. Bergner, of Ohio, entered the ministry from this church.

2. SALEM'S CHURCH.

This church is three miles east of Pine Grove, and is owned jointly with the German Reformed congregation. It was organized in the year 1783. A school-house was first built and also used as a place for preaching for a few years. In 1795 the foundation was laid for the first church. The work was carried on slowly. The dedication was on Ascension Day in 1797. This church was used as a place of worship for eighty-four years. In 1880 the cornerstone was laid for a new church. In 1881 it was dedicated to the worship of the Triune God. It is a beautiful country church, free of debt. There are over two hundred members in the Lutheran congregation. The members are all Pennsylvania Germans. There is not a foreigner among them. The services were formerly all in German, but of late years the preaching is partly in English. The first pastor on record was Rev. Andrew Schultze, who served from 1799 to 1802. He was succeeded by Rev. John Knoske, who remained until 1811. Rev. Geo. Mennig then became pastor, and remained such until the year 1833. Then followed Revs. J. F. Haesbert, 1834; W. G. Mennig, 1834 to 1839; A. B. Gockelen, 1839 to 1845; B. Sadtler, 1845 to 1848, and Julius Erhart, 1854 to 1856. In May, 1856, Rev. Elias S. Henry was elected pastor. He has now served for nearly thirty-seven years. The preaching is always in the afternoon. The attendance at services is uniformly good. The church is central in the congregation. There is a Union Sunday-school held in it. There are no debts on the church. A little farm is owned by the congregation. This church, as well as all the others in the Pine Grove charge, is furnished with organ and a fine bell. The present church council are G. W. Zerbe, Trustee; William Kemmerling, G. W. Subb, elders; William R. Nagel and Jonathan Schwartz, deacons. Mr. W. C. Heffner, from this congregation, is studying for the ministry.

3. St. Peter's Church, Pine Grove.

This church is owned in connection with the German Reformed. The building is of stone and is very substantial. This and St. John's are built of the sandstone found in the Swobes mountain near by. This church was put up in 1816. It has stood now for seventy-six years, but neither this building nor the St. John's, which was built almost fifty years ago, shows any yielding to the ravages of time. They look as if they could last for many centuries. Rev. George Mennig was the first pastor. He served the congregation until 1833. After his resignation there was discord in the church. Some members showed much zeal, but it was not according to knowledge. They were very much afraid of what was called, at times, "New Measures." They would not allow even a Sunday-school to be held in the church building. The books of the Sunday-school were carried out into the middle of the street. For a number of years men that were not connected with the Synod preached for the Lutherans. The following members of Synod preached at various times within the periods indicated, viz.: J. F. Haesbert, 1834; M. Harpel, between 1835 and 1838; W. G. Mennig, 1838 and 1839; A. B. Gockelen, between 1839 and 1845; J. M. Deitzler, 1846–1847; and Julius Erhart, 1854–1855. In the early part of 1855 Rev. Elias S. Henry was elected pastor. He has served in this capacity for almost thirty-eight years. There are almost two hundred members in this congregation. They live mostly in the country, whilst the members of St. John's live mostly in the town. There is peace and harmony between the two Lutheran congregations in the same village, having both the same pastor, and many attend services at both places. The church building was very much changed internally a few years ago. It is furnished with an organ and a very fine-toned bell. The present church council are: James Clemens, Daniel Lehman, trustees; James Hummel, Aaron Rehrer, elders; Lyman Croll and Jacob Lengel, deacons.

4. St. John's Church, Pine Grove.

The St. Peter's church, of Pine Grove, having informally called and admitted to their church a minister, acting under an *ad interim* license from the President of the Pennsylvania Synod, a number of the members, not approving of this action, resolved to secede from their connection, erect a new congregation, and build a new house of worship. Accordingly, they met on the evening of April 10, 1845, and formed themselves into a congregation under the name of "St. John's Evangelical Lutheran congregation of Pine Grove, Pa." The number of communicants was about thirty. Rev. B. Sadtler was its first pastor. He served the congregation, in connection with several others, until 1849. His successor was Rev. E. Breidenbaugh, who served until the year 1852. Rev. Elias S. Henry took charge September 21, 1852, and is, after forty years, still the pastor.

This congregation, in connection with Jacob's congregation, two miles west of Pine Grove, owns a very comfortable parsonage, on a lot fifty by two hundred feet deep. There have been improvements made during the last few years about the church which cost about $1500. The church has no debts. It has some hundreds of dollars in the treasury. The Sunday-school has also some money on interest. The congregation owns a cemetery of nearly ten acres of ground, in which many of the members of the other congregations in the town and vicinity own lots and bury their dead. The Sunday-school was organized in 1836—fifty-six years ago. There are still two connected with the school who were charter members, viz., Mr. William Forrer, the librarian of the school, and Miss Esther Conrad, the superintendent of the infant department.

A number of ministers went forth from this church and Sunday-school. Drs. F. W. Conrad and V. L. Conrad were formerly members of the church and superintendents of the school. Mr. John E. Graeff was a member, and superintendent of the school. He entered the ministry from here. Rev. James T. Kendall was a child of this church and the superintendent of its school. Rev. George C. Henry, of Des Moines, Iowa, was from his childhood a member of this congregation and Sunday-school. His sainted mother, Sarah Conrad Henry, had been superintendent of the infant department for twenty years, up to the time of her death. Her last request was, "Don't give up the church and Sunday-school in which I labored so long." Revs. Eli Huber and H. B. Wile were also raised in this Sunday-school.

The preaching was originally English and German, and it is so still. There is a German sermon every two weeks, and in the same time five sermons in English. There is a Society of Christian Endeavor connected with this congregation, of over one hundred members. This society has been supporting a native preacher in our mission in India for some years by paying $30 yearly. The English-speaking families take the *Lutheran Observer*. A number of *Missionary Journals* are also taken. There are about two hundred and forty members. A weekly German and a weekly English prayer-meeting are held. A prayer-meeting before preaching on Sunday morning has been kept up since 1858. The present church council are: M. H. Boyer, T. B. Hughes, P. F. Seidel, trustees; M. Richter, P. Haug, elders; and H. H. Christ, W. M. Druckmiller, deacons. John A. Richter and M. M. Dieffenbach superintend the Sunday-school.

XIX. SHOOP'S CHARGE, DAUPHIN COUNTY—SHOOP'S AND SALEM.

BY REV. W. L. HEISLER.

1. SHOOP'S CHURCH.

Shoop's church is situated in Lower Paxton township, Dauphin County, Pa., on the road leading from Harrisburg to Jonestown, about four miles east of Harrisburg. It is said that the first settlers in this community were Presbyterians. The Germans came here a little later. Few, if any, came directly from Germany. It is supposed that all the first of the German settlers were Lutheran and German Reformed, and that they came from what is now called Lebanon county. "These two denominations were at that time the only sects known here among the German settlers." "In the year of our Lord, A. D. 1783, these people united with each other in the erection of a house of worship—a union church building, which was finished and occupied in the year of our Lord, A. D. 1784." The church was built of logs, logged up, chinked, and covered with clap-boards.

On the first page of a very old book was written in German: "This book presented to the church by David Epler."

"*Church Book, Register of Births, Baptisms, Confirmations, and Deaths, began by Frederick Theodore Melsheimer, Evangelical Lutheran Preacher, Beckstein (Paxtang), the 26th day of April, A. D. 1783.*"

"*Soli Deo Gloria.*"
"*To God alone the glory.*"

This book was used by both congregations for the purposes indicated. The following was also written in this book: "Anno Domini 1794, February 22, the church was closed for repairs, and Stoffle Shoop and John Parthemore were appointed for the purpose of repairing the church." Parthemore charged for boarding shingle-makers, 25 days, £2 7s. and 5d. Shoop had the shingle-makers in board and received £2. After deducting charges for boarding shingle-makers, there was left in his hands April 13, 1794, a balance of 17s. There is also a receipt of June 23, from John Bim, for £26, for work done on the church.

In 1797 we also find a credit claimed by Christian Walborn

for £7, paid Peter Bobb for 2,800 feet of boards; also for £7 5s. 5d. for work at building.

We find on record a deed from Christopher Shoop and wife, of Lower Paxton township, Dauphin county, Pa., dated March 20, 1797, to Peter Bobb, Henry Myer, John Parthemore, and Jacob Milleisen, trustees for the United German Lutheran and German Reformed church in the township of Paxton aforesaid, for one acre and fifty perches, being the lot of ground on which the said church now stands, acknowledged August 12, 1797, at which date it was no doubt delivered; this showing that, although erected and occupied some time in the year 1784, it was not completed until 1797.

The building was large and substantial, built of logs, weatherboarded, and painted white, with comfortable pews, end and side galleries, the seating capacity being about eight hundred persons. It answered the purpose of the congregation, and was used by them until May 28, 1829, when the present church was erected as it stood before the late alterations were made, at a cost of $2,100. The building committee were John Elser, David Mumma, Frederick Shoop, George Hain, Jacob Shell, and Frederick Parthemore, treasurer.

The present building was enlarged and improved in 1883, and dedicated January 13, 1884. The building committee were Joseph Rudy, Daniel Metz, John Ebersole, John E. Horstick, Luther K. Lingle. The cost of improvement $5,224.68. Ministers present at the dedication were: Lutheran, Revs. J. H. Menges, J. G. Martz, an ex-pastor, E. Daron, an ex-pastor, and S. Dasher, pastor; German Reformed, Revs. A. S. Stouffer, pastor, D. Y. Heisler, an ex-pastor, and M. A. Smith, an ex-pastor. The address of welcome was made by Rev. A. S. Stouffer, and the historical address was delivered by Hon. David Mumma.

It is difficult to give a correct history of the pastors who served the Lutheran congregation from time to time, inasmuch as only a few of the pastors kept correct records. It is evident, says Mr. Mumma, that there was some service in this locality before the "Church Book," already referred to, was opened in 1783. There are some baptisms recorded as early as 1774, and one in every year (but one) down to 1782. The first one after the opening of the book was in May, 1783. But who performed the service of all but the last one we are unable to say. It is fair and reasonable to presume that it was done by visiting clergymen. After April 26, 1783, the Rev. Frederick Theodore Melsheimer was the regular Lutheran pastor, who subscribes himself as "Evangelical Lutheran Preacher, Beckstein," the latter being the name by which the church was then known. In fact the name Shoop's is not found in any record until we find it in the next church register, opened May 23, 1830. It is not so named in the deed. That is to "The United German Lutheran and Reformed Church, in township of Paxton." It is evident that at the date of the opening of the church register aforesaid, April 26, 1783, the church edifice was not yet commenced, and that it was finished in 1785.

It is a matter of tradition that the congregation for some time worshiped in Stoffle Shoop's house, until the church was finished and used for worship, and that before any regular organization existed traveling preachers frequently visited here and were entertained by Stoffle Shoop at his house, and held service there. Rev. F. T. Melsheimer officiated here as Lutheran pastor from April 26, 1783, to 1788. He recorded but one communion list, April 18, 1784, containing fifty-one names.

From 1788 to 1790 Rev. F. D. Schaeffer was pastor. From May 1, 1796, Henry Muehler (Moeller) was pastor. He subscribed himself "Pastor at Harrisburg, East Pennsboro and Beckstein" (Shoop's), and continued at Paxton (Shoop's) until 1803. In 1803 Rev. George Lochman held communion services here. He was then pastor at Lebanon. In 1804, November 24, Rev. J. F. Ernst officiated at communion services. At this time the congregation was evidently without a regular pastor. In 1805 Rev. John Paul Ferdinand Kramer held confirmation and communion services here. He subscribed himself as "der zeit pradiger"—preacher for the time being—"Berufen Lehrer, in Maytown, Lancaster county, St. Paul's." He officiated as pastor from 1807 to October 2, 1808. Here we are left without any record of services for four years. On Whit-Monday, 1813, Rev. F. C. Schaeffer records a service held by him as pastor of the church. From the fact that he was pastor at Harrisburg from November 22, 1812, to May,

1815, it may be inferred that he ministered here also during that time. On May 17, 1816, Rev. George Lochman became pastor, and continued until his death, which occurred in July, 1826. In 1826 Rev. Augustus H. Lochman succeeded his father as pastor, and continued until November 29, 1835, when he resigned.

Then followed: Rev. H. G. Stecher, from 1836 to April 2, 1847; Rev. L. Gerhard, May, 1848, to September 8, 1850; Rev. Charles F. Stoever, October 1, 1850, to October 28, 1854; Rev. George J. Martz, December 1, 1855, to December, 1868; Rev. H. D. Kutz, 1869 to May 28, 1871; Rev. E. Daron, April 1, 1872, to June 1, 1878; Rev. S. Yingling, June 9, 1878, to July, 1881; Rev. S. Dasher, September 18, 1881, to 1885; Rev. M. V. Shatto, November 10, 1885, to November 1, 1887; Rev. T. J. Frederick, January 2, 1888, to December 1, 1890; Rev. W. L. Heisler, April 1, 1890, to the present time.

It is said the first person that was buried in this graveyard was a woman who was killed by Indians, after being scalped by them.

There is no debt on this church. There is no parsonage belonging to the charge. The amount paid towards the pastor's salary is $408.00. It is supposed that English preaching was commenced in this church during the pastorate of Rev. Charles F. Stoever, about 1850. A Sunday-school was organized in this church at an early day.

The present officers of the church are as follows:

Elders—William Gerberich, Amos Fisler; Deacons—Morris Eshenour, George Machen; Trustees—Daniel Metz, Martin Kahler.

The Sunday-school numbers, at present, 100 scholars, 15 teachers, and the following officers:

Superintendents—G. S. Machen, G. Hetrick; Secretaries—L. B. Nye, David Hetrick; Librarians—William Saul, G. Hain; Treasurer—Alfred Crum; Organists—Miss Mary Horstick, Miss M. Gertie Fisher; Chorister—John A. Ebersole; Artist—Daniel Fisher.

During Rev. Mr. Kutz's pastorate a gracious revival of religion was enjoyed by this congregation. Many souls were happily converted during this revival, of whom many are still alive and are active members of the church. During Rev. Mr. Shatto's pastorate there was also a revival meeting held, and quite a goodly number of souls were converted to God.

2. SALEM'S EVANGELICAL LUTHERAN CHURCH, OBERLIN.

This church was organized in 1844, service being held in a school-house in the neighborhood until the church building was erected in 1846. September 12, 1846, a deed was made by Peter Brenner, Jr., and Rebecca, his wife, to Jacob Baker, Peter Brenner, Sr., George Hocker, Jacob Eshenour, Sr., and Conrad Peck, for the consideration of one dollar. The date on the corner-stone is September 12, 1846. There is no date on record when the church was dedicated. The church is a frame building, one story high, with an end gallery, a vestibule and a steeple. In 1877 the church was enlarged and improved at a cost of about one thousand dollars. There is no record of re-dedication.

The pastors have been as follows: Rev. J. Vogelbach, 1845 to September 22, 1847; Rev. L. Gerhardt, November 4, 1847, to October 1, 1850; Rev. J. Vogelbach, October 13, 1850, to April 11, 1852; Rev. D. Maier, April, 1852; Rev. George J. Martz, December 1, 1855, to October 27, 1868; Rev. H. D. Kutz, 1869 to August 18, 1871; Rev. E. Daron, April 1, 1872, to January 1, 1878, when he resigned and left; Rev. Samuel Yingling, June 1, 1878, to July 1881; Rev. S. Dasher, September 18, 1881, to 1885; Rev. M. V. Shatto, December 1, 1885, to November 1, 1887; Rev. T. J. Frederick, January 2, 1888, to December 1, 1890; Rev. W. L. Heisler, April 1, 1891, to the present time.

This congregation has always been in connection with Shoop's church. English preaching was introduced in this church when Rev. George J. Martz was pastor. There is no debt remaining on the church property. There is no parsonage belonging to the charge. This congregation pays $264 towards the pastor's salary. Five families take the *Lutheran Observer*. There is a Christian Endeavor Society in connection with the church, which is conducted by the young people.

The Sunday-school was organized March 29, 1874, at which time the following officers were elected: Superintendent, Frank C. Earnest; Assistant Superintendent, Christian Hess; Secretary, A. B. Dunkle; Treasurer, Henry Becker; Librarian, Jacob Reigert; Assistant Librarian, Mrs. Dobson.

The first session was held the following Sunday, April 5, 1874, at 1:30 p. m. The present officers are: Superintendent, Samuel A. Brehm; Assistant Superintendent, Jacob Reigert; Secretary, Elmore Handshaw; Librarian, Jacob E. Bishop; Assistant Librarian, Miss Maggie Hocker; Treasurer, George Hocker. There are at present twenty-one officers and teachers and two hundred and nineteen scholars.

The present officers of this church are as follows: Elders—Joseph Brehm, John Pifer; Deacons—Benjamin C. Hoover, John W. Shakespere, Jr.; Trustees—Michael Barnhardt, John B. Reed.

XX. ZION CHURCH, HARRISBURG.

BY REV. D. M. GILBERT, D. D.

Prior to the year 1787 the Christian people of all denominations in Harrisburg, then a town of about one hundred houses, worshiped together in a small log school-house which stood on the north corner of Third and Walnut streets, at the foot of what is now Capitol Hill. They enjoyed only such irregular and occasional services as might be obtained from visiting ministers.

On March 12, 1787, a subscription was opened to procure funds for the erection of the first church edifice of the town. The subscribers were largely Germans, members of the Lutheran and Reformed churches, and although others were granted certain privileges in it, the building was jointly owned and statedly occupied by the people of these two communions. The first church in Harrisburg, built of logs, was erected in the year above named, on lot No. 187 (corner Third and Chestnut streets), which was donated for the purpose, under certain reservations, by John Harris, the founder of the town. The building was 35 feet 5 inches by 30 feet 5 inches in dimensions, and was used jointly by the two congregations for about 27 years. After the death of John Harris, in 1791, his heirs released all their interest in the church lot to the Trustees of the Reformed and Lutheran churches for the sum of five shillings. Rev. A. Hautz became the first pastor of the Reformed church (and first resident minister of the town), while the Lutheran congregation was served, more or less regularly, by Rev. F. D. Schaeffer, of Carlisle. These two congregations appear to have been united in their temporal affairs and all church regulations from 1787 to 1795. In the latter year Rev. Henry Moeller became the first regular resident pastor of our church in Harrisburg, and with his ministry its *Protocol*, or *Register*, begins. The first entry in the record of baptisms reads: "*Benjamin*, born 20th Feb'y, baptized 29th March (1795). *Parents*, Benjamin Kurtz and wife Elizabeth."

In 1814, under the pastorship of Rev. Frederick Christian Schaeffer, the congregation, feeling that the time had come for them to build a church for their own exclusive use, purchased a desirable lot on Fourth street, between Market and Chestnut streets, which has continued to be the site of their church home to this day. On January 26, in the year named, a Building Committee was appointed, consisting of Christian Kunkel, Geo. Youse, Geo. Ziegler and Christian Stahl, who, on the 14th of the month following, contracted with Stephen Hills for the building of a handsome brick church. The corner-stone was laid June 22, 1814, the following ministers being present: Revs. George Schmucker, of Yorktown, Geo. Lochman, of Lebanon, H. Vanhoff, of Jonestown, W. G. Ernst, of Marietta, and J. P. Hecht, of Carlisle. The church was dedicated October 1, 1815, Revs. Schmucker, Vanhoff and Hecht taking part in the services of the occasion. The afternoons of October 16 and 17 were set apart for the renting of the pews, when, in the words of the original record, "to the complete surprise of everybody every pew was taken the first day." In 1816 the congregation sold their interest in the old church and lot to their Reformed brethren for one thousand dollars. In the year 1822 a large two-story brick schoolhouse was built on the lot at the side of the church, particularly for the accommodation of the Sunday school. In 1829 the church was improved by the building of a steeple upon it, in which a bell was placed, and on October 21, 1838, the entire edifice and the adjoining school-house were destroyed by fire. On the following day, in compliance with the request of the vestry and the pastor, Rev. Samuel Sprecher, the congregation assembled at the ruins, and promptly resolved that the church should be rebuilt. A committee was at once appointed to take general oversight of the enterprise, and so vigorously was the work prosecuted that on November 10 (Luther Day), 1839, the new Zion was dedicated. It was 64 feet front and 84 feet deep, with basement, lecture room and Sunday-school rooms. It was built of brick, covered with composition, painted white, and in the cupola hung two bells. It was in this new and spacious building, before its dedication, that the convention was held which nominated General W. H. Harrison for President and John Tyler for Vice-President of the United States. The edifice was remodeled and enlarged in 1867-68 at an expense of nearly forty thousand dollars, including the organ and a chime of eleven bells. It is now 104 feet deep by 64 front, and its tower and spire 175 feet high. At this time (September, 1892) a chapel extension is being added to the Sunday-school rooms and other improvements under way, at an estimated cost of six thousand dollars.

ZION'S PASTORS.

Between 1795 and the present time our congregation has been served by twelve regular pastors, as follows: Henry Moeller, from 1795 to 1803; John Dietrich Peterson, from April, 1803, to 1812; Fred'k Christian Schaeffer, from November, 1812, to June, 1815; George Lochman, from August 30, 1815, to the day of his death, July 10, 1826; Augustus H. Lochman, from April 2, 1827, to February 17, 1836; Samuel Sprecher, from June 6, 1836, to November, 1840; Charles W. Schaeffer, from January, 1841, to June, 1849; Charles A. Hay, from July 8, 1849, to September 4, 1865; George F. Stelling, from December 21, 1865, to July 1, 1875; Joel Swartz, from September, 1875, to 1880; Albert H. Studebaker, from February, 1881, to November, 1886; D. M. Gilbert, from December 1, 1887, to the present time.

ZION'S CHILDREN.

Our congregation has not only an extended, but a very creditable history. Ever zealous for the spread of the Redeemer's kingdom, she has been a faithful mother of churches. The first two pastors officiated at public service in the German language alone; but about the year 1812, yielding to the demand of many members for a change, the use of the English tongue was introduced. The English services steadily increased in number up to 1842, when scarcely one sermon a month was given in German. This state of things was far from satisfactory to the Germans, and both the English and the German portions of the membership having sufficiently increased in numbers, a friendly separation was effected, and on January 8, 1843, St. Michael's German Lutheran church was organized, with Rev. G. J. Martz as its first pastor. From that time forward the services in Zion have been, of course, altogether in the English language.

In 1863 a second German church (Zion) was organized several squares north of the Capitol, St. Michael's being on South Second street, in the lower part of the city.

Messiah Church, corner of Sixth & Forster streets, grew out of a Mission Sunday-school, founded on East State street, January 11, 1858, by the Sunday-school Association of Zion church. In March of that year a lot was leased and a small chapel built, in which, during the following winter, Dr. Hay preached on alternate Sunday afternoons. The congregation was regularly organized September 13, 1860, with Rev. E. S. Johnston as first pastor. On June 1, 1890, Messiah congregation established Augsburg Mission Sunday-school in the north part of the city, and within a year past dismissed about 100 members to form a church at that point, which, under the pastoral care of Rev. Dixon H. Geiser, is rapidly developing into a flourishing congregation.

Memorial Church, in East Harrisburg, had its origin in a like enterprise started by Zion Sunday-school Association in 1871, at 15th & Shoop streets. The congregation was regularly organized February 25, 1872, under Rev. S. Dasher, who is faithfully serving it to this day. Sixty-two members of Memorial church dismissed for that purpose organized Christ church, on South 13th street, March 23, 1890. Rev. T. L. Crouse is its pastor, and the congregation is going forward steadily and prosperously. Christ church, in turn, has under its care a Mission School at Brookwood, or East End, which it is hoped will, in due time, develop into the Third Lutheran church of East Harrisburg.

In the early part of 1887, and while without a pastor, Zion church dismissed about one hundred valuable and esteemed members to establish Bethlehem church, corner of Green and

Cumberland streets, in which portion of the city she had for some years previously maintained a Mission Sunday-school. Rev. W. H. Fishburn became the pastor of the congregation, which, within five years, has become numerically stronger than the mother church.

Ever watchful of her opportunities and desiring never to grow weary in well-doing, the congregation again, through her Teachers' Association, on November 11, 1888, (largely induced to the step by the interest and liberality of Mr. Jos. F. Young, one of her faithful members) started Trinity Mission, on South Ninth street. The Sunday-school rapidly grew to a membership of three hundred and fifty teachers and scholars, and the present pastor of Zion conducted service every Thursday night throughout the winter with encouraging results. Rev. M. L. Deitzler was called to take charge of the enterprise in connection with a mission at Steelton, and began his labors July 1, 1890. The congregation was formally organized May 17, 1891. Though yet partially dependent on the mother church and the Home Mission Board for support, Trinity has good prospects of becoming an assured success.

It will be seen from these brief notes that our Church in Harrisburg has been keeping pace with the growth of the city. Where, in 1843, we had one church (Zion), and one pastor, there are now nine churches (seven English and two German), each having a pastor, and reporting an aggregate membership of 3,228 communicants. The recent development has been very remarkable. Within five years we have averaged one new congregation every 15 months; and four handsome and costly church edifices and two spacious chapels (exclusive of the chapel extension now being added to Zion) have been erected among us within *four* years.

Almost every advance movement in this expansion of the past half century, it is proper to note, has been to some extent, and sometimes to a very large extent, at the expense of the mother church, as regards both members and money.

ZION AND THE SYNOD.

In her earliest history Zion church, as our old churches generally in this region, belonged to the Pennsylvania Ministerium. During the ministry of Rev. C. A. Hay, in 1857, she withdrew from that relation and became a constituent part of the Synod of East Pennsylvania. The records of this latter body will abundantly show that, notwithstanding much, and at times expensive, local mission work in which the congregation has been engaged, she has always been deeply interested in and faithfully borne her full share of the burden of the Synod's general work.

ZION'S PRESENT.

This congregation is now sharing, to some extent, in the experience common to old churches in growing cities. She finds herself, at the end of her century and more of life, somewhat disadvantageously situated with reference to the population generally and with reference to many of her own membership. Her stately edifice is rapidly being surrounded by business houses, instead of residences, and her territory has been so circumscribed by the younger organizations she has been instrumental in establishing in every direction about her, that rapid numerical increase of the congregation can scarcely be reasonably expected. But she does not complain, much less yield to discouragement. There are strength and vigor in the old church yet, as evidenced by the statistical reports for the year. She is still bringing forth fruit in old age—is engaged even now in enlarging her facilities for work among the children and youth upon whom she has a claim and, humbly looking to God for a continuance of the favor with which He long has so richly blessed her, still sets her face toward the future in earnest hope.

XXI. FISHERVILLE CHARGE, DAUPHIN CO. — ST. PETER'S, ST. PAUL'S, STRAW'S, MESSIAH, ST. JAMES', STAR OF BETHLEHEM.

BY REV. J. M. STOVER.

The Fisherville charge is located in Armstrong and Powell's valleys, Dauphin Co., Pa. The land is rolling, and in good cultivation. The roads are comparatively good. The people speak the Pennsylvania German dialect in most families. The English is also spoken and is gradually taking the place of the German.

The history of the churches upon this territory begins with the early settlement of these valleys, over one hundred years ago, but the "Fisherville Charge" was not formally organized until about the year 1848. It then included Messiah, Straw's and St. Paul's churches, and was served by the pastors of the Berrysburg charge until 1855, when it became an independent pastorate. It has since been served by the following pastors:

Revs. L. K. Secrist, 1855 to 1858; John H. Davidson, 1860 to 1862; M. Fernsler, 1863 to 1866; J. G. Breininger, 1867 to 1868; E. Daron, 1869 to 1872; F. Aurand, 1872 to 1874; S. S. Engle, 1874 to 1875; Chas. E. Hay, 1876 to 1877; J. K. Bricker, 1877 to 1879; A. B. Erhard, 1879 to 1883; M. V. Shatto, 1884 to 1885; H. A. Letterman, 1886 to 1889; J. M. Stover, 1890 to the present.

During the pastorate of Rev. Daron the charge became self-sustaining, and the present comfortable parsonage in Fisherville was built. The following ministers have come from this charge: Revs. N. A. Whitman, I. P. Zimmerman and I. H. McGann.

1. St. Peter's (Fetterhoff's) Church.

The record of this congregation gives an account of baptisms as early as 1788. About this time there was a log church erected near the present site of St. Peter's. In this rude building the two congregations, Lutheran and Reformed, worshiped for at least seventy years. We are told by tradition, that the church was used for public worship before it was completed, and that the young men were required to climb up at the wall and occupy the gallery during services. The reader will understand that this was not so difficult in an unplastered log house. The method of getting men to assist in building this church was somewhat different from what it is in our day. They worked in the forenoon and had shooting-match in the afternoon.

On Sundays, the early worshipers of this church came with their guns on their shoulders; not so much on account of the wily savage, as on account of the wildbeasts that might come across their pathway. For a number of years this was the only church in Armstrong Valley. The settlers of Powell's Valley worshiped here. From all around the people came, on horseback, or on the big wagon; more often on foot, walking many miles. It was nothing unusual for mothers to come from across the ridge with their babes on one arm, and their shoes on the other. They were accustomed to go barefooted, but put on their shoes, which they carried with them, before entering church.

But time brings about changes. Where once the old church stood, there are now tombstones marking the last resting-place of some of her members. Not far from this sacred spot there stands a handsome brick edifice, with tall steeple towering toward the skies. The corner-stone of this church was laid September 19, 1858. It was dedicated to the worship of God sometime during the following year. Rev. F. Waltz was the Lutheran pastor, and Rev. N. Bressler, the Reformed. This church, after undergoing extensive repairs, was re-dedicated on December 13, 1891, under the pastoral care of Rev. J. M. Stover, on the Lutheran side, and Rev. C. W. E. Seigle, on the Reformed side. The cost amounted to $2,100.

In the year 1846 the two congregations together purchased twelve acres of land, joining the old church lot. This land, in connection with a very pleasant home on the church lot, is calculated for the use of the sexton, and can not be used for a parsonage.

The venerable Nicholas Stroh, the oldest Lutheran minister in the United States, now in his ninety-seventh year, was baptized and confirmed in St. Peter's church, and all his relatives are buried in its graveyard. He was a brother of Mrs. Rev. Hemping. Among the many who are buried here we find the names of Rev. John A. Hemping and Rev. N. Bressler. Rev. Hemping was born and educated in Germany. He became the Lutheran pastor of this church in 1811, and served until 1847. He died in 1855, in the seventy-seventh year of his age. Rev. N. Bressler was the Reformed pastor for many years. He died in 1877.

St. Peter's church formerly belonged to the Lykens Valley charge, and to the old Pennsylvania Synod. But in 1869, through the influence of Rev. E. Daron, it came over to the General Synod, and was made part of the Fisherville charge. The principal reason for making this change was the inconvenience of being served by a pastor living in Lykens Valley, when at the same time there was a Lutheran pastor living in Fisherville and right among the members.

Up to this time the congregation had been served by the following pastors: Rev. Enterlein, 1795 to 1807; Rev. J. D. Peterson, 1807 to 1811; Rev. John A. Hemping, 1811 to 1847; Rev. W. G. Laitzle, 1841 to 1843; Rev. Jer. Schindel, 1843 to 1845; Rev. C. F. Stoever, 1845 to 1850; Rev. N. Jeager, 1850 to 1852; Rev. F. Waltz, 1855 to 1869. From 1842 to 1847 there were two parties in the congregation, each having its own pastor.

This congregation used to pay the trifling sum of twelve dollars per year for pastor's salary. It now, with a smaller membership, pays more than three times that amount per quarter.

2. St. Paul's (Bowerman's).

This congregation, located in Powell's Valley, was built in 1824, under the pastoral care of Rev. John A. Hemping and Rev. Gerhard. The church was built by Lutherans and Reformed, and the two congregations still worship in it.

3. Straw's.

Straw's church, in the upper end of Armstrong Valley, was erected in the summer of 1842. It was built by Lutheran members of the old St. John's church, who were unwilling to yield their convictions to the rulings of that church on "the new measures." This church stands in sight of the old one. It was at one time in a prosperous condition, but since a new church has been built at Jacksonville this congregation has been weakened, and of late years has not been served by regular preaching.

4. Messiah, Fisherville.

For several years previous to the formation of the "Fisherville Charge," there was trouble in St. Peter's church on account of revival methods. The congregation was divided. There was bitter feeling on both sides, and the result was that a new constitution was adopted, which forever prohibited the use of the anxious-bench in that church. In view of this fact, the excluded party resolved to build in Fisherville. Accordingly the corner-stone of a new church, named Messiah, was there laid on September 9, 1849. It was built as a Lutheran and Reformed church, and remains so to this day, but for some years the Reformed have had no organization here. This church was remodeled in 1885, under the pastoral care of Rev. M. V. Shatto.

5. St. James'.

This church was built by the Lutherans and Reformed in 1856. It is located at Carsonville, in the upper end of Powell's Valley. The first man buried in its graveyard was Jacob Bordner.

6. Star of Bethlehem.

The church at Jacksonville, in Armstrong Valley, known as "The Star of Bethlehem," was built in 1875. The lot was presented by Mr. G. W. D. Enders, of the Reformed church, and Mr. John Helt, of the Lutheran. The church, which cost originally about $2,500, is finely located, in good condition, and has been recently re-painted. The first officers on the Lutheran side were: Philip Enders, elder; Wm. Fitting, deacon; Daniel Enders, trustee. Those on the Reformed side were: Joseph Lyter, elder; Daniel Whitman, deacon; G. W. D. Enders, trustee. The Reformed have for some years had no organization here.

XXII. BERRYSBURG CHARGE, DAUPHIN CO.—SALEM, KILLINGER; SALEM, BERRYSBURG; ST. PAUL'S, MILLERSBURG.

BY REV. B. F. KAUTZ.

1. Salem (Wert's) Church, Killinger P. O.

This congregation, known formerly as "Wert's Church," is quite old, thought to be the oldest congregation in Lykens Valley. It is located in Upper Paxton township, two and one-half miles northeast of Millersburg, and seven and one-half miles west of Berrysburg. There are no old records preserved and we are obliged to depend for dates upon the memory of the older members. The date of its organization we have been unable to learn, but it lies back in the last century. "Grandfather Wert," whose descendants of the fourth generation are still living in the vicinity, presented sixty acres of land for church uses. The greater portion of this, with a dwelling house and barn erected upon it, was rented for many years. About 1870, when the project of building a new church was being agitated, all of this ground except ten acres was sold.

The present large two-story brick edifice, costing about $12,000, was erected in 1874; the former building, which stood a little distance away, was erected in 1812, whilst a few of the oldest members remember still the site of the first building, a small log church, abandoned in 1812, which stood a little distance from the second one. The list of pastors serving this church as far back as we could gather is as follows:

About the beginning of the century Rev. Andrew (?) Schultz was pastor of Salem and St. John's (near Berrysburg) and formed one class of catechumens for the entire territory, meeting them alternately in the two churches, and confirming seventy-six in one year. It is probable that Rev. John Paul Ferdinand Kramer served them about 1805, and Rev. John A. Hemping from 1811 until 1842. Then came Revs. W. G. Laitzle, 1842 to 1843; C. F. Stoever, 1846 to 1852; Jacob Martin, 1852 to 1853; D. Sell, 1853 to 1860; P. P. Lane, 1861 to 1862; G. P. Weaver, 1862 to 1863; C. A. Fetzer, 1863 to 1866; M. Fernsler, 1866 to 1878; Geo. C. Henry, 1879 to 1882; J. Fishburn, 1883 to 1890; B. F. Kautz, 1890 to the present.

2. SALEM CHURCH, BERRYSBURG.

This congregation sprang from St. John's Lutheran church (now of the General Council), standing about a mile from the town. There are no old records preserved, but from the recollections of the older members we gathered the data here given. The organization must have been effected about the year 1841 or 1842 by Rev. J. P. Schindel, then pastor of St. John's. The present church building, a one-story stone structure, was erected some time in 1844, in union with the Reformed congregation, and is still a union church. In 1875 it was enlarged and remodeled. Owing to the nearness of St. John's it has always been a weak congregation, having little territory. The list of pastors serving here is the same as that of Salem church at Killinger.

3. St. Paul's Church, Millersburg.

About sixty years ago, when Millersburg had a population of about three hundred, Father Hemping, pastor then of Lykens Valley charge, preached here occasionally in the German language in the old school-house About 1837 Rev. S. D. Finckel, residing at Middletown, came up to Millersburg about every four weeks and preached. In 1842 Rev. W. G. Laitzle, one of the founders of the East Pennsylvania Synod, who had been called to the charge in Armstrong Valley, crossed Berry's Mountain and preached here and in the valley church, now Salem or Killinger. In 1846 Rev. C. F. Stoever, of the Berrysburg charge, preached occasionally here during a pastorate of six years. From 1852 to 1853 Rev. Jacob Martin, of the same charge, preached here occasionally. Rev. D. Sell entered the Berrysburg charge in November, 1853, and began preaching regularly in the school-house. After laboring for a year he organized St. Paul's congregation in the latter part of 1854, with the following nine members: Simon Wert, Levi Miller, Christian Walborn, Daniel Martz, David Kramer, Mary Seal, Catharine Walborn, Sarah Hebel and Hannah Auchmuty. Simon Wert was chosen as elder, which office he has held continuously, and still holds at the present time, a period of thirty-eight years, and will hold it to his death. He is truly a prince in Israel. Through Rev. Sell's labors a church building was erected on Centre street, which is now occupied by the Reformed church. This building was dedicated on Christmas Day, 1856. Rev. P. Willard, of Danville, preached the dedication sermon. The first communion was held March 22, 1857, with fifteen communicants. Upon Mr. Sell's resignation Rev. P. P. Lane entered the charge, serving from 1861 to 1862. Mr. Lane was followed by Rev. G. P. Weaver, who served 1862–1863. Rev. C. A. Fetzer entered the Berrysburg charge April, 1863, remaining here three years. In December, 1866, Rev. M. Fernsler assumed the pastoral care of this charge.

The charge had consisted up to this time of Lykens, Berrysburg, Salem and Millersburg. In 1871 Lykens withdrew from the charge, leaving the three last-named congregations forming the Berrysburg charge. The same year, also, some difficulty having arisen between the Lutheran and Reformed congregations here in Millersburg, the question of separation came up, and after a lengthy discussion the Lutherans sold out their interest in the old church to the Reformed for fourteen hundred dollars ($1400).

Ground for the new church was broken in March, 1873. The cool judgment of all was that not more than $3000 at the best could be secured for a church, yet this weak little congregation built and paid for a building costing them about $16,000. The corner-stone was laid July 13, 1873. Besides the pastor there were present D. Sell, D. Kloss and U. Graves. In June, 1874, the basement was dedicated, Rev. Dr. Reinmund preaching the sermon. At the time of dedication there had been paid in cash $1000, with another $1000 in subscriptions.

During the six following years the congregation worshiped in the basement, and the work of finishing went on as they were able to raise the funds. Every year current expenses were met, interest on debt of $2700 paid, as well as pastor's salary and small subscriptions gathered for finishing the building.

In November, 1878, Rev. M. Fernsler, after a pastorate of twelve years, resigned. The charge remained vacant for eight months, when Rev. Geo. C. Henry, of the Theological Seminary, was called, and entered upon the charge in July, 1879.

Early in 1880, at a congregational meeting, it was resolved to finish the audience room; work was begun, and it was finally dedicated to the service of God November 14, 1880, Rev. F. W. Conrad, D. D., preaching the dedication sermon. A debt of upwards of $3000 was left to the congregation, which they just finished paying last year, and are now free of debt. In December, 1882, Rev. Geo. C. Henry resigned, and was followed by Rev. J. Fishburn, who served them from 1883–1890. In July, 1890, Rev. B. F. Kautz assumed charge.

XXIII. ST. MATTHEW'S CHURCH, PHILADELPHIA.

BY W. M. BAUM, D. D.

The first Lutheran preacher in Philadelphia of whom we have record was Rev. Gerhard Henkel, between the years 1720 and 1728. In 1732 Rev. John Christian Schultze officiated. In 1733 we meet with the name of Rev. John Caspar Stoever. From 1734 to 1737 there appears to have been a vacancy. In 1737 John Philip Streiter, though unordained, supplied the pulpit. In 1742 Count Zinzendorff presented himself as a Lutheran pastor, and received a call May 30th. He appointed John C. Pyrlaeus as his assistant, who was dismissed as early as July 29th. In August, 1742, Valentine Kraft, who had been dismissed from his office in Germany, succeeded in detaching a portion of the congregation. December 5, 1742, Dr. Henry Melchior Mühlenberg began his ministry. Kraft withdrew to Germantown and Zinzendorff returned to Europe. During 1843 St. Michael's church was built. January 26, 1745, Rev. Peter Brunnholtz became assistant pastor, and was soon left in sole charge of the city congregation, whilst Dr. Mühlenberg served the Trappe and New Hanover churches. July 26, 1753, Rev. J. D. M. Heintzelman became assistant pastor, holding the position until his death, February 9, 1756. Mr. Brunnholtz, long in feeble health, died July 5, 1757. In November, 1757, Rev. John Frederick Handschuh became pastor and served until his death, October 9, 1764. In November, 1761, Dr. Mühlenberg, who was still nominally pastor, was recalled, and remained until 1779, resigning the active ministry in 1774. October 28, 1765, Rev. Christopher Emanuel Schultze became assistant and remained until December, 1770. October 8, 1770, Rev. Christopher Kunze was elected third pastor. In December Rev. Schultze removed to Tulpehocken, and Dr. Mühlenberg's son, Henry Ernst Mühlenberg, became assistant. In 1773 he was elected third pastor, remaining such until April 8, 1779. April 4, 1774, Dr. Mühlenberg resigned, having served 16 years. In June, 1779, Dr. Justus Henry Christian Helmuth was elected as successor to Dr. Mühlenberg. Dr. Kunze removed to New York, 1784, and was succeeded by Dr. John Frederick Schmidt. The distinction between senior and junior ministers was removed. In 1794, December 26, Zion's church, built between 1766 and 1769, was destroyed by fire, but was immediately rebuilt, and re-dedicated November 27, 1796.

As early as 1796 demands for English services began, which culminated, in 1806, in the organization of St. John's church. Again in 1815 a new demand for English services arose, which, after a long struggle and bitter contention, resulted in the organization of St. Matthew's church in 1818.

Dr. Schmidt died May 12, 1812, and was succeeded by Rev. Frederick David Schaeffer, who served until 1834. Dr. Helmuth retired in 1822 and was succeeded by Rev. C. R. Demme.

St. Matthew's, Philadelphia, Pa.

The organization of St. Matthew's, Philadelphia, was consummated January 26, 1818, by the signing of the constitution on the part of those designing to enter it. Being without church accommodations, the academy building on Fourth street, between Arch and Market, was secured for use and occupied until 1830, when the edifice on New street, below Fourth, was dedicated. The congregation had no regular pastor until the year 1827, when Rev. Charles P. Krauth, Sr., began his ministry. The names of Rev. Christian F. Cruse and Rev. David Eyster, with others, appear as temporary supplies during this period. It was a time of difficulty and struggle.

The real life of St. Matthew's began with the securing of a permanent pastor. Being highly favored in obtaining the services of so able a divine and acceptable a preacher as Dr. Krauth, they soon emerged from their unsatisfactory surroundings in the old academy, and for nearly fifty years worshiped in the church on New street. The ministry of Dr. Krauth continued from 1827 to 1833, when he was called to Gettysburg, Pa., and placed over the newly-chartered Pennsylvania College as its President. An interval of some months occurred before a successor was secured, during which time the pulpit was occupied by the Rev. Simeon W. Harkey, then only a theological student. Rev. Jacob Medtart, of Martinsburg, Va., took pastoral charge of St. Matthew's in November, 1834. His ministry was attended with no little congregational agitation and disturbance, and terminated in 1838. Rev. Stephen A. Mealy, of Savannah, Ga., then took charge, but his views and methods were not entirely acceptable to many of the congregation, so that a mutual separation was not long delayed.

ST. MATTHEW'S EVANGELICAL LUTHERAN CHURCH, PHILADELPHIA.

Rev. Theophilus Stork, of Winchester, Va., became pastor in October, 1841. With his advent there came a new era of prosperity. Faithful labor, earnest evangelic methods, able and edifying ministrations in public and in private, brought gratifying results. The influence and the revenues of the church were largely increased. Additions were numerous, new fields of operation were needed and soon found, and a cluster of new organizations was the result, culminating in the establishment of St. Mark's Lutheran church on Spring Garden street, above Thirteenth, of which Rev. Stork became pastor, resigning St. Matthew's in 1850. Rev. Edwin W. Hutter was installed pastor of St. Matthew's September, 1850, and rendered an unbroken service of twenty-three years. He was admirably qualified for the field to which he was called. Under his fostering care its energies were quickened into vigorous life, and enterprise after enterprise was inaugurated. If Dr. Krauth stands forth as the scholar among the pastors of St. Matthew's, and Dr. Stork as the preacher, to Dr. Hutter unquestionably belongs the distinction of being the model pastor. He enjoyed in unusual degree the esteem, the love and the confidence of the congregation and the community. The period of his ministry was marked by internal peace and external activity. He died in 1873. Rev. William M. Baum, D. D., followed Dr. Hutter. He was installed in March, 1874, and continues in charge. This ministry is marked by the transfer, in 1876, of the congregation from New street to Broad and Mt. Vernon streets. A new and commodious church and chapel and parsonage have been erected, and with the exception of a small balance of the ground rent, all indebtedness has been canceled.

From its continuous anniversaries it appears that the Sabbath-school bears equal date with the congregation. No doubt, for a considerable time, this was the only bond of union, the only centre of operations for the new enterprise. For a period of forty-six years it had but one and the same superintendent, in the person of Martin Buehler, Esq., whose name deserves special mention in this sketch. At his death, in 1880, his personal friend and business partner, Mr. Charles P. Suesserott, took his place in the school. He also served until relieved by death in 1887. Since then his position has been filled by William J. Miller, Esq.

St. Matthew's has not only maintained its own congregational life unimpaired, but has been instrumental in the establishment of St. Mark's, St. Luke's, St. Peter's, Grace and Messiah Lutheran churches. It is now fully equipped for the most active and zealous service of the Master.

XXIV. EAST PETERSBURG CHARGE.—TRINITY, LONDONDERRY, IN LEBANON CO.; ZION'S, EAST PETERSBURG, AND GRACE, MANHEIM, IN LANCASTER COUNTY.

BY MR. L. M. PERVEIL.

1. TRINITY CHURCH, LONDONDERRY TOWNSHIP, LEBANON COUNTY.

Very little can be gathered concerning this church. The church record is very imperfect, and the old members have died away, leaving but a few who know anything about the congregation. As far as known, this church was erected in the year 1818, but the corner-stone of the present building was laid in 1842. The Building Committee were as follows, viz.: Jacob Missimer, John Baker, Joseph Porter and George Baker. Officers—Trustee, Jacob Missimer; Elder, George Baker; Deacons, Philip Keener and Jacob Yingst.

The congregation was served by Revs. L. Gerhardt, Martin Sondhaus, Wm. G. Laitzle, 1854-1859, Mark Harpel, 1859-1870, and others. For a long time the congregation was without a pastor. On September 22, 1872, Rev. J. Peter took charge of the few members left, and has been serving the congregation ever since (except from September, 1890, to June, 1891) with acceptance.

He has labored hard and faithfully, and the congregation, though not strong in membership, numbering only seventy, is active. May the great Head of the Church continue to prosper it.

2. ZION'S CHURCH, EAST PETERSBURG, LANCASTER COUNTY.

The East Petersburg congregation was organized by Rev. Reuben S. W. Wagner, and was named Zion's. The corner-stone was laid in the year 1847. In 1849 Rev. Wagner resigned, and Rev. J. H. Menges became the pastor, serving until February 11, 1852.

November 1, 1852, Rev. Adelbert Charles Roderico Rueter took charge of the congregation. Others followed, viz.: Revs. Jacob Albert, 1853-1855; J. H. Menges, 1855-1857; Geo. Haines, 1857-1858; Jno. Early, 1862-1863; Joseph Focht,

1864-1868; Jacob Kaempfer, 1868-1869, and S. S. Engle, 1870-1874.

August 9, 1874, the present pastor, Rev. J. Peter, took charge of the congregation, and has served them up to the present time with the exception of a brief period, from September, 1890, to June, 1891. The congregation has steadily increased, and is now in a prosperous condition.

The preaching is now conducted in both the German and the English languages, the latter taking the lead.

3. Grace Church, Manheim, Lancaster County.

This congregation is at this time but a year and a half old, and hence the history will be brief. It was formed by about forty-six persons who were regularly dismissed from Zion's Lutheran congregation of Manheim, and was organized April 4, 1891, by the Rev. W. H. Dunbar, of Lebanon, then President of the East Pennsylvania Synod.

The following officers were elected: Elders—S. D. Miller and George Gromlish; Deacons—T. S. Burns, S. Will, W. Zink and L. M. Perveil. The last named was chosen as Secretary.

Rev. J. Peter, of Bellwood, Pa., was authorized by the President of Synod to install the officers, which was done April 12, 1891.

A congregational meeting was called April 26, 1891, at which Rev. D. S. Kurtz, of Felton, York Co., presided. A unanimous call was then extended to Rev. J. Peter, which was accepted, and on the 1st of June, 1891, he entered upon his duties.

The members had left the old church without a penny; but, through the earnest work and self-sacrificing spirit of the pastor, the congregation soon moved forward. A small chapel, owned by the M. E. church, was rented for the time being. Soon an effort was made to purchase a lot suitable for a church, which work was accomplished in a short time. The corner-stone of the new building was laid July 31, 1892. The pastor was assisted by the Rev. G. J. Martz, of Lebanon. The church at this writing is almost ready for dedication, and will compare with any church in Manheim or with the majority in the East Pennsylvania Synod. The prospect of this congregation is bright.

XXV. LITITZ CHARGE, LANCASTER CO.—KISSEL HILL, NEFFSVILLE, LITITZ.

BY REV. I. W. BOBST.

The Lititz charge is composed of three congregations, Kissel Hill being the oldest, and the mother of two vigorous daughters, St. Paul's, of Lititz, and the Neffsville congregation. As is so often the case, the mother has made large sacrifices, to her own detriment, for the enrichment of her offspring. She has greatly decreased in her membership, whilst they are steadily increasing.

1. SALEM CHURCH, KISSEL HILL.

The Kissel Hill congregation was organized in 1823, and united with the Reformed element of the community in founding Salem union church. A lot was purchased of John Frank at a cost of $60.00, the corner-stone laid June 1, 1823, and a substantial brick church dedicated May 24, 1824. Rev. W. Baetes and Dr. Andrews (Lutheran) and Revs. Leinbach and D. Hertz (Reformed) were present on that occasion. In the style of the times it had a wine-glass pulpit, painfully suggestive to the ministry in this age of reform, and panel casing around the pews, symbolical of the rigid orthodoxy of its devotees. The cost of the edifice was $2,000. In 1848 a steeple with a bell was added, at a cost of $217.60. In 1872 the spirit of the age removed the grotesque pulpit and panels, and in 1887 the church was again repaired and carpeted.

The following are the pastorates: Rev. William Baetes, 1824 to 1839; Rev. Chas. P. Miller, 1839 to 1841; Rev. Christopher G. Frederick, 1842 to 1846; Rev. Chas. A. Barnitz, 1846 to 1852; Rev. Chas. A. Barnitz, 1853 to 1854; Rev. Chas. Rees, 1855 to 1856; Rev. D. P. Rosenmiller, 1857 to 1862; Rev. S. R. Boyer, 1862 to 1864; Rev. J. R. Focht, 1864 to 1868. Up to 1864 the preaching was nearly all in German.

From 1864 to 1871 the congregation vacillated between the General Council and the General Synod, a majority being in favor of the General Council. Rev. S. S. Engle became pastor about the year 1871, and preached for several years, gathering in quite a number of members. He was afterwards deposed from the ministry. Rev. J. Peter then took charge, and served the people faithfully till 1886. The pastorate of Rev. W. H. Lewars began October 15, 1886, and ended April 15, 1889. The present pastor, Rev. I. Walton Bobst, assumed charge June 1, 1889. The congregation in its palmiest days had about two hundred members. It now numbers about one hundred. The preaching is partly in German and partly in English.

2. St. Peter's Church, Neffsville.

In the spring of 1880 about thirty members of the Kissel Hill church amicably withdrew and formed the congregation of Neffsville. Through the influence of the sainted John Wechter, assisted by a noble little band of workers, the Neffsville church was erected. The corner-stone was laid during the summer of 1880, and the church dedicated June 26, 1881. Rev. J. Peter, the pastor, and Rev. R. W. Hufford, D. D., presided on this occasion. This congregation, though so recently established, has no reliable statistics. After Rev. J. Peter resigned, it was connected with the Millersville charge, and served as follows: J. V. Eckert, 1881–1882; F. Aurand, 1883; A. M. Whetstone, 1884–1885; J. W. Goodlin, 1887–1888. In 1888 the congregation severed its relations with the Millersville charge and connected itself with the Lititz charge. It has since been served by Revs. W. H. Lewars and I. W. Bobst, the present pastor, who took charge June 1, 1889. During the present pastorate the congregation has more than doubled, numbering now 154. This is largely due to the labors of its excellent Sunday-school Superintendent, Dr. E. H. Witmer, who has for twelve years assiduously inculcated Bible truths among the young of this community.

3. St. Paul's Church, Lititz.

August 4, 1885, a meeting was called for the purpose of discussing the feasibility of building a Lutheran church in Lititz. Rev. Peter, of the Manheim charge, occupied the chair. In pursuance of the action of this meeting, fifty-two members of the Kissel Hill church formed themselves into an independent congregation, and founded St. Paul's Lutheran church, of Lititz. The corner-stone was laid with appropriate ceremonies September 13, 1885, by Rev. Peter, assisted by Revs. Sylvanus Stall and John V.

Eckert. The dedication took place February 14, 1886. Rev. Eli Huber, D. D., preached the sermon and Rev. T. C. Billheimer, D. D., solicited subscriptions, securing $2,000, which covered all the indebtedness. The edifice cost upward of $6,000. The congregation demonstrated its enterprise by immediately erecting a commodious parsonage, at an expense of $2,200. Six hundred dollars of the subscriptions taken on dedication-day failed to materialize, which, together with the cost of the parsonage, left the congregation $2,800 in debt. This has been reduced during the present pastorate to $1,500. Shortly after the completion of the church Rev. J. Peter resigned. He was followed by Rev. W. H. Lewars, who entered upon his labors October 15, 1886, continuing faithfully three years and a half, when he was succeeded by the present pastor, Rev. I. Walton Bobst, who assumed charge June 1, 1889. The congregation now has one hundred and thirty-five members and is in excellent condition. The preaching is mainly in English, with a German sermon once a month.

XXVI. LIONVILLE CHARGE, CHESTER CO.—ST. MATTHEW'S AND ST. PAUL'S.

BY REV. M. S. CRESSMAN.

Chester County, Pa., was originally settled by two distinct classes of people—the English Quakers and the Germans. The former located in the southern part of the county, and the latter in the northern. The main line of the Pennsylvania Railroad now divides this district into two nearly equal parts, and, in a general way, may be regarded as the dividing line between the two distinctive elements of the county. In the section to the south the Quaker element still largely prevails, whilst in that to the north the descendants of the Germans still hold sway. It is accordingly in the northern part of the county that all our Lutheran churches are to be found, with the single exception of Trinity church, recently established at Coatesville, and this is on the border line.

Henry Melchior Mühlenberg organized the first Lutheran congregation in the county, to which the name Zion was given.

The early records being lost, the precise year of its organization is not known. It must, however, have been early in the ministry of this patriarch of American Lutheranism, as the erection of a new building was begun in the year 1771. The first edifice was made of logs, and was located in what was then known as Vincent Township, about five miles west of the Trappe. The site chosen was a commanding one, overlooking a large part of the counties of Berks and Montgomery.

When the Zion congregation was about to erect a new building, there arose a division of opinion as to the location, many desiring to remove some three miles further south. The result of this division was, that the Lutherans residing in Pikeland Township withdrew, and organized themselves into a separate congregation, erecting a log church in the year 1772, some ten miles southwest of Zion. This organization is known as St. Peter's. It was here that the first annual meeting of the East Pennsylvania Synod was held, October 15, 1842.

The two churches now composing the Lionville pastorate, St. Matthew's and St. Paul's, are the direct outgrowth of Zion's and St. Peter's congregations. The older of these, St. Matthew's, is now located in Upper Uwchlan township. It was organized in the year 1833, by Rev. Jacob Wampole, then pastor of Zion's and St. Peter's churches. It was the third Lutheran organization in Chester county, and the first to wholly use the English language. The original membership, sixty-six in number, came from the other two Lutheran churches; principally, however, from St. Peter's, in West Pikeland. About this time there was a general religious awakening in this vicinity. The Baptists and Episcopalians had begun the erection of places of worship. The Lutheran people felt the need of greater religious privileges than they were enjoying. Accordingly, a meeting was held in West Vincent township, January 1, 1833, to consider the propriety of erecting a church building, to be owned jointly by the Lutherans and the German Reformed. As the result of earnest and prayerful deliberation a piece of ground was purchased on the Conestoga pike for $50.00, upon which was erected a two-story stone church, 35x45 feet in size, with galleries on three sides, at a cost of $1,700.00. The corner-stone was laid May 27, 1833, Dr. C. P. Krauth, sr., preaching the sermon on the part of the Lutherans. On December 10, of the same year, the building was dedicated to the worship of the Triune God. Rev. P. F. Mayer, D. D., of Philadelphia, preached the sermon. The feast of dedication lasted two days, with three services daily, at each of which a sermon was preached. St. Matthew's became a part of Zion's charge, the pastor residing near the latter church, some ten miles distant.

Rev. Wampole continued as pastor till May, 1836, when he was succeeded by Rev. Frederick Ruthrauff. During the ministry of the latter Zion's church withdrew, and there was also a division in St. Peter's, owing to the introduction of what were known as "new measures" in church work. The members who withdrew from St. Peter's, some twelve or thirteen in number, erected for themselves a church building in close proximity to the mother church, and in connection with Zion's formed a new charge. These churches are now in connection with the Ministerium of Pennsylvania, and are served by separate pastors.

Previous to this division, under the leadership of Rev. Ruthrauff, steps were taken towards organizing a Lutheran congregation in Uwchlan township, near Lionville. February 9, 1838, a meeting was held at the house of Peter Acker, where the subject was discussed. At this meeting it was resolved "that in reliance on the help and favor of the Lord a house of worship be erected, to be owned jointly by the Lutherans and the Reformed." The name afterwards chosen was "St. Paul's Church in Uwchlan township." The location was on a piece of ground near the "White School House," donated for the purpose by Peter Stiteler. The building erected was of stone, one story high, 38x45 feet in dimensions, and cost $1,483.00. June 5, 1838, the corner-stone was laid, Rev. Jonathan Ruthrauff, of Lebanon, preaching the sermon. On November 6 and 7 of the same year, the building was dedicated. Rev. C. W. Schaeffer, D. D., LL. D., then pastor of St. Peter's church at Barren Hill, preached the dedicatory sermon. The pastor was assisted in these services by Revs. John P. Hecht and H. S. Miller. The formal organization did not take place till November 11, 1838, the first Lord's Day following the dedication. Sixteen persons composed the original membership, two of whom are still actively identified with the congregation.

They came from St. Peter's and St. Matthew's churches, mainly from the former. St. Paul's became a part of Zion's charge, which now consisted of four churches, St. Peter's, St. Matthew's, St. Paul's and Zion's, the pastor residing in the parsonage near the latter church until the separation in 1840.

At the time of the division, Rev. Ruthrauff became pastor of the three churches known as the Pikeland Charge, St. Peter's, St. Matthew's, and St. Paul's, the pastoral residence being in the vicinity of the former, and about five miles distant from the other two points. He continued to serve this field till June 13, 1843. He was succeeded, December 17, by Rev. John McCron, D. D., who continued as pastor till July, 1847, when he and Rev. D. Miller exchanged pastorates. The latter remained but two years, and was followed by Rev. Peter Raby, September 27, 1849.

Brother Raby served this charge faithfully for nine years, and was held in high esteem by his people. Under his ministrations substantial progress was made. It was through his instrumentality that a dissolution was effected in St. Paul's church between the Lutherans and Reformed, in the year 1852. The former disposed of their interest in the property to the latter for $700.00, and bought a small tract of land in the village of Lionville, about one mile distant. Here a commodious two-story stone building was erected, at a cost of about $4,000.00. The membership at this time was forty-two. July 31, 1852, the corner-stone was laid, and on January 1, 1853, the building was dedicated. The dedicatory sermon was preached by Rev. E. W. Hutter, of Philadelphia.

In the year 1858 Rev. Raby resigned, and on June 20 was succeeded by Rev. Samuel Aughey. Soon after Rev. Aughey became pastor, a division took place in the charge, St. Matthew's and St. Paul's withdrawing, and forming a separate pastorate This was in the year 1859. Rev. Aughey became pastor of the Lionville charge, St. Peter's calling Rev. Cornelius Reimensnyder as their pastor. In the year 1860 a parsonage was purchased by St. Paul's congregation, adjoining the church, for the sum of $1,500.00, where the pastor has continued to reside ever since.

In the year 1861 Rev. Aughey resigned, and on November 10,

Rev. Christian D. Ulery became his successor. The labors of this young brother extended over but a few months. Shortly after becoming pastor, he enlisted as member of a company of volunteers being formed in the neighborhood, and marched to the front in defense of a threatened Union. Being naturally of a frail constitution, he soon contracted a cold in consequence of exposure, which rapidly developed into pneumonia, from which disease he died, November 7, 1862, in the 31st year of his age. His body lies in the cemetery adjoining St. Paul's church.

January 4, 1863, Rev. S. Sentman became the spiritual guide of this flock. For seven and one-half years he ministered in holy things to this people. His memory is still cherished by those to whom he broke the bread of life. He resigned, July 1, 1870, to become principal of the Preparatory Department of Pennsylvania College, Gettysburg.

The charge was now vacant for almost a year, when on May 1, 1871, Rev J. R. Shoffner began his labors as pastor. He continued in this relationship till the year 1876. The last time this brother ever preached the word was to this people, May 24, 1891, having returned on a brief visit. This was just nineteen days before his death, which took place at Wilkesbarre, Pa., June 12, 1892.

After a vacancy of some months a pastor was secured in the person of Rev. H. S. Cook, March 11, 1877. The labors of this brother were abundantly blessed. The commodious new St. Matthew's church is his enduring monument. In 1878 Rev. Cook succeeded in effecting an amicable dissolution of the union existing in this church. The Lutherans sold their interest to the Reformed for $1,000.00, and at once purchased a plot of ground containing eighteen and one-half acres on a commanding elevation, about five hundred yards north, in the adjoining township of Upper Uwchlan, the original site being in West Vincent. Here the congregation proceeded to erect one of the finest church buildings in the county. It is of Gothic architecture, 42x95 feet in size, and has a seating capacity of about six hundred. The cost of the property was about $13,000.00. The corner-stone was laid in 1878, the dedication taking place on May 1 of the following year. On the latter occasion, Rev. John McCron, D. D., a former pastor, preached with more than his usual eloquence. At these services there were present twenty ministers, and though held on a week day the building was crowded to its utmost capacity, and the entire obligations liquidated, over $4,000.00 being subscribed.

In 1880 St. Paul's church was remodeled at a cost of $2,300.00. The re-dedication took place January 2, 1881, Rev. F. W. Conrad, D. D., LL. D., officiating. The Lionville pastorate has now two comfortable and convenient churches, the credit of which in a large measure is due to Rev. H. S. Cook. Under his ministry the congregations increased largely in membership. He was the first to introduce a systematic way of gathering the benevolent offerings of the people. The monthly envelope system he inaugurated continues in use to the present time, and has been the means of making this charge one of the most liberal in our synod. October 8, 1882, Rev. Cook, after a most successful pastorate of five years and seven months, took leave of this people, having accepted a call to Harrisburg.

December 1, 1882, Rev. W. F. Rentz took charge of the work in this parish, in which he continued till April 1, 1888, being then sent by the Board of Home Missions as missionary to Atchison, Kansas. Through his labors the people were much strengthened in all departments of church life and work. Here he has left many seals to his ministry. It was during his pastorate that the Sunday-school room of St. Paul's church was remodeled, at a cost of about $700.00.

April 8, 1888, the present pastor—Rev. M. S. Cressman—began his labors. Under his direction about $700.00 have been expended by the charge, in the improvement of the church properties. The pastorate is entirely free of debt, and meets all its obligations with promptness. It is composed of an intelligent and church-loving people.

Of the twelve pastors who have served this field, eight have passed to their reward, Revs. Aughey, Cook, Rentz and Cressman alone remaining in the church militant. Of the original members, but three are still among us, Thomas Rooke of St. Matthew's and Mrs. Catherine Oberholtzer and her sister, Miss Sarah Acker, of St. Paul's. At different times the churches have received legacies amounting in all to about $4,000.00. The estimated value of the property is $20,000.00. The present membership numbers 295 persons. In the Sunday-schools there are enrolled 238 scholars, and 41 teachers and officers.

XXVII. ST. JOHN'S LUTHERAN AND REFORMED CHURCH, FOGELSVILLE, LEHIGH COUNTY.

BY REV. J. A. SINGMASTER.

The above church was organized by members of the Treslertown, Jordan and Ziegel churches. Jacob Moyer and Judge John Fogel donated each three-fourths of an acre of land for a building site and burial place. At a meeting held October 4, 1834, it was decided to build a church. John Lichtenwallner and Daniel Schlauch, Lutheran, and Henry Mohr and Jacob Moyer, Reformed, were elected a building committee, and Solomon Fogel, treasurer. Benjamin Fogel, John Keck, Peter Musselman and Jonathan Mohr were appointed to solicit subscriptions.

The corner-stone was laid May 9, 1835, on which occasion Rev. Isaac Roeller and Rev. Joseph Dubs officiated. On the 31st of October, 1835, the church was dedicated, Revs. Roeller, Joshua and Gottlieb Jeager and Charles Y. Herman participating. The church is a substantial stone structure, with gallery on three sides, and seats about four hundred.

The first pastor, Rev. Isaac Roeller, was elected November 15, 1835. The first council consisted of Adam Litzenberger, elder, and Samuel Fetherolf, John Lichtenwallner, Jr., Henry Stettler and Daniel Kuhns, deacons.

Rev. Roeller resigned January 13, 1851, and was succeeded by Rev. Jeremiah Schindel, who was followed in 1859 by Rev. E. H. M. Sell. In 1861 Rev. O. Leopold became pastor. In 1874 the pastor and a part of the congregation withdrew and organized St. John's Evangelical Lutheran church

On account of the establishment of the latter church, the old congregation was no longer recognized by the Pennsylvania Synod, and hence was left without pastoral care. Rev. Wm. G.

Mennig, of the East Pennsylvania Synod, became pastor in 1877. He was assisted by Rev. C. E. Hay, who supplied the pulpit after Mr. Mennig became disabled until the church became a part of the Macungie charge, in 1884, with Rev. J. A. Singmaster as pastor. In July, 1886, the latter was succeeded by Rev. G. W. Fritsch, who continued pastor until March, 1891. Since then the pulpit has been supplied by Rev. J. A. Singmaster, pastor of St. Paul's, Allentown.

It is a remarkable fact that since the organization of the church in 1835, the Reformed part of the congregation has had but two pastors, father and son, Revs. C. G. and A. J. Herman, the former serving twenty-seven and the latter thirty-one years.

In 1878 the church was remodeled. Rev. J. M. Deitzler officiated at the re-consecration. November 29, 1885, was the occasion of the semi-centennial festival of the church, during which, among others, Rev. Dr. F. W. Conrad preached.

The services have always been held every two weeks, the Lutherans and Reformed alternating. The German language has been used from the beginning. The present Lutheran membership is about sixty, and there are nearly one hundred and fifty persons connected with the Union Sunday-school, of which Mr. A. W. Held has been the superintendent for many years. Rev. Cyrus E. Held, pastor of the Hamilton charge, entered the ministry from this church.

XXVIII. TRINITY CHURCH, GERMANTOWN.

BY REV. L. E. ALBERT, D. D.

The Evangelical Lutheran Church of St. Michael's, Germantown, dates its origin in the early part of the last century. It existed as a distinct organization, and was provided with its own place of worship previously to the year 1740. At that time there were about four hundred dwelling-houses in Germantown. The principal part of the population was German, but as the congregation was not favored with the ministry of a regular pastor, the number of members was small and the circumstances of the church not very flourishing. In the year 1742 the Rev.

Henry Melchior Mühlenberg arrived in Philadelphia and began his labors as pastor of the Lutheran church in that city. Soon after his arrival, the church in Germantown attracted his attention, and his interest in it was so earnest, that he took it at once under his pastoral care. Finding that his duties pressed too heavily upon him, he made arrangements to relieve himself of at least a portion of his pastoral care. Accordingly his assistant, Rev. Peter Brunnholz, who arrived from abroad in *1745*, took charge of the church in Germantown. So the pastorates are as follows:

Rev. Henry Melchior Mühlenberg, 1742-1745 ; Rev. Brunnholz, 1745-1751 ; Rev. Handschuh, 1751-1757. From 1757-1763, the accounts are musty, and the times stormy. Clearer skies came in 1763, for then pastor John Nicholas Kurtz served the congregation one year. He was followed by Rev. John Ludwig Voigt, 1764-1765 ; Rev. Jacob Van Buskerk, 1766-1769 ; Rev. John Frederick Schmidt, 1769-1786 ; Rev. John Frederick Weinland, 1786-1789 ; Rev. Frederick David Schaeffer, 1790-1812 ; Rev. John C. Baker, 1812-1828 ; Rev. Benjamin Keller, 1828-1835 ; Rev. John William Richards, 1836-1845.

Trinity Lutheran Church, Germantown.

Trinity Lutheran church is an offshoot of St. Michael's church of Germantown. It was organized with a membership of about thirty persons, February 28, 1836, when the vestry was installed by the Rev. Philip F. Mayer, D. D., then of St. John's church, Race street, Philadelphia. The names of the vestrymen were Thomas Haddin, Henry Goodman, Michael Trumbauer, David Heist, Henry Nicholas, Jacob Mehl, John Felton, George Heist, George Geysel and Joseph Heist. The original name of the church was the English Evangelical Lutheran church of Germantown. At first the congregation worshiped in the brick building at the corner of Main and Mill streets, now occupied by the Woman's Christian Association. While worshiping there it elected as its first pastor William N. Scholl, who had just completed his theological studies at the Seminary at Gettysburg, Pa. Mr. Scholl preached his first sermon in the brick building April 17, 1836. On June 2, 1836, he was licensed, at the meeting of the Synod of Pennsylvania at Easton, to preach the gospel. On June 12, he preached his introductory sermon from 1st Corinthians, 2d chapter and 2d verse: "For I determined not to know anything among you, save Jesus Christ, and him crucified." In the meantime the congregation had purchased the property at the corner of Main and Queen streets for the sum of $3,000.00 on which it immediately proceeded to erect a church edifice 45x55 feet, at a cost of $2,699.68. The corner-stone of this building was laid on May 15, 1837. Rev. Philip F. Mayer, D. D., and Rev. Jacob Medtart officiating at the morning services, and Rev. Charles W. Schaeffer at the afternoon. On December 3, 1837, the building was dedicated, the Rev. Dr. Mayer preaching the sermon from Psalms lxxxiv. 1 : "How amiable are thy tabernacles, O Lord of hosts!" The first communion was held on June 19, 1836, and the first accessions to the congregation were made on Whitsunday, May 14, 1837. The first baptism in the church under the Rev. William N. Scholl was that of Henry Ernest, son of Henry and Maria Goodman; the first marriage, that of Reuben G. Tomlinson to Hannah K. Shepherd; and the first burial, that of William Saunders, of Rising Sun. As a pastor the Rev. W. N. Scholl stood high in the estimation of his flock, being diligent in the discharge of his duties, and watchful of the interests committed to his care. His pastorate over the congregation extended from June 12, 1836, to March 5, 1840.

Rev. Mr. Scholl was succeeded by Rev. Samuel D. Finckel, who came to Germantown, May 28, 1840. His first communion was held June 7, 1840, and his last, December 1, 1843. His first recorded accessions to the church took place on September 5, 1840. On February 7, 1844, Mr. Finckel resigned the pastorate of the congregation. Although his pastorate was short in its continuance, the impress he made upon the congregation was remarkable. There was something in the very make of the man that told upon all with whom he came in contact. Genial in his manners, warm-hearted in his disposition, brilliant in intellect, and eloquent in speech, he drew men of all classes to him personally, and also attracted them to the house of God.

Rev. William F. Eyster became the successor of Mr. Finckel,

and assumed the pastorate on May 12, 1844. His first recorded communion is that of July 7, 1844. The largest accession to the church at any communion occurred during the ministry of Rev. Mr. Eyster. This was on April 16, 1848, when thirteen persons were received by adult baptism, twenty-eight by confirmation, four by renewal of profession, and seven by certificate from the Presbyterian church. At that time there was a wonderful awakening on the subject of religion in Germantown, and this church shared largely in the ingathering that followed. On August 14, 1851, Rev. Mr. Eyster resigned the pastorate of the congregation, to take charge of the church at Chambersburg. Mr. Eyster was a living embodiment of a Christian gentleman. Sincerity beamed forth in his speech and actions. To him a mean deed was impossible. Ever courteous, ever gentle, ever loving, ever forbearing and forgiving, he walked in his Master's footsteps and preached daily sermons by his constant exhibition of these Christian graces. At this present writing he is a resident of Crete, Salina county, Nebraska.

Mr. Eyster was succeeded by the present pastor, Rev. Luther E. Albert, who came to Germantown on November 23, 1851. His first recorded communion was held in the month of March 1858, when 95 persons participated in the blessed ordinance of the Lord's Supper. After a few years had elapsed, the congregation undertook the building of a new church edifice. The contract for the building, exclusive of the furniture and the spire, called for $13,500. The corner-stone was laid on October 11, 1856, the Rev. Philip F. Mayer, D. D., officiating. Among others who were present on that occasion were Rev. Theophilus Stork, D. D., and Rev. Edwin W. Hutter, D. D. At the dedication of the church, which occurred on October 12, 1857, Rev. John G. Morris, D. D., of Baltimore, Md., officiated. In 1867 the organ was purchased at an expense of $2,096.15, and in 1870 the church was frescoed. In 1886 the church was renovated and improved at a cost of $16,000. The growth of the congregation, in every direction, has been marked and steady. The number of those entitled to membership, at this present writing, is about 300. The active communing membership is about 250. The strength of the Sunday-school is as follows: officers and teachers, 46; scholars,

325. The present superintendent is Theophilus H. Smith. In connection with the church is a Woman's Home and Foreign Missionary Society, a Young People's Lyceum, and a Society of Christian Endeavor. The Board of Trustees consists of the following members: President, M. L. Finckel; secretary, F. Studenmund; treasurer, Jacob Green; associates, Theophilus H. Smith, Samuel Goodman, George Jenkins, William Martin, Theophilus Stork, William Maybury, David Barrows, Jr., Charles Longmire and Henry Yeager; assistant pastor, Rev. Clinton E. Walter. Such is a brief history of Trinity Lutheran church, Germantown. Thankful for the past, she moves on hopefully into the future.

XXIX. ST. MATTHEW'S CHURCH, READING.

BY MR. CHARLES H. TYSON.

Trinity Lutheran church, the mother church of St. Matthew's, as well as of all the other Lutheran churches of Reading, was founded in 1751 by German Lutherans. The early pastors were as follows: H. B. G. Wordman, 1752 to 1753; D. Schuhmacher, 1754 to 1755; J. C. Hartwig, 1757 to 1758; B. M. Hausihl, 1759 to 1762; J. A. Krug, 1764 to 1771; Henry Moeller, 1775; D. Lehman, 1779 to 1780; C. F. Wildbahn, 1782 to 1796; D. Lehman, 1796 to 1801; H. A. Mühlenberg, 1803 to 1829; Jacob Miller, 1829 to 1850.

For almost a century the worship was carried on in the German language. About the year 1842 the town had a large English population; the English language was spoken in the schools, in business transactions, and in social intercourse. The children, though of German parentage, were growing up in total ignorance of that language. A large number of the congregation discovered that their children were deriving no benefit from the worship and were wandering away to the English churches, which were the Presbyterian, the Episcopalian, and the Methodist. To prevent this loss to the Lutheran church, several members, with Dr. Diller Luther as spokesman, requested the pastor of Trinity, Rev. Jacob Miller, to hold English services at intervals of a month or six weeks. Rev. Miller was a pious, conscientious and earnest man; but, fortunately for us in this instance, very conservative in his views. Having been educated under the German system, and being somewhat advanced in years, he could not appreciate the importance of the situation. He refused absolutely to comply with their request.

ST. MATTHEW'S EVANGELICAL LUTHERAN CHURCH, READING, PA.

Earnestly desirous of accomplishing their object, they started an English service at 5th and Penn streets, in the Old State House, which was destroyed by fire in 1873. In order to secure a large attendance and also the co-operation of the English community, they held services in the afternoon, the English churches being open in the evening. The attendance from the beginning was large, and at length overtures were again made to the pastor of Trinity, which were again rejected. They now had no alternative except a separate permanent organization.

Rev. J. S. Schock, then lately graduated from the Seminary at Gettysburg, had acted as pastor of this little flock from its first gathering. He was young, talented, active, and eminently fitted for the hard task he had undertaken to perform. His salary when engaged was $300, which was afterwards reduced to $150, owing to the meagre resources of the congregation. The first council meeting was held in March, 1842, and the officers were Rev. Schock, president, Dr. Diller Luther, secretary, and Henry Haas, treasurer. The men most active in this movement, to whom St. Matthew's church is largely indebted for what she is to-day, were Dr. Diller Luther, John Hepler, Sr., Frederick Fox, Henry Haas, Peter Filbert, Henry Fry, Adam Rightmyer, Dr. S. S. Birch, Jacob Sallade, Peter Shanaman, Joseph Moyer, William Ziegler, Nicholas Mason, John German, Jeremiah Hagenman, Marks B. Scull, George Frees, Jesse Orner, Paul Ammon and Samuel Focht. The first communion was held in September, 1842, when 17 communicants presented themselves; at the same time a considerable number were confirmed. The first infant baptism occurred in 1842, Susan Yeager being the subject; the first marriage ceremony of which there is now any record was performed in 1843, and Levi Moser and Catharine Myers were the contracting parties. In spite of all difficulties and hindrances, the congregation grew rapidly. In 1843 an appeal was made to the other churches in Eastern Pennsylvania for aid in building a church. Rev. Schock was sent out as collector, and during his absence Rev. Kohler acted as his substitute. The church was begun in May, 1844, and dedicated on the 22d of December of the same year. The services were prolonged for several days, and many eminent divines were present, from Philadelphia, Baltimore, and other places; among these were Rev. J. G. Morris, D. D., who preached the dedication sermon, Rev. F. W. Conrad, and Rev. John McCron, who preached an impressive sermon from the text, "What think ye of Christ?"

The congregation increased in numbers slowly but steadily in their new home, notwithstanding some opposition on the part of outside parties. The following incident is related to show the feeling (now happily extinct) which existed on the part of the old toward the new congregation. The first death, that of Dr. Birch, occurred in 1845. As the plot surrounding the church was very small, the pastor first applied for permission to bury upon Trinity graveyard. Permission was granted, upon condition that the pastor of Trinity should conduct the services. Not deeming it proper to accept the conditions, the body of Dr. Birch was buried in the space on the eastern side of the church, from which it was afterwards removed to Charles Evans' cemetery. No incident worthy of mention occurred until 1849, when Rev. Schock received a call from New York City, resigned, and was succeeded by Rev. J. A. Brown. During Rev. Brown's pastorate, a schism arose in Trinity church and a large number seceded, some forming a new church and others swelling our membership. Among those prominent in this second period of the church's history were Major S. E. Ancona, Dr. Ulrich, Jacob S. Livingood, Esq., Messrs. Weida, Lindemuth, Craig and Lehman, and Mrs. Esther G. Otto, familiarly known as Mother Otto. In consequence of this diminution, the council of Trinity made propositions to our council looking to the return of our congregation to the bosom of the mother church, which were respectfully declined. Rev. Brown resigned in 1859, and was succeeded by Rev. Milton Valentine, during whose term the church was repaired; Rev. M. W. Hamma, from 1866 to 1869; Rev. Samuel Domer, from 1869 to 1872; Rev. J. M. Anspach, from 1872 to 1877; and our present pastor, Rev. T. C. Billheimer, D. D.

For many weeks after the first meeting of the congregation, the attention of the members was centered upon the growth of the church. Their children were scattered, some attending the Presbyterian, some the Methodist, and others the Union Sunday-school which had been opened by Judge Darling in the Old Court House on Penn Square. At length, early in December, 1842, several of the younger members of the church—Misses Eliza, Lydia and Louisa Filbert, Miss Hope Pettit, Miss Boyer,

Mr. George Frees, Mr. Jacob Boyer, and Rev. Schock—met in the office of Peter Filbert, Esq., and organized our Sunday-school, whose first regular session was held on the Sunday before Christmas. Dr. Diller Luther was elected president, Frederic Fox vice-president, Rev. Schock superintendent, Jeremiah Hagenman secretary, Mrs. McCombs directress, Jacob Boyer treasurer and A. Raiguel librarian. The school first met on Franklin street above 6th, in a building upon the site of the Reading fire-engine house. The attendance numbered about forty. The meetings were held in this building, then called the infant school, until early in the following spring, when the building was damaged by fire and the school was removed to the public school house at Chestnut and Carpenter streets. Here the sessions were held until November, 1844, when the church was so far completed as to allow the school to meet in the basement. On the day of its removal the school was addressed by several clergymen then attending the Synod held in our city. The school numbered 60 when they left Franklin street, 75 when they came to the new church, and about 100 when Rev. Schock resigned in 1849. The infant school was established in 1845 by Rev. Schock, and Mrs. John Craig, then Miss Eliza Filbert, was the first teacher. A celebration was held at High's Woods on the Fourth of July, 1845; a large table was set, and the whole congregation as one family celebrated the day. That celebration seems to have been kept green in the memories of the older members of the church.

Mr. George Frees, who had acted as superintendent in connection with Rev. Schock from the organization of the school, served until 1851, and was succeeded by Charles Davis, Esq., whose term continued only for one year. He was succeeded by Mr. Frederic Fox, who served for three years. Rev. Brown then became superintendent, and continued such until his resignation as pastor. Jacob S. Livingood, Esq., was then elected, who, after serving a short time, resigned in favor of his brother, William H. Livingood, Esq., who held the position until 1863. During the 15 years from 1848 to 1863, the school increased from a membership of 100 to that of 250. The pastor, Rev. Valentine, filled the position of superintendent from 1863 until he resigned in 1866. Mr. Frank Fichthorn was then elected, and served for 11 years—during the pastorates of Revs. Hamma, Domer, and Anspach. During Rev. Hamma's pastorate, the school numbered 400—a greater number than it ever had before or has had since. During the terms of Revs. Domer and Anspach the number fluctuated between 300 and 400. Mr. Fichthorn was succeeded in 1878 by Mr. Edward Scull, who served until January, 1888. Frank S. Livingood, Esq., was then elected and served until January, 1892, when he was succeeded by Mr. Jacob A. Buch, the present superintendent.

The first mission was organized in 1860, at 10th and Green streets, by Rev. Valentine and Mr. Frederic Fox, and soon grew from a membership of 17 to that of 175 in 1865. Owing to the resignation of Rev. Valentine and the removal from town of Mr. Fox, the school fell into other hands, and is now known as St. Luke's Lutheran church, a very flourishing congregation. The second mission, known as the Rose Valley Sunday-school, was organized in 1874 by Major S. E. Ancona, Mrs. Bessie Hunter, and Mr. Frank Fichthorn, and finally abandoned in 1879 as unfruitful. The third mission was founded in the winter of 1881, at 4th and Elm streets, by Mrs. A. S. Ladd, Rev. Daniel A. Shetler, and Mr. Cornelius T. Anderson. The membership numbered 30, and, upon Rev. Shetler's removal from town, he was succeeded by Mr. A. B. Yorgey in 1881, who was in turn succeeded by Mr. Edward C. Hecht in 1882. In 1886, when the movement had begun for the erection of a new chapel, this mission was merged into the main school.

During Dr. Billheimer's pastorate the congregation and school grew too large to be accommodated in the building at Franklin and Pearl streets, and under his leadership, in 1886, a fund was started for the erection of a chapel for the Sunday-school upon an adjoining property, but eventually the movement expanded into a fund for a new church. A lot was bought at 5th and Elm streets, and in April, 1889, ground was broken for the erection of a church and chapel. On January 19, 1890, the corner-stone was laid by Rev. W. H. Dunbar and the pastor, in the presence of the other clergy of the city and the congregation. On July 12, 1891, the building was dedicated by Revs. W. H. Dunbar,

H. W. McKnight, D. D., and Samuel B. Barnitz, with impressive ceremonies, and funds were collected to pay for the edifice. The congregation, headed by the pastor and council, marched in a body from the old to the new church. The new edifice is an imposing structure, built of stone, containing in front an auditorium with a seating capacity of 550 persons, with vaulted ceiling, beautiful windows, altar and pulpit, and comfortable pews and furniture. The chapel, with an entrance from Elm street and another from the auditorium, has two stories, upon the first of which is the lecture room and infant school, and upon the second story, a beautiful main school room with a gallery for the larger classes. Later results have justified the congregation in the erection of their new edifice, as the Sunday-school has grown so large that arrangements are now making to utilize the basement of the church for its use, in addition to the rooms already occupied. The whole structure when completed will cost about $65,000. The church and Sunday-school now number about 350 persons each, with indications of a steady increase in the future.

XXX. ZION CHURCH, LEBANON.

BY H. H. ROEDEL, M. D.

The earliest records of the Lutheran church at Lebanon are a marriage, February 25, 1731, and a death, April 28, 1734. About the years 1733–1735 the first efforts were made to gather the scattered Germans, who had settled around where the town of Lebanon now stands, into a congregation. Worship was conducted at a point about two and a half miles south-east of the present site of the town, where a house of worship was afterwards built, called "Die Kruppe Kirche." This edifice was occupied by the congregation until about 1768. In March, 1765, a lot of ground, within the present borough limits, was deeded for church purposes, by the Rev. John Caspar Stoever and others for the use of the Lutheran congregation for "the yearly rent of one red rose in June of every year forever hereafter, if the same shall be lawfully demanded." A school-house was built the same year, which was also used for church purposes. The church was probably erected about four years later. The corner-stone of the present edifice (Salem) was laid June 8, 1796. The regular pastors who served this congregation from the time of its location in the town until the organization of Zion church were as follows: F. A. C. Mühlenberg, 1773—1775; William Kurtz, 1775—1794; George Lochman, 1794—1815; William G. Ernst, 1815—1836; Jonathan Ruthrauff, 1836 to 1844.*

The views of church membership held by Rev. Ruthrauff differed widely from those entertained by many clergymen in this vicinity. Horse-racing, gambling and drinking to excess, were practices not infrequently indulged in by members of this community who claimed positions in the church as officers. The pastor, however, refused to install such. When expostulated with, he claimed the introduction of no new tenets, but referred to the formula for the government and discipline of the Evangelical Lutheran Church, of which they were a part. This proceeding was the origin of a long church strife. True, the issue was not claimed to be such. To speak or preach English, was almost looked upon as wicked. So prejudiced was the community against English preaching, that this was made the cudgel which the wily enemies of Sunday-schools, prayer-meetings and vital godliness used to enlist the sympathies and obtain the influence of church members against the introduction of the latter. So bitter did the feeling against the pastor and his adherents become, that the opposite party locked the church, forbidding the pastor to preach. This resulted in a suit at court, which eventually was compromised, the followers of the pastor accepting less than $800, for which they relinquished all right, title and claim to the church, graveyard and parsonage.

These members, with the pastor, formed the nucleus of a new church organization, which was incorporated by an Act of Assembly, dated March 14, 1844, the corporate name and title being, "The Evangelical Lutheran Congregation of the Borongh of Lebanon and its vicinity." Immediate steps were taken to build a church. A lot on the corner of Market, now North

---

* The facts above have been gleaned from the published History of Lebanon County.

Ninth Street and Spring Alley, was purchased by Mr. Jacob Stoever, a member of the Board of Trustees, from Mr. Jacob Schaffner, of Marietta, upon which to erect a suitable building. Little money was in circulation here at that time. Business transactions were carried on by barter. Labor was exchanged for produce, and produce for merchandise.

The members of the new church organization, with few exceptions, were poor. Yet, under such adverse circumstances, they undertook the erection of a church edifice, costing from twelve to thirteen thousand dollars. The excavations for foundation and cellar were made by the members, without the expenditure of one dollar in money. The Lord put it into the hearts of several parties (not members of the church) owning stone quarries, to give the members of the church the privilege of quarrying all required for the church, free of cost. Farmers (members of the church) did the hauling, while town members did the loading and unloading gratuitously. The officers of the Union Canal Company gave the privilege of gathering all the sand for plastering the church inside and out (the church was rough cast) at the water works, free of cost, and it was all delivered without the expenditure of a dollar in money—some members furnishing teams, others loading and unloading. The pastor's horse was in daily use for hauling the water necessary to make the mortar.

Among the church members were three carpenters, none of whom could subscribe a large sum of money. They agreed, however, to do a certain amount of work in the church. Augustus Reinoehl (now of Lancaster) did the necessary work in the basement; Henry Zimmerman, that of the church chamber; and Benjamin Moore, the woodwork at the roof and tower. Israel Karch did the painting at fifty cents per day.

The present generation cannot realize, much less appreciate, the sacrifices made by the original members of this church. Children denied themselves butter and fruit, selling these to obtain money to contribute to the church. Some worked after school hours for the same object. The pastor stimulated every member of the congregation by his own liberality. He not only gave much time, labor, and money (receiving only two hundred and forty dollars' salary while the church was being built), but even imperiled his health. With all the contributions of labor and money, when the church was completed and dedicated there remained a debt of over three thousand dollars on the building.

The salary and interest on the debt was a grievous burden. Nor was this all. A new church necessarily called for improved methods in church attendance. Pious parents desired to have their children not only accompany them, but occupy the same pew. This was looked upon as an innovation and seriously objected to. It was regarded as a design, on the part of some members, to select the best pews and deprive others of occupying choice ones. To prove this view erroneous, the party desirous of having their children sit with them proposed drawing lots annually for pews. This was acceded to, and indulged in for several years, much to the satisfaction of some and disgust of others. Now, the most liberal contributors objected. They were generally unfortunate enough to draw pews under the gallery, while contributors of sums less than one dollar annually, almost always secured the most desirable ones. This disposition of the pews existed until 1849, when the pastor, in consequence of ill health, was obliged to resign. Rev. A. C. Wedekind became his successor.

How to pay the interest of the debt and an increase of salary, was the question which presented itself to the trustees and the congregation at the annual meeting; besides, the pew question still remained unsettled.

Another year passed, the annual expenditures exceeding the income. No better, in fact no other plan seeming possible, it was determined to rent the pews annually, to the highest bidder, reserving ten free pews, five on each side of the middle aisle, (the choicest in the church) for the poorer members, so that none could complain of being deprived of the use of pews. This gave rise to our present pew system.

Upon the resignation of the Rev. Jonathan Ruthrauff, the congregation at Schaefferstown severed its connection with this charge, leaving only the Hill church in connection with Zion. This made it possible to have two church services every Sunday, the pastor preaching both German and English.

During the latter part of Rev. Wedekind's administration, which was of thirteen years' duration, the Hill church was added to the Annville charge, and Lebanon claimed the entire time of the pastor.

Rev. L. A. Gotwald succeeded Rev. Wedekind in April, 1863. It was during his administration that the congregation, after mature deliberation, deemed it best to sever the existing relation between the English and German members. The reason assigned was the difficulty of obtaining a pastor qualified to preach acceptably in both languages for the compensation we could pay.

This division gave origin to the Seventh Street Lutheran congregation. The English portion assisted them in building their first church, which was a frame structure. It has now been rebuilt in brick and is a very handsome church, with all the modern appointments. The trustees of the mother church manifested their kindly feeling by voting one thousand dollars towards the erection of this building. Rev. L. A. Gotwald served the congregation two years, and was succeeded by Rev. Daniel Schindler in July, 1865. The church services were now altogether English. During this administration, about 1866, the parsonage, situated on Chestnut street, between 10th and Spring streets, was purchased.

Rev. Schindler was succeeded by Rev. M. Rhodes, in March, 1867. He served the congregation very acceptably for five years, and was succeeded by Rev. J. F. Reinmund in November, 1872, during whose administration a new church was built (1875) at a cost of $30,000.00. The lecture and school rooms (of which there were three) were built in the rear of the church, admirably adapted to the wants of the congregation, and models of convenience and comfort. Dr. Reinmund served the congregation seven years, and was succeeded by our present pastor, the Rev. Dr. W. H. Dunbar, in May, 1880. The parsonage was thoroughly repaired, before his occupancy, at a cost of fifteen hundred dollars.

In 1891 an addition was built, consisting of a study, dining-room, etc., making it complete in all its appointments, at an expense of $2,000.00. The church was also re-modeled, beautified, and the interior enlarged. The organ was placed in the rear of the pulpit. This improvement cost $5,000.00.

During this administration the large and convenient Sunday-school rooms became crowded, and it became necessary to locate the Bible Department in the church chamber for a number of years. This arrangement was not sufficient to meet the growing needs of the schools. There being a vacant space 33x62 feet in the rear of the Sunday-school building, it was resolved to add a building in harmony with the balance of the church at a cost of $4,000.00. This has been done. All of the rooms have been renovated, painted, re-carpeted, furnished with chairs, etc., and the congregation now claims to have a suite of Sunday-school rooms second to none in the country.

The pastors of Zion trained many true yoke-fellows, who stood shoulder to shoulder and were in touch with them in every good word and work. Three entered the gospel ministry, the Revs. Wm. D. Roedel, Jacob Weidman, Johnson Groff.

SUNDAY-SCHOOLS.

The Sunday-school of Salem's church, which was held in what is now known as the Beneficial Hall, North Tenth Street, went bodily with the new church organization, and when the new Sunday-school rooms were ready for occupancy, provision having been made for two departments, another progressive step was taken—an infant school was organized. Notwithstanding the sneering remark made by one not friendly to the cause, "Who will nurse your babies?" it has been a decided success. The pastor's wife, Mrs. Jonathan Ruthrauff and Mr. John George, both veterans in the Sunday-school work, were its first superintendents, taking charge of the ten infant-school scholars present on the day of its organization, and nobly did they do their work. Many graduates of that infant-school are now holding positions of trust in the church here and elsewhere, and its impress for good has been stamped upon our community. Mrs. Mary Groff and Jacob Roedel were the color-bearers in the larger school. Both departments combined rarely averaged over 100 pupils. Soon, however, another department was organized, which occupied the lecture room. After the German members formed a new organization, the number was reduced somewhat. Gradually, yet steadily, the school increased in numbers—and had 250 enrolled in

1872; 302 in 1879. To-day there are over six hundred members upon its rolls. Two members of the original school, held in the Salem church prior to the separation, are now members of the Bible-class, Mr. Andrew Fasnacht and Mr. George R. Fauber.

MISSIONS.

The missionary contributions from this charge, consisting of Schaefferstown, Hill church and Lebanon, amounted to $8.00 in 1837. Systematic giving was early inculcated and continuously taught, until this part of the congregation's work gives evidence of early training and constant practice, as shown by reference to the synodical minutes of a recent date, where it may be seen that the contributions during the past year were $1,199.13.

XXXI. ENGLISH CHURCH, POTTSVILLE.

BY REV. E. G. HAY.

There were both Lutheran and Reformed church-going people in Pottsville prior to 1834. They spoke the German language, and occasionally were ministered to by visiting pastors of their own denominations, but until June 29, 1834, there was no attempt among either, as far as known, at anything like the organization of a congregation. At that time, Rev. Wm. G. Mennig began preaching to the people of both denominations in a block-house, used during the week as a school-house, and occupying the site of the present grammar school building, on the corner of Centre and High streets.

On June 18, 1837, all united in laying the corner-stone of a new frame structure on Third street as their common place of worship. Revs. George and William G. Mennig, of the Lutheran, and Rev. Thomas Leinbach of the Reformed church, officiated upon that occasion. On October 8 and 9 of the same year the church was dedicated, under the name of Emanuel's church. Revs. Thomas Leinbach and David Hassinger of the Reformed, and Revs. Daniel Ulrich, Jonathan Ruthrauff, Gottlieb Jeager and William G. Mennig, of the Lutheran church, officiated. Prior to 1850, the Reformed congregation withdrew, and located on West

Market street, leaving the church property in the hands of the Lutherans.

On May 16, 1847, some members left the pastoral care of Rev. Wm. G. Mennig and formed "The English Lutheran Congregation of Pottsville," under the Rev. Daniel Steck. There were eleven charter members, as follows: Mrs. Mary Bock, Mrs. Samuel Born, Mrs. Annie Born, Mr. Daniel Heil, Mr. Washington L. Heisler, Mrs. Sarah H. Heisler, Miss Barbara A. Heisler, Mr. Henry G. Kurtz, Mrs. Sarah A. Kurtz, Mr. John H. Kurtz and Mr. William Zern. The congregation worshiped for some time in a frame building on Second street, but in April, 1851, ground was

ENGLISH EVANGELICAL LUTHERAN CHURCH, POTTSVILLE, PA.

broken for the erection of the present building. Revs. E. Breidenbaugh and John E. Graeff assisted at the laying of the cornerstone, and Revs. B. Kurtz, D. D., A. C. Wedekind, and E. W. Hutter at the dedication of the completed structure, in the spring of 1852.

Rev. Steck remained until Nov. 26, 1857. He organized a Ladies' Mite Society that still exists, received into membership 182 persons, but left no other record of official acts.

Rev. W. H. Luckenbach was pastor from November 26, 1857,

to August 20, 1859. He received 43, baptized 31, officiated at 16 weddings and 26 funerals.

Rev. S. A. Holman succeeded, from August 23, 1859, to September 1, 1861. He received 36, baptized 39, officiated at 7 weddings.

Rev. Philip Willard, of Schuylkill Haven, supplied the congregation from June 1 to October 1, 1862, receiving 11.

Rev. Uriel Graves followed, serving from April 1, 1866, to July 6, 1868. He received 123, baptized 65, officiated at 4 weddings and 1 funeral.

The charter was changed July 27, 1866, allowing *all* members to vote at elections. Hitherto the men only had the privilege. A lot adjoining the church was purchased for $1,700.00. In April, 1867, an addition was built to the church, six feet wider than the rest of the building and twenty-eight feet in length, costing $6,000.00. $1,000.00 of this was paid under the present pastorate. The East Pennsylvania Synod convened with the congregation on September 25 of this year, but held its sittings in the Second Presbyterian church near by.

Rev. Daniel Steck again served the congregation from September 22, 1868, to July 17, 1870. He received 63 members, but left no further record.

Rev. J. Q. McAtee had charge from February 22, 1871, to November 8, 1877. He received 260, baptized 273, officiated at 79 weddings and 136 funerals. In December 13, 1876, a Young People's Sociable was organized, with a membership of 37. By February 19, 1872, the present parsonage was erected, at a cost of $4,697.26. It is a commodious, three-story structure, with pressed-brick front and brown-stone trimmings, and supplied with all modern conveniences. The Sunday-school room was re-floored, and re-seated with reversible pews in ash and walnut.

Rev. John McCron, D. D., was pastor from June 20, 1878, to August 1, 1880. He received 52, baptized 33, officiated at 24 weddings and 2 funerals.

Rev. E. G. Hay, the present pastor, took charge on November 28, 1880. He has thus far received 611, baptized 431, and officiated at 197 weddings and 324 funerals. According to the records, therefore, which might have been much more accurate, the pastors of this church have officiated at 489 funerals and 327 weddings; have baptized 862 children, and received into membership 1,437 persons.

Regretting that a lack of knowledge, even after a careful study of available records, prevents a fuller statement of leading events which occurred under preceding pastorates, we note the following under the present. Organizations effected: November 13, 1881, Children's Foreign Missionary Society, membership 120. April 28, 1886, Young People's Social and Literary Assembly, membership 31. December 1, 1886, Women's Missionary Society, membership 44. December 15, 1886, Young Ladies' Sewing Circle, membership 52. February 9, 1887, Young Men's Christian Association, membership 23. November 27, 1887, The Christian Workers—a children's mission-band—membership 50. October 13, 1890, Young Folks' Lyceum, membership 25. December 9, 1891, Young Ladies' Mission Band, membership 22. January 10, 1892, A Branch of Missionary and Church Extension Society of Lebanon Conference, membership 25. June 12, 1892, Young People's Society of Christian Endeavor, membership 25.

From September 20 to 26, 1882, the East Pennsylvania Synod was entertained by our people. On November 10, 1883, our congregation held a Luther Celebration in the Academy of Music in conjunction with the German Lutherans of this place.

On February 23, 1883, we paid off our debt of $2,000.00. On May 13, 1883, the pastor's salary was raised $200.00. November 10, 1883, new pulpit furniture was purchased at a cost of $200. March 1, 1884, the present envelope system took the place of a more cumbersome one. May 16, 1884, a handsome pipe organ was dedicated, Rev. F. W. Conrad, D. D., officiating. The instrument, and the changes necessitated by its introduction, cost $1,440.73. April 5, 1885, stained glass windows, at a cost of $400.00, were substituted for the plain ones hitherto in use. July, 1885, a tin roof was placed upon the church. In November, 1885, a renovation of the audience chamber was begun, which was completed March 27, 1886, at an outlay of $1,502.99. March 28, the room was re-dedicated, Rev. J. H. Menges officiating. In December, 1886, the pastor began the publication of a sixteen-page monthly congregational paper, entitled

The English Lutheran. It is in pamphlet form, and 700 copies have been issued monthly for these six years. Many interesting historical facts are preserved in its pages. February 6, 1887, the Sunday-school was re-opened for service after a complete renovation, including re-papering and the addition of handsome chandeliers. August 1, 1887, the pastor's salary was again increased by $200.00. February 26, 1888, a second department was added to the Sunday-school, consisting of fifty-one adult scholars. In April a new Sunday-school organ was purchased. In September, Rev. W. H. Dunbar officiated at the dedication of a new building just erected for our infant scholars at a cost of $1,333.00. In the same month the pastor completed a history of the congregation from its origin to that time. It is a cloth-bound volume of 167 pages, and embraces many valuable statistics carefully collated. During the winter of 1889 and spring of 1890, the old church tower was removed and replaced by the present handsome steeple, one hundred and eighteen feet in height, covered with copper and slate, and surmounted by a gilded crown. The cost was $1,600.00, and other concurrent improvements on the church front made an aggregate expense of $2,000.00. In June, 1892, additional changes were made in the Sunday-school room, costing $150.00, and on the ninth of October it was resolved to introduce steam heat at once into both church and parsonage at a cost of $850.00. The work is now in progress.

Our church is well located, and the congregation has long enjoyed the respect and sympathy of the community in all its efforts after material and spiritual prosperity.

XXXII. ZION CHURCH, DAUPHIN.

BY REV. M. L. HEISLER.

The following quotation, introducing the subject of the organization of a Lutheran and German Reformed congregation in the neighborhood of Dauphin, is from Dr. Wm. Egle's History of the counties of Dauphin and Lebanon :

"About 1770 a log house was erected on land owned by Robert McCord half a mile north of the present town (Dauphin), and on the site of the 'Hill Church Cemetery.'

"On October 11, 1796, an agreement was entered into whereby Mr. McCord stipulated to convey by deed said lot to the trustees of the Middle Paxtang Presbyterian congregation. This conveyance was made November 6, 1813, to Wm. Cochran, Wm. Forster and James Green as said trustees. The expenses of the erection (of the building) were principally met by the Scotch-Irish settlers, who were then the main farmers of this region. The congregation at one time was very large, and this old log (weatherboarded) structure held 200 persons. The increase of German settlers led to the Scotch-Irish Presbyterians removing, and the church edifice passed into the hands of the Lutheran and German Reformed, or was jointly owned by them and the remaining Presbyterians. It burned down in 1855, but for some five or six years previous had not been used for religious services."

The only information at hand concerning the pastors serving the Lutheran people in the old log church is, that at a period including 1830 Rev. Augustus H. Lochman preached there; and sometime prior to 1849, Rev. C. F. Stoever became pastor. The latter preached in the town of Dauphin, after the abandonment of the old log church, in the old Sons of Temperance Hall.

At a meeting held September 5, 1849, it was

Resolved, That in reliance upon the God of our fathers we undertake to build a house of worship for the joint use of the Lutherans and the German Reformed.

A building committee was selected, three from each congregation, viz.: Lutheran, D. Poffinberger, Elias Fertig, H. C. Sponsler; German Reformed, George Kinter, Geo. W. Urbin, Wilson C. Hyde.

The following resolution was passed at the same meeting:

Resolved, That the church be built on the lot of Mrs. Gross and part of the lot of Daniel Poffinberger, if needed.

At the same meeting two sets of officers, one for each congregation, were selected. The Lutherans were: Elders, Daniel Poffinberger and Samuel Miller; Deacons, H. C. Sponsler and Leonard Poffinberger.

On August 10, 1850, the corner-stone of the new church, named Zion, was laid with appropriate services. The exercises preparatory to the laying of the corner-stone were conducted in the Methodist church. The following-named ministers participated:

Rev. Mesick, Reformed; Rev. C. A. Hay, Lutheran; Rev. Moore, Presbyterian; Rev. Ludden, Methodist Episcopal; Rev. C. F. Stoever, pastor. Prayer was offered by Rev. Moore, and addresses were made by Revs. Mesick and Hay. Prayer was offered by Rev. Ludden, after which the meeting adjourned to the site of the new building. A hymn was sung, prayer offered by Rev. Mesick, and the pastor, after the usual service, exhibited, and then deposited in the corner-stone, Bible, Catechism of the General Synod of the Lutheran church, Catechism of the German Reformed church, list of contributors, pastor, building committee, elders, deacons, and members of the church, names of President of United States and Governor of Pennsylvania, county papers, *Lutheran Observer*, Minutes of 1849 of the Synod of Pennsylvania. The doxology was sung, and the benediction pronounced by Rev. Hay.

This church was dedicated February 2, 1851, Rev. Stoever and Rev. Schneck, of Chambersburg, conducting the dedicatory services. Rev. A. H. Lochman, of York, preached the morning sermon; Rev. Schneck preached in the evening; Rev. Calder, appointed missionary to China, also preached in the evening, and Rev. Hiester on Monday evening. Rev. C. F. Stoever continued to serve as pastor of this church until about September 1, 1852, serving it in connection with churches at Sandy Hollow, Wenrich's (near Linglestown) and Shoop's church. Rev. C. Nitterauer succeeded him, but remained only about a year. He was followed by Rev. Geo. J. Martz, who served until the latter part of 1867 or the beginning of 1868.

In September, 1867, this congregation severed its connection with the Synod of Pennsylvania, and was received by the Synod of East Pennsylvania at its convention in Pottsville. Rev. Martz was followed as pastor by Rev. H. D. Kutz in 1868, who resigned October 24, 1869. The connection of this church with the other churches—Wenrich's, Sandy Hollow and Shoop's—terminated with Rev. Kutz's pastorate. Rev. D. P. Rosenmiller then became pastor, and served until his death, September 25, 1880. Following Rev. Rosenmiller, Rev. H. A. Letterman became pastor in

October, 1882. He was the first minister who resided in Dauphin as pastor of the Lutheran church. He served a few years, but the burden of supporting a pastor alone rested heavily on the church and led to some difficulties from which it has not yet rallied. Rev. M. L. Heisler came in June, 1886, and has served as regular supply to the present time.

The original church edifice, erected in 1850, is still in a very good condition, and, owing to the present very gloomy industrial outlook of the town, will satisfy all demands for years to come. There has never been a parsonage attached to this church, and it may be added that it has never for any length of time indulged in any attachments of the kind that require legal interference for their dissolution. Whenever a debt was contracted, at once efforts were made to liquidate it by special subscription. For instance, the building after completion was soon cleared; the property has been kept in good repair, and usually the money for repairs has been ready when needed or soon after repairs were completed.

No regular records of benevolent contributions appear, though a few notices of synodical collections averaging in the earlier days $7.00 or $8.00. In 1868 Rev. McKnight visited the congregation in behalf of Pennsylvania College and collected $33.00. In 1878 the old bell was exchanged for a new one costing in position over $230.00, the difference being promptly paid. In 1880 the church was re-painted, carpeted, new blinds and lamps and fixtures put in, costing $241.16. In 1883 a new tin roof was put on, costing $162.50. In 1889 the church was papered, pulpit lowered, silver contribution plates procured, new blinds and new pulpit furniture at a cost of $76.26, and the Sunday-school room repaired and neatly carpeted, costing $60.00. These are given as evidences that the people have willingly paid to keep the house of God in good order.

The church has contributed regularly since 1886 to the various objects of benevolence of Synod. The amounts though small and scattered among various objects have always been freely given. The pastor's salary has averaged all through the years of its history about $300.00.

The preaching has always been in the English language, with the exception of a German sermon at rare intervals. No German

Reformed pastor ever regularly served the German Reformed part. Several visits were made by different ministers of that church, but their efforts soon lapsed and the German Reformed interest was by tacit consent, or rather by default, merged into the Lutheran, though the deed of the church property is to the joint Lutheran and German Reformed congregations. Such persons in the community as have any special interest in the Reformed church by virtue of early training or preference are now, and have been for years, identified with the Presbyterian church of the town.

The church has no indebtedness, and the property is worth between $2,000.00 and $3,000.00. It cost over $2,900.00, and by care and prompt repairs and improvements has maintained its value and could not be replaced for the amount of the original cost. Expenses are met by penny and special collections and by the efforts of the Ladies' Mite Society.

The Sabbath-school is small, and better furnished than the number of scholars would actually require. It has borne lately the bulk of the calls for objects of benevolence. Few church papers are taken. Several copies of the *Missionary Journal* and about eight copies of the *Lutheran Observer* are circulated among the little handful of members still left.

The membership, by death and removals, is dwindling in number, until the question of the survival of the church is assuming a perplexing interest. The membership now is about thirty-five, with a loss of seven within a month.

The industries of the place are dead. The young men are scattered all over the country in the bridge-building gangs of the various bridging firms of this and other states. The influences of such a life do not tend to lead these young men to take an active interest in the home churches, even when they are at home for a time. Yet the faithful still work on, hoping for a change to better things.

XXXIII. SECOND STREET CHURCH, COLUMBIA, LANCASTER COUNTY.

BY REV. WILLIS S. HINMAN.

The history of Lutheranism in Columbia dates from the year 1805, when Salem Lutheran (German) church was organized.

The first English service was held in the German church on July 1, 1849, when Rev. J. H. Menges preached to five persons. English services continued to be held monthly in the German church until February 5, 1850, when an English organization was effected by a small but earnest band, and in the spring of the same year the corner-stone of a new English Lutheran church was laid on the site of the present edifice. Rev. J. H. Menges continued as the pastor.

In 1859 the congregation withdrew from the Pennsylvania Synod and united with the East Pennsylvania Synod. At that time there were nearly 200 members, and a Sunday-school of about 400 scholars. In the following year Rev. J. H. Menges resigned, and from April 1, 1860, to the present time the church has been served by the following pastors: 1860–1863, Rev. E. Dorsey; 1863–1865, Rev. C. Reimensnyder; 1865–1870, Rev. W. H. Steck; 1870–1874, Rev. G. M. Rhodes; 1875–1877, Rev. I. C. Burke; 1877–1881, Rev. F. W. Staley; 1881–1888, Rev. W. P. Evans. The present pastor, Rev. Willis S. Hinman, began his duties June 10, 1888.

The church's history during this period has been a varied one, with alternating lights and shadows. In 1875, during the pastorate of Rev. I. C. Burke, the church was enlarged and improved at a cost of $10,000.00, one-half of which amount was unprovided for, and remained for many years a heavy burden to the congregation.

It was doubtless out of this financial trouble and circumstances connected with it, that differences arose in the congregation which culminated in a disruption in the spring of 1881, when nearly half of the members withdrew, including several of the church council, and organized a new congregation under the pastoral care of Rev. Samuel Yingling. The pastor of the old congregation, Rev. F. W. Staley, also resigned at the same time. After its organization the new congregation, being refused membership in the East Pennsylvania Synod, applied to the Pennsylvania Synod (General Council) and was received into that body, in which connection it still remains.

The old congregation, left with only about 150 members, and a Sunday-school of only about 125, and burdened with a debt of nearly $6,000.00, though discouraged was not disheartened, and with a band of determined and faithful people took up the work with vigor and hope. A new pastor, Rev. W. P. Evans, was called at once, who proved an earnest and efficient leader of the re-organized forces. During his pastorate the heavy debt was finally canceled on March 18, 1887. A special jubilee service was held, at which several addresses were made by local and visiting clergymen, and the canceled bonds and mortgages were publicly burned. The congregation now numbered 225 members, and the Sunday-day-school 300.

During the period spent in raising the debt nothing had been done to the church building, and it was now very much in need of repairs. After about a year's rest, during which time Rev. W. P. Evans had resigned, and the present pastor, Rev. Willis S. Hinman, had succeeded him, the needed work was undertaken, and completed at a cost of about $1,500.00, all of which was paid on completion of the work. The congregation had never had a parsonage, and in the summer of the following year, 1889, a handsome brick parsonage was erected on a lot owned by the congregation, adjoining the church, at an expense of nearly $4,000.00. In the fall of 1892 the lecture-room of the church was re-modeled at an expenditure of $1,200.00, and was re-dedicated November 20th, 1892.

During the struggle for the liquidation of the debt and the work of repairing and building, there was no diminution in the contributions for the support of the church. On the contrary, the salaries of the servants of the congregation have several times been increased, and the offerings for synodical and other benevolent objects have constantly increased from year to year. Indeed, the record of this congregation, especially since 1881, is one of which the church may well be proud. The membership has grown to 280, and, in addition to the services held in the church, a Sunday-school of about 80 members is maintained in the chapel at Kinderhook, about two miles from town, by some members of the congregation who live in that vicinity.

XXXIV. PALMYRA CHARGE, LEBANON COUNTY—PALMYRA AND BELLEGROVE.

BY REV. D. R. BECKER.

1. CHRIST CHURCH, BELLEGROVE.

The church at this place was erected in 1850, under the administration of Rev. A. C. Wedekind. It is beautifully located and well-built. The congregation, which now numbers 125, has been served by the pastors of various neighboring charges. Rev. J. M. Deitzler served for about a year in 1856. Rev. Christian A. Fetzer was pastor from 1860 to 1863, and Rev. J. M. Deitzler from 1865 to 1892, when the congregation was united with the recently organized church at Palmyra to form the Palmyra charge. Rev. D. R. Becker was then called, and entered upon labor in the united pastorate September 18, 1892.

2. ST. JOHN'S CHURCH, PALMYRA.

This congregation, composed of members formerly belonging to surrounding General Council and General Synod churches, was regularly organized June 19, 1890. The following persons constituted the inchoate organization: John Bordner, Martin Early and wife, Sarah, Dr. M. R. Fisher and wife, Marion C., Amos Henning, John Hipple, Hannah Horstich, Sarah Horst, D. B. Leslie and wife, Mary, with daughters, Alice C., and Anna L., John A. Ricker and wife, Malinda, Henry U. Seltzer and wife, Anna, John R. Seltzer, Jacob Snoke, C. F. Zimmerman and wife, Lizzie, and Levi Zimmerman.

The first Church Council of this congregation was duly installed by Rev. M. H. Stine, of Lebanon. It consisted of John Bordner, Martin Early, and Dr. M. R. Fisher, trustees; John A. Ricker and Amos Henning (secretary), deacons, and Henry U. Seltzer and Jacob Snoke, elders. D. B. Leslie was the acting chairman. The congregation was received into the East Pennsylvania Synod September 19, 1890, while in convention at Columbia. From the time of organization until fall the congregation worshiped fortnightly in the Academy, paying a rental fee of one dollar and fifty cents for each service. During the winter they worshiped in the United Brethren church, paying the same fee. In the spring of 1891 they returned to the Academy, and there, April 26, organized a Sabbath-school with a membership of twenty-eight. Dr. Fisher was elected superintendent.

The convention of the Lebanon Conference in the Academy, April 20-22, 1891, gave recognition, stability, and manifest impetus to the newly-formed congregation. The trustees, together with Jacob Snoke and Levi Zimmerman, constituted the Building Committee. They chose as their treasurer Simon L. Gingrich. The auspicious outlook for the incipient congregation prompted the committee to look for, as well as secure, an appropriate lot on which to erect a house of worship. In this they were not unsuccessful, for on the 8th of July, 1890, they procured from Peter B. Witmer, for the sum of six hundred dollars, a suitable and desirable site. The work of excavation and foundation was begun in the fall, but discontinued during the winter. In early spring it was resumed, and May 27, 1891, the corner-stone was laid. The officiating clergy were Revs. W. H. Lewars and W. H. Dunbar. Henceforth the work progressed steadily until May 29, 1892, when the neat, substantial stone structure was dedicated to the service of God. The acting pastor, Rev. W. H. Lewars, was assisted by Revs. M. H. Stine, J. M. Deitzler, W. H. Dunbar and R. W. Hufford, D. D., President of Synod, who preached the dedicatory sermon.

The success and steady growth of this congregation is due in great measure to the energy and tact of their acting pastor, Rev. W. H. Lewars, of Annville, in honor of whom the members procured and placed in commanding position a memorial window as a token of great respect and high appreciation.

The present incumbent received an invitation to preach for both the Bellegrove congregation and the Palmyra congregation, July 10, 1892. The two Church Councils mutually agreed, July 18, to accept the recommendation of Synod, published 1891, and form one pastorate. They elected their present pastor August 7. He accepted their call, and entered upon his ministerial duties in the Palmyra pastorate September 18, 1892. This pastorate receives aid from the "Lutheran Missionary and Church Extension Society of the Lebanon Conference" to the amount of two hundred dollars. The membership of this congregation at this writing is thirty-three. As recently as November 17 a Woman's Home and Foreign Missionary Society was organized, with ten members. Existing circumstances and present outlook augur well for this congregation.

XXXV. RIEGELSVILLE CHARGE, BUCKS COUNTY.— RIEGELSVILLE AND RAUBSVILLE.

BY REV. C. L. FLECK.

1. ST. PETER'S CHURCH, RIEGELSVILLE.

The history of the Riegelsville congregation, as an organization, dates from about 1851. Previous to this time, however, there was preaching in this locality by Lutheran and Reformed ministers in the school-house, which building was afterward constructed into a dwelling and is yet used as such. While there is no church record to this effect, it is the general testimony of those who can distinctly recall the events of that date, that there was preaching here in 1850 on Sunday afternoon, by Rev. J. McCron, who was at that time pastor of what was then called the "Straw church" (now St. James') in New Jersey. A private record gives the information that there was preaching as early as January 27, 1850, by Rev. Geo. Diehl, of Easton, and by Rev. McCron on March 24 of the same year.

From this and other intelligence given, it would seem fair to suppose that these brethren, both of whom are now "at rest," had a mutual understanding as to looking after the interests of the Lutheran church in this place. It was in this year that the Lutheran and Reformed people of this vicinity joined hands and erected a church building, in which they were to worship alternately. The work was begun in April, and the church was dedicated January 1, 1851.

Rev. McCron left no record of ministerial acts, but evidently he was interested in this people and in their new enterprise, for his name is engraved or moulded on the church bell. After the church was built he preached here from January to April, after which Rev. Diehl's services were rendered until July. It seems, however, that the latter served as a regular pastor, for the minutes speak of him as presiding over a meeting of the officers of the congregation, which assembled June 3, 1851, for the purpose of calling a pastor, which call they wished to have accepted "after the resignation of our present pastor, Rev. Geo. Diehl, shall go into effect;" and baptisms are recorded and referred to as "administered by the former pastor, viz.: Rev. Geo. Diehl of Easton." At some time during this interval, an organization was effected, but there is no reference to the fact more than that a Constitution was adopted May 20, 1850.

The "Call," previously mentioned, was sent to Rev. J. R. Willox, who had preached June 1, and was accepted. Rev. Willox labored in this field about ten years, with diligence and acceptability. He faithfully catechised the young and was accustomed to hold "protracted meetings." He preached at Finesville, Raubsville and Holland as outposts. Soon after entering upon his work here, he organized the Upper Tinicum congregation, where a church was built in 1852. This point was served in connection with Riegelsville until 1891. In 1856 a sore affliction befell his family, when in thirty-four days four of his children died from scarlet fever. Being the first regular pastor on this territory, the work was found difficult and discouraging; nevertheless it was pursued with fidelity and hopefulness, and with much prayer and sacrifice he sowed the seed, that then and afterward brought forth an abundant harvest.

In October, 1861, Rev. C. L. Keedy was elected pastor, who served the charge one year. Rev. Nathan Jaeger was the next pastor chosen. He entered upon his duties in March, 1863. In November of the same year, whilst driving to Easton, he was thrown from his buggy, and fatally injured. He died January 2, 1864, aged forty-three years, and was buried in the cemetery at Riegelsville.

In May, 1864, Rev. Theophilus Heilig, of Stroudsburg, became pastor. His time of service was twelve years and four months. At some time during this period the present parsonage was bought for $3,200.00. It is a very desirable property, a pleasant home, and a most commendable monument to the efforts of those who shared in its purchase.

In 1871, although the two congregations had been worshiping together in comparative peace, there was a growing desire to separate; consequently on January 20, 1872, at a congregational meeting, it was resolved to accept the offer of the sister denomination, and to purchase the right and title of the Reformed congregation in the church building and lot. The amount paid was $2,200.00.

Another important event in the history of this charge took place during this period. It was customary to elect a delegate to accompany the pastor to the annual meetings of the East Pennsylvania Synod; but on May 28, 1876, a delegate was elected to attend the Pennsylvania Ministerium, to assemble at Reading, June 10. This is the first and only mention of a delegate to this body. The minutes record no action of the congregation in effecting this synodical change, and that it was done contrary to their desire is shown by subsequent action; for on November 12, after a four weeks' notice, the congregation assembled, and, by a vote of thirty-three to two, decided to "return to the East Pennsylvania Synod, where they formerly belonged."

Rev. Heilig resigned August 27, 1876, and Rev. D. T. Koser became his successor, April 1, 1877. He served the charge until May 1, 1887. These were years of faithful labor, and resulted in the general upbuilding of the charge in membership, in benevolence, and in general efficiency.

In 1878 the church was repaired, principally the exterior, at a cost of about $1,300.00. This was the result of a congregational meeting, which took place on March 9, 1878, and was held to consider the question of repairing the old church or building a new one. Although there was a goodly number that favored the building of a new church, those who thought best to repair prevailed.

The church property was further increased in value, about this time, by the securing of a lot of ground near by, where quite a number of sheds have been erected by individual members, at their own expense, to afford protection to their teams in inclement weather. In 1861 the basement of the church was re-modeled at a considerable expense, being made much more cheerful and much better adapted to efficient Sabbath-school work. It was arranged so as to give the school the benefit of four different apartments.

It was during Rev. Koser's term of service that the Riegelsville congregation united with St. Paul's Lutheran church of Easton, and ran an excursion to Ocean Grove and Long Branch, which has been run annually up to this date, 1892.

In July, 1887, Rev. C. L. Fleck, of the Theological Seminary at Gettysburg, became Rev. Koser's successor. The charge consisted of the same points as that served by former pastors. There was to be preaching at Riegelsville three successive Sundays in the month in the morning, at Upper Tinicum every fourth Sunday, and at Raubsville every two weeks in the afternoon.

In view of the church needing some repairs, and because of a desire on the part of some to build a new church, a meeting was

ST. PETER'S EVANGELICAL LUTHERAN CHURCH, RIEGELSVILLE, PA.

called to consider the matter on December 1, 1888, almost ten years after the similar meeting above referred to. After carefully weighing the question, it was decided to build a new church. There was a little sentiment in favor of repairing the old church, but it was of such a yielding character, that it can be said with gratification that almost perfect unanimity prevailed throughout the entire time of building. The old church was torn down early in February, immediately after it was vacated. Work was begun on the new church early in spring, and the corner-stone was laid May 5, 1889. A sermon was preached by Rev. R. W. Hufford, of Easton, and remarks made by Rev. A. R. Steck, of Stewartsville, N. J. After vacating the old church, the congregation rented the G. A. R. Hall, which was destroyed by fire a few weeks after. The loss to the church was about $200.00, including organ, Sabbath-school library, clock, etc. They then secured Mechanics' Hall, where they worshiped until January 5, 1890, when the lecture-room of the new church was finished. The church was dedicated September, 1890. It cost over $12,000.00, besides the material used from the old church, and the voluntary assistance rendered by the members, in removing the old building, preparing the foundation, and hauling the material, etc. The architect was Rev. A. K. Felton, of the Lutheran church. The indebtedness is about $2,000.00.

When the congregation became settled in their new home, there was a desire manifest to have preaching every Sunday morning. Accordingly steps were taken to effect such an arrangement, and the Upper Tinicum congregation was requested to join with Nockamixon, which was then vacant, and form a new charge. The change was satisfactorily made, and took place in June, 1891, with the understanding that it should not affect the pastor's salary, which was then $700.00.

The Sunday-school is in a flourishing condition. Previous to building the first church, and while the two congregations worshiped together, it was a union school. It is now larger than both were then, and doing much more efficient work. For some years it has given a large proportion of its contributions to benevolence.

A W. H. & F. M. Society was organized in 1886 by Mrs. D. T. Koser, and has been doing a good work. It numbers about 50 active members and 6 honorary, and circulates at present 67 *Missionary Journals*. It has had co-operating with it, since 1888, a faithful little Mission Band.

In May, 1891, a Y. P. S. C. E. was organized. The young people are deeply interested in the movement, and it promises to leave telling effects for good. It numbers about 75 active and associate members.

Some twenty *Lutheran Observers* are taken in the congregation. But one member has studied for the ministry, viz.: Samuel T. Nicholas, who expects to graduate from the Theological Seminary at Gettysburg, in May, 1893. The congregation is of substantial growth, and promises to have a future history fully as creditable as that thus far recorded.

2. ST. PAUL'S CHURCH, RAUBSVILLE (UHLERSVILLE).

The history of this congregation dates from January, 1854, although there was preaching in the school-house back of Raubsville by Rev. J. R. Willox for an indefinite period previous to that time. This point has always been served in connection with the Riegelsville church.

On the afternoon of January 21, 1854, a few members of the Lutheran church living in Uhlersville and vicinity met in Peter Uhler's school-house for the purpose of organizing themselves into an Evangelical Lutheran Church. The reason given was, that there was no church of their own faith near enough for them to attend, and that there was need of English preaching in the neighborhood. The new organization was to be connected with the General Synod Lutheran Church, and with the Riegelsville charge, which was served at that time by Rev. J. R. Willox. It was to be called the Evangelical Lutheran Church of Uhlersville.

Such an organization was effected, and on Sunday afternoon, January 22, "immediately after the services of public worship," they elected church officers—one elder and two deacons. These were regularly installed the following Sunday. This movement seems to have been entirely satisfactory to the Riegelsville congregation, for on March 19, 1854, a meeting of the Council was held, "at which a resolution was passed unanimously to receive the proposal of the Uhlersville congregation, viz., that they pay $125.00 salary, and receive preaching twice a month, once in the morning and once in the afternoon." Mention is made of the installation of church officers again in 1860, "the only change in the council since the church was organized."

There is no account of officers being elected after that, and no mention is made in the minutes of the Riegelsville church of the Uhlersville congregation as such after September 22, 1861, when Rev. C. L. Keedy was elected pastor of the charge. The two following pastors were called with the distinct understanding that they were to preach at Riegelsville "twice a month in the morning," and in the afternoon of the same day "at such other place, or places, as the church council may direct." But while the organization, for some unknown reason, ceased to exist, there must have been preaching at this point regularly, for there is an unbroken record of ministerial acts performed by the different pastors.

The school-house, previously referred to, was used as a place of worship for over thirty years, but, it having become unfit for this purpose, it was decided, by those who were accustomed to worship here, to build a new church. This action was taken in January, 1887. The new building was to be located at Raubsville, as a more desirable site could be procured at that place. The corner-stone was laid on June 19, the former pastor, Rev. D. T. Koser, returning to officiate on that occasion. He was also present at the dedication of the church, January 22, 1888, at which time Rev. J. H. Menges, of Philadelphia, solicited contributions to meet the indebtedness. The cost of the church was $3,600.00.

A few years later, a bell was purchased at a cost of $190.00. When the bell was hung in the place designed and prepared for it when the church was building, it was found to be too low to sound well throughout the community. To obviate this it was decided by the congregation to build a steeple somewhat higher on the opposite corner of the church. This was completed and proved much more satisfactory. The cost of the improvement, and re-painting the exterior of the church, was over $500.00. A desire was now manifest on the part of the members to organize themselves into a congregation, remaining however a part of the Riegelsville charge. For this purpose a committee was appointed to meet the council at Riegelsville and request of them an honorable dismissal of the members in the vicinity of Raubsville, who desired to become members of the new organization. The request was granted, and the organization was effected, and subsequently was admitted into East Pennsylvania Synod as a separate congregation.

There has been a Sunday-school faithfully conducted in the community for many years. Previous to the building of the church it was held in the school-house, sometimes called the "Uhlersville church." During these days it was a union school. But when they entered the new church it became denominational.

A W. H. & F. M. society was organized October, 1888, by Mrs. C. L. Fleck, which continues to be in a flourishing condition. There are twenty-eight members, and twenty-five *Missionary Journals* are taken. There are in the congregation five subscribers to the *Lutheran Observer*. Although this congregation is small, it is in a fair condition to be of great usefulness.

XXXVI. MINERSVILLE AND TREMONT CHARGE, SCHUYLKILL CO.

BY REV. J. C. TRAUGER.

1. ENGLISH LUTHERAN CHURCH, MINERSVILLE.

The English Evangelical Lutheran congregation of Minersville was organized in 1851. The following-named brethren constituted the first council: Elders: Daniel Hoch, Isaac Straub; Deacons: Levi Deitrich, Joseph Weaver.

The members of the new organization withdrew from the German Lutheran church on account of a strong desire for English services, which were prohibited in the mother church. The congregation first worshiped in a small Baptist church on South street, then in what was known as "Odd Fellows' Hall," on the corner of South (East) and Sunbury streets. They were supplied with preaching services by Rev. Daniel Steck, the resident pastor of Pottsville English Lutheran church. During this time the present church building was erected and, in the autumn of 1853, dedicated to the Triune God. Daniel Hoch, Mrs. Hoch and Harriet Straub are the only members still living and in vital connection with the present congregation.

The first regular council meeting after the completion of the present church structure took place on November 20, 1853, and they decided to extend a call to Rev. J. K. Kast at a salary of

$325.00. Rev. Kast accepted the call and became the first pastor that same year. His ministry with this infant organization lasted until 1855. The next pastor was Rev. Jacob Steck, who was called immediately after his predecessor's resignation, and remained until March 3, 1857. Rev. M. Sheeleigh was called August 3, 1857, and remained to July, 1859. His successor, Rev. E. A. Auld, entered upon his duties as pastor January 1, 1860, and served the congregation until about January 1, 1864. Rev. H. C. Shindle became his successor, receiving his call June 5, 1864, and labored in their midst until April 1, 1868. Rev. Chas. Fickinger fell in line September 1, 1869, and made a brief stay up to September, 1870. Rev. R. Weiser inaugurated his ministry here November 1, 1870, and continued until the end of his active service for the Master, May 28, 1872. During an interim here Rev. J. Q. McAtee, pastor of Pottsville English Lutheran church, supplied the pulpit every couple of weeks in the afternoon. Rev. J. B. Anthony was the next regular pastor, from June 1, 1874, to November 21, 1875. Rev. McAtee, of Pottsville, was now chosen as their officiating clergyman, serving to September, 1877. Rev. A. N. Warner, from September 29, 1878, when called, to May 26, 1879, and Rev. I. P. Neff, March 29, 1880, to December 1, 1881, complete the list of administrations up to the time when a union was effected with Tremont English Lutheran congregation. The formation of these two churches into a charge began under Rev. I. P. Neff. The first pastor called by the joint councils was Rev. Washington L. Heisler, and his ministry with this persevering congregation extends over a period of four years, from February 11, 1883, until February 1, 1887. Rev. G. G. M. Brown took charge August 15, 1888, and remained a little over a year, up to December 1, 1889. Rev. J. C. Trauger received his call in February 1890, took charge on July 1 of the same year, and is still laboring with these kind and liberal people.

The congregation has a membership of about 120, and an *active* membership of about 106. There are about 25 *Lutheran Observers* taken and all use the Augsburg Lesson Helps in Sundayschool work.

2. St. John's Church, Tremont.

St. John's English Evangelical Lutheran church of Tremont,

Pa., dates back for its origin to the year 1853. The Lutheran congregation then organized by Rev. E. S. Henry, the resident pastor of Pine Grove, consisted of sixteen members, of whom only Mr. and Mrs. Zachariah Batdorff are at present in active membership.

The services were regularly conducted in both German and English. In the year 1855, the church edifice, in which the German Lutheran congregation still worships, was completed.

In the year 1861, the German part of the Lutheran congregation organized themselves into a separate congregation and called a pastor. The English part did likewise, and took the name of St. John's English Evangelical Lutheran church of Tremont. Both congregations lived peaceably with each other and worshiped in the same building until 1866, when St. John's congregation sold their interest in the church which they held in part with the Presbyterians. They then bought the so-called "stone church," now the commodious place of worship of the St. John's English Lutheran congregation. This church building had been originally commenced (about 1848) as a union church, Lutheran and Reformed, but, as the old Presbyterian church completed by the Lutherans before, so this stood in an unfinished state, awaiting Lutheran hands to complete the work. This church the St. John's congregation purchased and began to finish in 1866. An agreement was entered into with Z. Batdorff to complete its erection, after which the congregation was to purchase the same.

The first council recorded, which held its first meeting January 15, 1860, was composed of the following brethren, and held their first meeting January 15, 1860:

Elders—Isaac H. Alter, William R. Reece; deacons—Christian Lawer, John E. Lehman; trustees—John A. Seltzer, Jacob Gruber, Jr., Frederic Wolfe. In all probability there were councils before, and many meetings, but the minutes have been destroyed or lost. The first pastor was Rev. S. Jesse Berlin. He was elected in December, and entered upon his duties February 1, 1867. During the ministry of this faithful brother the congregation was brought into regular connection with the East Pennsylvania Synod of the General Synod. Rev. Berlin, being in delicate health, was forced to resign October 1, of the same year. He remained in Tremont until his decease, which occurred February 6, 1868, at the early age of thirty-seven years.

The church edifice was not completed until 1868, and was then deeply involved in debt. The consecration services were held January 1, 1869, Rev. F. W. Conrad, D. D., of Philadelphia, preaching the sermon, being assisted by Rev. E. S. Henry, of Pine Grove, and the pastor. The pastor during this time was Rev. Frederick Klinefelter, of Philadelphia. He took charge January 1, 1868, and resigned about January 1, 1872. Rev. Henry C. Grossman was extended a call from the congregation on March 2, 1873, and accepted. His labors extended over a period of three years, to March 2, 1876. Brother Grossman's successor was Rev. Henry L. Dox. He formally accepted May 31, 1876, and resigned October 26, 1878. During the interim which followed, Rev. G. J. Martz, of Lebanon, and Rev. I. P. Neff, of Minersville, supplied the congregation with preaching. On July 31, 1881, after services, Rev. I. P. Neff officiating, it was decided to announce services every two weeks, provided it was agreeable to Minersville, where Rev. Neff was the pastor. This was the origin of the present union of the St. John's Lutheran congregation of Tremont with the English Lutheran of Minersville in a single charge. On December 1, in the same year, Mr. Neff removed to Shenandoah, leaving Tremont and Minersville congregations vacant. They now proceeded jointly to call a pastor. Rev. W. L. Heisler, who was thus elected, took up his abode in Tremont, February 11, 1883, and served these earnest people until February 1, 1887. Rev. G. G. M. Brown, who was next called, took charge August 11, 1888, and worked for the building up of the charge with great energy and zeal until December 1, 1889. In February, 1890, the present pastor received the call to carry on the work, so faithfully begun and carried on hitherto. He has for two years and a half labored with pleasure and encouragement among this Christian people, both at Tremont and Minersville. The membership at Tremont at present is 89 members in good and regular standing. There are 20 *Lutheran Observers* taken in this congregation, and the Sunday-school is prosperous, using the Augsburg Lesson Helps.

XXXVII. ZION CHURCH, LYKENS, DAUPHIN COUNTY.

BY REV. P. S. HOOPER.

The first minister who represented the Lutheran church in this vicinity was Rev. C. F. Stoever, who preached occasionally in Lykens and the neighboring town of Wiconisco. He was on the Berrysburg charge from 1845 to 1850. Rev. N. Jeager, the next pastor on the same charge, effected an organization of the congregation at Lykens and Wiconisco, remaining from 1850 to 1852. He was followed by Rev. J. Martin, who did not preach at either Lykens or Wiconisco—devoting his whole time to the work in the Berrysburg pastorate. This continued, however, only one year; for on November 2, 1853, Rev. D. Sell took charge of the Berrysburg pastorate—and gave much of his time to this field. After consolidating the membership of the two towns—Lykens and Wiconisco—he proceeded to erect a house of worship in Lykens. This building was a substantial brick structure in which the congregation worshiped for about a generation. It was built in 1859. Mr. Sell remained the pastor until April 1, 1861. Rev. P. P. Lane next came in charge, on April 1, 1861, and remained one year—to April 1, 1862. The next was Rev. G. P. Weaver, who took charge April 1, 1862, and also remained only one year, resigning April 1, 1863. Rev. C. A. Fetzer entered the field and took up the work April 1, 1863. He served the charge until April 1, 1866. Next came Rev. M. Fernsler, who arrived on the Berrysburg charge December 2, 1866, remaining until April 1, 1871, at which time Lykens and Williamstown were made a separate charge, afterwards called the "Lykens Charge," which was served by Rev. D. Kloss from April 1, 1871, to April 1, 1877. Rev. J. A. Wirt arrived and took charge June 1, 1877. He was succeeded May 15, 1883, by Rev. M. L. Heisler, after whom came Rev. W. H. Fishburn, June 1, 1886. Previous to the giving of the call to Mr. Fishburn, the partnership of the two congregations —Lykens and Williamstown—was dissolved, each place calling its own pastor. Mr. Fishburn remained in charge at Lykens eleven months, and was followed, July 10, 1887, by Rev. Herman F. Kroh, who remained at his post until August, 1889, when he resigned. Soon afterward a call was extended to Rev. Philip Stansbury

Houper, the present pastor, who entered upon his duties January 1, 1890. During his pastorship, the old church edifice, which had well served its generation, was torn down and the present modern structure, at a cost of about $10,000.00, was erected on its site, upon which there remains an indebtedness of about $2,000.00. A good parsonage adjoins the church lot.

Preaching was formerly in German and English. The attempt to dispense with the German occasioned at times no little disturbance, but the present pastor, who was known to be unable to preach German, was elected with only one dissenting voice.

ZION EVANGELICAL LUTHERAN CHURCH, LYKENS, PA.

Since then, no German sermon has been preached, and there is no apparent demand for any.

There are four societies, Woman's Home and Foreign Missionary Society, Young People's Society of Christian Endeavor, Junior Young People's Society of Christian Endeavor, and Church Aid Society.

Sixty-eight copies of the *Lutheran Observer* are taken, six of the *Lutheran World*, four of the *Lutheran Evangelist*, and twenty of the *Missionary Journal*.

The Sunday-school numbers about 300—with no history known to the present pastor of great value to posterity.

XXXVIII. FIRST CHURCH, STEWARTSVILLE, N. J.

BY REV. WM. E. FRY.

Stewartsville Lutheran congregation was organized in the year 1852. Rev. James McCron, then pastor of St. James' church of Phillipsburg, N. J., deserves credit for encouraging some of his own members, who lived in the vicinity of Stewartsville, to form a separate organization and build a church. He, and afterwards his successor, Rev. John Plitt, preached once in two weeks in the Stewartsville school-house, and the Presbyterian minister from Greenwich church supplied the intervening Sundays. Rev. Dr. Reynolds, of Easton, preached occasionally. The church was built after the Presbyterians had completed theirs, but before the organization of the Lutheran congregation. On August 28, 1852, at a meeting held in the church building at Stewartsville, the organization of the congregation was effected with the assistance of Rev. Plitt, chairman, who, with Philip E. Weller and John Kase, was appointed upon a committee to draft a constitution, which was immediately presented and unanimously adopted. The following were elected: elders, John Fulmer, John Kase, Philip E. Weller; deacons, George H. Weller, William S. Kase, Isaac Zellers, Charles R. Thompson. September 25, 1852, a meeting of the congregation was held to elect trustees, "for the purpose of being legally incorporated." The following were elected: John Fulmer, Jr., Thomas Thatcher, John Fritz, Matthias Pickle, George Scott, William Hulshizer, Henry Snyder, Jr.

Rev. D. M. Henkel, the first pastor, took charge April 8, 1855. On Sunday, June 17, he administered the Lord's Supper to fifty-two persons, and on the same day began the Church Record. The pastor was called for one year, and at the end of that time another call was extended to him for the succeeding year, so that at the end of each year the "call" was renewed.

The pastor was required to preach two sermons every Sunday, one every Sunday forenoon, and one every two weeks on Sunday evening during the winter in the church at Stewartsville, and at stated times at different stations within bounds stated by church council. The salary was $400.00 without parsonage. Rev. Henkel relinquished his charge May 30, 1859, and was succeeded by Rev. Joseph Barclay, September 1, 1859, who received a salary of $550.00 with parsonage. About this time a parsonage was procured through the efforts of the committee appointed, Matthias Pickle, Alva Kase, Chas. R. Thompson, Enos Mangle, for the sum of $700.00, not including the cost of the building of the stable. The congregation took part in the formation of a synod in the State of New Jersey, and at a meeting of the church council, October 2, 1859, sent as delegates Rev. Barclay and George H. Weller.

The resignation of Rev. Barclay took effect November 1, 1863, and the pastorate of Rev. Matthias Sheeleigh began June, 1864. December 18, 1864, Wm. Kase, chairman of a committee, reported to the Joint Council that there was not room enough to put such additions to the parsonage as were needed to make it a convenient size. The old parsonage was accordingly abandoned and a new one built at the cost of $4,000.00. Rev. Sheeleigh resigned his position as pastor April 27, 1869. He was succeeded by Rev. J. R. Sikes, who took charge November 1, 1869, at a salary of $700.00 with parsonage and donation the first year, and $800.00 with parsonage and a subscription amounting to about $50.00 the second year. The pew rents were increased twenty-five per cent. The new edition of the hymn-book was for the first time used. Rev. J. R. Sikes vacated the charge September 8, 1872. The next pastor, Rev. P. Rizer, of Hummelstown, Pa., received a unanimous call at a salary of $700.00 and parsonage. The church at his coming in 1873 belonged to the New York and New Jersey Synod, but to the East Pennsylvania Synod before his leaving. He relinquished his pastorate May 17, 1877.

Rev. William Kelly assumed charge October 1, 1877. The church was then warmed with stoves, but very soon furnaces were substituted. A modern pulpit took the place of the old-time "swallow" pulpit. The great square posts which supported the galleries were replaced by iron columns. Another aisle was added. A centre chandelier was put in by Mr. Howard Melick and wife, as a memorial to Mr. William Kase. The melodeon was removed and a pipe organ put in its place. The floor was newly carpeted. The heavy wooden pillars which supported the basement were superseded by iron ones. The walls of the church were painted. The shed for horses in the churchyard was put up, and trees now growing round the church were planted. The parsonage was painted inside and outside. A debt of nearly $300.00 was paid off. Rev. Kelly organized the Mite Society, which assisted in improving the financial condition of the church. He succeeded in interesting the congregation in the work of the Synod, and raised as apportionment money during the second half of his ministry about $75.00 per year. The Church Record shows 70 new members, 55 baptisms, 22 marriages, 55 burials. His successful pastorate ended March 1, 1884.

Rev. L. H. Geschwind assumed charge June 1, 1884. September 20, 1884, at the semi-annual meeting of the congregation, the collectors were ordered to pay over all salary collected to the secretary, who should pay the same to the treasurer. At the semi-annual meeting April 4, 1885, it was decided that hereafter the church building shall not be used for any purposes but those for which it may be required by the congregation itself, except with the consent of two-thirds of the Joint Council given at a meeting formally called. A new Sunday-school library was furnished. In the Church Record the following was entered: new members 9, baptisms 14, marriages 5, burials 5. Rev. L. H. Geschwind vacated his pastorate November, 1885.

Rev. A. R. Steck assumed charge July 4, 1886, and relinquished it July 1, 1891. During this pastorate a number of improvements were made. A pulpit recess was built by Mr. Howard Melick and wife, and the pulpit was re-furnished by Mrs. Catharine Kase. The church was re-painted and frescoed. Mr. John H. Kase put in a beautiful stained-glass window as a memorial to his father, John Kase, and his brother William. Mrs. Samuel Carhart presented the church with a baptismal font. A more systematic method of giving was introduced. For the first time the Sunday offering was received both morning and evening. Envelopes were sent out quarterly for the raising of the synodical apportionment, which was gradually increased from $75.00 to $190.00 The Church Record has the following entered upon it: new members 87, baptisms 55, marriages 11, burials 43.

Rev. W. E. Fry assumed pastoral duties August 16, 1891, at

the salary received by the two former pastors, $700.00 and parsonage. The following improvements were made: a new platform built for the choir; the walk in front of the church and around it paved with stone, through the efforts of the King's Daughters; the parsonage painted outside by the congregation, and partly papered and painted inside by the Woman's Missionary Society. The Church Record is as follows: new members 18, baptisms 10, marriages 7, burials 18.

The following are the societies of the church: the Woman's Home and Foreign Missionary Society, organized by Mrs. Susan Steck in 1887; the Children's Mission Band, which in 1892 erected in Africa a chapel costing $50.00; the King's Daughters, organized by Miss Bertha Melick. All of these societies were organized during the pastorate of Rev. A. R. Steck. The Young People's Christian Endeavor Society, senior and junior Bands, were organized under the present pastorate.

The church has proved itself loyal to the East Pennsylvania Synod, to which it has belonged since the pastorate of Rev. P. Rizer, and has done well in meeting its apportionment, which for the past year was $204.25. The membership is 189. The Sunday-school numbers 90, teachers and scholars. There are two prayer-meetings, held on Wednesday evening and Sunday evening before service. During the past eighteen years there have been union services with the Presbyterian church on Sunday evening—services held alternately in each church. There are two preaching points, New Village and Good Springs, each of which is supplied by the Presbyterian pastor at Stewartsville, the Methodist pastor at Broadway, and the Lutheran pastor at Stewartsville. There is preaching by the Lutheran pastor at each point once in four weeks. Services are held every Sunday morning in the Lutheran church at Stewartsville. Value of church property, $10,000.00. Indebtedness on graveyard, $150.00. The Joint Council is composed of the following members: elders, Daniel Bloom, Abraham Hance; deacons, Isaac Shipman, Samuel Scott, Robert Hance, Howard Melick, John H. Hulshizer; trustees, C. R. Thompson, Robert Stone, John Smith, George Dutt, George Carhart, John Lomping, Maurice McFerren; secretary of church and council, Henry L. Frey; treasurer, Howard Melick.

XXXIX. ST. JOHN'S CHURCH, LANCASTER.

BY REV. B. F. ALLEMAN, D. D.

The earliest history of Lutheranism in Lancaster is preserved in the records of Trinity church. The pastors of this venerable congregation, up to the time of the establishment of St. John's, were the following; John Caspar Stoever, 1736-1740; John Frederick Handschuh, 1748-1751; John Siegfried Gerock, 1753-1767; Justus H. C. Helmuth, 1769-1780; G. Henry Ernst Mühlenberg, 1780-1815; Christian F. Endress, 1815-1827; John C. Baker, 1828-1853.

The organization of St. John's Evangelical Lutheran church was partly the outgrowth of a Sabbath-school established in the western section of the city, in the spring of 1852, by a number of the younger members of Trinity Lutheran church.

The school opened with twenty-two scholars, under the superintendence of Mr. J. S. Crumbaugh, a graduate of Pennsylvania College, and at that time principal of the Lancaster High School, and student of theology with Dr. Baker.

The size of Trinity congregation, the inability to furnish comfortable sittings for all its members at the public worship, the desire to develop Lutheran interests in growing parts of the city, and other considerations, led to the agitation at different times of the organization of another Lutheran congregation.

The first meeting for this purpose of which we have record was held April 2, 1853, when those present resolved to constitute themselves a nucleus for such an enterprise, and, to give permanency to their action, at once elected officers, who were to serve for six months or until a more complete organization might be effected.

On the 18th of May following, one committee was appointed to draft a constitution and by-laws, and another to solicit funds for the erection of a church edifice. On June 15, on motion of Mr. G. M. Zahm, the new organization unanimously adopted the name of "St. John's Evangelical Lutheran Church."

By this time Mr. Crumbaugh had been licensed to preach the gospel by the Pennsylvania Synod, and, as he had already endeared himself to those interested in this new enterprise, he was chosen as their pastor, and at once entered upon his labors.

The work of erecting a house of worship was vigorously pushed forward, with Messrs. John F. Shroder, Henry Baumgardner and G. M. Zahm as the Building Committee. The site chosen was the one still occupied by the congregation, at the corner of Orange and Arch streets. The first worship was held in Fulton Hall, and afterwards, until the completion of the lecture-room, by courtesy of the Moravian congregation in their church edifice.

The corner-stone of the new building was laid with impressive ceremonies October 9, 1853, Revs. B. Kurtz, D. D., G. F. Krotel and H. Harbaugh, D. D., officiating.

On March 5, 1854, the lecture-room was opened for service, Rev. G. F. Krotel preaching the sermon, and on December 24, 1854, the entire building, having been completed, was solemnly dedicated to the worship of God. On this occasion the pastor was assisted by Revs. F. W. Conrad and B. Sadtler.

The new structure cost about $20,000.00, and was considered one of the finest places of worship in the city. Thus equipped with a church home, this devout and energetic pastor and his little flock, with limited resources and considerable opposition, entered upon a series of heroic struggles for permanent existence and usefulness. Hitherto the congregation had been in connection with the Pennsylvania Synod, but at a meeting held May 29, 1855, it was resolved that application be made for an honorable dismission, with the view of seeking more congenial synodical relations.

This application was presented at the next convention of the Pennsylvania Synod, at Harrisburg, but it met with determined opposition, and a decision was postponed for one year. However, at the next meeting of this body, in Lancaster, the request was granted, and the congregation united with the Synod of East Pennsylvania, at Hughesville, September, 1856.

While this change was most agreeable to the congregation, and won for it new friends, it also intensified the opposition of those who had been unfavorable to its organization. At this time the outlook was very discouraging. There was the burden of a heavy debt, to be borne by a congregation numerically and financially weak; then the pastor was incapacitated by failing health, which necessitated the engagement of an assistant (Rev. Lewis Hippee), who served but six months; and, finally, on March 19, 1857, the pastor himself resigned. It was thought that a change of employment might be beneficial to him, but he was a victim of consumption, and died January 13, 1859, beloved and lamented by all his people.

But St. John's had been *planted*. The tree was small, and many of the conditions of its growth and development were unfavorable, but it *grew*, and its thrift and fruitage are due, under God's blessing, largely to the faithful husbandmen who have cared for it. St. John's has been served by the following pastors: Rev. J. S. Crumbaugh, April 2, 1853, to March 19, 1857; Rev. Lewis Hippee, assistant, October, 1856, to June, 1857; Rev. D. Steck, January, 1858, to July, 1862; Rev. A. C. Wedekind, January, 1863, to September, 1865; Rev. W. V. Gotwald, July, 1866, to June, 1869; Rev. B. C. Suesserott, January, 1870, to January, 1876; Rev. R. W. Hufford, May, 1876, to November, 1880; Rev. S. Stall, February, 1881, to May, 1887; Rev. B. F. Alleman, June, 1887, to the present time.

During the ministry of Mr. Steck, the condition of the congregation was much improved. His eloquent preaching drew large audiences, the number of communicants was almost doubled, and the Sabbath-school became the largest, save one, in the city. In one year (1860) eighty-two persons were admitted to church fellowship, which increased the membership to two hundred and fifteen. "Then already," we are informed, "the congregation had risen, in point of influence and Christian activity, to a position rivaling the oldest religious organizations of the community."

Although otherwise prosperous, the financial condition of St. John's was (1863) very depressing. The original debt had not only not *decreased*, but by a "sad misfortune," and unexpectedly to the congregation, it had largely *increased*—to more than $6,000.00.

In this respect the field was by no means inviting to Mr. Wedekind. But he pursued an aggressive ministry, stimulated all departments of the church's activity, and, while he had the satisfaction of realizing an advance in spiritual matters, he could also rejoice in the great achievement of liquidating the entire indebtedness of the congregation. "Owe no man anything," was his motto, and the irrepressible *Ladies' Aid Society* his chief human helper.

As with other pastors of St. John's, Mr. Gotwald's earnest efforts were blessed with seasons of gracious revival. The "church grew and multiplied." There was revival in *worship*, and in work. As never before the benevolence of the congregation was developed. In 1868 (Jubilee year) $4,000.00 were contributed for all purposes. Of this sum, $2,100.00 were devoted to benevolence, $400.00 being given to the cause of beneficiary education alone. At the suggestion of Mr. Gotwald, a Sabbath-school was organized in the northwestern part of the city. The school prospered, and after his death (June 9, 1869,) the congregation built for it a chapel to his memory, which was dedicated January 30, 1870. The school was named "Gotwald Memorial Mission," has been under the superintendence of Mr. John H. Kline for many years, and numbers 150 scholars and teachers.

The pastorate of Mr. Suesserott was characterized by practical work. The city was districted, and committees were appointed to aid the pastor in the spiritual care of the people. The "Bellefonte System" for benevolent work was introduced, and this doubled the contributions the first year of its trial. Special attention was given to beneficiary education, one young man being supported by the congregation alone for a season. The discipline of the church was faithfully enforced, special attention was given to the poor, and the church edifice was repaired and thoroughly renovated. Mr. Suesserott died January, 1867.

Owing to the protracted illness and death of his predecessor, Mr. Hufford found a field requiring earnest work. Vigorous effort, however, soon rallied the people, and the church prospered. A debt of $1500.00 was removed, various improvements were made in the lecture and infant school-rooms, and about the church building externally. One hundred and three were added to the membership, and the finances of the church were improved. As, by the action of the council, the penny collections were made the source of benevolent funds, no progress was made in that direction.

One of the most significant events in this period of St. John's history, was the adoption of *The Order of Worship* provided by the General Synod. Hitherto, the congregation had been strongly anti-liturgical, and the change at first threatened serious results. But since that time the greater part of the Service has been used, and to-day the congregation holds a conservative position with regard to worship.

The succeeding pastor, Mr. Stall, having given considerable attention to the subject of church finances, and to methods of church work, endeavored to bring his people to more systematic effort, and to greater liberality in their work. As a result of these efforts the sum of $3177.60 for all purposes was reached in a single year, while the amount contributed to benevolence was about $800.00.

Improvements were made in the church property at an expense of $1800.00, the Sabbath-school contributed two-thirds of the expenses of a beneficiary student for a time, and a parsonage was purchased which cost $5000.00. Two thousand dollars were paid on this purchase, the Ladies' Aid Society contributing one-half of that amount.

A Young People's Society, and a Boys' Society were organized. Sunday funerals were abolished, and an effort was made to establish a new congregation at Gotwald Memorial Mission.

Under the present pastorate the debt on the parsonage has been removed, and so has the old church building. On account of an unmathematically-designed roof, the walls were bowed, and the structure otherwise injured. It was inspected, condemned, and torn down. The old building is gone, but not its hallowed memories, nor the spirit of the fathers who reared it. There stands to-day on the same spot a sanctuary which bespeaks the homage and faith of our people. The corner-stone was laid September 7, 1890, by Rev. W. H. Dunbar, president of Synod, assisted by Revs. C. L. Fry and Dr. J. Max Hark.

On Sabbath, October 4, 1891, the beautiful chapel was consecrated by Rev. Dr. R. W. Hufford, then president of synod, assisted by Drs. H. W. McKnight, Revs. W. H. Dunbar, S. Stall and H. H. Weber.

St. John's has long since taken a prominent position among her sister churches in the East Pennsylvania Synod. She has been active in all the benevolent operations of the church. She has sent at least five sons, and as many daughters, into the ministry. She entertained the General Synod once, and the district synod four times. She has lost none of her prestige in the community. She has three hundred and sixty members, four hundred scholars

ST. JOHN'S EVANGELICAL LUTHERAN CHURCH, LANCASTER, PA.

and teachers in her Sabbath-schools, and is well organized for her work. She has a flourishing Young People's Society of Christian Endeavor numbering one hundred and four members, an efficient Ladies' Aid Society, and an active Woman's Home and Foreign Missionary Society. Recently death has dealt harshly with her, financial misfortune has crippled her, and her temple is not yet finished. But she is not disheartened. She looks back over the history of the past, and *thanks God*. She looks forward with the spirit of her fathers, and *takes courage*.

XL. SEVENTH STREET LEBANON CHARGE, SEVENTH STREET AND MT. ZION.

BY REV. P. C. CROLL.

1. SEVENTH STREET CHURCH, LEBANON.

This is a daughter of Zion Lutheran church of this city. All her original members were former members of that congregation. When, in 1866, the mother church decided to discontinue the use of the German language in her public services, a number of her older members, speaking this tongue and preferring its use in public worship, peaceably withdrew, and, with the consent and direction of the church council, made efforts to establish a German mission in the then extreme northern portion of the city. Accordingly an organization was effected on May 2, of the same year. The meeting for organization was held at the house of Mr. Geo. Barry, where a constitution was adopted, and a pastor elected in the person of Rev. J. M. Deitzler. At first the name proposed by the mother church was adopted, viz., "The German Mission of Zion's Church of Lebanon." Later, this name was changed to "Zion's German Church," and, still later, during the pastorate of Rev. Stine and at its incorporation, to that of "Seventh Street Lutheran Church."

For a season after its founding this Mission worshiped in the house where the enterprise was born, which, because it was used for worship by other struggling church societies, received the name of the "Union Church," and was often called the "Union House of Prayer."

The first officers were the following: trustee, Christian Howerter; elders, Henry Roland and George Patschke; deacons, George Garte, Conrad Roller, Benjamin F. Harpel and Peter Leslie.

In 1867 a neat frame church building was erected on the corner of Seventh and Weidman streets, where the congregation had secured a large and valuable lot. To meet urgent demands in the liquidation of the church debt, all this valuable patch of ground, save the small corner now occupied by the church building, was gradually, but unduly and unwisely, disposed of in building lots.

The pastor, serving a large country charge, was at first enabled to preach but once in four weeks; later, once in two weeks; and during the last years of his pastorate, once every Sabbath. This, and the exclusive use of the German language for a long period, go far in explaining the comparative slowness of progress during the first decade and more of the congregation's history. Only when the English language was introduced and proper care was given to the young people, and, finally, when a pastor settled among this flock, did the congregation manifest a healthy and substantial growth in numbers.

In 1882 this church, under the direction and by the help of the Lebanon Conference, and by the union with it of a small country

SEVENTH STREET EVANGELICAL LUTHERAN CHURCH, LEBANON, PA.

church at Mt. Zion, Lebanon county—hitherto a part of another pastorate—became the centre of a separate pastoral charge, with the pastor's residence here. Rev. Deitzler accordingly resigned this congregation, and in the spring of 1883 Rev. M. H. Stine, of Norwich, Conn., was called as the second pastor. He assumed charge May 1 of the same year. During his pastorate of nine years great progress was made. The charge became self-sustaining, after two or three years' help by the Lebanon Conference. A brick parsonage was built the first year at a cost of $2,700.00. The Sunday-school rapidly increased in numbers and manifested a spirit of work. In 1885 an infant-school room was attached to the rear of the church, and the following year a pipe organ was purchased for use in public worship. In 1888 the old church was replaced by a larger and finer church building of brick—having a commodious and beautiful audience chamber capable of seating six hundred people, a Sunday-school room, and separate apartments for the infants, the library, and the pastor's study. The lower floors were dedicated in December of the same year, and the church proper on September 15, 1889. The structure was completed at a cost of about $12,000.00, including furnishings, frescoing, and the heating of church and parsonage by steam. Of this amount, the present indebtedness on the entire property is about $3,400.00.

The growth of the membership has been commensurate with the outward improvements. From a communicant membership of fifty-seven in 1867, and of about ninety in 1882, it has steadily grown to about two hundred and seventy-five at the present time, and the Sunday-school to over three hundred.

In June, 1892, Rev. Stine resigned the charge to accept a call from our church at Los Angeles, Cal., and the congregation, in August of the same year, elected Rev. P. C. Croll, of Schuylkill Haven, Pa., as his successor, who assumed charge October 1, 1892.

At present more than half the public services are conducted in English, and, out of twenty classes in the Sunday-school, but one is taught in German. The church is well organized, having all the usual working and devotional societies, is bright with hope, and fresh with the vigor of a young life, kept steady by its admixture with age and experience.

2. MT. ZION CHURCH.

This church, located about five miles north of Lebanon, and since 1883 a part of the Seventh Street Lutheran pastorate, came into being in 1854 under the following circumstances: When in the previous year the "Ziegel's" Lutheran church of this place— which had existed for the previous two generations as an exclusively Lutheran congregation, belonging synodically to the Ministerium of Pennsylvania and Adjacent States—proposed the re-building of their edifice, the Reformed people living in this neighborhood, and by marriage closely related to this flock, who had previously enjoyed occasional privileges of conducting worship here, proposed to contribute their quota towards the new building, provided equal rights should be deeded them to the property. This offer the Lutherans refused. In consequence, the Reformed, and such Lutherans as were joined with them by marriage or sympathy with the new project, resolved to build a new and union church within the shadow of the old, with equal rights to both parties. The enterprise succeeded, and in 1853 and 1854 a plain brick church was erected on an eminence at the edge of the village, costing, besides much gratuitous labor, several thousand dollars. It is known as "Zion's Union Church of Mt. Zion."

Among the principal instigators in its erection were Samuel Goshert (after whom the village is commonly called) and Henry Hornish—both Reformed members, the former of whom donated enough land for church-plot and burial purposes. The building committee consisted of Samuel Goshert, Henry Hornish and Samuel Horn, on the Reformed side, and John Phillips, Henry Phillippy and John Olewein, on the Lutheran side.

The Lutheran congregation has from the beginning held its membership with the East Pennsylvania Synod, and has constituted a part of four different pastoral charges, viz.: Womelsdorf, Annville, Myerstown and Seventh Street, Lebanon. Its pastors have been Revs. J. M. Deitzler, Uriel Graves, G. J. Martz, W. I. Cutter, E. Lenhart, P. C. Croll, M. H. Stine, and now again P. C. Croll.

The Reformed pastors have been Drs. Thos. H. Leinbach and C. H. Leinbach, and Rev. Welker. Since 1891 it has constituted a part of a new charge in the Reformed Church, which is at present without a pastor.

The Lutheran membership, which has always been the weaker, has been varying from forty to ninety communicants. At the last celebration of the Lord's Supper seventy-four communed. The people are agricultural in their pursuits, devout and church-loving. In worship the German language is used, but a Union Sunday-school conducts all its exercises in English.

The church is built after the model of country churches, with galleries on three sides, and a pipe-organ at the end, opposite the pulpit. The building is in a good state of repair and is free from debt.

XLI. ZION'S CHARGE, ASHLAND, SCHUYLKILL CO. ZION'S, ASHLAND, AND HUNTERSVILLE.

BY REV. G. W. FRITSCH.

I. ZION'S CHURCH, ASHLAND.

This church was organized by Rev. Jacob J. Weber, who was born at Wurtemberg, Germany, and came to America in 1847. In 1857 the East Pennsylvania Synod sent him as missionary to Ashland, where, June 14, he preached his first sermon. Four days later he organized Zion's with 125 members. In connection with this church he served for some years the congregation at Mahanoy City (General Synod), and those at Mahantongo, Tief Creek and Ringtown, belonging to the Synod of Pennsylvania.

The services of Zion's were held in the stone school-house of Ashland until 1860. The first class of catechumens was confirmed in the English Methodist church building. In 1860 a small church was put up on the corner of 14th and Market streets. The corner-stone of this church was laid by Dr. C. A. Hay, of Harrisburg, and Dr. A. C. Wedekind, of Lebanon. For this church Pastor Weber collected money in the congregations of the brethren Hay, Wedekind, Strube, Henry and Link, where he was kindly received and assisted.

In 1869 this building was removed and the present commodious church erected. The corner-stone of this church was laid October 10, 1869, on which occasion the Revs. Reuben Weiser of Mahanoy City, G. A. Hinterleitner of Pottsville, H. C. Grossman, of Port Carbon, and the pastor, were present. The dedication of this church took place May 29, 1870. Dr. Wedekind, of New York, and Rev. Sanner, of Tremont, officiated. For this building no money was collected from others. In 1887 a large steeple and a bell were added, the Sunday-school room enlarged, stained windows put in the church, and the same papered. The Sunday-school of this congregation was organized in the year 1860 with eight members. Mr. Wm. Burmeister was its first superintendent, filling that office until 1878, when Mr. F. E. Heintze was elected, who is still the efficient superintendent of the school, which now numbers about 300.

Rev. Weber served this church up to 1891 (a period of thirty-four years), when, on account of great feebleness, he felt compelled to lay down his work. A unanimous call was extended to Rev. G. W. Fritsch, then serving the Lyons charge, who entered this field with his family April 14, 1891. He was installed pastor of the congregation by Rev. P. C. Croll, of Schuylkill Haven, who preached in the German language to a large and appreciating audience.

Until the present pastor was called, all the services were conducted in the German language. But in view of the young of the church, who were rapidly becoming anglicised, and in view of some losses on this account, the church had decided that the new pastor should preach German in the morning and English in the evening of every Sabbath. Although the introduction of English was a wise and necessary step, it was nevertheless reluctantly taken by not a few.

It is to be remarked in this connection that nearly all the parents of Zion's came from Germany, and from the province of Pomerania. They came to Ashland to work in the coal mines. Many families were helped over the ocean by their relatives. This occurs even yet occasionally. At present, however, the work and wages are rather poor and discouraging, the men often being allowed to work only three days a week, and having a certain percentage deducted even from that. Many say they cannot now live and pay as they go. A goodly number of this church own their plain houses, having paid for them when times were more favorable. Some who formerly worked in the mines are now successful business men.

This congregation not having a parsonage when Rev. Fritsch took charge of it (Rev. Weber living in a house of his own), it decided within less than four months to erect one back of the church. A beautiful frame house, with modern improvements, was ready to be occupied by the following February, when the happy and grateful pastor-family took possession. The ground belonging to the church, the building was put up at a cost of $2,500.00, leaving a present indebtedness, on account of scant earnings, etc., of about $1,500.00. The membership of this church at present is easily 500, when those are looked upon as members who count themselves as such and think they have a right to be so judged.

The congregation has now a general prayer-meeting, conducted every Wednesday evening in both languages, the German preponderating. It is fairly well attended. Prayers are offered by both sexes.

In the spring of 1892 a Society of Christian Endeavor was organized by the pastor, which is conducted in the English language, with the privilege given to those who wish it, to use the German. This society has so far been quite successful and a great encouragement to the pastor. It has a membership of over fifty at present.

A Children's Mission Band has also been organized by the pastor's wife, who is assisted by several faithful ladies of the church. This band is made up of little girls who come together every Saturday. Sewing is also taught, and the articles made are sold in town. To this mission band meeting, which was something new in its way, children from all the different Protestant churches in town are coming, showing much interest and delight in its operation.

The pastor also meets the little boys, from six years up to the catechetical class, every Saturday from ten to eleven a. m. These boys are known by the name of Little Soldiers.

The congregation has also a sewing circle, organized in 1890. This faithful band of workers has furnished the church with a beautiful altar set. For benevolence, Zion's has raised this year (1892) $204.11.

The salary, paid in monthly installments, is $750.00 and parsonage, in addition to a small amount received from the congregation at Huntersville.

Finally, it may be said of this church that, while in many respects it is not up to many of our General Synod churches, it is however making progress, and the pastor has reason to feel encouraged as well as discouraged in his work.

2. HUNTERSVILLE.

In 1891 Rev. G. W. Fritsch, pastor of Zion's church, of Ashland, organized a small congregation in the village of Huntersville, a short distance west of Ashland, which for the present meets in the public school-house. Divine service is held every three weeks. This little flock contributed $60.00 towards the support of the pastor during the last year.

XLII. ST. JAMES' CHURCH, CHALFONT, BUCKS CO.
BY REV. GEORGE SILL.

St. James' Lutheran Church was organized, and a commodious structure for divine worship built, in the year 1857, under the supervision of Rev. John W. Hassler, then pastor of St. Peter's Lutheran church, North Wales, and St. John's Lutheran church, Centre Square, Montgomery county. There were about fifteen charter members, among whom were the following: Martin Eckhart, George Delp, David Barnett, Charles Eckhart, William Biddle and Samuel Delp.

Rev. Hassler served this church as pastor to the year 1863, when he became chaplain of the 112th Regiment, Pa. Volunteers.

Rev. Peter M. Rightmyer became his successor in the same year, and served this charge four years. At his resignation, St. Peter's and St. John's united in calling a pastor, and so leaving St. James without a minister to break unto them the bread of life and administer the holy sacraments. The congregation was too weak in membership to support a minister by itself, and so called Rev. G. M. Lazarus, of Quakertown, to supply it with the means of grace for a time indefinite. This arrangement continued from 1869 till 1871.

Rev. C. Pitman Whitecar was elected pastor February 9, 1871, and installed May 21 of the same year, serving the church "one year, nine months and seven days."

Rev. R. F. Kingsley became successor to Rev. Whitecar, January 1, 1874, and resigned September 22 of the same year. Rev. H. M. Bickel was called to the pastorate some time during the year 1874, and served the charge till autumn, 1875.

A certain Mr. Hertzel, professing to be a minister of the Reformed church, offered his service as supply until such time as the church could get a regular Lutheran pastor, which offer was accepted by the members of the church. His stay was two years, viz., 1876 and 1877, during which time seeds of discord and strife were sown which have proved a great hindrance to the prosperity of the church.

Rev. B. B. Collins received and accepted a call from St. James' church December 30, 1877. After three years and nine months of faithful labor among these people, he resigned the charge on October 2, 1881.

Rev. Wm. S. Delp supplied the church with the means of grace for some months after Rev. Collins resigned and vacated the charge.

Rev. J. A. Hackenberg accepted a call July, 1882, and served till March, 1883.

Rev. E. S. Morell commenced his labors here in 1883, which continued until July 30, 1888, when he resigned the charge.

Shortly after Rev. Morell vacated the church, Rev. Jno. R. Williams served as a supply for some months, the exact time not being recorded. On his departure, the Philadelphia Conference of the East Pennsylvania Synod made arrangement with Rev. H. M. Bickel to supply the charge until such time as they could see their way clear to call a pastor. May 11, 1890, a call was extended to and accepted by Rev. George Sill, who is still serving as pastor.

One of its members has gone out of this church into the ministry, Rev. William S. Delp.

The church building is a very substantial one of stone. There remains upon it a debt of four hundred dollars. The pastor's salary is three hundred dollars per annum.

The number of members is variously estimated, from forty to sixty. They are widely scattered, some very remote from the place of worship, so that it is not possible for them to attend services. Thus isolated, they lose interest in and love for the church and her institutions, and their influence and beneficence are in a great measure lost to the cause of Christ. The number of active, communicant, and contributing members may be put down at from thirty to thirty-five.

XLIII. ST. JAMES' CHURCH, ASHLAND, SCHUYLKILL COUNTY.

BY REV. W. M. B. GLANDING.

This congregation was organized by Rev. W. L. Heisler. He had been engaged in business at Minersville, Pa. The Lebanon Conference, at its meeting in Harrisburg in March, 1858, requested him to visit Ashland, Pa., look after some English Lutheran families which had moved there, and hold prayer-meetings among them. He arrived April 11 of that year, and conducted religious services in a frame school-house on the corner of Fifth and Walnut streets. A Lutheran Sunday-school was organized May 2, with twenty-seven scholars and nine teachers, at the home of Abel G. Swift, who was the first superintendent.

ST. JAMES' EVANGELICAL LUTHERAN CHURCH, ASHLAND, PA.

The congregation itself was organized with fourteen members June 16. The first Church Council consisted of Geo. H. Helfrich, elder, and J. Logan, deacon. On December 6, 1859, the court granted the petition for a charter of incorporation with the legal name of "*English Evangelical Lutheran Church of Ashland.*" This church from its beginning has held all its services in the English language.

Rev. Heisler, having received "*ad interim*" license from Rev. A. C. Wedekind, D. D., President of East Pennsylvania Synod, and having prosecuted his theological studies privately, was licensed by the Synod in the fall of 1858. He also visited

Ringtown and Miller's school-house in Catawissa Valley, Gordon, Mt. Carmel and Locust Dale, respectively from three to twelve miles distant. From these services held in school-houses several flourishing congregations have resulted. The membership of the Ashland congregation increased to 67.

In June, 1859, three lots were purchased for $550.00 on the corner of Ninth and Market streets. Here was erected a frame church building of one room at the cost of $1500.00, which was dedicated November 6, 1859. Rev. Heisler resigned December 29, 1861, having served about three and one-half years.

The second pastor was Rev. F. A. Barnitz, who labored just two years, from February 1, 1862, to February 1, 1864. The steeple was built and the bell was bought. The debt on the church lot was paid. Mt. Carmel and Ringtown were then connected with this pastorate.

The third pastor was Rev. James R. Sikes. His services lasted from May 1, 1864 to November 1, 1867. On September 25, 1864, the council resolved that it would be better for the pastor not to supply the Mt. Carmel church. A Sunday-school was sustained at Locust Dale. On December 25, 1864, the council passed a motion that the pastor recommend to the congregation at the next congregational meeting the propriety of adopting semi-monthly experience meetings. This action was ratified.

One of the marked features of this pastorate was the exercise of the right of discipline. Thirteen members were excommunicated and a number were suspended. A committee was appointed to admonish the "lukewarm members." Excessive use of intoxicating liquors, dancing, and attendance at a circus, were specially prohibited. Very positive action was taken towards those members who indulged in these offences.

The fourth pastor was Rev. S. Curtis. He came about February 15, 1868, and remained two and a half years. The basement of the church was built. The infant Sunday-school was started by Mrs. Curtis in a carpenter shop on Middle street above Eighth.

The fifth pastor was Rev. J. A. Hackenberg, who began his ministrations April 1, 1871, and ended them May 1, 1875. During the summer of 1871 the parsonage was erected, at a cost of

$4,000.00, and was occupied in December of the same year. Religious services were held in Gordon, where a Lutheran congregation soon afterwards was organized.

The sixth pastor was Rev. O. D. S. Marcley. His pastorate began August 15, 1875, and terminated March 1, 1878.

During the year 1876, $2,700.00 of the debt was paid. In the winter of the same year the Lutheran congregation of Gordon was organized with 33 members. These two churches then formed the English Ashland pastorate. The Mt. Carmel congregation was served only the one year before the departure of Rev. Marcley.

The seventh pastor was Rev. D. E. Rupley, who had just been ordained by the Susquehanna Synod. He began his labors about July 1878, and remained until May 1, 1879.

The eighth pastor was Rev. J. H. Weber, from Schoharie Co., N. Y. He served from November 1, 1879, to September 1, 1887.

In June 1881, a successful effort was made to remove a debt of $1,200.00 on the parsonage. The Young People's Christian Association was organized March 9, 1883. This has been very helpful to the material and benevolent interests of the church. It will soon celebrate its tenth anniversary.

On June 10, 1883, it was resolved to build a new church. On Sabbath, June 17, at the celebration of the 25th anniversary of the congregation, this movement was inaugurated, when the sum of $3,519.00 was promised. The corner-stone was laid on June 22, 1884. The basement was occupied on November 2. The church was dedicated January 18, 1885. The cost of the building, with windows, organ and furniture, was $10,133.93. On November 4, 1883, the council instructed that the proper legal action be taken for changing the charter name to "*St. James' Lutheran Church.*"

On March 1, 1886, the Gordon congregation, which had so grown in membership and ability that it could support a minister, withdrew from this pastorate. The Ashland congregation at once increased the salary to the amount before the division.

The ninth pastor was Rev. E. Felton. He served from October 16, 1887, to September 1, 1889. The basement of the church was repaired and re-seated in the early part of 1889.

The tenth pastor is Rev. W. M. B. Glanding, who had lately

been Professor of Mathematics and Natural Science in Midland College, Atchison, Kansas. He began his labors on October 1, 1889, and is still serving the congregation.

On February 10, 1890, the Young People's Society of Christian Endeavor was formed as an adjunct of the Young People's Christian Association. This Society was reorganized on October 13, 1892, as a separate association.

The Woman's Missionary Society, after a silence of ten years, was revived on February 14, 1890.

A debt of $1,250.00 has been removed. On September 11, 1892, the pastor burnt, in the presence of the congregation, all the bonds, mortgages and notes against the church.

This congregation has been built up under the influence of the evangelistic system. The "revival service" has been employed in connection with the Lutheran method of catechisation.

The special organizations have proven very serviceable to this church. The Ladies' Aid Society began in Rev. Heisler's pastorate. It has contributed to the material interests of the church about $4,400.00.

Two young men of the church are at the institutions of learning in preparation for the Gospel ministry. The Young People's Christian Association is educating a native at Guntur, India.

The approximate amount of money contributed in all for general expenses, real estate and buildings, is $51,000.00. The estimated value of the property at present is $20,000.00. The membership increased from 14 in 1858 to 228 in 1892.

The accessions have been 749, and the losses 521.

The benevolent contributions have increased from $30.66 in 1870 to $284.32 in 1892.

The Sunday-school has advanced from 34 to 250 members. The superintendents of the Sunday-school were the following: Abel G. Swift, Jeremiah Logan, Isaac I. Wagner, Henry S. Boner, Theo. F. Barron and Charles F. Russell, the latter still serving.

The Home Missionary Board gave this church aid for a few years in the early part of its existence.

This history closes November 1, 1892, covering a period of thirty-four years and four and a half months.

XLIV. ST. MATTHEW'S CHURCH, SCHUYLKILL HAVEN.

BY REVS. P. C. CROLL AND J. A. SINGMASTER.

The mother of St. Matthew's Lutheran church is the Jerusalem church on the turnpike, known for many years as the old "White Church," a name no longer applicable to the present modern brick edifice. This church was one of the very oldest in the county. Its early pastors were Revs. George Mennig, 1821–1836; Wm. G. Mennig, 1836–1851; Frederick Waltz, 1852–1854; Julius Erhart, 1854–1865. The original St. Matthew's congregation, however, did not emanate directly from the "White Church." On account of inconvenience of location and insufficient accommodations, together with other reasons, a union congregation of Lutherans and Reformed determined to leave the old church and found another in town. They accomplished their design in the erection of St. Paul's church, now St. Ambrose Roman Catholic church. Before 1851 there had been but little English preaching in the Lutheran church, but then Rev. Daniel Steck, the English Lutheran pastor at Pottsville, began to hold services in St. Paul's every two or four weeks in the afternoon. The adherents of Mr. Steck had and claimed no right to the possession or use of the church building, enjoying the privilege of its use only with the consent of the regular pastor, Rev. W. G. Mennig, and his people. During Rev. Steck's ministry here there was no regular or permanent organization of the English congregation. There were, however, about a score of persons who considered themselves identified with this movement.

St. Paul's church, after the departure of Revs. Mennig and Steck, began to decline. Coldness and discord finally issued in dismemberment and the enforced sale of the edifice, at one-third its cost and about one-fourth its value, to the Schuylkill Haven School Board. The Board, finding it ill-adapted for school purposes, finally disposed of it at an advance to the Roman Catholics.

During Dr. Steck's pastorate there were several extensive revivals of religion. His ministry closed here in 1857. For a year following there was no regular English preaching. In the minutes of the East Pennsylvania Synod, of 1858, we find :

"Resolved, That we recommend Bro. Eli Huber to the promising field of Schuylkill Haven."

Accordingly, on October 17, 1858, Rev. Eli Huber took charge as the first pastor. He found twenty-nine persons ready to enter into a permanent organization. After several futile efforts to reunite the German and English interests by preaching in both languages, the English members withdrew from St. Paul's, leaving it to its impending fate. Of the twenty-nine, whose names are not all remembered now, Andrew Keefer was most prominent. Dr. Steck said of him: "He, more than any other, was the father

ST. MATTHEW'S ENGLISH LUTHERAN CHURCH, SCHUYLKILL HAVEN, PA.

of the English movement." His varied ability, extensive experience, and ardent love for the church, fitted him for leadership and success. During the summer of 1859, the lot upon which the church stands was purchased for $500.00. The contract was signed on June 20 by Messrs. A. Keefer, Samuel Haak, John Worts and C. H. Dengler. The corner-stone was laid, August 17, by the pastor and Dr. Wedekind, of Lebanon; and the church was dedicated in February, 1860, the sermon being preached by Rev. E. W. Hutter, of Philadelphia.

The congregation passed through great straits in paying for the property. Weak and poor, they labored against odds. Several hundred dollars were contributed by churches at Easton and Greencastle. Finally, the Board of Church Extension came to the rescue with a loan of $500.00, which, after several years, was repaid in full.

At the close of the first year, there were 50 members, 62 Sunday-school scholars, and $300.00 paid as pastor's salary. At the close of the second year there were 100 members, 102 Sunday-school scholars, and $500.00 paid as salary.

Rev. Huber's ministry closed December 4, 1860, he having accepted a call to Danville. Rev. P. Willard succeeded, taking charge April 27, 1861. At the close of his third year there were 94 members and 150 scholars. The salary was probably $600.00, of which the Home Mission Board contributed $100.00 in 1863, and $58.50 in 1864. Rev. Huber resigned in March, 1864.

On April 25, 1864, Rev. J. B. Keller, of the Theological Seminary, received a call, which he subsequently declined.

Rev. G. P. Weaver took charge August 1, 1864. He represented the church before Synod as small, composed principally of females, and unable to support a pastor without missionary aid, the membership being 80, and school numbering 140. He received about $100.00 per annum from the Home Mission Board. He left abruptly in April, 1866.

The fourth pastor, Rev. A. Yeiser, was elected May 14, 1866. He accepted the call, but completed his studies at Gettysburg before assuming full charge. He entered upon his work August 19. From his sixth anniversary sermon we learn that $10,390.00 were contributed during that time for all purposes, including the re-modeling of the church at an expense of $3,250.00. From other sources we learn that during the four subsequent years of his ministry about $4,000.00 were raised, making a total of about $14,000.00 in ten years. He reported 64 members the first year, added 232 new members, and reported 240 members at the close of his ministry. The salary was never large, being $600.00 the greater part of the time and $720.00 the remainder.

Under Rev. Yeiser's administration the church became thoroughly established and made great progress in various ways.

"He died in the city of Philadelphia while under medical treatment, February 29, 1876, in the full triumph of that same faith in which he had lived." For several months preceding Rev. Yeiser's death, Rev. J. B. Anthony acted as his assistant. He entered upon his duties December 1, 1875, and supplied the pulpit for six months, to June, 1876. After Rev. Yeiser's decease the congregation elected Rev. J. A. Singmaster, still at the Seminary, April 19, 1876. From July 1 to September 1, Mr. F. W. Staley, a theological student, acted as supply.

Rev. J. A. Singmaster took charge September 1, 1876. During his ministry the church enjoyed several refreshing revivals. In spite of a great financial crisis, the material prosperity of the congregation advanced considerably. A commodious and elegant parsonage was erected, and gas was introduced into the church, as well as minor improvements made, during his administration. After a pastorate of six years, two and a half months, he accepted a call from the Lyons charge, his resignation going into effect November 13, 1882.

The following statistics cover the term of this administration, and represent the numerical strength at its close:

Infant baptisms, 110; additions to membership, 103; losses, 70; number of communicants, 201; strength of Sunday-school, 236; contributions by Sunday-school, $1,367.86; all charitable and benevolent contributions, $1,846.00; local expenses, $11,-311.00; total, $13,157.00.

Rev. P. C. Croll took charge December 1, 1882. During his pastorate the church grew steadily in numerical and financial strength. Over two hundred souls were added to the membership, and the period was marked by great activity and general peace. A remaining debt on the parsonage was liquidated, considerable improvement made to the grounds, and the church wholly re-built. The grand total of over $26,000.00 of money was collected in this period for all purposes. This pastoral relation was severed, after nearly ten years of successful work, October 1, 1892. The pastor removed to Lebanon, Pa., whither he was called by the Seventh Street Lutheran church. Statistics at close of administration, and covering its term, are as follows:

Infant baptisms, 170; additions to membership, 209; losses,

by death and removal, 186; number of communicants, 224; strength of Sunday-school, 218; contributions by Sunday-school, $2,728.35; all charitable and benevolent contributions, $3,129.43; local expenses, $23,038.39; total, $26,167.82.

XLV. MESSIAH (FORSTER STREET) CHURCH, HARRISBURG.

BY PROF. L. O. FOOSE.

Messiah Lutheran church, of Harrisburg, Pa., formerly the Second English Evangelical Lutheran church, grew out of a mission Sunday-school, and its origin can best be reached by tracing the rise and development of this school.

On January 11, 1858, the project of establishing a mission Sunday-school in the upper end of (the then borough of) Harrisburg was brought before the Sunday-school association of Zion church by Mr. Wm. Parkhill, and a committee was appointed to inquire into the expediency of the movement, with instructions to organize a school immediately if found to be advisable. On February 1, following, the matter was brought to the notice of the vestry of the church. This body regarded the movement with much favor, and the hope was expressed that the school could be so located, if possible, as to attract the population from both sides of Capitol Hill. The hope was also expressed that it would serve as a nucleus for another church, the need of which was becoming more and more apparent. On February 8, 1859, one week later, the Association of Zion School was informed by the committee that a school had been opened in a rented building at the corner of State and Cowden streets. The following persons were then elected as officers and teachers of the new school for the ensuing year: Superintendent, Mr. E. Byers; assistant superintendent, Mr. John Heim; treasurer, Mr. Wm. Duncan; librarian, Mr. Wm. A. Parkhill; assistant librarian, Mr. D. L. Duncan; teachers, Mr. George Garberich, Mr. Wm. D. Martin, Mr. Geo. T. Murray, Mr. Chas. Ossman, sr., Mr. Wm. Parkhill, Miss Mary Landis, Miss Mary J. Ossman, Mrs. Mary Eyster and Mrs. Wm. Sayford. Others were added as necessity required, but their names have not been left on record. The school grew so rapidly that on the fourth Sunday the rooms on the first and second floors of the building were filled. It became evident at once that larger accommodations must be secured in the near future.

At the next meeting of the joint Sunday-school Association steps were taken to secure a lot on which to build a chapel for the use of the school. In March, 1859, the lot at the corner of State and Fourth streets, on which the Baptist church now stands, was leased for five years.

The undertaking met with the favor of the vestry and membership of Zion church, a loan was secured, and steps were at once taken to erect a cheap wooden chapel on the lot leased. This building was completed during the early summer, and dedicated and occupied by the school in July. For some time thereafter services were held in the chapel on Sunday afternoon and Thursday evening by Rev. C. A. Hay, D. D., pastor of Zion church. A mite society was organized by the teachers of the school to raise funds to pay for the building. By mutual agreement, it was thought best that a pastor should be secured to take charge of the work of the mission, and accordingly the vestry of Zion church extended a call to Rev. Joshua Evans for this purpose. The call was accepted, but before entering upon his labors here Rev. Evans re-considered his action and declined. Rev. E. S. Johnston was then called, who entered upon his duties June 24, 1860. A congregation of 64 members was organized September 13, 1860, sixty-one of whom brought letters of honorable dismission from Zion church.

The new church thus began its independent existence, and Rev. Johnston became its pastor, devoting his whole time and energy to its welfare. A Sunday evening prayer-meeting was organized, which has been kept up, except for short intervals, ever since. A constitution was adopted the following January, and the necessary steps were taken to unite with the East Pennsylvania Synod.

About this time a lot was purchased for a permanent church home, on Elder street, and partly paid for. Not long afterward, however, it was rendered unavailable for church purposes by the opening and grading of Forster street, which passed through it at the intersection with Elder street. The chapel had been paid for, but the lot on which it stood had been sold, and a few months afterwards the chapel was sold. Another lot was bought, on Forster street near Sixth, and steps were at once taken to erect a two-story stone edifice as the future home of the congregation.

By April, 1864, more than a year after the ground was broken, the building was so far completed as to enable the congregation to use the basement, but it was not finished until 1867, when on July 12, it was dedicated. In the meantime Rev. E. S. Johnston resigned, November 1, 1866, and Rev. G. W. Halderman became pastor January 13, 1867. The congregation at this time numbered about 150 members, and in the erection of this church had passed through one of the severest ordeals of its existence. It had a church home, but this was heavily mortgaged with debt. Three years later, January 24, 1870, Rev. Halderman resigned. The congregation was without a pastor until September 28, 1870, when Rev. F. P. Tompkins was elected pastor, who served in this capacity until April, 1873, when he resigned. The pulpit was supplied until September, when Rev. L. M. Heilman was elected pastor, who entered upon the duties of his office November, 1873.

During this pastorate, which lasted for ten years, new life and zeal were infused into the congregation. Nearly all of the debt on the church building, which had become very burdensome, was paid. The building was enlarged, to make room for the increased membership. It was also thoroughly overhauled at very considerable expense. The children and young people of the congregation were regularly instructed in the catechism and the doctrines of the church, missionary societies were organized, the people grew in piety and spiritual power, the Sunday-school increased greatly in numbers and in efficiency, many of the young people from time to time united with the church and identified themselves with its work, and the blessing of the Lord was everywhere manifest. At the close of this time the membership had increased to over 400, and the Sunday-school to nearly 500. Rev. Heilman resigned June, 1883.

In October of the same year Rev. H. S. Cook became pastor, and served the congregation in this capacity until January, 1888, when he resigned. During this time the remainder of the debt was paid, and the lot on which the present church building stands was purchased. The temporal and spiritual work of the church was carried along very much as during previous years. April 1 of the same year Rev. T. T. Everett, D. D., became pastor. The church building soon proved too small for the audiences that attended the public worship, and it was evident to all that a larger audience room was a matter of necessity. For some time the congregation was in a quandary, whether to endeavor to remain in this building until the lot recently purchased had been paid for, and a fund sufficiently large to erect a new building had been secured, or to build at once. The latter course was adopted, at the risk of incurring a heavy debt, and a two-story brick chapel, 100 feet by nearly 60 feet, was erected. It was dedicated April 13, 1890. The building has been well furnished and well equipped for church work, and will answer the needs of the congregation until the entire structure, of which this is only a part, is completed. In March, 1890, the name of the congregation was changed from "The Second English Evangelical Lutheran church" to "Messiah Lutheran church." In June of the same year the Augsburg Lutheran Sunday-school was organized in the northern part of the city as a missionary enterprise of the congregation. At the time of Dr. Everett's resignation, December 18, 1890, the congregation numbered about 600 members, and the Sunday-school had an enrollment of over 800.

Rev. Luther DeYoe became pastor September 6, 1891, and still continues in this relation. January, 1892, about 100 members were honorably dismissed, at their own request, to organize the Augsburg Lutheran church. During the last year large numbers have been added to the church. The membership now numbers over 700, and the Sunday-school enrolls over 900. The congregation is in a very prosperous condition.

The following are the various organizations at work in the church at present : Weekly Prayer meeting, Senior Christian Endeavor organization, Junior Christian Endeavor organization, Young Men's League, King's Daughters, Woman's Missionary Society, Young Ladies' Mission Band, Children's Missionary Society, Ladies' Mite Society, society for liquidation of debt, consisting of nearly 20 committees, and the usual senior and junior catechetical classes.

XLVI. ST. PAUL'S CHURCH, STONE CHURCH POST OFFICE, NORTHAMPTON COUNTY.

BY REV. I. H. McGANN.

St. Paul's Lutheran Church of Centreville, (Stone Church P. O.,) Pa., was informally organized February 2, 1860. A meeting was called to be held in the second story of an old school-house that stood in the centre of the village of Centreville. About forty men responded to the call, all of them nominally members of the German Reformed and Lutheran congregations, known as Christ's Church. This call was occasioned by the vigorous denunciation of the views held, services demanded, and methods of worship desired, by a respectable minority in each of the above-named denominations. After some preliminary discussion, Reuben Schoch was elected president, and Jesse Pearson, secretary of the meeting. It was resolved that they unite in one body, to be called "New Measure Lutherans."

Samuel Hilliard moved that a church be built near Centreville. This motion was amended by Jacob Kunsman, to read that two churches be built, one at Richmond and another at Williamsburg, Pa. Notwithstanding the wisdom of the amendment, it was voted down, and the original motion carried unanimously.

George Baker moved that a committee of four be appointed to solicit funds for the erection of the proposed building. The president appointed John Schoch, Reuben Wagner, Theodore H. Ink, and Abraham Schmell.

On February 10, nine days after the first call, another meeting was held. The Committee on Finance reported $2,803.50 subscribed. Philip Pearson was the first to subscribe, and pledged himself for $100.00; Jacob Pearson and Joseph Emory followed with like sums. Then there was a deep silence, when the three persons named doubled their pledges. This gave a new impetus, and large subscriptions followed in rapid succession. The new church being an assured fact, specifications were presented, and Jacob Pearson and Joseph Stahley were appointed a building committee. The formal organization now took place. A church council of six elders and four deacons was elected and organized.

The elders were Daniel Emory, Abraham Schmell, Reuben Schoch, Jesse Pearson, and Jacob Deiterich; the deacons, John C. Pearson, William Jacoby, Ephraim Dutt, and Christian Brodt.

Rev. J. J. Albert, a former pastor of the First Lutheran congregation, was consulted. He recommended Rev. John I. Burrrell, then a theological student at Gettysburg. The Council sent a committee to confer with a similar organization at Martin's Creek, Pa. It was agreed that the organizations at Centreville and Martin's Creek would unite in one pastorate. An election was held in Joint Council April 14, 1860, and Rev. Burrell received a unanimous call. The newly-elected pastor entered at once upon the arduous work before him with unflinching zeal.

The Church Council was convened June 18, 1860, and named the new organization, "St. Paul's Evangelical Lutheran church." Arrangements were made to lay the corner-stone July 4, and on November 10, 1860, St. Paul's, amid great rejoicing, was solemnly dedicated to the service of Almighty God. In the meanwhile the M. E. church was offered and used for preaching purposes. Articles of incorporation were granted March 28, 1861. A protracted service followed immediately on the dedication of the church. A precious revival was the result, and on January 13, 1861, the Lord's Supper was administered to two hundred and twenty-eight persons. Special services were conducted in neighboring school-houses; many were savingly converted and added to the growing congregation, and at the next communion season St. Paul's enrolled her largest number of members.

The outbreak of the Civil War became the occasion of difficulties and discouragements which seriously interrupted the progress of the congregation. The pastor tendered his resignation February 8, 1875, and accepted a call to Brooklyn, N. Y., where he died a few years afterward.

About this time St. Paul's withdrew from her former pastoral relation with Martin's Creek and Ackermanville congregations, and formed a separate pastorate. It continues so up to this time.

On September 20, 1875, the congregation extended a call to Rev. H. R. Fleck to become pastor of their now distracted field. Rev. Fleck's labors were eminently successful. He succeeded, in a large measure, in restoring peace and good will among the members, and many others were brought to a saving knowledge of the truth and added to the church. After six years of patient and devoted ministerial labor, he resigned the charge. During Rev. Fleck's pastorate, on January 30, 1876, the congregation changed its synodical relations from the New York and New Jersey Synod to the East Pennsylvania Synod.

Rev. P. S. Hooper was the next pastor, who remained with the people about eighteen months. He was followed by Rev. C. S. Trump, who entered the field January 31, 1883. During the spring and summer of 1883 the church edifice was re-modeled and the interior beautified. The church was re-opened August 5, 1883. Rev. Trump presented his resignation September 1, 1888, to take effect in thirty days.

The next pastor was Rev. J. T. Gladhill, who, owing to ill health, resigned August, 1891, having been pastor about two years and six months. He succeeded in bringing most of the young people of the congregation into church fellowship, and his work will tell for the future.

The present pastor, Rev. I. H. McGann, began his labors March 1, 1892. The congregation now numbers two hundred and twelve members. The people seem united and willing to work. There is a spirit of improvement and advancement manifest, and the congregation, during the vacancy of seven months before the present pastor was called, erected an iron fence facing the public road for a distance of 243 feet, re-papered the parsonage, laid stone walks, and made various other needed improvements.

St. Paul's has furnished to the ministerial ranks Rev. Ephraim Dutt, Rev. W. H. Dunbar, D. D., Rev. John Wagner, Rev. Jacob S. Paul, Rev. Charles B. Gruver. Mr. George Uhler is now a student at Gettysburg preparing for the ministry. George D. Stahley, M. D., Professor of Hygiene and Physical Culture in Pennsylvania College, is one of her sons, as was also Mr. Alvin Schmell, a very promising young man, who died while a theological student at Gettysburg in 1890.

Material aid in the preparation of the above has been received from an excellent and detailed history of the congregation, written by Prof. B. F. Reasley, ex-Superintendent of Public Instruction in Northampton county, and read by him at a congregational jubilee held August 18, 1892.

XLVII. LYONS CHARGE—LYONS, PLEASANTVILLE, MOHRSVILLE, AND STRAUSSTOWN, IN BERKS COUNTY; MACUNGIE AND UPPER MILFORD, IN LEHIGH COUNTY.

BY REV. J. A. SINGMASTER.

The Lyons charge consists of six small congregations in Berks and Lehigh counties. The present church membership numbers 263, and the Sunday-schools, teachers and scholars, about 650. The German language is used at the regular services. In the Sunday-schools English predominates, and it is used also more or less frequently at special preaching services on Saturday and Sunday evenings.

The charge was formed by Rev. A. D. Croll in 1868, and consisted of congregations then organized by him at Lyons, Macungie and Pleasantville, together with the Mohrsville Union church, established in 1864. Salem was at first only a preaching station, but formed a separate organization in 1872. Strausstown was not added to the charge until 1878.

The formation of this charge was the result of a great revival of religion during the ministry of the sainted Rev. A. D. Croll. In the year 1862 he became the pastor of six country congregations, known as the Lobachsville, DeLong, St. Peter's, Hereford, Longswamp and Hill churches, located in Berks county, and adhering to the Synod of Pennsylvania. He exercised a wonderful spiritual influence throughout his large charge, in awakening, converting and edifying souls. For five years he continued the faithful and popular pastor of this large field. Calls to more inviting and prominent churches did not induce him to leave his important work. He had, however, serious difficulties to contend with. None of the congregations held prayer-meetings, in which he so ardently believed. His methods began to arouse opposition on the part of some of his people, as well as from his clerical brethren.

In the meantime Pastor Croll found his connection with the Synod of Pennsylvania growing less congenial. Its well-known disapproval of "revivals," the comparatively rigid type of Lutheranism which it advocated, the cold formalism prevalent in many of its congregations, together with other reasons, induced Mr. Croll to withdraw from the old Synod in March, 1868. He immediately proceeded to gather his adherents into new organizations, excepting at Mohrsville, where the entire congregation followed him. He was received, with his five congregations numbering 200 members, into the East Pennsylvania Synod in September, 1868. A period of great religious activity followed. During the succeeding six years, hundreds were converted and spirituality promoted in wide circles. Contributions grew phenomenally for that region. Besides supporting their pastor from the start without missionary aid, and building new churches, the offerings for the benevolent objects of the Synod amounted to $400.00 per annum. The power of the Holy Spirit was further manifested in the call of young men to the ministry. During the eight brief years of Mr. Croll's pastorate, three of these became pastors and two others had almost completed their preparation. Since then two more have entered the ministry, and another candidate is preparing. Thus, in the twenty-five years of the history of the Lyons charge, it has rarely been without at least one candidate for the ministry.

The tremendous labors of Mr. Croll soon broke down his frail body. With the words, "Is this dying? No, sweet living," upon his lips, he passed away June 19, 1876, aged 38 years. His death was a severe blow to his congregations, which had now increased in membership to 335. The protracted illness of Mr. Croll, frequent changes of pastors, long vacancies, the wide separation of the churches, and various other causes, have to some extent depleted the membership, but there is yet much pure "salt" there. The sketch of the charge will be amplified in the brief notes on the individual congregations here following.

1. St. Paul's Church, Lyons Station.

This congregation was organized by Rev. A. D. Croll, in 1868, out of adherents who followed him from the De Long congregation at Bowers. The corner-stone of the substantial two-story brick church was laid June 1, 1868. Mr. Croll's pastorate extended from 1868-1876. Rev. W. I. Cutter and others supplied the charge until the former was elected pastor, in July, 1877. He was succeeded in February, 1878, by Rev. E. Daron, who resigned January 1, 1880. Rev. D. E. Reed was the next pastor, for less than a year. Rev. W. H. Lewars succeeded him, April 10, 1881, and resigned January 24, 1882. Rev. Wm. G. Mennig acted as supply for some months. On November 15, 1882, Rev. J. A. Singmaster took charge, and remained until April, 1885, when he resigned for the purpose of serving the Macungie charge, which had been formed by the withdrawal of Macungie and Salem from the Lyons charge and the addition of St. John's, Fogelsville. Rev. George W. Fritsch, who had been called to the ministry through the instrumentality of Rev. A. D. Croll, became pastor in the summer of 1885. After serving the charge about six years, he resigned in March, 1891. Since then the pulpit has been temporarily supplied by Rev. G. J. Martz, of Lebanon. Revs. W. R. Wieand, of Altoona, P. C. Croll, of Lebanon, and Morris F. Good, of the Theological Seminary, entered the ministry from this church.

2. St. John's, Pleasantville.

The history of this congregation is much like that of the foregoing. It was organized under similar circumstances by Pastor Croll in 1868, with a small membership which withdrew from congregations in the vicinity. For ten years the congregation worshiped in a hall. Their neat brick church was built during the pastorate of Rev. E. Daron. It has had the same pastors as the church at Lyons Station.

3. St. Matthew's Church, Macungie.

St. Matthew's church was organized in 1868 by about 100 people who separated from Solomon's Lutheran and Reformed church, under the leadership of Rev. A. D. Croll. In 1869 a brick church, seating about 400 people, and costing $6,500.00, was erected upon land donated by James Singmaster. The pastors have been the same as those of St. Paul's, Lyons. During the pastorate of Rev. J. A. Singmaster, this church, with Salem and Fogelsville, formed the Macungie charge for about a year and a half (April, 1885, to September, 1886). After his resignation it re-united with the Lyons charge, of which Rev. G. W. Fritsch was the pastor. During the pastorate of Rev. E. Daron a frame chapel was erected. This congregation has given to the ministry Rev. J. A. Singmaster, of Allentown, and Rev. O. C. Roth, of Baltimore. Another of its young men has recently consecrated himself to the same work. Since 1881 the church has sustained a flourishing Woman's Missionary Society.

4. SALEM CHURCH, UPPER MILFORD.

This church is situated about three miles south-east of Macungie. Its original membership separated in 1868 from a neighboring church, called St. Peter's, whose history dates back to 1770. For four years Rev. A. D. Croll, whom they followed from the old church, preached occasionally in their houses and barns. Their names, however, were enrolled in St. Matthew's, Macungie. In 1872 they organized separately and built a comfortable stone church, with basement, seating about 250 people. It has always had the same pastors as Macungie.

5. UNION CHURCH, MOHRSVILLE.

The Union church of Mohrsville, Berks county, Pa., was founded in 1864 by members of the Union church at Shoemakersville, from which they withdrew on account of dissatisfaction with the election of an "independent" pastor. Messrs. John Snyder, Isaac H. Mohr, Seth Zimmerman and Isaac K. Becker, were elected as a building committee and erected a brick church, thirty-six by forty-eight feet, with basement and gallery. The dedication took place May 7, 1865.

The Reformed held their first election for pastor in January, 1865, and chose Rev. Aaron Leinbach.

The Lutherans elected Rev. B. E. Kramlich in February, 1865. He resigned June 24, 1867. Rev. A. D. Croll was then elected pastor, being a member of the Synod of Pennsylvania. At his second appointment he announced that he could not accept a call, in view of his intention of changing his synodical relations by uniting with the East Pennsylvania Synod, unless the congregation would hold another election. He was again unanimously elected, and served the church with the greatest possible acceptance until the time of his death in 1876. During the ministry of

Rev. A. D. Croll, the church was connected with the Lyons charge.

After his death Rev. J. A. Singmaster, pastor at Schuylkill Haven, supplied the pulpit for about two years. Rev. E. Lenhart became pastor on July 9, 1878, and the congregation, by a re-districting of various charges, was assigned by Synod to the Womelsdorf charge, consisting of congregations at Womelsdorf, Strausstown, Mohrsville, Myerstown and Gosherts. He was succeeded by Rev. Philip C. Croll in 1879, whose pastorate extended to December, 1882. Rev. I. B. Crist took charge in September, 1883, and labored until June 1, 1885. By a new arrangement, Mohrsville and Strausstown were now added to the Lyons charge, consisting of four churches. Rev. G. W. Fritsch became pastor in the summer of 1885, and terminated his pastorate April 1, 1891, since which time the pulpit has been supplied by neighboring pastors.

The church edifice was re-modeled in 1886 at a cost of $1,400.00, all of which was paid on or before the dedication. The improvements consisted in raising the floors, thus bringing the basement above ground, and in removing the side galleries. Since then, shedding has been erected to the rear of the church, and the cemetery improved. The introduction of new reversible seats into the Sunday-school room is now contemplated.

The membership numbers at present fifty-eight, and the Union Sunday-school over a hundred. On account of the frequent changes of pastors and the present vacancy, the membership has been somewhat depleted. This little congregation has always been very zealous in the work of the Lord. It has given one of its young men, Rev. Wm. H. Lewars, the present Secretary of the Synod, to the ministry of Christ.

6. St. Paul's Church, Strausstown.

This congregation was organized by Rev. J. M. Deitzler, in 1861, with a few members who withdrew from Zion Union Lutheran and Reformed Church. At a meeting held on July 15, Messrs. John Strauss, Jonathan G. Reber, Michael Miller, John Boltz, and Dr. W. J. Schoener, were appointed a building committee. Within a week they had purchased a lot for the church and cemetery and begun building operations. The corner-stone of a frame church was laid in August. Suitable sermons were preached on this occasion by Revs. A. C. Wedekind, E. S. Henry, and J. M. Deitzler, the pastor. The church was finished and consecrated in November, Rev. P. Willard assisting the pastor in the services. During the following winter the membership increased to seventy by means of a great revival.

Rev. Uriel Graves succeeded Rev. Deitzler as pastor on April 1, 1865. He resigned March 6, 1866. From this date to Nov. 15, 1868, when Rev. G. J. Martz became pastor, the church was dependent upon supplies. The charge consisted at this time of churches at Womelsdorf, Schaefferstown, and Strausstown. Rev. Martz continued pastor for about nine years. During 1877, Rev. W. I. Cutter supplied the pulpit. Rev. E. Lenhart became pastor July 9, 1878. Since then it has been served by the same pastors as Mohrsville.

XLVIII. MARTIN'S CREEK CHARGE, NORTHAMPTON COUNTY, LOWER MOUNT BETHEL AND ACKERMANVILLE.

BY REV. WM. HESSE.

1. TRINITY CHURCH, MARTIN'S CREEK (LOWER MT. BETHEL).

The Mt. Sion church of Lower Mount Bethel, was jointly controlled by Lutherans and German Reformed. It was built in the year 1837. Rev. Andreas Fuchs was the first pastor, serving until 1850. His preaching was all in German. He was succeeded by Rev. Mark Harpel, whose preaching was partly English and partly German. Rev. Jacob Albert entered upon the duties of pastor as successor of Mr. Harpel early in 1855, remaining until the fall of 1859. His preaching was mostly English, and of a spiritual character. Rev. J. I. Burrell was next chosen, under whose preaching a great awakening took place.

In 1864 a number of members, with the pastor, withdrew from the old church and organized a new congregation, electing the following as a Church Council:

Trustee: Abram Shimer. Elders: Christian Buzzard, George

Racely, Joseph Engler, Charles Ziegenfuss, Robert G. Morris. Deacons: David Hinkle, Joseph Kiefer, William Snyder, John Riegel, Samuel Hile, Joseph K. Snyder.

The following were appointed as a Building Committee: Rev. J. I. Burrell, pastor, Drs. Asa K. Seem, Abram Shimer, Christian Buzzard, Joseph Kiefer, Jr., William Snyder.

The corner-stone of the new church was laid in 1864, in the immediate vicinity of the old building, Rev. Luther Albert, of Germantown, Pa., preaching in the morning, Rev. R. A. Fink, of Lewisburg, in the evening, Rev. Duy, of New Germantown, N. J., officiating in the formal act of laying the corner-stone, and Rev. R. B. Forsman assisting in the services.

The consecration of the new building took place on Thursday, December 8, 1864, Rev. F. W. Conrad, D. D., of Chambersburg, preaching able sermons morning and evening. Rev. J. I. Burrell read the dedicatory service. A number of other ministers were present. The pastor and congregation belonged to the New Jersey Synod. At a joint council meeting of Upper and Lower Mount Bethel, held March 19, 1862, it had been agreed that Lower Mt. Bethel pay the sum of $500.00 toward building a parsonage at Centreville, Pa., which amount was to be refunded in case of a division of the charge.

On May 29, 1875, a joint congregational meeting was held, at which it was decided to divide the charge, and a committee was sent to Synod to secure its sanction of the division. The first congregational meeting of Trinity, after the division, was held July 31, 1875, for the purpose of electing a pastor. Rev. J. H. Leeser was chosen, during whose pastorate the synodical relation was changed from the New Jersey to the East Pennsylvania Synod, and a fine parsonage erected by the church. Rev. J. H. Leeser resigned, to take effect May 3, 1877. Rev. S. Stall received and accepted a call August 25, 1877, and took charge on the 28th of the same month. He resigned November 20, 1880, to take effect December 8 of the same year. Rev. F. W. Staley was chosen as pastor March 25, 1881, and entered upon his duties April 1. Rev. A. R. Glaze took charge October 1, 1885, and resigned May 26, 1889. Rev. William Hesse, the present pastor, entered upon his duties November 10, 1889.

The present amount paid for support of pastor is $700.00 and parsonage; from all sources $900.00. There is no indebtedness on either of the church buildings, and the Sabbath-school is in excellent working order, with an enrollment of 152 scholars and 23 teachers and officers. Nine church papers are taken. Two young men are now entering school to prepare for the ministry, Mr. Herbert D. Shimer and Mr. John I. Burrell Hummer. One other young man, Daniel Hinkel, now teaching school, hopes also to prepare for the sacred office.

2. Zion's Church, Ackermanville.

The Zion's congregation of Ackermanville, Pa., was organized by Rev. J. I. Burrell in the year 1871. A church was built, jointly with the Evangelical Association, in the year 1872. This is a weak congregation. It was formerly connected with Centreville church, but has been connected with the Martin's Creek charge ever since the division of the Centreville charge, in 1875. The Sabbath-school is in excellent working order, and numbers about eighty, of whom we report forty to Synod. One young man of this congregation has entered the ministry, Rev. B. F. Kautz, of Millersburg, Pa.

XLIX. MESSIAH CHURCH, PHILADELPHIA.

BY REV. E. HUBER, D. D.

Messiah Lutheran church, Philadelphia, had its origin in a Sunday-school established December 18, 1859, by members of St. Matthew's Lutheran church, during the pastorship of Dr. E. W. Hutter. In honor of its first and devoted superintendent, C. Y. Barlow, it was named, "The Barlow Mission of St. Matthew's church." The school was carried on for six years before any decided steps could be taken toward organizing a congregation. After several preliminary meetings, a public meeting was held December 12, 1865, at Thirteenth and Oxford streets, at which it was determined to rent a hall on Broad street and to hold prayer-meetings regularly in the same. During January, 1866, the organization of the congregation was completed by the adoption of a constitution and the election of church officers. Under the name of " Messiah Lutheran Church," the congregation was admitted into the Synod of East Pennsylvania in the fall of 1866, Dr. Theophilus Stork, Sen., representing it at that meeting.

MESSIAH EVANGELICAL LUTHERAN CHURCH, PHILADELPHIA, PA.

Regular services were held for nearly a year by means of such supplies as could be procured, until November 1, 1866, when Dr. F. W. Conrad took charge of the congregation, thus becoming its first pastor. Under his ministrations the church grew rapidly in numbers and in influence, the main part of the present house of worship was erected, at the southwest corner of Sixteenth and Jefferson streets, and the services hitherto held in a hall near by were, in the early part of 1870, transferred to its Sunday-school room. After serving the congregation for a term of six years, Dr. Conrad resigned the pastorship of the church, and was succeeded in December, 1872, by Rev. J. R. Dimm.

In consequence of reverses in business among some of the members, the congregation had become severely crippled in its financial affairs, and, unable to meet its obligations, was in danger of losing its church property—a bill of sale having, in fact, been fastened upon its walls by the sheriff of the city. From this misfortune the church was happily saved by the indefatigable efforts of the pastor and Mr. Christian A. Snyder, the treasurer of the congregation, who, during the short time allowed them, raised $4,000.00, the sum required to redeem the property.

After serving the congregation for nearly two years Rev. Dimm resigned July 1, 1874, and was some time after succeeded by Dr. Joel Swartz, who remained pastor of the church till called to Zion's church of Harrisburg. After a considerable interval Rev. Eli Huber, of Nebraska City, was elected to succeed Dr. Swartz, and entered upon his duties in the congregation the first Sunday of March, 1876.

About two years later the work of finishing the church building was begun, and brought to completion in April, 1879. The following constituted the Church Council at the time: William Boyer, Henry Boyer, Henry S. Boner, V. L. Conrad, J. B. Downing, W. H. Fry, A. Hartranft, H. S. Jones, J. T. Monroe, C. A. Snyder, Henry Wile, and John Wiseman.

The expense incurred in the finishing of the church was about $23,000.00, and, as there was a previous indebtedness of over $8,000.00, upwards of $31,000.00 had to be made up by the congregation. Over half of this amount was secured by subscriptions and collections, and by the sale of certain lots, and the balance of $15,000.00, was borrowed on mortgage, individual members of the council making themselves responsible for the payment of the interest. By the aid of the Ladies' Sinking Fund Society the interest has been regularly paid, and by successive annual collections of about $1,000.00 each, the sum borrowed has been gradually reduced to about $5,000.00. The church building thus secured cost about $63,000.00 in all—and is a beautiful, commodious and well-finished structure.

The present membership of the congregation is about 315 ; the number of scholars in the Sunday-school nearly the same.

The Messiah church also contributed very freely toward the erection of the new building of Pennsylvania College, at Gettysburg, the sum given being nearly $6,000.00. A memorial window by the Sunday-school, a fine clock in the tower, and the endowment of the professorship of English Bible, are abiding testimonials at Pennsylvania College to the liberality of this congregation. The whole amount thus secured for Gettysburg out of the congregation is not far from $35,000.00.

The pastor of the church, having been elected to fill the professorship thus endowed, resigned the congregation, and preached his farewell sermon the first Sunday in September, 1892, exactly sixteen years and six months after preaching his introductory sermon.

On the first Sunday in December of the same year, the work thus laid down was taken up by Rev. Milton H. Valentine, of Bedford, Pa., who is the present pastor. That the blessing of God may abide upon this congregation unto the end, is the hope and prayer of the writer of this sketch.

L. ST. JOHN'S CHURCH, MAHANOY CITY, SCHUYLKILL COUNTY.

BY REV. I. P. ZIMMERMAN.

Until 1867 but one Lutheran congregation had an existence in Mahanoy City, and that was composed largely of foreign and Pennsylvania Germans. In the winter of 1866 and 1867 the pastor, Rev. I. C. Burkholder (now Burke), conducted a series of revival meetings, upon which God's blessing rested in a special manner, resulting in the conversion of one hundred and thirty souls. This, to many a new measure, in connection with some other trouble existing in the congregation, resulted in a division of its members, and the establishment of a second Lutheran church in Mahanoy City, with the Rev. I. C. Burkholder as pastor. Accordingly, on August 7, 1867, a new organization was effected, seventy-nine members signing the constitution, under the name of "St. John's English Evangelical Lutheran church of the General Synod."

This new organization at once went to work to secure lots and build for themselves a church. In the meantime they continued to worship in the old church to which they formerly belonged. The lots were secured from the Philadelphia & Reading Coal and Iron Company, the congregation paying six hundred ($600.00) dollars for one lot and the company donating the other. In the same year the congregation reared upon these lots a frame structure for a church, at a cost, when completed, of $4,500.00. Rev. I. C. Burkholder remained pastor of the congregation until April, 1869, when he resigned. During the two years of his pastorate of the new congregation, several protracted efforts were held, and by this means and catechisation forty-three more members were added.

A vacancy now occurred, continuing until October, 1869, when Rev. Reuben Weiser became the pastor. He remained in that position until January, 1871. During Rev. Weiser's pastorate a few German sermons were preached, which was about all the preaching in that language the congregation ever had.

In February, 1871, a call was extended to Rev. D. Beckner, of Antes Fort, Pa., which was accepted, and he entered upon his duties as pastor March 13, 1871.

In the summer of 1872 the church was papered and re-painted. In the fall of 1873 a parsonage was built on the same lot upon which the church now stands. The following year, 1874, the church was carpeted, and gas introduced.

Rev. D. Beckner resigned May 1, 1875. During the few months' vacancy which followed, the Sunday-school conducted an excursion to Fairmount Park, Philadelphia, and netted $656.00, which was appropriated to the local indebtedness, and Sunday-school library.

On October 1, 1875, Rev. J. M. Steck took charge as pastor. The congregation, though having advanced greatly in temporal affairs, had not gained much in membership, as Rev. Steck reports an enrollment of seventy-seven on taking charge, and a Sunday-school of ninety, mostly little children. When he resigned, March 1, 1880, he reports 127 members of the congregation, and the highest number present at any time in Sunday-school, 264.

During this pastorate, in 1879, the church was enlarged by the building of a brick front twenty by forty-two feet. New pews were placed in the auditorium, walls papered, floor re-carpeted, new pulpit furniture secured, and heaters placed in the cellar. The cost of the improvements was $2,900.00. Rev. H. Ziegler, D. D., preached the sermon at the laying of the corner-stone of the new front. Rev. W. W. Criley delivered the sermon at the re-dedication of the church as now enlarged and improved, Rev. John McCron, D. D., preaching in the evening.

While pastor of the congregation, Rev. Steck began preaching at Delano, Pa., and received fourteen persons into church fellowship, mostly married persons.

Mr. Newton H. Follmer, who subsequently prepared for the ministry and is now pastor of the Yeagertown charge, Mifflin co., Pa., was received as a member of the congregation in 1876.

Upon the resignation of Rev. J. M. Steck, a call was extended to Rev. J. W. Lake, who accepted and entered upon the field March 1, 1880. His pastorate, however, proved a very brief one, as his resignation was tendered and accepted June 1, 1881.

A vacancy of seven and a half months now occurred, when Rev. Wm. H. Lewars accepted a unanimous call tendered him January 15, 1882. A pastorate of four years and nine months was the result of this union, when, on October 15, 1886, Rev. Lewars severed his connection with the congregation.

During this pastorate a balance of indebtedness on the parsonage was paid.

A Literary Society was organized by Rev. Lewars, which still continues its semi-monthly meetings at the homes of a number of the members, and is aiding the congregation much financially and socially. The benevolence also exceeded that of former years.

After Rev. Lewars' resignation the congregation remained without a pastor until May 1st, 1887, when the Rev. J. R. Sample took charge, but remained only three months.

On September 1, 1887, Rev. I. P. Zimmerman, the present pastor, took charge. At this time the congregation numbered one hundred and twenty-eight members, but preaching at Delano, which had been discontinued, was soon resumed, and twenty-eight members re-enrolled, making a total of 156. The relation now formed proved a very pleasant one indeed. The first year, a large catechetical class was formed, which resulted in an accession of sixty souls on Easter, 1888. The salary of the pastor was advanced from $700.00 to $750.00 the first year. In the summer of 1888 an addition of four rooms was built to the west end of the parsonage, and the home of the pastor supplied with bath-room, etc. At the same time the church was re-papered and painted, the cost of all the improvements to church and parsonage being about $1,700.00. The re-opening of the church took place on October 14, 1888. The sermon was preached by Rev. J. A. Wirt, of Hughesville, Pa., and the money solicited by him more than covered the indebtedness.

On January 1, 1888, a Woman's Home and Foreign Missionary Society was formed, and on February 29 of same year, a Young Ladies' Mission Band was organized, both of which are doing good work. The latter is educating a boy in India.

During the short pastorate of Rev. J. R. Sample, a Band of Hope was organized among the children, which was subsequently changed into a Loyal Temperance Legion, and has rendered good service, with a membership of over one hundred.

In the first year of the present pastorate the envelope system was introduced in raising money for benevolent purposes. This at once brought system into the work, and in five years the amount raised has increased from $166.62 to $579.48. In April, 1890, the church was re-carpeted. At a congregational meeting in May, 1890, the salary of the pastor was increased from $750.00 to $900.00.

In October, 1890, a Young People's Society of Christian Endeavor was organized with seventeen members, which has had a steady growth, numerically and spiritually, now numbering sixty members. This society is educating a young man in India.

On the suggestion of Mr. A. B. Wagner, Secretary of the church council, that body appointed at their meeting, the first Monday evening in September, 1891, a committee of eight, four ladies and four gentlemen, known as the Christian Helper Committee, whose duty it shall be to look after the sick, poor, negligent and timid of the congregation, and make special effort for their encouragement. This committee has proved itself very helpful to the pastor in church work.

In August, 1891, the pastor succeeded in influencing eight families to place as many memorial stained-glass windows in the auditorium.

On September 6, 1892, a Junior Society of Christian Endeavor was organized with twenty-seven members. The Sunday-school has been growing gradually, now numbering three hundred. The present membership of the congregation is three hundred in good standing. The salary paid at present is $900.00, parsonage, water rent, and fuel. The number of *Lutheran Observers* taken is fifty-eight; the number of *Lutheran Missionary Journals* taken, ninety-two. The congregation is free of debt. The value of church property is $10,000.00.

The present year's benevolence is $549.48. One candidate is in preparation for the gospel ministry, Mr. Fred. R. Wagner having entered upon a course of study at Missionary Institute, Selinsgrove, Pa., August 25, 1892.

LI. BETHANY CHURCH, MILLERSVILLE, LANCASTER COUNTY.

BY MR. HENRY BOWMAN.

The history of our General Synod Lutheran church in Millersville, Pa., begins with an unhappy division, which took place after the formation of the General Council in 1866. As a result, both parties were left numerically weak, and the work of the church materially crippled. At the time of the division Rev. J. R. Focht was pastor in charge, who, with a minority of the members, on January 22, 1867,

"Resolved, to remain in connection with the General Synod, believing that by so doing we can best promote the spiritual welfare of the congregation."

They were, in consequence, ejected from their church-home and compelled to organize and build for themselves. For a number of years the little band (about fifty) were subjected to the inconveniences and disadvantages of worshiping in a hall. In the meantime Rev. Focht resigned the charge, and Rev. J. Kaempfer was called, who commenced his labors as pastor June 1, 1868. He, however, remained only a short time, and the congregation was then supplied, until 1875, by Rev. B. C. Suesserott, then pastor of St. John's in Lancaster city. After his death the work was taken up by Rev. W. S. Porr, at that time pastor of St. Stephen's of Lancaster. Under his pastoral direction a neat brick church (thirty-five by fifty-five feet) was erected at a cost of about $3,000.00, and dedicated, free of debt, some time in the early part of 1877. Having once more a church home of their own, the congregation entered anew upon its mission among the churches. After a successful pastorate of about six years, Rev. Porr resigned October 1, 1880. The congregation again turned to the pastor of St. John's in Lancaster, and arranged with Rev. R. W. Hufford for their supply. This, however, was soon terminated by a call of the pastor to Easton, Pa. Synod now recommended a union of Millersville with the Neffsville congregation, and the two were served by a number of pastors. Rev. J. W. Eckert, from March 1, 1881, to about the close of 1882. Rev. F. Aurand entered the charge November 4, 1883, and remained less than one year. Then, in September, 1884, Rev. A. M. Whetstone accepted a call, and remained until December 1, 1885. But the union of the two congregations never appeared very congenial, and hence Neffsville refused to co-operate any longer, and applied to another pastorate for their supply. Synod, being very accommodating, passed the matter by, and left Millersville again unable to support a regular pastor. Having, however, the advantage of a State Normal School in the place, the congregation has not been long at any time without a regular supply. February 11, 1887, Rev. J. W. Goodlin, then of York, Pa., accepted a unanimous call from the congregation, and moved to Millersville. With this arrangement the people were happy, but only soon to be sadly disappointed, when in a little less than two years their beloved pastor received and accepted a call to Tyro, Ohio. For about six months following Rev. Herbert C. Alleman, then a theological student, supplied the congregation. In September, 1889, Rev. A. W. Lentz moved to Millersville, in order to take a needed rest. His services were soon secured, and he has continued with entire pastoral care until the date of this history.

LII. GRACE CHURCH, PHILADELPHIA.

BY REV. J. H. MAIN.

During the year 1867 Rev. P. Willard, Rev. F. Klinefelter and other ministers preached statedly for a short time to congregations which met in a hall on the north-west corner of Thirty-fifth and Haverford Streets, West Philadelphia. In February, 1868, Rev. S. A. Holman, under the auspices of a missionary society composed of members of St. Matthew's, St. Andrew's and Messiah churches, Philadelphia, commenced preaching in the above hall. Under his ministry twenty-one members of the Evangelical Lutheran church formed themselves into an organization, known as "Grace Evangelical Lutheran Church," on April 5, 1868. During his administration, in July, 1870, a lot on the southeast corner of Thirty-eighth and Mt. Vernon streets was taken on mortgage, and immediately the congregation, with about $300.00, which they had themselves contributed and received by collections, began to build a brick chapel. The corner-stone was laid in July, 1870, and the chapel consecrated November, 1870, at which latter date over $500.00 was raised. The entire cost of the chapel was $3,200.00. Contributions were solicited during the months of February and March, 1872, and sufficient was raised to pay off the entire remaining indebtedness.

Services were held in the above-named chapel until November 9, 1873, when Rev. Holman relinquished the charge, and, with twenty of its members, who withdrew, formed another organization, known as "Calvary." The Sunday-school and week-day services were kept up by the members, and the pulpit supplied occasionally by ministers of the Lutheran and other churches.

The congregation remained in this condition for one year, when, at a meeting of the Philadelphia Conference held in the chapel November, 1874, Rev. P. Raby was appointed to supply the charge temporarily and report to the conference from time to time its condition and prospects. As this arrangement was of the nature of a supply for an indefinite period, and as Rev. Raby was in poor health, he reported the charge vacant and urged conference to provide a regular pastor.

At a special meeting of Conference it was resolved unanimously to appropriate $400.00 for one year, with the expectation that the congregation would raise $200.00 more for support of a pastor. Brother Raby at the same time was appointed missionary for one year. He accepted, taking charge May 23, 1875. From the close of this term until the fall of 1877, the charge was without a regular pastor. The Sunday-school and prayer-meetings were kept up, with a minister occasionally filling the pulpit.

In the fall of 1877 the present church building at Thirty-fifth and Spring Garden streets was purchased from the Presbyterians by the Board of Church Extension, with a mortgage of $7,000.00, $3,000.00 being paid by the Board, who still hold the deed.

After a number of repairs on the building, the congregation called Rev. J. H. Menges as pastor, who accepted, entering upon the work in February, 1878. He served the congregation until July, 1891. Rev. J. H. Main, the present incumbent, preached a trial sermon September 6, 1891, was called in the same month, and entered upon the work of the charge October 25, 1891. May the blessing of Christ, the Head of the Church, abide with this people forever!

LIII. ST. PAUL'S CHURCH, EASTON.*

BY REV. R. W. HUFFORD, D. D.

One of the least edifying things ever seen, in this world of infinite variety, is a church quarrel. It would be pleasant to be able to say that such a thing is unknown. The demands of truth, however, forbid such felicitous romancing. Not a few of the churches now doing good work had their origin in the throes of unseemly strife. The swarm went forth because of a disturbance within the hive.

---

* NOTE.—The first Lutheran pastor whose labors are upon record in what is now the city of Easton was Rev. John Justus Jacob Berkinstock, 1740 to 1748. From the latter year until 1868, when St. Paul's was organized, the

St. Paul's is a child of Christ Evangelical Lutheran Church; but when the child left the old home there was no marked display of parental and filial tenderness. The trouble was, there were two parties in the mother church; the one in sympathy with General Council Lutheranism, the other decidedly General Synod in its preferences. Christ Lutheran Church had belonged to the Synod of East Pennsylvania, and, thereby, to the General Synod, for many years. But in the ecclesiastical unrest of 1866 and 1867 a movement started, that finally took Christ Church into the General Council, and supplied the place thus left vacant by the organization and building of St. Paul's.

Considerable bitterness of feeling was engendered, and some things were said and done that no follower of the Master can recall with pleasure. But time—"that makes all things even"— has done his kindly work, and the two churches and their pastors, though in different Synods, are on friendly terms to-day, and we trust that no cause of strife will ever again disturb them.

The first minute in the record-book of St. Paul's is dated April 17, 1868, and is as follows:

"A meeting of the members of the Lutheran Church was held this evening in the First Baptist Church. The meeting organized with the election of Mr. John Eyerman as Chairman, and C. E. Hecht, Secretary. Mr. Eyerman stated the object of the meeting to be to consult together as to our duty, in view of the distracted condition of so many Lutheran families, and the withdrawal of other entire families from any Lutheran communion. He urged all who loved the Lutheran Church, to consider well whether it was not our duty to organize a third Lutheran congregation in Easton, in which all could unite."

original St. John's congregation was served by the following ministers: Revs. Henry Melchior Mühlenberg and John Nicholas Kurtz, 1749; Rudolph Schrenk, 1749–1754; Bernard Michael Hausihl, 1763–1764(?); Christian Streit, 1769–1779; J. Frederick Ernst, 1780–1782; Solomon Friederici, 1782–1798; Augustus Herman Schmidt, 1799–1801; Christian F. L. Endress, 1801–1815; John P. Hecht, 1815–1845; John W. Richards, 1845–1851; C. F. Schaffer, 1851–1856; Benjamin Sadtler, 1856–1862; B. M. Schmucker, 1862–1867.

The pastors of Christ Lutheran Church from its establishment until the same date were: George Diehl, 1843–1851; Charles Smith, 1851–1854; E. Greenwald, 1854–1867; W. P. Ruthrauff, 1867–1870.

After further consideration, a resolution, offered by Mr. Henry Bender and seconded by Mr. J. M. Dreisbach, "that we will form ourselves into a Lutheran Religious Society," was adopted by a unanimous vote.

At this meeting steps were also taken to rent the Baptist church for alternate Sabbaths, organize a Sunday-school, and raise money for necessary expenses. A committee was appointed to secure pulpit supplies. The temporary organization thus effected was soon superseded by a permanent organization, which was chartered as "St. Paul's (Third) Evangelical Lutheran Church of Easton." The charter members, regularly dismissed from Christ church, numbered forty-nine. Shortly afterwards quite a large additional number was received from the same church.

The first sermon to the new congregation was preached May 24, 1868, by Rev. Theophilus Stork, D. D., of Philadelphia. On the following Sabbath, May 31, Rev. Henry N. Pohlman, D. D., of Albany, N. Y., President of the General Synod, occupied the pulpit. Thus, at the beginning, the new enterprise received aid and encouragement by the presence and counsel of two of the most prominent clergymen of the church.

At a congregational meeting, held August 13, 1868, the first church council was elected, consisting of four elders, viz., John Eyerman, Henry Bender, George Sweeny and John Armbrust; and four deacons, viz., James M. Dreisbach, David Pyatt, D. B. Miller and R. H. Bixler. At this meeting also the Rev. Joseph H. Barclay, of Red Hook, N. Y., was unanimously chosen the first pastor of St. Paul's. He received all the votes of the male members present—the ladies having, at a previous meeting, unanimously decided "that it was their duty to abstain from participating in any election." This preference on the part of the female members was afterwards embodied in the Constitution of the church, except that they are permitted to vote at the election of a pastor. All other elections are conducted by the male members in good standing.

Rev. Barclay's pastorate began December 1, 1868, when he was installed by Rev. Drs. E. W. Hutter, of Philadelphia, and A. C. Wedekind, of New York, and continued to October 1, 1872, nearly four years. During this time the church building on North

ST. PAUL'S EVANGELICAL LUTHERAN CHURCH, EASTON, PA.

Fourth street was erected, at a cost of about $13,000.00. Its dedication took place January 9, 1870. The dedicatory sermon was preached, contrary to the usual custom, by the pastor himself—not from choice, however. The services of Drs. John McCron, of Baltimore, and A. C. Wedekind, of New York, had been engaged for the occasion; but, at the appointed time, Dr. McCron was kept away by sickness and Dr. Wedekind missed the train! It was during Dr. Barclay's pastorate that a mission was started on College Hill which has since developed into St. Peter's (Fifth) Lutheran Church of Easton. After serving churches in Baltimore, and Dayton, Ohio, for about fifteen years, Dr. Barclay died in Baltimore, October 13, 1887.

The second pastor of St. Paul's was Rev. Harvey W. McKnight, called from Newville, Pa. He was elected almost unanimously (but one negative vote being cast). November 6, and took charge of the church a few weeks later, December 1, 1872. The church was not less fortunate in the choice of its second pastor than it had been in its choice of the first. Pastor McKnight's ministry in Easton lasted seven years and five months, and was marked by decided success. He was popular in his congregation and outside of it, and received large accessions to the church. He found the church burdened with a debt of $7,000.00, the greater part of which was paid before the close of his pastorate.

May 1, 1880, the pulpit of St. Paul's again became vacant, the pastor having accepted a call to the First English Lutheran church of Cincinnati. This second pastor of St. Paul's is well known to-day as the Rev. Doctor McKnight, President of Pennsylvania College at Gettysburg.

After an interim of seven months, during which the congregation heard quite a number of candidates—two of whom declined calls extended—the third pastor was chosen, in the person of Rufus Ward Hufford, then serving St. John's Lutheran church, Lancaster, Pa. The election was held October 18, 1880, the candidate receiving all the votes cast but one. On the first Sunday of December following, the newly-elected pastor entered upon his work in Easton. Twelve years have passed since that time, but the third pastorate of St. Paul's has not yet ended.

After its close will be a more befitting time to write its history.

The communicant membership of the church is about two hundred and seventy-five. The elders at this time are Eli M. Fox, Samuel Kleinhans, Alvin F. Nolf and Ephraim Myers. The deacons are John F. Hess, William A. Lanterman, John Manning and George W. Hartzell. During the past year the church gave $502.40 to benevolence—$1.86 per member.

The Sunday-school numbers about two hundred, teachers and scholars. One member of the school is now a junior at college preparing for the gospel ministry in the Lutheran church. A Christian Endeavor Society, organized within the past two years, has fifty-five members and is an efficient aid to the church, being at present enrolled in the number of those that have volunteered to support our last missionary to India. A Dorcas Society of forty members, and a Young Girls' Mission Band, complete the list of organizations within the church.

LIV. EMANUEL'S CHURCH, WILLIAMSTOWN, DAUPHIN COUNTY.

BY REV. J. A. ADAMS.

This congregation began to exist in the year 1871. About the first of April of that year, Rev. Daniel Kloss began to conduct services here in school houses and in churches of other denominations, as these places were available. Some time during the last of April an organization was effected, numbering about twenty members, with the following officers: Elders—E. W. Zerby and Frederick Shindler; Deacons—Alfred Keiser and Charles Highland; Trustees—W. Koenig, J. Hartman and J. Erdman. On May 7, 1871, a constitution was adopted, and the name, "Emanuel's Evangelical Lutheran Church," agreed upon for the congregation.

This congregation was served by Rev. Kloss in connection with that of Lykens, the two constituting "The Lykens Lutheran Pastorate," the pastor preaching once a Sabbath at Williamstown, and receiving as salary from this congregation $175.00, $200.00, and $225.00 per annum. Brother Kloss served this congregation until some time in the spring of 1877, his resignation having been accepted on March 22. During his ministry of six years the church record shows the following: Infant baptisms, 87; confirmations, 68; marriages, 10; burials 26.

A lot was purchased, and a church building, thirty-five by fifty-five feet, was erected thereon, the corner-stone of which was laid A. D. 1874, and the building completed during the year, at a cost of about $2,500.00, about $900.00 remaining unpaid at the close of Brother Kloss' labors in the charge.

During the month of May, 1877, Rev. J. A. Wirt was called as pastor of the charge, who served "the Lykens Lutheran pastorate" until January 1883, a period of about five years and eight months, when he tendered his resignation. Rev. Wirt labored in the Williamstown congregation with great acceptance to the people and good results. He received as salary from this congregation $200.00 and $266.66 per annum. We can not, however, give a detailed account of accessions and losses during his stay with this people as pastor, as we have a record only of infant baptisms and burials, the former numbering 62 and the latter 27. During this pastorate the debt of nine hundred and some dollars, resting on the church property when Rev. Kloss left, was liquidated, and the church property repaired and improved at a cost of between five and six hundred dollars, all of which was paid before Rev. Wirt vacated the charge.

Rev. M. L. Heisler was called as Rev. Wirt's successor, began his labors in May, 1883, and continued to be the pastor until April, 1886, a period of about three years. He received as salary from this congregation $300.00 per annum. During Rev. Heisler's labors in the pastorate the Church Record gives the following: Infant baptisms, 33; confirmation, etc., 17; marriages, 4; burials, 16. Within the same time the church property was repaired and improved, at a cost of between one hundred and two hundred dollars.

At a congregational meeting held December 31, 1885, Emmanuel's Evangelical Lutheran congregation of Williamstown, up to this time a part of "The Lykens Lutheran Pastorate," decided to separate from the Lykens congregation, and in itself constitute a charge and support a pastor. At a joint council meeting of "The Lykens Lutheran Pastorate," January 1, 1886, this action of the Williamstown congregation was made known. There being no objection on the part of the Lykens congregation, the desire of the Williamstown congregation was cheerfully granted, the arrangement to go into effect April 1, 1886.

On February 28, 1886, Rev. M. S. Romig was elected pastor. He began his labors April 1, and continued his ministry among this people until January 1, 1888, a period of one year and nine months. He received as salary six hundred dollars per annum, out of which he was to pay the rent of a house. The Church Record gives as the result of his labors the following: infant baptisms, 45 ; confirmations, etc., 44 ; burials, 21.

The congregation was without a pastor, being served only by supplies, from January 1, 1888, until April 1, of the same year, when the present pastor, Rev. J. A. Adams, began his labors in this relation. During his ministry (April 1, 1888, to September 1, 1892, the date of this writing), a period of four years and five months, the church-book records the following: infant baptisms 79, confirmations, etc., 101, marriages 15, burials 30, losses by letter, etc., 40. The congregation now numbers 147 members. It has a circulation of between forty-five and fifty copies of church papers among its members. During the time of the present pastor's ministry, a good and pleasant parsonage, conveniently located, has been purchased by the congregation, which, with repairs and improvements, has cost not less than eighteen hundred dollars, all of which has been provided for. The salary of the present pastor is six hundred dollars and parsonage.

A Sunday-school in connection with the congregation was established about the same time that the congregation was organized. It has been doing a good work, and now numbers about two hundred members. A little over a year since, a Young People's Luther Alliance was organized, which continues to exist and to be helpful to pastor and people.

It is worthy of note that Mr. E. W. Zerby, who is a member of the congregation at present, was one of the original members of the organization, and has been in connection with the congregation ever since, serving most of the time as an officer, and as superintendent of the Sunday-school.

LV. MEMORIAL CHURCH, HARRISBURG.

BY REV. S. DASHER.

This enterprise was begun about the middle of November, 1867, by a number of Sunday-school workers of the Zion Lutheran Church of Harrisburg, then under the pastoral care of Rev. G. F. Stelling. The Sunday-school was organized in a small school-house on the Jonestown Road, near the present location of the church. Its sessions were held in the morning during the entire year, until about four years ago, when they were changed to the afternoon.

On September 17, 1868, Mr. Shoop and wife conveyed to the Trustees of the Zion church the lot of ground situated at the corner of Fifteenth and Shoop streets in the said city, fronting 100 feet on Fifteenth street and 105 feet on Shoop street, on which the present church building stands. On this lot of ground a chapel was erected by the Zion Lutheran church under the supervision of the above-named pastor, the corner-stone of which was laid on September 28, 1868, and the superstructure completed about June 1, 1869. It was a one-story frame building, with seating capacity for about 225 persons. It was set apart and consecrated under the name and title of the "Lutheran Jubilee Chapel." On the same day, the Sunday-school entered its new and then commodious home, and continued efficient and successful work up to the close of the year 1871, when the council and pastor, Rev. G. F. Stelling, D. D., of Zion Lutheran church, tendered a unanimous call to Rev. S. Dasher. After many earnest entreaties the call was accepted, the salary being $600.00, and the pastor required to find his own residence.

The first sermon was preached by the pastor, on the morning of January 7, 1872, from the text, Psalm xx. 5, "In the name of our God we will set up our banners." There were at this date one hundred and twenty officers, teachers and scholars in the Sunday-school, and a canvass of the territory discovered thirty-five persons who claimed to be Lutherans.

On February 25, 1872, a meeting was called in the chapel for the purpose of effecting an organization. The attendance was large. Rev. G. F. Stelling, who had been invited by the pastor to be present, opened the meeting with appropriate religious exercises. Mr. J. Amos Fisler was called to preside, Mr. Uriah Brown was chosen to act as secretary, and, after the object of the meeting had been stated, thirty-five names were enrolled, and a constitution was submitted and adopted. Eight officers were elected, as follows: Messrs. J. Amos Fisler, J. Potteiger, and C. A. Walters, elders; Messrs. David Mumma, U. H. Brown, and I. W. Hoover, deacons; U. H. Brown, secretary, and David Mumma, treasurer. The work was for some time partially supported by the mother church.

In June, 1885, an application was made and a charter granted, and the church thereupon became self-sustaining. The name was changed to "The Memorial Evangelical Lutheran Church of Harrisburg, Pa."

On July 6, 1886, the proper officers of Zion church conveyed the lot of ground on which the chapel stood to the new corporation for the consideration of one dollar.

On March 17, 1890, sixty-two of the members of the church made application to the council for letters of dismissal, for the purpose of forming a new congregation and locating in a more central place. Among the number were three trustees, one elder, one deacon, and the secretary, superintendent, and a large number of the teachers of the Sunday-school. Their request was granted. Within a short time after, seven more applied for dismissal and were transferred to the new congregation. This left the old church in a weak state, numerically and financially, but it rallied once more, and, with the material left, about 120 members, many of whom had little experience in church affairs, took hold of the work. It was evident, however, that something must be done to infuse new life into the remnant. After earnest thought, prayer, and well-matured plans, ground was broken in the latter part of April, 1891, on the old location, for a new building, the corner-stone of which was laid June 28, 1891, and the work of rearing the superstructure pushed as rapidly as possible to completion.

On February 14, the house was set apart and dedicated to the worship of the Triune God, in the presence of about 800 people.

The morning sermon was preached by Rev. C. S. Albert, D. D., of Baltimore; the evening sermon, by Rev. W. H. Dunbar, of Lebanon. The finances were in charge of Rev. J. A. Wirt, of Hughesville, Pa., and the consecration was performed by Rev. D. M. Gilbert, D. D., of Harrisburg, Pa. The building cost about $14,000.00 and the furnishing thereof about $3,000.00. The seating capacity of the main auditorium is 423. In the Sunday-school building there are three departments, with a seating capacity of at least 600. The main room of the Sunday-school is so constructed that it can be used in connection with the auditorium, which then affords a seating capacity of about 800. This house, built on a beautiful location, towers heavenward as a monument of self-denial and great sacrifice. When the subscriptions are all paid, there will be an indebtedness of between $7,000.00 and $8,000.00. The property, at a low estimate, is worth $20,000.00. The amount of salary now paid the pastor is $600.00, and he is required to find his own home.

The Sunday-school numbers 285 scholars and 30 officers and teachers, and has two departments. A third department will soon be formed.

There are three societies connected with the church, namely, the Ladies' Aid Society, the Christian Endeavor Society, and the Mission Band, all of which are doing good service for the Master.

The present membership of the church is 169, made up of hard-working people, most of whom are of the Lord's poor.

The progress of this work has been slow but steady. For at least eighteen years there were great hindrances. Far to one side of the populous district, with no sidewalks or pavements, and only one street leading to the church, progress was difficult. After a while the old chapel became too small and uninviting; but, thank God, all these things are of the past, and in the near future this beautiful church will be in the centre of a large population.

Up to September 20, 1892, there have been received by regular modes of the church, nearly five hundred persons. The pastor up to that time baptized 450 children; united 462 couples in holy matrimony, and officiated at 744 funerals. He served, in connection with this work, the Shoop's congregation, four miles east of the city, and the Oberlin church, four miles southeast of the city, every two weeks for the term of four years.

Hitherto the Lord has been with this work. To Him be all the glory. His servants take courage and go forward in His name.

LVI. CALVARY CHURCH, WEST PHILADELPHIA.

BY REV. S. A. HOLMAN, D. D.

Calvary Lutheran church, West Philadelphia, was organized May 10, 1874. The congregation at first worshiped in a hall at the corner of Fortieth street and Lancaster avenue. The church

CALVARY EVANGELICAL LUTHERAN CHURCH, WEST PHILADELPHIA, PA.

edifice, south-east corner of Forty-third and Aspen streets, was subsequently built by the congregation, and dedicated to the service of God, December 12, 1875. Recently, an offer having been made for their church, it was sold, and a lot on the south-west corner of Forty-first street and Mantua avenue was purchased. A new church is now being erected, which, it is expected, will be finished May 1, 1893. The location of the new building is several squares north-east of the old church. It is near the Forty-first street station of the Pennsylvania railroad, and a few squares south of Fairmount Park. The church has a front on Forty-first street of sixty-one feet, and extends back, for the present, to a depth of fifty-four feet, there being about forty-five feet in the rear of the church on Mantua avenue, over which it is expected, in the future, to extend the building. The church is built of red pressed brick, with the arches over the windows and doors of Pompeian brick. The membership of the congregation is 120; scholars and teachers in Sunday-school, 274. Rev. S. A. Holman, D. D., has been pastor of the congregation since its organization.

LVII. ST. STEPHEN'S CHURCH, LANCASTER.
BY REV. E. MEISTER.

St. Stephen's German Lutheran church is the youngest Lutheran congregation in Lancaster. Its house of worship, which is situated on the corner of Duke and Church streets, measures 49x75 feet, and has a steeple and spire 172 feet in height. The congregation was organized July 19, 1874, at which time the necessity of a second German Lutheran church was felt. There were only seventeen families at the above-named time to start the new church. Its first officers and church council were Messrs. Adam Oblender, John Ochs, C. P. Krauss, W. C. F. Sheer, Peter Dietz, Henry Zimmermann, John Landau, Bernhard Kuhlmann, B. F. Adams, A. Grötzinger, Jacob Lutz and William Gelzenlichter. The congregation is connected with the East Pennsylvania Synod and through it with the General Synod. Its first pastor was Rev. W. S. Porr.

In 1880 he was succeeded by the present pastor, Rev. E. Meister. Until 1881 the services were held in the lecture room, and on March 13–16, 1881, the main audience room of the church was dedicated. On Trinity Sunday of the following year the church was completed, and beautified with a large pipe organ. The membership of St. Stephen's now is nearly 400 souls. There is connected with this church an excellent Sunday-school, includ-

ST. STEPHEN'S EVANGELICAL LUTHERAN CHURCH, LANCASTER, PA.

ing a flourishing Bible class ; also, under the supervision of the pastor, is a Youths' and Ladies' Society, designed to further the interest of this young but enterprising congregation.

LVIII. ST. PETER'S CHURCH, COLLEGE HILL, EASTON.

BY REV. C. R. TROWBRIDGE AND REV. W. H. DUNBAR, D. D.

In 1870 St. Paul's Lutheran church, Easton, Pa., Rev. J. H. Barclay, pastor, erected a mission chapel on Porter street, near High street, College Hill. It was a frame building of twenty-four by forty feet, with a recess seven feet wide in front, five feet in rear, and three and six-tenths feet deep. The Building Committee were C. Edward Hecht, David B. Miller, Amandus Schug, and William Sweeny, of St. Paul's church. The chapel was finished and dedicated in the fall of 1870, Rev. Dr. F. W. Conrad preaching the dedicatory sermon. This building was afterward changed into and used for some years as a parsonage. It was then sold, and is now used as a private dwelling. In this chapel a Sunday-school was at once established. From the first the work was attended with the most encouraging success. Preaching services were held as those in charge were able to secure some one to break to them the Bread of Life. An occasional sermon was preached by Rev. Dr. Barclay. During the years 1870–1873 the population of College Hill increased with great rapidity. The idea was conceived, and received with great enthusiasm, to organize a congregation. Action was at once taken by St. Paul's Church Council, Rev. H. W. McKnight, pastor, to effect such organization. In July, 1874, a meeting of the people was held in the chapel, at which it was decided to organize the new congregation.

On motion of Ephraim Bower, the name adopted was, "St. Peter's Sixth Lutheran Church of Easton." It was originally designated "Sixth," because there were five Lutheran churches in existence in Easton before this one. It was afterward discovered that the colored church was designated "The First Colored Lutheran Church," and the title of St. Peter's was changed in the charter to the "Fifth Lutheran Church of Easton." The first Church Council consisted of P. A. Shimer, Ephraim Bower, Amandus Steinmetz and James H. Buell, elders; and Edwin Sandt, Isaac Snyder, Noah Deitrich, Daniel Brinker and Van Selan Walter, deacons. These officers were installed in the latter part of July by Rev. H. W. McKnight. Rev. W. H. Dunbar was called as first pastor on Friday, August 28, 1874, and preached his first sermon on the following Sabbath. The congregation was received into the East Pennsylvania Synod at Pottsville, September 9. On May 1, 1875, the congregation was regularly

ST. PETER'S EVANGELICAL LUTHERAN CHURCH, EASTON, PA.

chartered by the Court of Northampton county. The first communion was held October 18, 1874. The number communing was twenty-eight. The whole membership was thirty-six.

At the request of some of the good people, it was determined by the Council that a monthly German service be held. The pastor conducted the first German service on Sunday morning,

October 11, 1874. It was the only such service held. At a meeting of the Church Council, held during the following week, a motion was offered, and without a word of comment, unanimously carried, that there be no more German preaching. The pastor profited by the experience, and has never attempted to preach German since. We can not but think that, so far as the congregation was concerned, the action was wise.

The congregation having grown with great rapidity, early in the spring of 1875 it was decided to build a new church. A Building Committee was appointed, with power to raise money and to carry on the work. The committee consisted of A. Steinmetz, P. A. Shimer and Ephraim Bower, with William Werkheiser as treasurer of the building funds. A lot on the south-east corner of Porter and High Streets was purchased for $1,500.00 by Mr. John Eyerman, of St. Paul's church, and presented to the congregation, upon which it was decided to build. The corner-stone of the new building was laid June 19, 1875. The services were participated in by Rev. H. W. McKnight, of St. Paul's, Rev. Ph. Pfatteicher, of Zion German Lutheran church, Rev. S. Henry, Secretary of the East Pennsylvania Synod, and Rev. Dr. W. C. Cattell, President of Lafayette College. The new church was completed in January, 1876. It is a beautiful and commodious brick building with Sunday-school room adjoining, costing about $12,000.00. It was dedicated January 16, 1876, Rev. Dr. F. W. Conrad preaching the dedicatory sermon.

It is due to Mr. John Eyerman to say that his heart was in this enterprise from the first, and most liberally did he encourage it. In addition to the $1,500.00 for the lot upon which the new church was built, he paid a subscription of $1,500.00 to the new building; at the dedication he subscribed $300.00, and paid for one of the large windows. It was his expressed wish that a mortgage of $5,000.00, held by him against the congregation, should be canceled as soon as a remaining indebtedness of $3,000.00 over and above the mortgage was paid. This wish was carried out through the kindness of Mrs. Eyerman after his death.

After the dedication of the new church, a debt of $5,000.00 remained on the building. The panic of 1874 was just beginning to be felt. Laboring men were without work, and business men had to husband all their resources to keep themselves afloat. It was a severe struggle for the young congregation to meet its obligations. The sacrifices made for the church during those years are seldom surpassed. Rarely have a people given more liberally and worked more faithfully.

The first communion service in the new church, January 23, 1876, was the sixth in the history of the congregation. The number of communicants was 59; the whole number of members, 76. At the next communion, April 16, the number of communicants was 87, and the whole number of members, 116. Rev. W. H. Dunbar resigned in May, 1880.

Rev. H. B. Wile, a graduate of the Theological Seminary at Gettysburg, became pastor in August, 1880. Under his pastorate the church was freed from debt. In September, 1880, the old chapel was changed into a suitable parsonage. This old chapel-parsonage was sold in the fall of 1885, and the present commodious brick parsonage was erected, adjoining the church. Upon the representations of Rev. Wile, and at the earnest solicitation of the congregation, the East Pennsylvania Synod gave $1,000.00 towards the debt on the church, and in 1884 the entire burden was lifted. During the summer of 1884, and prior to the meeting of the East Pennsylvania Synod in Easton in the fall, the church was re-painted and repaired at a cost of $450.00. Rev. Wile resigned September 9, 1885.

Rev. J. B. Keller, of Williamsport, Md., was elected pastor in January, 1886, and assumed charge the following March. He resigned in January, 1888, after a term of not quite two years. During his pastorate the membership increased some forty or more.

Rev. Chas. R. Trowbridge, of Trenton, N. J., was elected pastor on May 18, 1888, and assumed charge of the work on August 22, 1888. During his pastorate, seventy-four were added to the membership of the church. On October 25, 1891, a brick addition, sixteen by twenty-two, to the Sunday-school room, for the use of the infant school, was thrown open and dedicated, free of debt. The total cost was $450.00. Rev. R. W. Hufford, D. D., and Rev. T. C. Pritchard, assisted in the dedicatory services. Two young men of this congregation have entered the ministry. They are Rev. Chas. M. Sandt, formerly pastor at Gordon, Pa., temporarily residing at Easton, and Rev. C. E. Walter, who is now the assistant pastor of Trinity Lutheran Church, Germantown, Pa.

The ladies of the congregation deserve much credit for their activity in efforts to assist in meeting the financial obligations of the congregation. At various times Aid or Mite Societies have done good work, and have raised a great deal of money by their labor. On November 1, 1891, a Society of Christian Endeavor was formed, with some twenty or more active members. A Circle of King's Daughters is also in existence among the young ladies of the congregation. During the winter of 1890-1891, a Circle of King's Sons maintained semi-monthly prayer-meetings among the young men of the congregation with some success.

The salary paid to the pastor at present is $650.00, with parsonage, a total of perhaps $750.00 or $800.00.

The Sunday-school consists of two departments—the primary, with three officers and teachers and eighty-five scholars; and the intermediate, with twenty-three officers and teachers and one hundred and four scholars.

The present indebtedness on the parsonage is $1,250.00, and on a house and lot adjoining the parsonage, also owned by the congregation, $950.00, making a total indebtedness of $2,300.00.

LIX. ST. JOHN'S, STEELTON, DAUPHIN COUNTY.

BY REV. M. P. HOCKER.

St. John's Evangelical Lutheran congregation of Steelton, Pa., dates its history from January 31, 1875, when, in the old brick school-house until recently standing on South Second street, a congregation was organized by Rev. E. Daron, who was then serving what was known as the Shoop's pastorate, and who had preached in the school-house at stated periods before this date. A Sunday-school had been organized as early as November 22, 1874, with about twenty pupils. The first officers of the school were: Superintendent, F. C. Earnest; Secretary, John A. Mc-

Clure ; Librarians, C. A. Dobson and Martin Sharlock ; Managers, Jacob Felty, Henry Lenhart, Mrs. Dobson, and Mrs. Sharlock ; Treasurer, Jonas Books.

When the congregation was organized a few months later the following Church Council was chosen : Trustees, Jacob Lenhart, David Sloop, and Henry Miller ; Elders, Christian Harm and F. C. Earnest ; Deacons, J. A. McClure and Martin Hocker ; Treasurer, Jonas Books.

ST. JOHN'S EVANGELICAL LUTHERAN CHURCH, STEELTON, PA.

The congregation was united with the Shoop's pastorate, and Rev. Daron became the first pastor. From its beginning the congregation gave evidences of intense activity, and, though few in numbers, arrangements were very soon made to build for themselves a chapel on Locust street, near Second, which building, though several times enlarged, still serves the congregation as a place of worship. The corner-stone was laid on August 15, 1875, and the completed building was dedicated on December 19 of the same year.

Too much praise cannot be given to the few devoted, zealous members who gave themselves so earnestly to this new enterprise. They laid the foundations of that which, under the blessing of Providence, developed into what we now so greatly enjoy. Some of the charter members are still with us, and have the rare satisfaction of working amid abundant fruitage in the garden of their own planting. The debt of gratitude on our part is not limited to members of the Lutheran church. There were those of other denominations who labored with and for this struggling congregation. The names of Mr. and Mrs. Dobson, especially, are most gratefully mentioned by the pioneers in this work whenever reference is made to those days of small things.

Rev. Daron, after serving the congregation a little less than three years, resigned January 1, 1878, and was succeeded by Rev. Samuel Yingling, who took charge June 1, 1878. The latter served the congregation until September 6, 1880, or about two years and three months. About this time the congregation became a distinct pastoral charge, having separated from the Shoop's pastorate.

Rev. Wm. S. Porr became the third pastor, and entered upon his duties October 1, 1880. After serving the church with commendable zeal and remarkable activity for two years and two months, he resigned November 30, 1882. During his ministry, and by his personal efforts largely, the chapel was beautified and rendered much more cheerful. At the close of his administration, and nearly eight years from the date of the organization, the congregation numbered about seventy-five members, with a Sunday-school of about one hundred and fifty.

From the last of November, 1882, until the middle of July, 1883, the congregation suffered from the demoralizing condition of being without a pastor; for, although the present pastor accepted a call February 1, he could not, prior to the above date, exercise any pastoral care, being still a member of the Senior class in our Theological Seminary at Gettysburg, from which institution he was graduated in the latter part of June, 1883, having in the interval, however, served the congregation as a supply. Entering upon his duties in July, 1883, and making a house to-house visitation, in company with our beloved and now sainted brother, D. B. Lupfer, about fifty adherents to the church were found, a number of members having recently removed.

Thus began the second half of the congregation's history up to date. Under the very special blessing and favor of God, during the last nine years the congregation has had a prosperous career. Although we have lost many members by removal and for other reasons, some of which will be referred to later, yet we number over four hundred members to-day, with a Sunday-school of nearly six hundred.

The following marks of prosperity may be noted : net growth of membership, from 50 to 405 ; of Sunday-school, from 150 to 580. The church building has been twice enlarged, and the main body of the church has been beautified. A site for a new church edifice has been bought and paid for at a cost of $5,100.00, not including interest on borrowed money.

The congregation has always responded to worthy appeals for contributions to the various operations of the church at large. We have always met our apportionment, and, with one or two exceptions, have exceeded it every year. We have not been unmindful of the poor. The pastor's salary has been regularly increased, from $500.00 the first year, to $1,000.00 several years ago, and is promptly paid every month.

By the aid of our council, especially that of our deacons, who seem to realize the responsibility of their stewardship and try to keep the church free from debt, the financial condition of our congregation is excellent.

We have also built and already partly paid for a chapel on South Second street, where the mother congregation has organized a mission church, and for several years prior had maintained a Sunday-school, for one year supporting a missionary on the ground.

We have never aimed merely at numerical growth, for, while we believe that the church is the divinely ordained institution in which, by the faithful use of the means of grace, men are to be saved and prepared for heaven, yet our council has regularly stricken from the roll the names of those who have given unmistakable evidence that they were not striving to walk in the faith, and who have persisted in a wilful dereliction of duty in the face of patient forbearance and sincere efforts to reclaim them.

We have sustained heavy numerical losses during the past several years, by the death of prominent members and the removal of others from the locality. We dismissed a number to assist in organizing St. Paul's mission. By the organizing of the German Lutheran congregation several years ago we lost some members, and when St. Mark's congregation was organized we gave letters of dismissal to six male and fifteen female members.

Our Church Record reveals the gratifying fact that we have received into church fellowship in the last eight and a half years 575 members, an average of nearly 68 each year. Of these, 163 were received by letter, 132 by profession of faith, 86 by baptism, 192 by confirmation, and 2 by restoration. During this time 315 infants were consecrated to God in holy baptism, 123 marriages solemnized, and the pastor officiated at 169 funerals.

The congregation has entered upon the eighteenth year of its existence under most encouraging circumstances. The past year was, in many particulars, the most prosperous. Perfect harmony prevails. There seems to be a disposition on the part of most of our members to respect each other's opinions and regard each other's feelings, a disposition that must characterize the true Christian and the congregation that would expect the blessing of heaven upon their work.

The initiatory steps have been taken to build a large and handsome church edifice for the comfort and increased facilities of the congregation. It is not considered wise to hasten this important work unduly; but by careful, deliberate counsel, accompanied by harmonious, concerted action, we confidently hope to realize, in the near future, what we so ardently desire and so greatly need, viz.: a commodious and attractive house of worship. With gratitude and extreme delight we note that one year ago the congregation gave their first candidate for the holy ministry, Webster C. Spayde, whom they supported one year in the preparatory department at Gettysburg.

May the rich blessing of God continue to abide with us!

LX. CENTRAL CHURCH, PHŒNIXVILLE, CHESTER COUNTY.

BY REV. JOHN KLING.

The Central Lutheran church of Phœnixville, Pa., was organized by Rev. S. S. Palmer, pastor of the Pikeland church, on December 5, 1875, with eleven members. The following is the list of names: Mrs. Elizabeth Tustin, Mrs. Sarah Auld, Miss Jane Auld, Miss Annie Rixstine, Miss Sarah Wells, Mrs. Mattie Caveny, William E. Caveny, Mrs. Emma C. Gregg, Mrs. Sophia King, Henry Rixstine and Thomas King.

The following-named brethren constituted the first official board of the church: Thomas King, William E. Caveny, Harmon Kanouse, Henry Rixstine, Jonas Tustin, William C. Dettra, Benjamin F. Auld, Davault Beaver.

The first sermon looking toward the organization was preached by the aforesaid minister in May, 1875, in the Mennonite church, corner of Main and Church Streets, permission having been granted through the earnest efforts of Thomas King, a member of the Pikeland congregation.

At a regularly-called meeting held on December 25, 1875, the Mennonite congregation (being about to abandon their work in the town) unanimously agreed to convey their church property to the Lutherans upon the following conditions, viz.: That the latter should assume the indebtedness upon the property, and that they should hold the property for divine worship. These conditions were unanimously accepted by the Lutherans. In accordance with an act of the State Legislature, passed in 1873, and by action of the courts of Chester county, on May 17, 1878, the church became an incorporate body. The circumstances which led to the organization were such as are common in nearly all growing towns, viz.: Lutherans were coming in from the surrounding country, locating in the town, and going into churches of other denominations.

The congregation has been served by the following-named pastors: Rev. S. S. Palmer, from December 5, 1875, to August, 1880; Rev. W. M. Baum, Jr., from October 1, 1880, to January 29,

1883; Rev. Philip S. Hooper, from March 1, 1883, to August 1, 1886; Rev. H. C. Grossman, from November 1, 1886, to November 1, 1890.

The present pastor, Rev. John Kling, commenced his labors February 19, 1891. The church has not been associated with any other in pastoral relation.

The building is of stone, and was erected by the Mennonites in 1789. It was repaired by them in 1873, and again repaired by the Lutherans in 1890.

The congregation has no parsonage. Present indebtedness is $320.00. The amount of salary paid the present pastor is $800.00, and $15.00 monthly toward the rental of the pastor's house.

The Sunday-school, previous to the organization of the church, was known as a Union school; but after the organization it immediately became Lutheran, with about fifty members. The first superintendent of this newly-organized school was Wm. E. Caveny.

A Woman's Home and Foreign Missionary Society was organized in 1885, during Rev. Hooper's pastorate, which continues its work.

In May, 1890, a Young People's Society of Christian Endeavor was organized, which is, indeed, a source of great and efficient help in the work of the church. We also have what is called a "Good Will Society," which is not only of a social character, but of financial aid.

About forty copies of the *Lutheran Observer* are taken by the congregation, thirty copies of the *Missionary Journal*, and one hundred copies of the *Lutheran Sunday-School Herald*.

The present membership of the church is 164, and the present condition and outlook are quite encouraging to both pastor and people.

LXI. ST. PAUL'S, GORDON, SCHUYLKILL COUNTY.

BY REV. A. R. GLAZE.

Gordon is situated in the west-central part of Butler township, Schuylkill county, Pa. It bears its name in honor of Judge Gordon, of Reading. The first congregation for religious worship was assembled in a school-house in the outskirts of the village (now a borough), about 1854, by Rev. Joseph Adams, who was located in Northumberland county and was a member of the Northumberland Presbytery. He preached at Gordon every two weeks for several years. There were a few Methodist families in the village; and, during the ministrations of Rev. Adams, a union Sunday-school, composed of Presbyterians and Methodists, was organized in the same school-house and conducted very successfully.

The first Methodist preaching at Gordon was in the year 1857, by Rev. J. A. DeMoyer, who was stationed on what was then the Catawissa circuit of the Baltimore Conference.

Rev. Robert C. Bryson, of Ashland, became the successor of Rev. Adams, serving also the Presbyterian congregation at Gordon.

It was not long until the school-house became too small to accommodate the children for the public school. Then a new school-house was built nearer the centre of the village.

In the year 1859 a Methodist society was organized. Worship was held every two weeks alternately in the new school-house by the Presbyterians and Methodists for about a year. The various preachers supplying the Methodist society from time to time came from the surrounding towns. Rev. Bryson continued to serve the Presbyterians, whose church outnumbered the Methodists. When it was thought expedient to erect a church edifice, a vote was taken by the citizens to decide which denomination should have the choice of building. It was decided in favor of the Presbyterians, who, in 1860, built the church beside the public school-house, on the lot presented by the McKnights of Reading, and secured a clear title for the same. The edifice cost about $2,500.00. The Northumberland Presbytery donated $1,000.00 towards the enterprise. This edifice remained in possession of the Presbyterians until December 2, 1872, when, on account of their decrease in membership, caused by many removals, it was sold to the Methodists, who had by this time increased in membership, for the sum of $1,300.00.

In the meanwhile several Lutheran families appeared in the

place. These, with the surviving Presbyterians, were served successively by Revs. Sikes, Curtis, and Hackenberg, pastors of the Lutheran church at Ashland. An Episcopalian minister of Ashland, by the name of Washburne, also served them for a while. In 1876 the church, being involved in debt, was sold, and purchased by the Lutherans for $600.00, the Methodist Society being compelled to seek a shelter elsewhere.

The Lutheran church at Gordon was organized by Rev. O. D. S. Marcley, September 3, 1876, with thirty-three members. The following were the officers elected at the time of its organization: Elders, Thomas Rasbridge and W. H. Anthony; Deacons, George F. Rick, Charles F. Hoffman, Joseph L. Harper, Edward G. Ebling, Boaz Dreher, and Frederick Rice. Rev. O. D. S. Marcley was elected its first pastor. From the time of its organization until February 3, 1886, it formed a part of the Ashland pastorate, and Rev. Marcley was succeeded as pastor May 16, 1878, by Rev. D. E. Rupley, and he, November 1, 1879, by Rev. J. H. Weber.

During the ministry of the last-mentioned pastor, a revival, in February of 1880, resulted in general good and thirty-four additions to the church. An organ was purchased in June, 1880, for $250.00. In December, 1880, another great revival was experienced in this church. In December, 1881, a church fair was held, from which $565.00 were realized. In August, 1882, began the work of remodeling the church edifice. This consisted in removing the gallery, putting in stained windows, painting the exterior and papering the interior, securing new pulpit and altar furniture and a new chandelier, at a total cost of $1,000.00. The church was re-dedicated October 29, 1882, free from debt, Rev. F. W. Conrad, D. D., preaching the dedicatory sermon.

October 11, 1885, it was resolved at a joint council meeting that this church separate from the Ashland church and become an independent pastorate no later than July 1, 1886. Accordingly, Rev. J. H. Weber tendered his resignation, to take effect on the date named. He, however, closed his successful services for this people, February 28, 1886, with a morning communion service and the addition of seven members. He found the congregation with 42 members, and left it with 106, and in a prosperous condition.

A bell was purchased in 1878, at a cost of $160.00, and a parsonage was bought, December, 1885, of Mr. George Hudson, for $1,400.00. On the latter, $1,000.00 remain unpaid.

Rev. W. G. Thrall, of South Valley, N. Y., became the first pastor belonging exclusively to the St. Paul's Evangelical Lutheran church of Gordon, and began his labors March 1, 1886, under the most flattering prospects.

A union Sabbath-school had been organized April 2, 1876, with sixty-eight scholars and seven teachers. W. H. Anthony was elected its first superintendent, and held the position many years. Rev. Thrall, while pastor, contended for a separate Lutheran organization. The school is to-day thoroughly Lutheran in name and character, and, under the superintendency of Mr. Thomas Rasbridge, is in a prosperous condition, with one hundred and fifty scholars and twenty-nine officers and teachers. Rev. Thrall ended his labors for this people in December, 1887. Rev. C. W. Sandt was elected as his successor, and served from July 1, 1888 to December 1, 1891.

On the night of March 28, 1890, the church building, along with the school-house, was destroyed by fire, the fire originating in the latter. Then, by the painstaking effort of pastor Sandt, his estimable wife, and a devoted people, a new church edifice was erected where the old building stood, at a cost of $10,000.00. This new house of worship, built of brick, having a large audience-room, with a seating capacity of 350, and a convenient Sunday-school room in the basement, unique in design, magnificent in style of architecture, beautiful in finish, stands as a monument to the zeal and loyalty of a little band of devout followers of the Lord Jesus Christ. It was dedicated to the worship of Almighty God, Sunday, September 27, 1891. Rev. Wm. M. B. Glanding, of Ashland, Rev. J. H. Menges, of Philadelphia, and Rev. J. H. Weber, D. D., of Sunbury, conducted the dedication services.

Rev. A. R. Glaze became the first pastor of the new church, entering upon his work January 1, 1892. The success of his first year's work may be seen in the parochial report to Synod. The synodical apportionment was met, and nineteen new members have been added to the church.

The Presbyterian society at Gordon ended with the disposal of their church property to the Methodists in the year 1876; the Methodist society has a fine church edifice and a beautiful and well furnished parsonage standing side by side in the centre of the borough; but the Lutherans have the most beautiful, substantial and commodious church building in the place, with a suitable lot at the side, donated to the church by Mr. Thomas Rasbridge, one of its original members, for a parsonage.

From September, 1891, to September, 1892, this congregation was, in the Providence of God, enabled to cancel orders to the amount of $5246.19. Its present indebtedness amounts (November, 1892) to $4287.28. The estimated value of its church property is $12,000.00, and its communicant membership is 130. This, with a flourishing Sunday-school, brightens the hope for its future.

LXII. MT. EDEN CHURCH, LANCASTER COUNTY.
BY REV. J. V. ECKERT.

Mount Eden Evangelical Lutheran church is located about thirteen miles south-east of Lancaster, Pa. The church building was erected in the year 1878, and was the result of services held, at intervals of several weeks, in Bowery school-house, Eden township, Lancaster county, by Rev. J. V. Eckert, during the period of about one year. The people began to feel the need of a church, and in the month of March, 1878, a meeting was held to consider the matter, and it was decided to build a Lutheran church, in which, when not used by the Lutherans, other evangelical denominations should have the privilege of holding religious services.

Rev. J. V. Eckert, Benjamin B. Myers, Joseph Wimer, Jacob Eckman, and Samuel A. Keen were appointed the building committee. The corner-stone was laid in the month of May, 1878, and the church building was completed in October of the same year; but in consequence of a severe equinoctial rain-storm, which did considerable damage to the building, it was not dedicated until May, 1879.

The ministers present at the laying of the corner-stone were

Rev. J. V. Eckert, Lutheran, Rev. J. A. Cooper, Methodist, and Rev. W. G. Cairnes, Presbyterian. Those present at the dedication were Rev. J. V. Eckert, Lutheran, Rev. S. E. Herring, Lutheran, and Rev. W. G. Cairnes, Presbyterian.

The building is of brick, covered with slate, and is thirty-five by forty-three feet in dimensions, with a cemetery of one-half acre connected with it, and hitching-ground enclosed with suitable fencing. The cost of the building was about $2,000.00, and the entire ground was donated by Levi Rhoads, of Bird-in-Hand, Lancaster county, who owns the farm from which the ground was taken. The church building is beautifully located in the country, and the burying-ground is of a sandy, barren soil, and free of stones.

After the dedication of the building a congregation was organized by the election of James Creswell and Joseph Wimer, elders; David Haverstick, Jr., and George Gaul, deacons; Benjamin B. Myers, Jacob Eckman and Samuel A. Keen, trustees.

The original members at the organization were James Creswell, Elizabeth Creswell, David Haverstick, Sr., Elizabeth Haverstick, Joseph Wimer, Elizabeth Wimer, Abraham Myers, Ann Herr, John Carnathan, Levinia Carnathan, David Haverstick, Jr., Elizabeth Haverstick. Rev. J. V. Eckert was elected pastor, and has remained such up to the present time.

The people of the community in which the church is located were previously rather destitute of church privileges, and therefore unaccustomed to attend any services regularly. They have, since the erection of the building and organization, manifested an awakened interest in religious services.

The congregation at present consists of about forty-five members, and is an incorporated body, the charter having been granted by the court February 14, 1887. The field of religious work is limited. Material advancement is difficult, as the locality is not wealthy. The church is now only thirteen years old. It has had no basis of traditional Lutheranism, and therefore will require time to engraft itself well in the community.

LXIII. FIRST LUTHERAN, SHENANDOAH, SCHUYL-KILL COUNTY.

BY MR. WM. A. KEAGEY.

The First English Lutheran church of Shenandoah, Pa., was organized December 18, 1881, in Egan's Hall. The following were enrolled as members: J. H. Kurtz, Jacob Glover, John C. Glover, H. L. Neff, Henry Miller, Mrs. J. H. Kurtz, Mrs. Jacob Glover, Mrs. John C. Glover, Mrs. H. A. Swalm, Mrs. D. W. Glover, Mrs. I. P. Neff, Miss Mary Glover, Miss Maggie Glover, Miss Robena Glover, Miss Sue C. Neff.

Rev. I. P. Neff was chosen as pastor. The following officers were elected by acclamation: Elders, J. H. Kurtz and H. Miller; Deacons, Jno. C. Glover and H. Neff; Secretary, J. C. Glover; Treasurer, J. H. Kurtz.

At 1:30 o'clock on the same day, the Sunday-school was organized, with J. H. Kurtz as superintendent, Henry Miller, assistant superintendent, John C. Glover, treasurer, Maggie Glover, secretary, and the following as teachers: Robena Glover, Annie Kurtz, Mary John, Geo. Kurtz and John C. Glover.

A congregational meeting was called on April 1, 1883, for the purpose of devising plans for building a church. J. C. Glover was appointed as a committee to solicit money for the purpose of building, and at the same meeting secured $374.00. On May 8, 1883, the congregation bought a lot from J. H. Kurtz for the consideration of $1,250.00, and the following persons were appointed by the pastor, Rev. I. P. Neff, as a building committee: J. H. Kurtz, Jacob Sanders, Henry Miller, Geo. Wagner, Jno. C. Glover.

The next minutes are dated September 30, 1883, with Rev. Walter Miller in the chair. On March 12, 1884, fifteen hundred dollars was received from the Board of Church Extension. Rev. Walter Miller resigned October 14, 1885. On January 31, 1886, Rev. D. A. Shetler became pastor, and continued up to July 10, 1888. On June 10, 1889, Rev. D. B. Treibley was elected pastor of the church, and served until August 1, 1891. Rev. M. H. Havice was then called to the charge. He entered upon his work here December 1, 1891, and is the present pastor.

The church appears to be now on a good footing and should prosper. The membership is about ninety. The Sunday-school numbers over one hundred. The sermons of the pastor are appreciated, and the congregation is harmonious.

LXIV. BETHANY (FORMERLY ELIZABETH MONROE SMITH MEMORIAL) CHURCH, PHILADELPHIA.

BY REV. S. G. SHANNON.

Bethany is one of the youngest churches in the north-western section of the city of Philadelphia. It is not yet ten years old, and these have been years of toil, self-denial and anxiety to the little band of faithful soldiers of the Cross. Of this church it can truthfully be said: "They have come up through much tribulation." A preliminary meeting was held at the residence of R. I. Heim, October 22, 1883, looking toward the organization of a General Synod Lutheran Church somewhere in the north-western section of the city. The following persons were present: R. I. Heim, C. F. Reinstein, W. H. Faunce, George F. Bultman, Jas. Lehman and George C. Bultman, Jr. After considerable deliberation, R. I. Heim was elected chairman, G. C. Bultman, Jr., secretary, and W. H. Faunce, treasurer, in order to carry the project to a more complete and successful end.

Several meetings were held in private residences, and one public meeting in the Independent M. E. church on Ridge avenue, near Twenty-fifth street, October 28, 1883, which was addressed by Rev. L. E. Albert, D. D., Rev. W. M. Baum, D. D., Rev. E. Huber, and Rev. J. H. Menges. This meeting proved a great stimulus toward a permanent organization, which was effected November 4, 1883, with eighteen members, in a hall at No. 2529 Ridge avenue.

Rev. John R. Williams became pastor, and held the first regular service in the aforesaid hall the same day.

He was formally installed as pastor, January 3, 1884. A constitution for the better government of the newly-formed congregation was adopted on Wednesday evening, January 23, 1884.

At a congregational meeting held September 21, 1884, it was resolved to make formal application to be received into, and become an integral part of, the *East Pennsylvania Synod.* This resolution, with a formal application, was presented to Synod, which was then in session at Easton, Pa., by R. I. Heim, and the congregation regularly admitted.

BETHANY EVANGELICAL LUTHERAN CHURCH, PHILADELPHIA, PA.

On December 1, 1884, by action of a committee appointed for the purpose, of which R. I. Heim was chairman, the lot at the corner of Twenty-fifth street and Montgomery avenue was purchased, for the sum of $7,333.33.

On January 5, 1885, the congregation was incorporated under the corporate title of "The Memorial Lutheran Church of Philadelphia."

At a congregational meeting held June 10, 1885, it was resolved to erect a chapel on the recently purchased lot, whereupon Rev.

J. R. Williams, Lewis H. Bolton, C. F. Reinstein, R. I. Heim and C. E. Bauder were appointed a building committee to carry out the design of the congregation. Accordingly, a contract was entered into with J. M. Anderson, of Philadelphia, for the erection of a stone chapel forty by seventy feet, for the sum of $6,000.00, which sum was increased $500.00 by deviations from the original design.

The chapel (a cut of which is herewith presented) was completed and dedicated to the service of Almighty God April 11, 1886. Rev. J. C. Zimmerman, Secretary of the Board of Church Extension, and Rev. F. W. Conrad, D. D., editor of the *Lutheran Observer*, officiated on the occasion, other Lutheran pastors of the city assisting the pastor *loci*.

The requisite amount of money to satisfy the claims of the contractor was not realized on the day of dedication, and, after the most strenuous self-denial and sacrifice on the part of members, the congregation was unable to meet the demands or longer carry the debt.

On May 30, 1886, the contractor notified the council that he would place a builder's lien on the church, which was promptly executed. On September 6 of the same year an advertisement of sale was placed on the church door, and on September 20, 1886, the sheriff of Philadelphia sold the building to J. M. Anderson's attorney, Samuel Baker, for the sum of fifty dollars ($50.00) subject to the claim against it, deeded the same to the said Anderson, and at the same time served a notice on the congregation to vacate the premises, or lease the same from him at a rental of $60.00 per month in advance. This was disheartening to the little band of earnest workers who had invested their all for the purpose of having a church home, and they were almost ready to disband. Some of the more enthusiastic members thought they could see day dawning in the distance, and believed there was yet a future for a General Synod Lutheran church in the north-western part of this great city. They encouraged the weaker ones to hold on, even though the future looked dark and unpromising. After much prayer and deliberation, the congregation determined to make another heroic effort. Having no church home, and there being no other alternative, the congregation resolved to pay the rent demanded, which they did for nearly five months, during which period an amicable arrangement was effected between the contractor and the congregation, and, according to agreement, the church was re-sold by the sheriff of Philadelphia, December 28, 1886, for the sum of $5,050.00, R. I. Heim becoming the purchaser for the congregation.

The congregation, now once more in possession of their own church home, sought assistance and sympathy from philanthropic persons. Overtures were made to the (now deceased) benevolent John F. Smith, of Broad Street, Philadelphia, who generously came to the rescue. A proposition was made to memorialize the chapel to his deceased wife, Elizabeth Monroe Smith, on condition that he would pay $4,000.00, which he did.

At a congregational meeting held March 6, 1886, it was resolved to change the corporate title to the "Elizabeth Monroe Smith Memorial Evangelical Lutheran Church of Philadelphia." Accordingly, a petition, dated May 2, 1887, was sent up to the Court of Philadelphia, praying for a change of charter, and on June 2, 1887, the Court granted the prayer of the petitioners, and the chartered title was changed to the above. Rev. John R. Williams resigned as pastor September 23, 1888, the resignation to take effect on the 30th day of the same month.

At a congregational meeting held January 2, 1889, Rev. S. G. Shannon, of Sunbury, Pa., was unanimously elected pastor, and a call was extended to him at an annual salary of $1,400.00, the Home Mission Board agreeing to pay seven hundred of the above amount the first year. After due deliberation the call was accepted, and he entered upon his duties as pastor of the congregation April 4, 1889, and was formally installed June 2, 1889. Rev. E. Huber, D. D., pastor of Messiah Lutheran church of Philadelphia, delivered the charge to the pastor, and Rev. H. M. Bickel, office editor of the *Lutheran Observer*, delivered the charge to the congregation.

At this time a mortgaged debt of $10,500.00 rested on the church property. A systematic effort was engaged in to liquidate this bonded indebtedness, which was only partially successful, on account of the Memorial Title of the church. Mr. Smith had died, meanwhile, and persons not related to Mrs. Smith hesitated to contribute to the completion of the work. This was reported to the East Pennsylvania Synod, and at its meeting held at Middletown, Pa., September 16–22, 1891, the following was offered by Rev. H. W. McKnight, D. D., LL.D.:

"*Resolved*, That a committee of five be appointed to unite with the pastor and church council of the Elizabeth Monroe Smith Memorial Lutheran Church of Philadelphia, in the effort to induce the Smith heirs to pay the indebtedness on the property."

The President of Synod appointed as such committee Rev. R. W. Hufford, D. D., Rev. H. W. McKnight, D. D., LL.D., Rev. Eli Huber, D. D., Mr. Henry S. Boner and F. A. Hartranft, Esq. This committee, in company with the pastor, Rev. S. G. Shannon, held a colloquium with Mr. Monroe Smith, son of John F. Smith, deceased, and representing the estate. This meeting was fruitless so far as the liquidation of the debt was concerned, but an agreement was effected to join in a petition to the court to remove the Memorial and change the chartered title, providing the congregation thought best. Accordingly a congregational meeting was held November 11, 1891, at which it was unanimously decided that it was to the best interests of the congregation to secure a release of the said Memorial and a change of the corporate name.

A joint petition of the congregation and Monroe Smith and Mary A. Smith (now Combs), children and heirs of John F. Smith, deceased, through their legal attorney, was presented to the court, praying a change of corporate title from "The Elizabeth Monroe Smith Memorial Evangelical Lutheran Church of Philadelphia" to "Bethany Evangelical Lutheran Church of Philadelphia." The prayer of the petitioners was granted by Court No. 1 of Philadelphia, January 6, 1892.

At a regularly-called congregational meeting held May 18, 1892, it was

Resolved, To enlarge our church capacity by the erection of a permanent building on the rear of the lot.

The pastor was appointed to canvass for funds for this purpose. This canvass is now in progress, with what result time alone will tell.

LXV. BETHLEHEM CHURCH, HARRISBURG.

BY REV. W. H. FISHBURN.

In February, 1875, Rev. George F. Stelling, D. D., then pastor of Zion Lutheran church, Harrisburg, Pa., originated a movement in the Sunday-School Association of his charge, having for its object the establishing of a mission school in West Harrisburg, "to care for the Lutheran interests in that part of the city." The result of the steps taken was the organization of Bethlehem Lutheran Mission Sunday-school, on April 4, 1875. It first met in a rented room on Broad street. Mr. L. H. Kinnard was chosen superintendent; Mr. James M. Miller was the secretary, and Dr. Charles T. George was the teacher of the Bible class. A corps of faithful and efficient co-workers made steady progress. Many of the first workers in the Mission "remain unto this present, but some are fallen asleep." The Mission School occupied the rented room for eleven years. The discouragements, the trials and disappointments, the headaches and heartaches, the self-denials and thankless labor—with efforts to do good frequently misunderstood and unappreciated—that were encountered in those years by the faithful mission workers, cannot be detailed. Yet the school was kept alive, the laborers hoping that a better time would come.

The plot of ground now occupied by chapel and tabernacle, at the corner of Green and Cumberland streets, was purchased in 1879, but it was not until 1885 that a contract was made for the erection of the first building for Sunday-school and other purposes. The corner-stone of the chapel was laid on August 23, 1885, by Rev. A. H. Studebaker, then pastor of the mother church, and on March 21, 1886, the structure was dedicated by the same minister. This building, which is of brick, with brown-stone trimmings, in Romanesque architecture, is forty-five by ninety-five feet in dimensions, and was comfortably furnished. A week after the dedication, the Sunday-school was transferred to its first *home*, and officers and teachers realized that their labors had not been in vain.

In the fall of 1886 a weekly prayer-meeting was established; a few months later the workers in the school, together with a few others in the western part of the city, feeling that the distance to Zion was great, that the mother church could spare them, and that a Lutheran church was needed in this locality, expressed a desire for a separate organization. Overtures were made to the church council of Zion, having this end in view, the mother church gave her consent, and on March 5, 1887, the Court of Dauphin county granted a charter to "Bethlehem Lutheran church of Harrisburg, Pa." The charter was granted on March

BETHLEHEM EVANGELICAL LUTHERAN CHURCH, HARRISBURG, PA.

5, on Saturday. On Tuesday, March 8, just three days afterwards, a congregational meeting was held for the purpose of electing a pastor, and it resulted in the election, by a unanimous vote, of Rev. William Haller Fishburn. A call was extended to him, and, after mature deliberation, he accepted it.

The formal organization of Bethlehem Lutheran church took place on May 15, 1887, when pastor Fishburn preached his introductory sermon. Zion church was closed that day, and the entire membership was present with Bethlehem, to wish the new-born child God's blessing. Prof. Knoche, the organist of Zion, with the choir of Zion, led the singing. The children of Albert and Catharine Hummel presented the new congregation with a silver communion service, in memory of their parents; and the Bible class of Dr. C. T. George made the church a gift of six silver plates for the offerings.

On the following Sunday, May 22, pastor Fishburn received one hundred and six members into full communion with the church, eighty of whom came by certificate from Zion church. From this date services were regularly held in the unpretentious chapel, which, although large, soon became overcrowded. The officers in the first church council were as follows: Trustees, Dr. Charles T. George and L. H. Kinnard; Elders, Alexander Blessing and Adam Reel; Deacons, James M. Miller, Henry Fraley, Charles M. Singer, Charles C. Schriver, James H. Lytle and Charles Y. Fink; Treasurer, Alexander Blessing; Secretary, James M. Miller.

The crowds soon became so great that the chapel was altogether too small to accommodate them. A larger building became imperative. But the congregation did not feel able to erect a large building of costly material. Mr. Fishburn suggested a "Tabernacle" of wood, built to accommodate 2,000 or more people, and so constructed that it could afterward be covered with some incombustible material. He preached about the needs of the congregation, and in June, 1889, when the organization was only two years old, it was decided to build a big tabernacle. Plans were approved, and the contract let to Joshua Sweeger, of Newport. The new building, with its furnishings, cost $25,000.00. It was formally dedicated to Almighty God on November 2, 1890, the pastor's father, Rev. Jeremiah Fishburn, of Elizabethtown, conducting the services of consecration. The tabernacle is the most beautiful church building in Harrisburg. It is seated with assembly chairs that are convenient and comfortable, and so arranged that all their occupants are brought within easy hearing distance of the preacher. Wide stairways lead from the pulpit platform to the galleries, which are also seated with assembly chairs. In the front, facing the pulpit, is the choir gallery, on which is a magnificent three-manual organ, containing 1859 speaking pipes.

The main auditorium is lighted by fifty-seven windows of cathedral glass of richest colors. The pulpit is of brass, and is on the large platform between the stairways.

In the new building the congregation's growth has been rapid. On the first Easter after dedication 106 new members were received; and on the following Easter, 193. Members have been received every time the communion has been celebrated. The total membership is now between 700 and 800.

From time to time pastor Fishburn has found it necessary to increase the number of men in the working council of the church, until it now numbers 2 trustees, 4 elders, 12 deacons, 12 advisers, 12 third committeemen, 60 auxiliaries, a treasurer, and the pastor, —in all, 104 men. The city has been divided by the pastor into twelve wards, and over each ward a committee of eight men is placed. A complete directory of the church and all its auxiliary societies is published annually. There are in connection with the church a Mite society, a Social Circle, a Christian helpers' society, a senior and junior Young People's Society of Christian Endeavor, a Sewing society, and other organizations, all of which make the outlook for the future most encouraging.

LXVI. IMMANUEL CHURCH, NORWOOD, DELAWARE COUNTY.

BY REV. E. S. MORELL.

Norwood is a suburban village, situated in Delaware County, Pa., on the Philadelphia, Wilmington and Baltimore Railroad, about eight and a half miles from Broad and Market Street Station, Philadelphia. In the former part of June, 1888, Rev. E. S. Morell, pastor of the St. James' Lutheran Church at Chalfont, Bucks County, Pa., visited Norwood, and ascertained that there was no religious organization there save a few Methodists, who held religious services in a room of a vacant dwelling-house, and that a large proportion of the population were of Lutheran persuasion. Regarding it as a promising field for mission work, he held a consultation with the brethren in Philadelphia, and a self-appointed committee, consisting of Rev. Wm. M. Baum, D. D.,

Rev. Eli Huber, D. D., Henry S. Boner, Superintendent of the Lutheran Publication House, and Rev. E. S. Morell, visited the locality. After a careful observation, all were favorably impressed, and decided that a Mission of our church should be started at once. A communication was then sent to Rev. Jacob A. Clutz, Secretary of the Board of Home Missions, directing his attention to it. In the meantime, permission was obtained from the public school directors to hold meetings in the school building. Circulars were then distributed throughout the community, in-

IMMANUEL EVANGELICAL LUTHERAN CHURCH, NORWOOD, PA.

forming them that a Lutheran Sabbath-school would commence on the following Sabbath afternoon, and also requesting the parents to assemble there on Sabbath evening.

The attendance at the first session of the Sabbath-school was nine adults and twenty-eight children. An organization was then effected, with Chas. G. Boekenkamp, a staunch Lutheran, as its Superintendent. In the evening, about sixty adults were present, and a preaching service was conducted by Rev. E. S. Morell. On July 29, 1888, Rev. Jacob A. Clutz, Secretary of the Board of Home Missions, was present at the morning and evening service.

He preached in the morning, and Rev. E. S. Morell in the evening. When, before closing the service, Rev. Clutz asked for an expression by a rising vote, of the willingness of those present to co-operate in the work of a Mission enterprise, there was a unanimous response.

After the return of the Secretary to Baltimore, the Board of Home Missions sent a commission to Rev. E. S. Morell to commence the establishment of a Lutheran Mission at Norwood, Delaware County, Pa., September 1, 1888. The organization of a church was formally effected, September 30, 1888, with twenty-two members, after which a church building-lot in a central locality was purchased for five hundred dollars. Upon this lot the corner-stone for a church building was laid with appropriate services, May 1, 1889, the sermon being preached by Rev. Eli Huber, D. D. The church building was dedicated November 10, 1889, Rev. J. H. Menges preaching the dedication sermon and conducting the financiering. Subscriptions to the amount of $1,010.09, were secured during the day. The total cost of the church building and ground was $5,114.47, which was covered by donations and subscriptions, except about $1,775.00, of which $775.00 has since been paid off, leaving the church encumbered at present with a mortgage of $1,000.00, at five per cent. interest

The present communicant membership is sixty-nine, with a Sabbath-school of one hundred and forty-eight officers, teachers and scholars. Rev. E. S. Morell is the pastor, his salary being six hundred dollars, of which the Board of Home Missions pays three hundred. The members of the Church Council are: Trustees, Chas. G. Boekenkamp, Frank W. Taylor, Dr. J. N. Wunderlich, Theodore Kreeger, Sr.; Elders, John Harrison, Henry Schroeder, Dr. Geo. F. Baier; Deacons, Walter L. Orwig, Chas. H. Boekenkamp, Thos. W. Pennypacker, Jacob Meier.

LXVII. ALL SAINTS' CHURCH, PHILADELPHIA.
BY REV. F. P. MANHART.

In December, 1888, a Lutheran Sunday-school was organized in a building on Sixteenth street, near Cayuga, in the northern part of Philadelphia. The building had been erected by Mr.

Wm. F. Shaw, a large publisher of music, who expected to have a permanent Moravian church established in it. An effort by the Moravians to establish such a church failed ; succeeding efforts to maintain a union Sunday-school languished. Mr. Frank A. Hartranft, an attorney-at-law, and a member of the Messiah Lutheran church, was invited to take charge of the Sunday-school. He did so in December, 1888, with the understanding that the school would become Lutheran, and that the property would be deeded to trustees appointed by the Philadelphia Conference, to be held in trust by them for a congregation to be formed, and to be connected with the Synod of East Pennsylvania.

The conditions were met. The property consisted of a lot thirty four by one hundred and sixty-eight feet, having upon it a building thirty-four by one hundred and twenty-eight feet. It was encumbered by a ground-rent and mortgage, together amounting to $6,200.00. Through the efforts of the Conference and Mr. Hartranft, regular services were maintained from December, 1888, to April, 1889. In February, 1889, Rev. Frank P. Manhart, of Bloomsburg, Pa., was asked to become pastor. He accepted, and commenced his labors on Sunday, April 7, 1889. On April 14 a congregation was organized with seventeen members. It was based upon the doctrinal position and polity of the Synod of East Pennsylvania and the General Synod. On Wednesday, the 17th, a congregational constitution and the name, " All Saints' ", was adopted. (Three adjacent streets being named St. Luke's, St. Mark's and St. Paul's respectively, a desire was felt to secure a name apropos to local surroundings.) A Church Council consisting of the following was elected : Elders, Frank A. Hartranft, Esq., Charles G. Marshall and Hamilton Bingham ; Deacons, Charles C. Hess, Sam. J. Lauber and A. J. Rudolph. The congregation was received into the Synod of East Pennsylvania in September, 1889. At the time of this writing it numbers seventy-seven communicants, and an enrollment in the Sunday-school of two hundred.

On June 1, 1892, it took title to a plot of ground about one-half acre in size, and fronting on Germantown avenue and Cayuga and Nineteenth streets. The cost, $6,000.00, was hardly more than half its market value. It is admirably located, and with its ample proportions offers the best site for the permanent home of All Saints' in its section of the city.

The Common Service has been in continuous use from the beginning. Available "Lutheran material" has been scarce in the neighborhood. In the membership are persons formerly connected with eight different denominations. The neighborhood greatly needs a church of the generous and progressive character which All Saints' aims to maintain.

LXVIII. ST. MATTHEW'S CHURCH, ALLENTOWN.

BY REV. CHAS. E. HAY.

In response to a call appearing in the daily papers of Allentown, Pa., about one hundred persons assembled in a vacant store-room at No. 830½ Hamilton street on the evening of February 4, 1890, to consider the propriety of organizing another English Lutheran church. Mr. Francis S. Wilt was called to the chair, and Mr. Wm. J. Frederick was appointed secretary. It was unanimously decided to establish a congregation to be in connection with the General Synod. Several hundred dollars were provisionally subscribed toward the necessary current expenses for one year. A further meeting was held on February 11, when a provisional form of constitution was adopted and Rev. Chas. E. Hay, who had just resigned as pastor of St. Paul's, was invited to hold services in the store-room on the following Sunday, February 16. The invitation was accepted. Bare floors and unpainted chairs did not in the least detract from the fervor of the enthusiastic and reverent worshipers who filled the room at the appointed hours. During the following week a large, furnished, third-story hall, at the corner of Eighth and Hamilton streets, was rented for an indefinite period at $2.00 per week, the free use of the above-mentioned store-room being kindly granted by its owner, Dr. H. A. Grim, for all meetings during the week.

On February 23, after a brief service, a congregational meeting was held, at which a formal organization was effected and the following were elected as church officers: Elders, P. K. Grim, F.

S. Wilt, H. D. Biever and Edwin Fetzer; Deacons, C. J. P. Bittner, J. C. Kleinsmith, W. J. Frederick, L. O. Shankweiler, I. W. Leiby and J. Lehrman. These brethren were installed at the evening service, and, at a congregational meeting which immediately followed, nominated for the office of pastor Rev. Chas. E. Hay, who was unanimously elected.

ST. MATTHEW'S EVANGELICAL LUTHERAN CHAPEL, ALLENTOWN, PA.

On the afternoon of the same day a Sunday-school was established, with a total enrollment of one hundred and twenty-seven, and a temporary organization with seven officers and eighteen teachers. The church council organized on the following day by electing Mr. P. K. Grim as treasurer, Mr. H. J. Michael as secretary, and Mr. C. J. Bittner as financial secretary.

On March 14, a plot of ground 80x126 feet, at the corner of Tenth and Maple streets, was purchased for $4,200.00, upon the rear of which it was decided to erect a brick chapel 40x75 feet in dimensions. The corner-stone was laid on Whitsunday, May 25, the congregation and Sunday-school marching in a body from the hall to the site. Addresses were delivered by Revs. R. W. Hufford and C. A. Hay, D. D., the pastor conducting the official ceremony, and Revs. J. A. Singmaster and S. A. Repass, D. D., assisting. The Allentown band orchestra kindly furnished appropriate music. The members of the congregation at this time, whose names were deposited in the corner-stone, numbered, with the class of seven catechumens just confirmed, 151. Of these, 133 had withdrawn from St. Paul's congregation.

The completed chapel, costing about $6,000.00, was dedicated October 26, Rev. W. M. Baum, D. D., of Philadelphia, officiating with the pastor. The Sunday-school was addressed in the afternoon by Dr. Baum and Revs. J. A. Singmaster and M. H. Richards, D. D. On the following evenings divine services were conducted, appropriate sermons being preached by Revs. T. C. Billheimer, D. D., C. R. Trowbridge, R. H. Clare and W. H. Dunbar.

The chapel is a neat and substantial structure, with a seating capacity of 450. The large front window was presented by Mr. W. J. Frederick as a memorial of his three bright boys who have been called to the better world. The pastors of the Easton Conference, by personal contributions, provided for two windows, in honor of Revs. A. D. Rowe and C. A. Stork, D. D. The remaining windows were, by the generosity of friends, inscribed to the memory of Rev. G. F. Stelling, D. D., Mrs. Eliza Hay Morris, Mrs. Eliza Ebert Hay, Rev. A. H. Lochman, D. D., Rev. J. A. Brown, D. D., LL. D., Daniel K. Grim, Mrs. Rebecca Young Billmyer, Rev. D. J. Hauer, D. D., Daniel Eppley, Rev. Samuel Yingling, Mrs. Hannah Roth. The central window in the gallery was inserted by the members of the Bible class, in memory of Mr. Franklin K. Kern, who had done efficient service for years as instructor of the English Bible class in St. Paul's. The pulpit furniture was a gift from Messrs. Francis and Frank D. Wilt, the elegant carving being the handiwork of the latter. Organs were presented by Messrs. W. J. Frederick and Irvin F. Kemmerer. Blackboard, clocks, communion services, pulpit Bible and hymn-book, besides many contributions of cash or its equivalent, attested the good-will of members and friends.

The Board of Church Extension granted a loan of $3,000.00 without interest for five years. Beyond this there remains less than $900.00 of indebtedness.

The Board of Home Missions has made an annually decreasing appropriation towards the pastor's salary.

The congregation now numbers one hundred and eighty-three, and expects to become self-sustaining by April 1, 1894.

The Sunday-school has always been a very prominent factor in the work of the Mission. A full organization was not effected until the completion of the chapel, when the following were elected as officers and teachers: General Superintendent, the pastor; General Secretary, J. C. Kleinsmith; General Treasurer, H. D. Biever; Ushers, E. Fetzer, J. H. Millar. Infant Department—Superintendent, I. W. Leiby; Organist, Mrs. L. O. Shankweiler; Teachers, Mrs. Henry Heckman, Mrs. J. B. Frederick, Mrs. C. W. Kleinsmith, Mrs. J. H. Millar, Mrs. C. J. Heckman, Miss Annie M. Weaver. Intermediate Department—Superintendent, W. J. Frederick; Assistant Superintendent, F. S. Wilt; Secretary, J. C. Kleinsmith; Treasurer, H. D. Biever; Librarian, G. H. Schillinger; Organist, Mrs. C. E. Hay; Teachers, H. D. Biever, F. S. Wilt, J. Lehrman, Mrs. H. D. Biever, Mrs. C. E. Hay, Misses Ella Merkle, Hannah Merkle, Millie M. Spatz, Maggie E. Spatz, Emma R. Frederick, Minnie M. Kuntz, Laura A. Weaver. Bible Class—Superintendent, L. O. Shankweiler; Secretary, J. H. Millar; Treasurer, C. J. P. Bittner; Enumerator, G. B. Frederick.

The entire enrollment of the school is at present about three hundred. There are three active organizations which are rendering valuable assistance, *i. e.*, a Ladies' Aid Society, a Young People's Society and a Band of Little Helpers. A parish paper has been found a most useful auxiliary.

St. Matthew's is the seventh Lutheran congregation in a community of 28,000, though but the second in which the English language is exclusively used. Its growth cannot be phenomenal in numbers, but promises to be steady and substantial. Pastor and people labor in entire harmony, and a spirit of hopefulness prevails, which, under the blessing of God, is the surest pledge of a useful and prosperous future.

LXIX. CHRIST CHURCH, HARRISBURG.

BY REV. T. L. CROUSE.

This church was organized March 23, 1890, at a meeting presided over by Rev. D. M. Gilbert, D. D., pastor of Zion Lutheran church, Harrisburg. Sixty-two was the number of members at the time of organization. Sixty of this number had withdrawn from Memorial Lutheran church, believing that there was room for another Lutheran organization in the eastern portion of the city. After the organization, steps were at once taken looking to the erection of a church building. Soon a piece of ground was purchased at the cost of fifteen hundred dollars. In July the ground was broken, and on Sunday afternoon at four o'clock, August 17, 1890, the corner-stone of the new building was laid by the pastor, Rev. Theodore L. Crouse. Rev. E. J. Wolf, D. D., of the Theological Seminary, Gettysburg, was present and delivered an address.

The pastor, Rev. T. L. Crouse, was elected April 23, 1890. He preached his first sermons to the congregation Easter Sunday, April 6, on which day the first communion was celebrated, and several persons received into the church. Rev. Crouse took regular charge of the work July 3, 1890.

All the services of the congregation, including Sunday-school and Wednesday evening prayer meeting, were held, for a period of about eleven months, in one of the upper rooms of the Webster public school building, located at the corner of Thirteenth and Kittatinny streets.

March 15, 1891, the church building was dedicated, Rev. W. S. Freas, of York, preaching the dedicatory sermon. Rev. H. H. Weber, Secretary of the Board of Church Extension, had charge of the finances. About sixty-four hundred dollars were pledged and contributed on that day. Previously about thirty-six hundred dollars had been paid in or subscribed, which, with the contributions and pledges on the day of dedication, covered the cost of the building and lot, which was something more than ten thousand dollars.

The membership at that time numbered ninety-four. The building was set apart to the worship of God by the pastor. The following ministerial brethren took part in the services of the day: Revs. W. S. Freas, H. H. Weber, J. W. Richard, D. D. (who preached in the evening) and F. L. Bergstresser. Rev. S. Dasher was also present both morning and evening.

Three years' time was given in which to pay the subscriptions. The congregation's present indebtedness is something less than four thousand dollars. It does not own a parsonage. The congregation has been self-supporting from the beginning.

The Sunday-school work was begun one week after the organization of the congregation. Two weeks after this, or three weeks from date of organization, a Sunday-school was established in a school house in East End, about ten squares from the location of the church building. Revs. M. P. Hocker, President of the Harrisburg Conference, and F. L. Bergstresser, were present at that meeting. Mr. W. H. Hoerner was elected superintendent of this Sunday-school, which position he also held in the other and older school. These schools have an enrolled membership respectively of about 325 and 80.

The *Lutheran Observer* is read in about forty families, and the *Missionary Journal* pays its monthly visits to a few of the homes of the people. The Augsburg Sunday-school literature is used in both schools.

The Young People's Society of Christian Endeavor numbers about eighty members. It is active and helpful. The Ladies' Aid Society, whose history begins with the history of the congregation, has been instrumental in raising annually a large sum of money. Besides helping to pay the indebtedness on the church building, this society has been paying the interest on all borrowed money.

LXX. ST. MARK'S CHURCH, CONSHOHOCKEN, MONTGOMERY COUNTY.

BY REV. J. F. SHEARER.

In the fall of 1889 Rev. A. H. F. Fischer, pastor of St. Peter's Evangelical Lutheran church of Barren Hill, Pa., looking over the field of Conshohocken, so long neglected by the Lutheran Church, and learning of a number of Lutheran families there, felt the necessity of doing something for their welfare. The matter was brought before the Philadelphia Conference, by which body it was referred to a committee consisting of Mr. Fischer and Rev. M. S. Cressman, pastor at Lionville, Pa. They visited the place in December, 1889, and secured the M. E. church for the holding of a service two weeks later, at which time the pastor of St. Peter's preached. After another interval of two weeks, services were again held by Mr. Fischer, and a committee was appointed to secure a hall for the purpose of starting a mission Sabbath-school. The newly-dedicated hall of the W. C. T. U. on Third Avenue was procured, and a Sabbath-school was organized, with Mr. J. S. Moser as superintendent, while the general pastoral supervision of its interests was under the care of the pastor at Barren Hill. Preaching services were conducted every two weeks in the afternoon by Mr. Fischer, until the February meeting of Conference, when arrangements were made to have the ministers of Conference serve the mission until the June meeting.

The mission in the meanwhile made encouraging increase in numbers, and on the evening of April 15, 1890, the committee called a meeting of the members of the mission in the hall for the purpose of organizing a congregation. After the singing of Hymn 202, "I love Thy Zion, Lord," and the reading of the 84th Psalm by Mr. Fischer, Mr. Cressman offered prayer, and then stated the purpose of the meeting. The names of twenty-five persons were enrolled. The constitution, as recorded in the church-book, was adopted *seriatim* and then unanimously as a whole. The organization was completed by electing the following temporary officers: President, J. S. Moser; Secretary, J. J. Becker; Treasurer, J. K. Streeper.

On April 22 a meeting of the congregation was held at the residence of J. S. Moser, and the name, "St. Mark's Lutheran church of Conshohocken," was unanimously selected. At this meeting the following officers were also elected: Elders, Wm. P. Ely and J. S. Moser; Deacons, Eugene A. Fillman, J. J. Becker, Mark Staley and Jacob K. Streeper.

In July Mr. J. M. Francis, a theological student at the Seminary at Gettysburg, was engaged to supply the pulpit, which he did very acceptably until the first of September, when he returned to the Seminary to pursue his studies. From the first of September to the first of December, the mission was supplied with preaching by different ministers of Philadelphia Conference. In the month of November a call was extended to Rev. J. F. Shearer, of Somerset, Pa., to become pastor of the mission. He accepted, and took charge December 1, 1890.

In November, 1892, one of the most desirable lots for church purposes, located on Fifth avenue, at the corner of Harry street, was purchased by the congregation, with the view of erecting a church building thereon as soon as possible. A building committee was selected, consisting of J. F. Shearer, Wm. P. Ely, J. S. Moser, J. Warren Schlichter and I. J. Moyer, who at once took steps to secure a plan for a church building. The plan submitted by Mr. Isaac Purcell, an architect of Philadelphia, seemed in the opinion of the committee to be well adapted to the needs of the congregation, and was unanimously adopted.

July 25, 1892, ground was broken for laying the foundation of the church, and on Sunday, September 11, the corner-stone was laid. The Lutheran ministers present on this occasion, and taking some part in the service, were Drs. Baum, Albert, Holman, Revs. A. H. F. Fischer, S. G. Shannon and J. F. Shearer. Drs. Baum and Albert delivered appropriate and impressive addresses. The ministers of the Presbyterian, Episcopal, Baptist and Methodist churches of this place were also present to commend the work of the mission.

The church building is now under roof. It is of Conshohocken limestone, beautiful in design, modern in its appointments, and universally admired by the citizens of the town. It also compares quite favorably with the other churches of the place. It is expected that the church will be ready for dedication by the month of May, 1893. The membership of the church now numbers 83. The Sabbath-school has on its roll 215 scholars, and has, perhaps, an average attendance of 150.

Many of the citizens have manifested their interest in the mission by liberal contributions toward the church building. The members of the mission are not possessed of great wealth, and many of them deserve commendation for the self-sacrificing spirit manifested in their efforts to give our beloved church an honored and a commanding position among the denominations of the place. Some of our people are among the most earnest Christian workers of the town, and are highly respected for their work's sake. If the entire indebtedness of the church is to be removed in a reasonable time, they will be compelled to ask aid from others outside of their own town. Such an appeal would merit a patient hearing and liberal response.

LXXI. TRINITY CHURCH, COATESVILLE, CHESTER COUNTY.

BY REV. W. H. STECK.

Trinity Lutheran church, of Coatesville, is in large measure the outgrowth of Blessing Sunday-school, which was organized in an old mill on the property of Paul Blessing, some fourteen years previous to the organization of the church. The Sunday-school was undenominational, and Mr. John Hope continued to be its faithful superintendent from its organization until it was merged into the Lutheran church.

Up to the year 1890, no special attention had been given to the matter of establishing a Lutheran church at this point. For some years previous to that date a few individual members had wished and hoped for a church of their first love, but, as of the original settlers of old Chester county very few were Lutherans, these scattered children of the Church of the Reformation had to wait long for the full realization of their hopes.

Early in the year 1890 Mrs. J. A. Hope called upon Rev. M. S. Cressman, of Lionville, and secured his services to preach what, so far as the record shows, was the first Lutheran sermon ever preached in Coatesville. A few months afterwards the attention of the Philadelphia Conference was called to this inviting and seemingly very promising field, and Rev. L. E. Albert, D. D., Rev. B. F. Alleman, D. D., and Rev. M. S. Cressman were sent "to spy out the land." Encouraged by the report they brought, the Conference appointed Rev. W. H. Steck temporarily as missionary to look up the field, and report back to the Conference the prospect, and whether the opportune time had come for organizing a mission in the new field. After a careful canvass of the territory, steps were taken to organize at once.

The organization was effected June 9, 1890. Though numbering only seventeen, there being among the few some made of the stuff of which Gideon's three hundred were made, they decided to secure a lot and build, their motto being that of other successful builders: "For we are able."

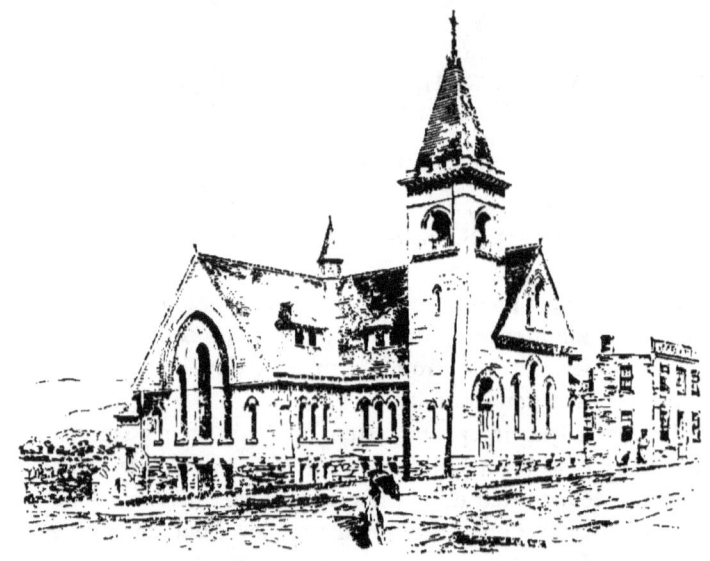

TRINITY EVANGELICAL LUTHERAN CHURCH, COATESVILLE, PA.

This little determined band proved their faith by their works, and on Sunday, November 1, 1891, the corner-stone was laid with appropriate ceremonies. Rev. J. M. Steck, brother of the pastor, preached the sermon, most appropriate and eloquent, to a large audience in the Coatesville opera house. Over $500.00 was raised on the day of the laying of the corner-stone.

The work of building went on encouragingly. Several thousand dollars had been subscribed, the Ladies' Aid Society, which had been doing splendid work, had raised about one thousand dollars, the lot had been paid for, and all were fully convinced that the time had come when Lutheranism would have a local habitation as well as a name in the town of Coatesville. September 1, 1890, the Home Mission Board appointed Rev. W. H. Steck as their regular missionary in the new field, who has continued his work as such up to this time, September 21, 1892.

On Sunday, June 19, 1892, the church, of which the accompanying cut is a good representation, was dedicated. Rev. H. H. Weber, Rev. A. Stewart Hartman, Rev. J. M. Steck, Rev. M. S. Cressman and the pastor, Rev. W. H. Steck, participated in the joyous feast of dedication, Mr. Cressman preaching the dedication sermon, which was most appropriate and well received by an audience that filled the house to overflowing. On the day of dedication about $3,500.00 were subscribed, leaving only a little more than $2,000.00 to raise upon the lot and new building, which cost over $13,000.00. To encourage the little flock in their undertaking, the Board of Church Extension has loaned them $2,000.00 for five years without interest.

The following were the church officers at the time of organizing: Elders, John S. Hope, Paul Blessing and Fred. Schulmeister; Deacons, F. N. Kurtz, James J. Mentzer and William Mann; Trustees, Roland Strode, John Heffner and August Brunninger.

LXXII. ST. MARK'S CHURCH, STEELTON, DAUPHIN COUNTY.

BY REV. W. L. RUTHERFORD.

St. Mark's Lutheran Mission, at Steelton, Pa., although quite young in years, is not without a remarkable and interesting history. Its birth and nurture are traced back to the untiring efforts and patient labor of Rev. E. Daron. For a number of years Rev. Daron had been teaching, with great success, a Bible class in St. John's Lutheran church, in the same place. While actively engaged in teaching this class, which was rapidly growing in interest and numbers, even to overflowing, circumstances led to his retirement from the position. A few weeks later, a committee waited on him, tendering a request to organize a Union Bible Class. He consented to do all that he could, on condition that they should use the International Lessons and submit to his accustomed way of teaching, as previously conducted in the

Sunday-school of St. John's Lutheran church. On the following Sunday, a Union Bible Class, thirty-one in number, was organized, which on the second Sunday had an enrollment of sixty-two members.

For about six months Rev. Daron taught this class in the Red Men's Hall, South Front street. The class then met for about one year in the Public Reading Room, No. 144 North Front street. During this time Rev. Daron faithfully taught the same doctrine and precepts as previously taught in his ministry and Bible teaching. In this class were men and women who had not attended divine services for many years. The exercises were always opened and closed with singing and prayer. While this teaching was conducted, the plan of salvation was clearly set forth in all its simplicity, and the great value and importance of the sacraments—Baptism and the Lord's Supper—were fully explained. The necessity of church membership, and the great importance of Christian activity, were also taught. After a number of conversions, a desire was awakened among the members of the class to organize a new congregation. A committee was accordingly appointed to call some minister to preach the gospel. But at this juncture all efforts and plans were frustrated by circumstances beyond control, which often cast shadows of gloom and doubt on the younger members.

Early in January, 1891, Rev. M. G. Earhart received an invitation to preach to the class in the public reading-room. After kindly responding, and holding service twice on Sunday, January 11, 1891, he was urged to return on the following Sabbath. After a consultation with the President of Synod, two services were held on the Sabbath following, January 18. It was then proposed that Rev. Earhart preach regularly, with a view of organizing a new congregation in the near future. The attendance and interest manifested by the people seemed to justify this move.

On March 8, after an appropriate discourse by Rev. M. L. Deitzler, the new organization was effected by installing a church council, and receiving thirty-eight of the Bible Class and fourteen by certificate as members of the organization, under the name of St. Mark's Lutheran Church, of Steelton, Pa.

Rev. Earhart served this devoted flock faithfully until December 30, 1891, when he passed peacefully away to his eternal rest.

On February 21, 1892, W. L. Rutherford, then a student in the Theological Seminary at Gettysburg, received a call to serve these people. In a few weeks the call was accepted, and on the first of June following, he assumed full charge of the duties incumbent upon his sacred office.

On June 1, 1892, when the newly-elected pastor took charge of this mission entrusted to his care, he found an enrollment of fifty-four communicant members. With two losses since then, one by death and another by removal, and with sixteen accessions, the mission has attained a membership of sixty-eight communicants. The growth cannot be rapid under the existing circumstances. Compelled to worship in the Grand Army Hall, on a third floor, under a tin roof, some idea may be formed of the inconveniences incurred. With all the difficulties and obstacles, however, with which we have to contend, the general interest is maintained, with a reasonable degree of progress in every line of work. The Sunday-school is growing, and has at present a roll of 171.

The Young People's Christian Endeavor Society, recently organized, is active and doing a good work. The women of the congregation have organized and are working in various ways for the mission under the name of "The Ladies' Benevolent Society."

The salary paid by our congregation is $300.00 per year, $200.00 being given by the Board of Home Missions, making in all $500.00.

Comparatively few church papers are taken, but this part of the work is improving and will no doubt be satisfactory in the near future.

The progress of our organization has been very much impeded by the want of a proper place of worship. We are yet, owing to adverse circumstances, without a church home, but we have utmost confidence in the future. It would be exceedingly difficult for us at present to secure, even at an exorbitant price, a lot suitable for our location. This disheartening fact has become generally known, but we are earnestly and zealously working, knowing that duty is ours and results are God's.

LXXIII. CHRIST'S CHURCH, BRIDGETON, CUMBERLAND COUNTY, N. J.

BY REV. J. EUGENE DIETTERICH.

Bridgeton, N. J., has a population of about twelve thousand. Until recently there was but one Lutheran church in the city, and that was German. But there were not many Germans in Bridgeton, and the young people were growing up in the use of the English language and desired English preaching, which was denied them in their own church. Hence they lost interest and many withdrew to other churches or neglected all church duties. Then, too, quite a good many English Lutherans were continually moving to Bridgeton from other places, and especially from Friesburg, ten miles distant.

These conditions suggested the idea of planting a new English Lutheran congregation in the city. Arrangements were made to have Rev. J. Eugene Dietterich, pastor at Friesburg, preach in the hall of the Cohansey Lodge, I. O. O. F., near the court house, on February 1, 1891. The service was held at 4 o'clock p. m., and about one hundred persons were present. The Odd Fellows kindly allowed the free use of the hall until a permanent place of worship could be secured. Grosscup's Hall, in the centre of the city, was then sub-leased from the W. C. T. U. for ten dollars per month, and the first sermon was preached there on February 22, 1891. Mr. J. N. Spence and Mr. Geo. Miller assisted in a canvass of the city, and on Palm Sunday, March 22, 1891, in the evening, in Grosscup's Hall, the new congregation was regularly organized by Rev. J. Eugene Dietterich, with the following members: Mr. and Mrs. John G. Bauer, Mr. and Mrs. F. W. C. Meyers, Miss Linnie Meyers, Mr. and Mrs. J. N. Spence, John D. Fisher, Wm. A. Bauer, Mr. and Mrs. Chas. Lutz, Mrs. Kate Maier, Mr. and Mrs. D. E. Christopher, Mrs. Mary Maier, Mr. and Mrs. Edward Sparks, Miss Minnie L. Miller, Miss Emma Bauer, Chas. W. Richards, Miss Susie Cramer.

A constitution was adopted, and the following council elected: Elders, John G. Bauer and F. W. C. Meyers; Deacons, J. N. Spence, John D. Fisher, Wm. A. Bauer and Chas. W. Richards.

The first communion was held the following (Easter) Sunday,

at which time Miss Alice Maier, Mrs. Henry Seibert, George Maier, Jr., and Geo. W. Finlaw were admitted to membership by confirmation.

Rev. J. Eugene Dietterich, pastor of the Friesburg church, was asked to supply the new congregation with preaching until a regular pastor could be secured. He consented to do so, and until October 1 preached every Sunday in the morning and evening at Friesburg, and in the afternoon at Bridgeton.

The second communion was held May 24, 1891, at which time four persons were confirmed.

In June, 1891, the Philadelphia Conference of the Synod of East Pennsylvania was entertained by the new congregation, and passed resolutions endorsing the work and pledging assistance.

Application was now made to the Home Mission Board of the General Synod for help, and that Board made an appropriation toward the support of a pastor and commissioned Rev. J. Eugene Dietterich as missionary, the commission bearing date October 1, 1891. The congregation unanimously accepted this arrangement. Rev. Dietterich resigned his charge at Friesburg and moved with his family to Bridgeton.

Mr. Wm. A. Bauer was sent as a commissioner to the meeting of the East Pennsylvania Synod held at Middletown, Pa., September 16–22, 1891, to ask that the new congregation be received as an integral part of that body. It was so accepted, and Mr. Bauer enrolled as delegate.

Because of the interest shown by Rev. G. W. Enders, D. D., a former pastor of the German Lutheran church of Bridgeton, and because of the assistance which he and his congregation gave to the new organization, the congregation voted that he should select the name by which it should be known, and he named it "Christ's," in honor of the congregation which he is serving in York, Pa.

The next communion was held January 3, 1892, at which time eight persons were admitted to membership, and since that time six others have been added.

The winter's work was greatly hindered by the uncomfortable and uninviting condition of the hall, and it was found to be absolutely necessary that a church be built as soon as possible. At an Orphans' Court sale on April 29, 1892, a lot was bought on

Bank street, near Commerce street, a very favorable location. The price paid was $1600.00. A successful effort was now made to secure the money to pay for the lot, and application was made to the Church Extension Board for help to build the church. The Board in reply made a proposition, which the congregation ventured to accept, and a plan was at once adopted for the new building, bids called for, and the contract placed.

The corner-stone was laid on Sunday afternoon, October 9, 1892. Rev. S. G. Shannon, of Philadelphia, preached the sermon, and was assisted in the exercises by Rev. S. J. McDowell and Rev. H. Lisse, of the Lutheran church, and by some of the pastors of other congregations in the city. At this service over five hundred dollars were secured in cash and subscriptions.

The work has been pushed rapidly, and the new church will be dedicated about January 15, 1893. The building is of frame, with slate roof, is Gothic in style, will cost five thousand dollars, and will seat three hundred and fifty persons. Quite a number of people have signified their intention to become members of the congregation as soon as it worships in the new church. There is a Young People's Society connected with the congregation, having over fifty members.

The outlook for the development and growth of the congregation is excellent. The church will probably be dedicated free of debt, with the exception of the amount borrowed from the Church Extension Board, and it is hoped and expected by pastor and people to make the congregation self-sustaining by October 1, 1893, when it will have been on the funds of the Board just two years.

LXXIV. HARRISBURG AND STEELTON CHARGE—TRINITY AND ST. PAUL'S.

BY REV. M. L. DEITZLER.

On November 11, 1888, Rev. D. M. Gilbert, D. D., pastor of Zion Lutheran church of Harrisburg, with a few of his workers, organized a mission Sabbath-school at 1038 South Ninth street, with Jos. F. Young as superintendent. The school grew rapidly.

Within two years three necessary additions were made to the residence in which the school was held. The average attendance for the first year was 105, for the second 205, and for the third 218. The Board of Home Missions appointed Rev. M. L. Deitzler, July 1, 1890, to take charge of this work as pastor, in connection with St. Paul's mission school at Steelton. On May 17, 1891, seven members from Zion's congregation, with thirty-nine others, nearly all non-church-members, were regularly organized into a congregation. At the end of the first year the congregation numbered seventy, reducing the appropriation of the Board of Home Missions for pastor's salary from $300.00 to $200.00.

Trinity congregation was regularly admitted to the East Pennsylvania Synod at its annual meeting in Middletown, September, 1891.

The congregation was chartered September, 1892, and worships in the chapel where the work was begun. A lot of ground, 60x100 feet, with the chapel, is the generous gift of Mr. Joseph F. Young and wife to the congregation. The mission is now, and has been from the beginning, generously supported by Zion Lutheran congregation.

2. St. Paul's Church, East Steelton, Pa.

On January 1, 1890, Rev. M. P. Hocker, pastor of St. John's Lutheran church, with others of his congregation, organized a mission Sabbath-school in a private residence in East Steelton, which promised then, and has since proved, to be a true and hopeful home mission field.

November 30, 1890, was dedicated a neat and commodious chapel, erected by St. John's congregation for the work, at a cost of about $2,000.00.

Rev. M. L. Deitzler was appointed by the Board of Home Missions, July 1, 1890, to take charge of this work as pastor, in connection with Trinity Mission, Harrisburg, Pa.

May 17, 1891, a church organization was effected, with eleven members, nearly all from St. John's congregation. St. Paul's congregation was regularly admitted to the East Pennsylvania Synod at its annual session held at Middletown, September, 1891 uniting with Trinity Lutheran congregation of Harrisburg, Pa., to form the Harrisburg and Steelton Mission. The congregation numbers at present fifteen, while the school has grown from twenty to an average attendance of eighty.

Substantial building improvements, constantly and rapidly made on the territory of this mission, present a hopeful prospect for the congregation in the near future.

LXXV. AUGSBURG CHURCH, HARRISBURG.

BY REV. D. H. GEISER.

Augsburg Lutheran Church, Harrisburg, Pa., had its origin in a mission Sunday-school planted in West Harrisburg by zealous members of Messiah Lutheran church (Forster street) in June, 1890, with W. L. Gardner as superintendent. In less than two years the school enrolled 455 pupils, officers and teachers. Its sessions were held in Kelker Street Hall. The demand for a new Lutheran church in this part of the city was irresistible. Accordingly the Augsburg congregation was organized January 10, 1892, with 98 members, 92 of whom were dismissed for that purpose from Messiah Lutheran church, with cordial good wishes. Those prominently interested in the new organization had already, through Mr. W. W. Davidson, secured from a generous lady the spacious lot on the corner of Fifth and Muench streets for $8,500.00.

The corner-stone of the new church-building on this lot was laid June 19, 1892. The first pastor, Rev. Dixon H. Geiser, was called from the seminary at Gettysburg, and took charge July 1, 1892. The church was dedicated November 20, 1892. The building is of frame, 90 by 45 feet, and with furniture, gas fixtures, steam heat, fencing, etc., cost $6,600.00. It occupies nearly the central portion of the ground, leaving a large space on either side for further use. The congregation was self-sustaining in every respect from the beginning. Its present membership is one hundred and forty-nine.

LXXVI. EBENEZER EVANGELICAL LUTHERAN CHURCH, BERBICE, BRITISH-GUIANA, S. A.*

BY REV. J. R. MITTELHOLZER.

Mission work in the past two centuries has received its impulse largely from colonization. The Lord has stirred up in the minds of mankind enterprises of this character, by which the word of truth was to be disseminated, and reach the most distant parts of the earth. Early geographical discovery brought to light lands and people unknown to the apostles and their immediate

---

* NOTE.—In response to an earnest request from the synodical historian, the pastor of our church at New Amsterdam has kindly furnished the following brief autobiographical details:

I am a native of British Guiana, born in June, 1840. My father, Jan Vincent Mittelholzer, was born in the colony, but of German parentage. His father, C. M. Mittelholzer, came to this colony at an early time from Switzerland. Both my father and grandfather were planters. Nor am I aware of any of my elder male relatives ever having entered the Christian ministry.

My own choice of a profession, at first, was that of engineering, which I pursued with great zeal for a time. I was then a boy of 14 years. My course, however, was providentially diverted. An English missionary, the Rev. H. B. Ingram, having seen a small engine of wood constructed by me, took me under his personal care and tuition, with the view of educating me in the higher mathematics, so as to fit me more thoroughly for a professional engineer. After conducting some examinations in the mathematics, the good English minister was taken away from the colony. But I was provided for. Another minister, the late Rev. John Dalgliesh (a Scotchman) took me, but he thought it best for me to study literature, as well as the sciences, and teach in the schools. I now became a teacher of the young, and taught for many years, having successfully passed examinations under the Government Inspector of Schools. It was whilst so engaged, in connection with the London Missionary Society, that, favorable reports reaching the Directors of said Society, I was by them directed to study classics, theology, etc., etc., in preparation for the work of the Christian ministry. Thus it will be seen that at the first my education was directed for specific objects, and by an all-wise Providence then became blended into the work of the Christian ministry, thus qualifying me to work in a country like this, where a minister must be "made all things to all men," that he may "by all means save some."

Another incident which I consider most providential in my life is that my father and his brother were both of them "postholders" (high military officers) under the Dutch colonial government, having command of the Indian militia, etc. Thus becoming at an early age acquainted with the ways of

successors. The discovery of America by Christopher Columbus incited the European nations to move westward and southward in quest of new fields of industry. As the Christians traveled to these newly-discovered regions, they carried with them the banner of the Cross, and, planting it on heathen soil, signalized to the great foe of mankind that the holy war had reached thus far.

South America as well as North America has seen Jehovah's banner unfurled, and the bold armies of the prince of darkness gradually retiring before the advancing arms of Jesus of Nazareth ; and, if not entirely, yet to some extent evil is mitigated and many souls are saved.

In the early part of the sixteenth century, Guiana was visited by the Europeans. Foremost among them were the Spaniards. "Pope Alexander the Sixth, the illustrious 'Borgia,' had, on May 2, 1493, issued a bull granting to King Ferdinand of Spain possession of all lands which had been then, or might be thereafter, discovered to the west of the ideal line drawn from the North to the South Pole, starting a hundred leagues west of the Azores—discoveries west of this line to be held as belonging to Spain, and those in the opposite direction to Portugal.

"'The explanation of the issue of such an edict from Rome is to be found in the circumstance, recorded by Washington Irving, that 'During the crusades, a doctrine had been established among the Christian princes, according to which the Pope, from his supreme authority over all temporal things as Christ's Vicar on earth, was considered as empowered to dispose of all heathen lands to such Christian potentates as would undertake to reduce

the Indians, and aided by the influence which my father and uncle wielded over them, I have been enabled after the lapse of so many years to do successful missionary work among these people. Truly

> "God moves in a mysterious way
> His wonders to perform."

I have worked hard, and am still working hard every day, to recover for our Church the ground which had been lost. May the Lord spare me to see Lutheranism take a firm hold of the country, all the obloquy which our adversaries had heaped upon us completely wiped off, and the glory of the Lord fully restored in his Zion here and in the colony of British Guiana.—J. R. M.

them to the dominion of the Church, and to introduce into them the light of religion.' "—*Rodway & Watt's Annals of Guiana.*

According to the same authority quoted above, Alonzo de Ojeda, who "sailed from Port S. Mary, May 20, 1499," was the first who reached the north-east coast of South America, somewhere about Surinam (Dutch Guiana), and sailed along the coast up to the Orinoco and thence to the Island of Trinidad. But the great bell, whose stirring tone really inspired European nations to make exploration voyages to Guiana and trade along the coasts, was the gilded story told by dying Juan Martinez of his journey inland, in which he was conducted by Guianians (who had rescued him from perishing in the river Orinoco) into the famous city, "the houses of which were covered with shining gold, stretching as far as his eyes could reach. The place was situated on a great lake or inland sea, called Parima, the sands of which were golden; from which circumstance, together with the abundance of precious metal he saw in and on the dwellings of the people, he named it ' El Dorado.' "

Whether this visionary city was a mirage or the invention of Martinez, his story got abroad into the northern countries, and the result was the outfitting of a number of expeditions in search of this El Dorado. Guiana became an attractive country. The famous Sir Walter Raleigh also made voyages to this region, in hope of discovering a supposed remarkable and prolific gold mine. Sir Walter really believed in the gold-fields of Guiana. Nor was his notion chimerical. Strange to say, nearly three centuries after Sir Walter Raleigh's first expedition to this land, gold is now turning up somewhat plentifully in Guiana, both Dutch and British; and in the latter colony there is a river known as the " Barima " (no doubt the ' Parima' of Martinez). If the city El Dorado do not turn up, it is evidently showing its golden sands. But alas for the thousands who are fast becoming buried in that " sordid dust !" Our gold fields are crowded with people from the cities and villages. Again and again the sad tidings are announced in our papers of the upsetting of boat-loads of human freight, and thus precious souls in quest of "gold that perisheth"—souls who for gold have long neglected divine worship—are being hurried into eternity to meet their God. But what is still more sad, is the fact that there is so much demoralizing influence amongst the gold-diggers.

Guiana, however, did not become a real colony, it appears, before the year 1624.

"By a Grant of the States General in 1602 the Merchants of Zeeland, Van Peere, Van Rhee, De Moor, Lampsius, De Vries and Van Hoorn were allowed freedom of convoy to their vessels which were trading to Guiana and the West Indies."

The first man who is said to have taken firm footing on Guiana soil was Captain Gromweagle in 1616. He died in 1664, "having governed the country for 48 years." The settlement of Berbice, however, was under Abraham Van Peere, the son of Jan Van Peere, in 1627.

Guiana occasionally changed hands, sometimes taken by the English, the French, and again restored to the Dutch. It was in 1803 that the English took final possession of the entire colony.

Guiana is divided into British, Dutch and French. British Guiana consisted of three colonies, Berbice, Demerara and Essequibo. These were united into one colony in 1831. Now it is entitled the *Counties* of Berbice, Demerara and Essequibo.

FOUNDING OF THE LUTHERAN CHURCH.

"It being ascertained in the year 1743 that there were then residing in the colony a number of individuals professing the unaltered Augsburg Confession of Faith, it began to be considered by them that, although they lived in peace and harmony with each other, they nevertheless were like so many scattered sheep without a shepherd."

The colony, now British Guiana, was at that time under the Netherlandic government, and the colonists were Dutch as well as German. The established church in those early days was the "Dutch Reformed."

These Lutherans felt it desirable to make application to "their High Mightinesses, the States General of the Netherlands," for permission to exercise religion after the Augsburg Confession. They were encouraged in their good desire by the fact that in that same year the Lutherans in Surinam (Dutch Guiana, S. A.) had succeeded in obtaining from the Netherlands a similar privilege.

The most energetic spirit in this Lutheran movement was Mr. Ludewyk Abbensetts "who, from his unremitting exertions and persevering zeal in the cause, may with strict justice be looked upon as the founder of the Lutheran congregation in Berbice." This gentleman called a meeting of his co-religionists for the purpose of considering and adopting measures that might be deemed most conducive to the attainment of their object. This meeting was convened at his own house on October 15, 1743, when it was resolved, "that petitions should be forwarded to the Honorable the Court of Policy (the colonial legislature), and to the Most Honourable the Directors of the Colony, and their High

EBENEZER EVANGELICAL LUTHERAN CHURCH, BERBICE, BRITISH-GUIANA, S. A.

Mightinesses the States General of the Netherlands, praying for the privilege of the free exercise of their religion ; and that at the same time applications should be made by letter to the Reverend Consistory, of Amsterdam, soliciting their aid and co-operation in this urgent matter, and also their good services in procuring a clergyman for the community."

Respecting the last request, the Consistory advised that the appointment of a clergyman should be deferred until the Berbice brethren had secured sufficient funds and property for the support and maintenance of their establishment. This was, beyond all doubt, a wholesome advice, as matters afterwards amply proved. Meanwhile, however, "the Hon'bles, the Directors of the Colony," were pleased to grant their application under the proviso—"that the clergyman to be chosen and engaged by them should, previous to his departure to the Colony, be presented to them (the Directors) for their approbation and confirmation; that the expenses of the salary of said minister, and also of the church or building to be erected or used for the purpose of divine worship, should be defrayed by the members of the congregation themselves, and not at the charge of the Directors; that they should, moreover, contribute to the ordinary church (the Dutch-Reformed) fund equally and in the same proportion as all other inhabitants." The collecting of these rates was urged rigorously upon the Lutherans in the year 1790, when "the Colonial Receiver-General was instructed to proceed summarily against them for arrears of acre-money."

Notwithstanding these hard stipulations, the Lutherans were only too much rejoiced at the permission to exercise their religion. Their next business was to raise the necessary funds for the support of their church establishment. Having obtained permission of His Excellency, the then Governor of the Colony, to convene a regular financial meeting of their body, it was agreed upon amongst them that each individual should contribute a sum of money at once or annually towards what was required. This resolution was so energetically carried out that eight years afterwards their favorable report to the Consistory in Amsterdam procured the services of the Rev. J. H. Taerkenius. Their first pastor arrived in the colony in October, 1752.

One difficulty was now settled. The next immediately presented itself. So connected are the several events of human life. In this case there was the lamb, there was the priest, but where was the altar on which to celebrate the service? Funds were at hand to meet the minister's salary, the minister was now amongst the flock, but where was the CHURCH? They wanted to build one, but where were the means? In vain did they apply to the local authorities for assistance in this urgent matter. The Lutheran community was, once for all, fully convinced that the colonial authorities were determined not to countenance Lutheranism in the colony if they could help it; hence, if the former were to succeed, they must depend instrumentally on their own hands, with the help of God. But ever, as the emergency demands in all great and good movements, the proper man for its promotion appears. In this trying situation one of the members of their body, Mr. John Reynhout Reymers, willingly offered his spacious mansion for the performance of divine service.

Notwithstanding all the discouragement they had received at the hands of the local authorities, the members of the Lutheran church beautifully exemplified their Lord's injunction—" Bless them that curse you ; do good to them that despitefully use you and persecute you." Having succeeded in building a church with their own funds at Fort Nassau, then the capital of the colony of Berbice, situated about seventy miles up the river and about the same distance from the present town, " they cheerfully allowed the use of their church to their brethren and fellow-Christians of the Reformed or established church, who had but one place of worship, situated at some distance from the town and higher up the river." So, also, when in 1763 the great slave rebellion threatened the colony with total ruin—for the infuriated slaves in their mad career burnt all the houses in the Fort and left standing only the Lutheran church and the buildings connected with it—the Lutherans permitted their parsonage to be occupied as a temporary residence of the Governor, and the out-buildings as hospitals for the sick and wounded. For eleven years' use of their buildings the only mitigation of hard feelings against the Lutherans was that the government did not press them so much for arrears of acre-money.

Prior to the appointment of a minister, the Lutheran community had planned a fairly well organized body of administrators for the care of the church properties in course of acquisition, as well as for general management of the affairs, correspondences with the authorities in Europe, etc. The six persons, under the designation of " Directors," were Messrs. Schiermerster, Dietzhold, Speelmain, Abbensetts (the founder), Meyners and Rertomis. On the arrival of the first minister, the Rev. J. H. Taerkenius, at a meeting held October 25, 1752, and at the motion of the minister, the

FIRST ECCLESIASTICAL VESTRY

was formed. The minister proposed to re-elect the six directors with the addition of "four elders and two deacons out of competent members well known to the directors," so that they may be in accord with the church ordinance. Of these first elders elected only one name is given, viz.: "J. L. Van Stoken, etc., etc., etc."

The vestry was elected for two years; the election took place in December, and the installation on New Year's day. It appears that the community appointed one of these vestrymen as treasurer and book-keeper for one year, at the end of which term his accounts must be rendered to the vestry or consistory. Likewise, another member was appointed as church warden or inspector of the church building.

Like our tropical climate, with its alternations of sunshine and shade, the Lutheran community passed through various vicissitudes, at times very trying. Within the brief period of twenty-seven years four ministers had served, an average service of scarcely seven years each. The names, times of arrival, etc., are as follows:

1. The first minister, the Rev. John Hendrick Taerkenius, arrived in the colony October, 1752; died in the colony 1754.

2. The Rev. J. J. M. Groshmer arrived in the colony May, 1756; died in the colony March, 1760.

3. The Rev. S. F. Miller arrived in the colony October, 1761; left the colony April, 1763.

4. The Rev. J. A. Glendtkampt arrived in the colony May, 1777; left the colony January, 1779.

5. The Rev. —— Junius.

These clergymen, appointed at the request and guarantee of the vestry in Berbice, served up to the year 1840, when it appears, failing to obtain any more supplies from Holland, the Berbice Lutherans had recourse to offer their pastorate to the Rev. Alexander Riach, of the Presbyterian church. Mr. Riach was sent to Holland to study the Dutch language. At his return to the colony and assumption of his duties as a Lutheran, he was to preach alternately in the Dutch and in the English language, it being the transition period from the former to the latter. In certain times the services were conducted in both the Dutch and the German languages. A great interval appears to have elapsed between the departure of the Rev. Mr. Glendtkampt and the appointment of the Rev. Mr. Junius. The marriage register of Mr. Junius contains records from 1832 to 1840. Also of Mr. Riach's appointment I am unable to give the precise date. But about the year 1852 Mr. Riach became personally known to me. At this time he was in the Presbyterian ministry. Again another great interval occurred, when the Lutheran congregation was without a minister for twenty-five years, during which period the Wesleyans were permitted to use the Lutheran church, manse and other buildings, and were allowed by the vestry the amount of £100 per annum to assist their ministry, but this sum was afterwards reduced to £50.

I shall revert to the state of the Lutheran congregation during the Wesleyan gratis tenancy of the church, etc., and shall say something about the origin of the congregation's

CONSOLIDATED FUND.

About the year 1774, matters became very depressing, and the Lutherans were reduced to a condition almost similar to that experienced before 1743. Failing to obtain any help from the local government, many of their best supporters had become poor, and some had returned to the mother country. Matters were wearing a sad aspect. Indeed, that same year, " the members of the vestry were obliged *to bind their persons and goods* by a formal deed, as a security for the payment of the minister's salary and the fulfilment of other stipulations," before the consistory in Amsterdam could be prevailed upon to engage and send them out a clergyman.

A project which had been mooted in 1753 was now deliberately adopted, viz.: to acquire in behalf of the Lutheran community, and put into cultivation of coffee, a piece of land, the proceeds of which, "by the blessing of God, may afford a more certain and permanent source of revenue for the support of their church and maintenance of a minister," etc. Messrs. H. J. Buse, P. Schwetzer and Nelis Anderson (members of the vestry) were in April entrusted with the business of giving effect to the resolution. Having obtained from the Colonial Government a piece of land, Mr. Botzen, an elder of their church, undertook to lay out the land and put it in cultivation gratis. After the death of this right noble-minded elder, Mr. Heilen came forward and took it up on the same disinterested principle. As acre-money became a very severe pressure indeed, on one occasion, Mr. Janch, another of the elders, offered, together with his brother vestry members, to pay this money out of their own private means. It was resolved to purchase the estate which they had cultivated, as a permanent possession of the church, and Mr. Buse, having exerted his influence in Amsterdam, obtained for the purchase from Messrs. J. A. Pool & Co. a sum of 15,000 guilders (the Dutch guilder 40 cents in American currency). This effort was so blessed that in the course of a few years a very respectable revenue was insured. After the resignation of the Rev. Alexander Riach, the estate was sold, and the proceeds, toge ther with the amounts obtained from season to season for coffee, were invested in shares in the British Guiana Bank. There was a time when the dividends amounted annually to five thousand dollars. But this capital has been from time to time reduced, and to such an extent that the present does not exceed two thousand five hundred dollars per annum (an amount sufficient to maintain a respectable ministry). Of course, this yield in the way of dividends varies at times as the money market rises and falls.

During

THE WESLEYAN OCCUPATION OF THE LUTHERAN CHURCH,

as stated above, for the period of twenty-three years, the Lutheran church had died out. Her members were scattered amongst the several denominations; some united with the Presbyterians, others with the Episcopalians, the Congregationalists and Wesleyans. When Lutheran services were re-opened in the fall of 1875 the actual number of Lutherans was twelve. Even this infinitesimal remainder of the grand old establishment became still further reduced, so that although several members were confirmed by the Dutch Lutheran minister of Surinam (Dutch Guiana), at my assumption of this pastorate there were only eleven members. The male portion was reduced to four. The church regulations require that there shall be at least three members to form a quorum of the vestry, and it appears that at one time the vestry was reduced to *that bare quorum*, so that had a death occurred among them—there being no Lutheran minister to confirm other members—the vestry would have become extinct, and the entire Lutheran community would have collapsed. This illustrates the evil of allowing any church to be without a minister for any lengthened period, an evil which we trust this congregation will never again experience.

THE REVIVAL OF LUTHERANISM

took place in the year 1875. In that year an old and long-standing administrator died, owing the church funds a sum not inferior to $20,000.00, of which amount $15,000.00 was recovered from his life policy. The vestry, by some extraordinary charity, divided (of this latter amount) amongst the few members the sum of $5,000.00. Great dissatisfaction was created. Some, considering themselves unfairly dealt with (although the male members had received large amounts of gratuity), made representations to the government that the administrators were wasting the Lutheran Church funds. At once the government instituted a " Commission of Inquiry into the Lutheran Funds." This commission interdicted any further wasting of the old funds of the church, and ordered that " the Lutheran Church *should be re-opened, and the moneys put to the use for which they were originally intended*, and thus fulfill the object of the founders."

The vestry was thus compelled to accept one of two alternatives, either to do as the commission recommended, or allow the church properties to be taken over by the government, and appropriated to other uses for the benefit of the public. The vestry wisely chose the first alternative, and immediately invited Rev. John Sauder, minister of the Lutheran Church in Surinam, Dutch Guiana, to re-institute Lutheran services. Mr. Sauder came over, re-opened the services, confirmed a few new members, added one more vestry-man to save the quorum, and advised the vestry to endeavor to obtain the assistance of some local clergyman to keep up the services at extra-canonical hours, as might be convenient. The vestry then sought my help at extra hours, to continue the Lutheran services. Meanwhile, Mr. Sauder returned to Parimaribo (capital of Surinam, D. G.). After three years' experiment of visits at distant intervals from Parimaribo, the vestry passed a formal resolution, empowering the administrators to give me the refusal of their pastorate. These administrators gave as their reasons for calling on me: first, that they were satisfied with my temporary ministrations; and secondly, that, from my being directly descended from the old German colonists, a good connection between the past and present would be realized in my person. This selection, I was afterwards informed, gave universal satisfaction. This testimony was borne by the Attorney-General of the colony, Sir Wm. Haynes Smith, now Governor of the "Windward Islands."

Matters progressed comfortably (after my confirmation in Surinam as a Lutheran) for eight years, during which time the church prospered and increased. But in the year 1878 broke out

THE GREAT PERSECUTION,

which culminated in our application to and connection with the East Pennsylvania Synod, U. S. A. This marks a very important period in the work of Lutheranism in this colony, and therefore is worthy of record.

The year 1878 opened upon this Lutheran Church under the cloud of ecclesiastical war. The financial meetings of the vestry had been neglected for a number of years, and in vain had I endeavored to induce the administrators to convene a financial meeting and lay before the vestry a statement of the church's monetary status. At first the chief administrator promised, but deferred. The church, the manse, and other buildings were allowed to run to thorough dilapidation; and I feared that, should things continue so much longer, the church and manse would go beyond recovery. My insisting upon a statement of the finances being given led to the project of casting me off, to consummate which the administrators, in defiance of the vestry and general members, demanded, through a lawyer, my dismissal. The battle was now fairly set, and, anticipating what the result for the congregation would otherwise be—its direct dismemberment—I decided to resist, and replied to their document that I did not intend to surrender the Lutheran church unless it was the wish of the majority of the members, and unless compensation were made to my satisfaction.

At a "general meeting" great indignation was expressed by members at the unwarranted action taken by the two administrators. Their lawyer was now irritated, and resorted to the most vehement measures. The vestry had appealed to the Legislature to institute an ordinance for the protection of the old Lutheran properties, which were on the verge of ruin. The vestry had also, by a formal resolution, interdicted the bank from paying any more of the church's money to the recalcitrant administrators, whom the election at the general meeting had replaced by other officers.* The prosecuting lawyer also issued a countermanding order to the bank. He appealed to the Legislature to be permitted to appear at its bar and plead the cause of his clients. I represented the vestry and appeared in *propria persona*, together with our attorney, to resist the church's opponent. The Legislature decided for the church.

The lawyer next appealed to the judges of the Supreme Civil Court for an interdict against me. Thus he managed to cause delay, and kept matters pending for three long years, trusting that being kept so long out of my salary (for the bank was advised to pay the moneys to neither party till the matter was settled by the judges) I would in disgust vacate the pulpit. We were thus besieged. But the Lutheran church was still vocal, and all her services were regularly conducted, to the utmost surprise of all lookers-on. The Lord helped us. How I managed to sustain a large family without a penny of my salary, and, thank God, cheerfully discharge my solemn duties, the Lord only knows. It is now to myself mysterious!

Just four months before the judges brought the case to hearing and decision, the vestry had put itself in communication with the President of the East Pennsylvania Synod for recognition. And just a week after the three judges delivered their able and learned

---

* These newly elected administrators were Messrs. Charles A. Hicken and Thomas Campbell Douglass. The other members of the vestry who stood side by side with their pastor, and brunted all this attack, were Messrs. Michael Floris, James Samuels, Christian Ben and Hugh McDonald, to whose fidelity testimony is borne by this record.

"Decision on the Lutheran Matter"—a decision worthy of record in the Church's archives—a letter came from the United States announcing our

RECOGNITION BY THE EAST PENNSYLVANIA SYNOD,

which led to the consummating event of official connection with the Synod.

This act was the *coup de grace* to the church's triumph. This connection, which was effected September 18, 1890, will be ever memorable in this church's history.

The church now has several missions amongst the Aboriginal Indians in the interior amidst their forest homes. They are known as Bethel, Mt. Hermon, Mt. Carmel, Bethesda and Mt. Lebanon.

The Lord bless the Synod which came unknowingly but timely to the rescue of this distant but not unimportant branch of the great Lutheran Church! May our Zion flourish to the honor and glory of her divine Master, whose kind and ever-watchful providence had guided her from her commencement, protected her amid crushing dangers and changing scenes, and once more revived and established her! May she ever prove a satisfaction and credit to the venerable Synod with which she is connected.

And now, "unto the King eternal, immortal, invisible, the only wise God," who delivered us from our distress and gave us again a lively hope in his work, "be honor and glory for ever and ever." Amen.

STATISTICAL TABLE.

SHOWING THE PROGRESS OF THE SYNOD BY DECADES.*

	1842.	1852.	1862.	1872.	1882.	1892.	East Pennsylvania and Susquehanna Synods Combined, 1892.
Ministers on the Roll	11	34	56	56	67	92	129
Pastors within the bounds of Synod	10	28	49	41	51	73	110
Churches	24	41	114	60	103	119	188
Stations		19	19	11	10	9	13
Prayer Meetings	11	58	135	87	97	154	226
Students for the Ministry				†17	14	38	60
Catechumens Instructed		†696	1,102	262	1,617	2,577	3,977
Infant Baptisms	179	517	1,132	1,070	1,144	1,440	2,055
Adult Accessions	272	705	1,157	922	1,340	2,600	3,786
Adult Losses		235	371	557	790	1,795	2,506
Communicant Membership	1,513	4,747	12,599	10,422	13,166	19,571	29,143
Sunday Schools, Lutheran	13	30	60	47	63	97	152
Sunday Schools, Union		19	80	43	43	35	53
Officers and Teachers		†637	2,099	1,595	1,903	2,619	3,929
Scholars		†3,970	13,009	11,317	16,162	21,377	32,203
Contributions		†	$1,869 33	$3,910 26	$10,793 66	$21,990 25	$29,336 37
Estimated Value of Church Property					†	1,599,450 00	2,086,500 00
Indebtedness						206,168 17	239,168 17
Local Expenses		†$15,558 00	$17,252 22	$38,577 42	$62,496 33	218,372 14	277,907 82
Benevolent Contributions	$554 50	2,887 71	11,192 22	13,181 34	14,191 56	25,422 51	36,446 91
Total Contributions		†$18,445 71	$28,444 44	$51,758 76	$76,687 89	$243,794 65	$319,878 73

*The Susquehanna Conference of this Synod withdrew in 1867 and formed a separate organization, since known as the Susquehanna Synod. As its territory was all originally embraced in that of the Synod of East Pennsylvania, we have appended to the above Table a final column presenting the combined statistics of the two Synods for the year 1891-1892.—*Committee.*   † Not reported in earlier years.

PAROCHIAL REPORT OF THE EAST PENNSYLVANIA SYNOD.

PAROCHIAL.

Pastor's Name and Address	Congregations, Names of	Churches	Stations	Prayer Meetings	Students for Ministry	Catechumens	Death	Certificate	Excommunication and other losses	Infant Baptisms	Adult Baptisms	Confirmations	Certificate	Restoration	Communicant Membership	Estimated Value of Church Property	Indebtedness	Local Expenses for All Objects	Index No. See line with corresponding No. on page below
J. A. Singmaster, Allentown	St. Paul's	1		1		52	13	5	10	26	1	29	3	5	449	$35000 00	$2000 00	$889 00	1
Charles E. Hay, Allentown	St. Matthew's					57	7	4	10	15	1	8	3	5	180	10200 00	4252 34	2417 03	2
W. H. Lewars, Annville	1st Ev. Luth. and Hill Church	2		2		10		4	10			3	6		219	20000 00		1400 00	3
Melanchthon Coover, Ardmore	St. Paul's					13		2		6	2	3	10	5	147	27000 00	4000 00	4091 01	4
W. M. B. Glanding, Ashland	St. James			2		56	13	8	26	24	2	23	21	6	228	20000 00	1600 00	3195 68	5
G. W. Fritsch, Ashland	Zion's			2		100	2	3		88		50	4	2	402	8500 00		3440 00	6
	Huntersville (sup'y)					12	2	4	2	7		3	2		50			70 00	7
B. F. Kautz, Millersburg	St. Paul's			2		8				4		1			118	15000 00	800 00	606 15	8
	Salem									1			1		103	3000 00		350 00	9
	Berrysburg					18		1							80			218 30	10
J. Eugene Deitterich, 129 N. Laurel St., Bridgeton, N. J.	Christ's Eng. Luth.			2				4	2	2	2	5			42	1500 00		1832 00	11
Geo. Sill, 2634 N. 11th St., Phila delphia, Chalfont Charge	St. James	1		2	1	15	3			4		3	1	1	40	5600 00	400 00	537 93	12
W. H. Steck, Coatsville	Trinity Lutheran			2		34		4		12	10	9	2	14	100	13000 00	4500 00	7230 78	13
J. F. Shearer, Conshohocken	Second Street			2	1	8	3			10	4	10	2		280	20000 00	1000 00	5014 42	14
M. L. Heisler, 1211 Kittatinny St., Harrisburg, Dauphin Charge	St. Mark's			2												7500 00	5300 00	1637 60	15
	Zion								1	2			5		75				16
R. W. Hufford, D. D., Easton	St. Paul's			2	1	20	3		13	6		11		4	41	3000 00		346 18	17
Chas. R. Trowbridge, College Hill, Easton				2				2		12				11	275	20000 00		2600 00	18
J. Peter, Manheim, Lanc. Co.	St. Peter's	1		2		25	3	2	11	10		6	5		175	16500 00	2250 00	975 00	19
	Grace, East Peters burg and Hill	3		2		38	8	3		9		23			216	10000 00		4487 90	19

PARAROCHIAL REPORT OF THE EAST PENNSYLVANIA SYNOD.—*Continued.*

Index Number.	SUNDAY-SCHOOL.				Contributions		BENEVOLENCE.												
	Lutheran.	Union.	Officers and Teachers.	Scholars.	For Support of School and Local Objects.	For Benevolence.	General Synod.	Synodical Treasury.	Home Missions.	Foreign Missions.	Church Extension.	Board of Education.	Beneficiary Education.	Woman's Missionary Society.	Pastors' Fund.	Orphans' Home.	External Objects.	Total Benevolence.	Grand Total.
1	1	..	54	542	$298 14	$248 46	$6 00	$40 00	$89 06	$80 00	$80 00	$22 00	$60 40	$80 00	$18 00	$36 00	$84 69	$596 15	$1476 15
2	1	.	35	264	265 37	89 82	1 20	8 00	19 29	18 31	18 50	1 10	8 00	....	2 00	9 60	27 29	113 29	2530 32
3	2	..	50	285	125 0	56 31	3 45	23 00	40 04	23 17	35 75	12 65	17 00	....	12 33	50 07	70 41	287 87	1687 87
4	1	..	19	148	188 71	87 45	5 25	25 60	37 00	32 00	42 31	19 25	2 50	163 20	5 75	24 15	53 00	409 44	4500 48
5	1	..	21	260	122 92	65 71	3 40	20 50	40 65	45 52	46 50	14 00	45 00	14 75	11 50	22 50	20 00	284 32	3180 00
6	1	..	30	272	90 00	100 00	3 30	16 70	33 16	42 53	35 00	10 09	33 00	....	6 46	22 00	15 86	218 01	3658 01
7	..	..	....	....	....	....	......	....	....	4 44	....	....	....	....	....	....	....	4 41	74 44
8	1	..	19	175	100 00	51 50	1 18	12 75	17 00	17 00	22 25	....	12 00	23 08	5 00	9 00	13 75	133 01	739 16
9	1	..	15	80	10 00	44 75	1 23	3 00	6 00	6 00	30 00	....	6 00	....	1 00	7 00	....	60 23	410 23
10	..	1	12	85	12 00	....	26	3 00	7 00	6 87	4 00	....	4 00	....	2 00	1 00	....	28 13	246 13
11	1	..	10	40	37 00	21 40	......	4 00	3 00	5 00	21 40	....	1 00	....	....	....	1 00	35 40	1867 40
12	1	..	17	91	54 56	....	60	4 00	8 80	8 00	8 00	2 20	4 00	....	1 80	2 60	1 00	41 00	578 93
13	1	.	26	112	185 00	....	90	6 00	13 20	12 00	12 00	3 39	9 00	....	2 70	3 90	....	63 09	7293 87
14	2	..	54	360	199 02	161 52	4 65	31 00	68 20	62 00	69 75	17 05	46 50	....	13 95	20 15	44 00	377 25	3391 67
15	1	..	21	160	110 00	30 00	90	6 00	13 20	12 00	13 50	3 30	9 00	....	2 70	11 87	25 00	97 47	1734 47
16	1	..	9	30	20 89	6 50	......	2 36	2 50	2 50	2 21	....	....	....	....	3 45	6 50	19 52	365 70
17	1	..	29	175	193 98	108 75	7 65	51 00	162 80	109 95	98 00	28 05	50 00	....	22 95	32 00	25 00	527 40	3127 40
18	1	..	26	189	135 01	47 86	2 70	18 00	28 07	28 07	28 07	9 90	1 00	....	8 10	11 70	3 75	139 36	1114 36
19	2	1	39	408	479 90	8 00	90	4 00	13 20	12 00	12 00	3 30	9 00	4 25	2 70	8 05	20 00	89 40	4577 30

PAROCHIAL REPORT OF THE EAST PENNSYLVANIA SYNOD.—Continued.

Pastor's Name and Address.	Congregations, Names of	Churches	Stations	Prayer Meetings	Students for Ministry	Catechumens	Death	Certificate	Excommunication and other losses	Infant Baptisms	Adult Baptisms	Confirmations	Certificate	Restoration	Communicant Membership	Estimated Value of Church Property	Indebtedness	Local Expenses for All Objects	Index No.
J. M. Stover, Fisherville, Dauphin Co.	Messiah	1		1		12	1	1	1	11					63	$2000 00		$423 04	20
	St. Peter's	1				10	3	2	2	16		3	2	4	55	4500 00		1585 00	21
	St. Paul's	1							1	1				4	26	600 00		187 00	22
	St. James	1								2				1	17	300 00		80 00	23
	Star of Bethlehem	1								2		7		1	24	2000 00		130 00	24
J. A. Singmaster (supply), Allentown	St. John's, Fogelsville			2		18	5	5		3		4			57	3000 00		390 00	25
S. J. McDowell, Friesburg, N. J.	Emmanuel									2		10			180	10000 00		107 00	26
L. E. Albert, D. D., Germantown.	Trinity						1	6		21		16	5		356	60000 00	$8000 00	6141 92	27
A. R. Glaze, Gordon, Schuylkill Co.	St. Paul's, Christ's, Hamilton, St. John's, Bart'nsv'l Zion's, Broadhydsv'l St. Mk's, Appenzell Mt. Acton	6		1		30	1	1		18		16			130	12000 00	4257 28	5160 19	28
Cyrus E. Held, Sciota, Monroe Co.	Tannersville					49	25	10	2	23		49			342	22000 00	400 00	950 00	29
D. M. Gilbert, D. D., 311 Walnut St., Harrisburg	Zion	1		2		75	10	10		13	9	12	22		573	60000 00		5339 87	30
Luther De Yoe, 423 Forster St., Harrisburg	Zion	1		5			8	22		63	40	102	45	5	724	42000 00	14150 00	7470 81	31
S. Dasher, 53 N. Thirteenth St., Harrisburg	Messiah	1		2		190	1	3	3	36	3	19	20	2	169	20000 00	8000 00	10879 26	32
W. H. Fishburn, 1015 Green St., Harrisburg	Memorial	1		4		65	10	16	3	45	47	131	48		719	60000 00	10900 00	7891 99	33
Theodore L. Crouse, 1246 Derry St., Harrisburg	Bethlehem, Christ	1		2		134 55	2	7		28	7	11	29		171	12000 00	4000 00	1554 46	34

PAROCHIAL REPORT OF THE EAST PENNSYLVANIA SYNOD—Continued.

Index Number	Lutheran	Union	Officers and Teachers	Scholars	For Support of School and Local Objects	For Benevolence	General Synod	Synodical Treasury	Home Missions	Foreign Missions	Church Extension	Board of Education	Beneficiary Education	Woman's Miss. Society	Pastors' Fund	Orphans' Home	External Objects	Total Benevolence	Grand Total
20			24	90	$113 00	$3 40	$1 95	$1 87	$18 00	$2 00	$10 40	$1 00	$1 44			$2 02	$18 00	$69 74	$183 74
21			15	55	25 00				3 00	12 00	8 33		5 42			1 66	2 15	31 08	1646 72
22			6	60	12 00				4 00	1 00	2 20		1 39		$5 00		11 66	10 82	197 68
(23)			7	55	25 00						1 00		2 50					2 12	98 50
24			9	40	45 00	1 34			2 00	5 00	4 44						63	12 72	142 72
25			10	143	40 00			5 00	7 00	7 00	7 00	5 00	4 50		1 35	3 00	6 00	35 90	223 30
26			25	219	80 00	27 00	45 60	48 00	75 22	48 00	48 00	13 50	36 00	$68 50	10 80	15 00	22 46	258 00	365 00
27			46	325	341 92	22	3 60	50 00	344 81	570 00	180 00	171 00	105 00		33 00	18 00		379	5321 69
28			29	150	81 33	33 28	1 20	2 00	17 60	16 00	16 00	4 40	12 00		3 60	2 20		86 00	5246 19
29		5				3 75	9 25	15 00	33 00	30 00	30 00	8 25	36		6 75	9 75	2 00	174	1121 92
30	1		82	540	719 55	465 59	18 00	120 00	264 00	240 00	240 00	66 00	120 00	264 62	54 00	78 00	1240 59	2772 63	8312 48
31	1		90	973	758 26	273 91	9 00	60 00	132 00	120 00	120 00	33 00	90 00	73 80	27 00	40 00	117 28	822 50	8292 89
32	1		30	295	312 69	48 00	1 50	7 00	19 30	16 00	19 50	2 50	12 00		4 50	7 00	5 00	93 00	10972 56
33			58	502	514 53	31 79	4 95	33 00	22 00	66 00	46 00	12 10	49 50	42 00	14 85	21 45	167 10	533 80	8347 39
34	2		33	350	208 58	55 00	1 05	11 00	25 75	22 00	24 02	10 00	16 50		4 95	28 50	5 75	150 12	1704 58

PAROCHIAL REPORT OF THE EAST PENNSYLVANIA SYNOD.—Continued.

Pastor's Name and Address.	Congregations, Names of	Churches	Stations	Prayer Meetings	Students for Ministry	Catechumens	Death	Certificate	Excommunication and other losses	Infant Baptisms	Adult Baptisms	Confirmations	Certificate	Restoration	Communicant Membership	Estimated Value of Church Property	Indebtedness	Local Expenses for All Objects	Index No. See line with corresponding No. on page below.
M. L. Deitzler, 631 S. Front St., Harrisburg	Trinity, Harrisburg	1		2		13	2	13	136	4	1	17		9		56	$2500 00		$853 00	35
	St. Paul's, Steelton					6				2				4		13	2000 00	$500 00	204 28	36
Samuel S. Diehl, Kintnersville, Bucks Co.	Nockamixon*													1		300	13500 00		850 00	37
H. G. Snyder, Hummelstown	Upper Tinicum*																			
A. H. F. Fischer, Lafayette Hill	Zion's					42	1	2	3	9		11	3	3		203	8000 00		1292 17	38
Montgomery Co.																				
B. F. Allemaa, D. D., 233 West Chestnut St., Lancaster	St. Peter's			2		12														
	St. John's			1		60	6	5	29	17	8	5	4	4		225	20000 00	39 45	2683 34	39
E. Meister, Lancaster	St. Stephen's					14	12		2	31	4	23	9			340	55000 00	20000 00	3880 77	40
W. H. Dunbar, D. D., Lebanon	Zion			2		40	6	2	1	12		22	24			365	24000 00	10000 00	2515 32	41
M. H. Stine, Lebanon, nine months	7th St. Lutheran												13	1		451	50000 00		4776 28	42
	Mt. Zion					38	4	2	{15 2}	22	3	34	9	1		275	8000 00 {1556 00}	3400 00	1981 09	43
Mark S. Cressman, Lionville	St. Matthew's			2		20	1	1	65	5		1	3	3		80				
	St. Paul's						1			10	8	23				255	20000 00	1500 00	1491 62	44
I. W. Bobst, Lititz	St. Paul's, Lititz					40	1		51	3		3	24			130	7000 00		700 00	45
	Kissel Hill					2	1			3		30	2			92	2000 00		350 00	46
P. S. Hooper, Lykens	Neffsville			2		65	6		15	4		15	13			148	2000 00	2000 00	500 00	47
	Zion		1	1		30	2	6		28		13				272	13500 00	150 00	3500 00	48
	Lyons						2	2		4						43	6300 00		173 00	49
	Macungie			2			1				2					67	7000 00		244 00	50
Geo. J. Martz, Lebanon	Salem			1						3						37	3000 00			51
	Pleasantville				1		3		10			2				35	6000 00		125 00	52
	Mohrsville			2	2				6				2			58	3000 00		264 09	53

* Benevolence reported in Springtown charge. † Reported in Riegelsville charge.

PAROCHIAL REPORT OF THE EAST PENNSYLVANIA SYNOD.—Continued.

Index Number.	Lutheran.	Union.	Officers and Teachers.	Scholars.	For Support of School and Local Objects.	For Benevolence.	General Synod.	Synodical Treasury.	Home Missions.	Foreign Missions.	Church Extension.	Board of Education.	Beneficiary Education.	Woman's Missionary Society.	Pastors' Fund.	Orphans' Home.	External Objects.	Total Benevolence.	Grand Total.
35	1		36	275	$156 00	$19 98	$ 45	$3 00	$6 00	$5 00	$5 00	$1 65	$4 50		$ 35	$1 95	$20 73	$52 25	$465 23
36	1					8 24	15	1 00	2 25	2 25	2 25	55	1 50		45	65	8 47	18 97	223 25
37	1		14	80	89 17														850 00
38	2		33	350	206 25	37 63	2 50	20 00	27 83	25 00	39 62	10 00	40 00	74 00	10 00	20 15	66 53	194 50	1486 67
39		4	22	119	65 41	82 16	4 50	15 00	49 00	44 00	55 50	10 00	46 31	163 62	13 50	25 30		403 64	2036 98
40	2		51	372	1300 14	160 82	7 60	66 00	130 00	130 00	147 00	7 50	93 83	201 86	29 70	42 90	60 00	818 15	4098 92
41	1		27	225	284 16	40 00		5 00	5 00	5 00	5 00	25 19	5 00			5 00	250 00	90 00	2905 32
42	1		58	619	459 68	254 73	10 00	50 00	100 00	140 00	123 25		119 50		41 85	131 48		1199 13	5975 41
43	2		30	350	445 44	7 00	4 35	19 87	205 88	85 00	40 00	20 00	18 00		29 70	19 85	7 25	212 12	2193 21
44	1		41	228	148 75	96 00	8 00	30 00	87 08	85 00	97 88	9 25	78 90	67 37	24 30	51 80	70 00	620 42	2112 04
45	1		32	213	175 00	35 00		15 00	33 00	30 00	47 50		22 50	21 00	6 75	24 00	90 00	231 25	1781 25
46	1		12	80	10 00	11 81	2 25	3 00	12 00	14 98	21 80		5 00		7 25	15 51		131 61	3631 61
47	1		27	130	175 00	14 51	2 07	1 91	20 00	22 94	10 00	20 00		33 35			50 00	141 07	683 07
48	1		30	150	80 00								21 87			25 00			
49	1		13	154	25 00													49 00	313 09
50	1		25	90					19 50	19 50	10 00								
51	1		22	45															
52	1		10	86	52 82	25 56													
53	1		23																

PAROCHIAL REPORT OF THE EAST PENNSYLVANIA SYNOD.—Continued.

PASTOR'S NAME AND ADDRESS.	CONGREGATIONS, NAMES OF	Churches.	Stations.	Prayer Meetings.	Students for Ministry.	Catechumens.	Death.	Certificate.	Excommunication and other losses.	Infant Baptisms.	Adult Baptisms.	Confirmations.	Certificate.	Restoration.	Communicant Membership.	Estimated Value of Church Property.	Indebtedness.	Local Expenses for all Objects.	Index No. See line with corresponding No. on page below.
Rev. I. P. Zimmerman, Mahanoy City	St. John's English Lutheran	1		2	1	30	4	5	16	2		21			300	$10000 00		$1763 83	54
J. H. Menges, 2510 Spring Garden St., Philadelphia, Manheim charge	Zion's	1		2	1	50	4	3	1	6	1	13	1	1	146	20000 00		13809 00	55
William Hesse, Martin's Creek	Trinity																			
	Zion's												13		225	7500 00		1043 00	56
W. H. Harding, Maytown	St. John's, Maytown					61	5	2		14	2	16	13		135	6000 00		649 21	57
F. W. Staley, Middletown	St. Luke's, Bainbridge					43	2	1	25	14	1	15	5		95	3000 00		477 50	58
A. W. Lentz, Millersville, (supply)	St. Peter's					40	3	4		14	9	25	30		347	35000 00	4300 00	688 89	59
J. C. Trauger, Tremont	Bethany																			
	Tremont, St. John's					5	1	2	21	4	4	5	1		43	2500 00		450 06	60
Schuylkill Co.	Minersville					22	1	1	31	11	1	4	7		90	5000 00		675 00	61
John V. Eckert, Lancaster	Mount Eden					19	1	4	18	13		3	4		120	2000 00		250 00	62
	Ebenezer, N. A.														46	2000 00	500 00	225 00	63
J. R. Mittelholzer, New Amsterdam, Berbice, British Guiana	Bethel																			
	Mt. Hermon	5	6		1	47	8	3	14	26	6	47	10	3	257	46400 00	1053 50	7008 05	64
	Mt. Carmel																			
	Bethesda																			
	Mt. Lebanon																			
E. S. Morell, Norwood	Immanuel	1		1		5	1	3		11	3	6	3		63	6000 00	1000 00	1391 71	65
W. M. Baum, D. D., 630 N. Broad St., Philadelphia	St. Matthew's	1		2		25	4	5	14			13	17		296	200000 00	15000 00	24022 20	66

PAROCHIAL REPORT OF THE EAST PENNSYLVANIA SYNOD.—Continued.

Index Number.	Lutheran.	Union.	Officers and Teachers.	Scholars.	SUNDAY-SCHOOL CONTRIBUTIONS: For Support of School and Local Objects.	For Benevolence.	BENEVOLENCE: General Synod.	Synodical Treasury.	Home Missions.	Foreign Missions.	Church Extension.	Board of Education.	Beneficiary Education.	Woman's Missionary Society.	Pastors' Fund.	Orphans' Home.	External Objects.	Total Benevolence.	Grand Total.
54	1		30	270	$255 02	$173 50	$4 25	$22 00	$70 75	$45 00	$72 00	$17 60	$48 00	$129 95	$14 40	$53 50	$39 31	$807 31	$2571 14
55	1		95	550	58 67	39 84		8 00	7 84	6 00				6 00		26 00		45 84	1045 84
56	1		26	192	63 00	14 71	2 50	22 00	15 00	15 00	16 25	10 00	5 00	5 00	6 00	7 10	8 75	93 60	1136 60
57	1		27	173	121 35	15 78	1 80	12 00	26 40	21 00	29 00	6 00	18 00	9 00	5 40	7 80	23 18	159 18	1285 99
58	1		15	92	40 00	51 46	5 40	36 00	79 20	72 00	72 00	19 80	54 00	10 00	16 20	50 55	26 45	470 62	6359 51
59	1		48	75	760 00	116 52													
60	1		10	70	36 00	46 02	1 12	4 00	17 00	16 00	10 00	1 33	5 00		2 19	17 00	36 00	117 19	567 19
61	1		20	139	110 00	47 12	1 12	4 50	16 50	15 00	15 00	4 34	11 15		3 36	4 87	1 22	80 72	755 72
62	1		16	103	70 00			7 00	16 50	15 00	15 00		11 15		3 37	4 88	1 87	80 73	830 73
63	1		14	55	35 00			1 00										1 00	236 00
64			15			32 05					5 00								7013 05
65	1		21	124	167 21	16 61	75	5 00	9 73	5 00	6 88	1 04	7 50		2 25		1 25	40 00	1341 71
66	1		36	302	220 30	584 17	18 00	120 00	327 92	240 00	296 83	66 00	230 00		54 00	108 00	181 82	1642 57	2564 77

332   EAST PENNSYLVANIA SYNOD.

PAROCHIAL REPORT OF THE EAST PENNSYLVANIA SYNOD.—Continued.

PAROCHIAL.

Pastor's Name and Address.	Congregations, Name of	Churches.	Stations.	Prayer Meetings.	Students for Ministry.	Catechumens.	Deaths.	Certificate.	Excommunication and other losses.	Infant Baptisms.	Adult Baptisms.	Confirmations.	Certificate.	Restoration.	Communicant Membership.	Estimated Value of Church Property.	Indebtedness.	Local Expenses for All Objects.	Index No. See line with corresponding No. on page below.
									Losses.		Accessions.					Finances.			
F. Huber, D. D., Gettysburg	Messiah, 16th and Jefferson Sts., Phila.				3		4	17	84	11		8	8	17	313	$80000 00	$5500 00	$1143 46	67
Phila., (now vacant)	Grace, 35th and Spring Garden	1		2		35	1	7	112	8	4	31		29	190	30000 00	10000 00	2500 00	68
J. H. Main, 3801 Haverford St., Philadelphia	Calvary	1		2		10	3	4	21	2	1	4	4	33	120	12000 00	4200 00	1457 29	69
A. Holman, D. D., 505 N. 40th Philadelphia	Bethany	1		2	1	23	1	5	16	10	1	14	5	5	157	17000 00	9500 00	2359 87	70
S. G. Shannon, 2923 Montgomery Ave., Pa.	All Saints			2		12		1		12	2	6	25	5	77	18000 00	12290 00	1501 14	71
Frank P. Manhart, 1824 Cayuga St., Philadelphia	St. James	1		1	1	10	8	2	6	13	2	9	2	2	200	10000 00		1400 00	72
T. C. Pritchard, Phillipsburg, N. J.	Central Lutheran	1		2	1	28	2	2	21	1		12	3		164	25000 00	329 00	1283 80	73
John Kling, Phoenixville	Palmyra, St. John's	1												8		28	5700 00	3000 00	2700 00	74
D. R. Becker, Palmyra, Lebanon Co.	Bellegrove,* Christ																			
J. A. Hackenberg, Kimberton	St. Peter's Centennial	1	2	1	1	20	2	4	8	5		6	4	4	153	12000 00		900 00	75
Elias S. Henry, Pine Grove	St. John's Jacob's Salem's	4		3	1	125	25	10		133	4	73	12	12	634	18000 00		1950 00	76
P. C. Croll, Schuylkill Haven	St. Peter's St. Matthew's		2	2		26	8	4	3	35	2	10	4	4	224	15000 00		1394 42	77
E. G. Huy, Pottsville	English Lutheran			2		18	10	2	7	30	6	12	2	21	495	22000 00		2617 62	78
T. C. Billheimer, D. D., Reading	St. Matthew's			2		17		2	12	19	3		21	9	349	60000 00	30000 00	2107 00	79

* Reported in Union Deposit Charge.

PAROCHIAL REPORT OF THE EAST PENNSYLVANIA SYNOD.—*Continued.*

Index Number	Lutheran	Union	Officers and Teachers	Scholars	For Support of School and Local Objects	For Benevolence	General Synod	Synodical Treasury	Home Missions	Foreign Missions	Church Extension	Board of Education	Beneficiary Education	Woman's Missionary Society	Pastors' Fund	Orphans' Home	External Objects	Total Benevolence	Grand Total
67	1		29	241	$279 50	$287 63	$7 50	$50 00	$110 00	$100 00	$100 00	$27 50	$75 00		$22 50	$22 50	$255 02	$700 02	$4933 48
68	1		25	236	300 00	42 00			14 00	14 00	25 00					21 00		73 00	2575 00
69	1		24	250	187 92	104 47	2 10	10 30	27 57	25 00	25 00	7 70	21 00	$39 60	3 00	5 20	127 97	222 21	1729 55
70	1		33	349	288 95	139 12	1 20	8 00	17 60	16 00	40 00	4 40	12 00	19 60		5 80	2 00	129 00	2188 32
71	1		18	157	175 51	33 77	75	4 25	11 00	9 10	10 00	2 75	6 50		2 25	15 12	12 35	64 85	1565 49
72	1		20	175	120 00	51 44	5 00	5 00	14 30	45 00	23 53	10 00	10 00	15 40	10 00	15 12	12 00	265 55	1695 55
73	1		17	125	60 00			15 00	20 00	20 00	27 20		19 24	17 10	5 34	10 00	33 00	167 48	1461 25
74	2		10	40	56 00												56 00	56 00	2736 00
75	1		18	150	75 00	45 00	2 00	16 00	20 40	70 00	50 00	5 00	15 00		11 00	15 60		173 00	1075 00
76	3		80	750	350 00	157 00	4 00	25 00	68 00	62 00	60 00	10 00	40 00	57 00	10 00	27 00	217 00	525 00	2473 00
77	1		28	190	162 49	190 21	3 60	24 00	12 37	18 84	31 00	10 00	36 00	25 00	10 04	25 00	10 00	337 85	1732 15
78	1		45	451	405 46	119 35	5 00	40 00	20 00	62 00	71 17	15 00	60 00		12 00	29 30	25 00	417 37	2064 37
79	1		41	345	232 00		7 95	53 00	100 00	50 00	50 00	20 00	42 00		25 00	31 30	13 25	391 50	3298 52

PAROCHIAL REPORT OF THE EAST PENNSYLVANIA SYNOD.—Continued.

Pastor's Name and Address	Congregations, Names of	Churches	Stations	Prayer Meetings	Students for Ministry	Catechumens	Death	Certificate	Excommunication and other losses	Infant Baptisms	Adult Baptisms	Confirmations	Certificate	Restoration	Communicant Membership	Estimated Value of Church Property	Indebtedness	Local Expenses for All Objects	Index No. see line corresponding No. on page below
C. L. Fleck, Riegelsville, Bucks Co.	St. Peter's Evan. Lutheran St. Paul's	1 1		2 1 1	1 1	20 17	2	4	1	16 21	4	13 17	4	4	622	$15000 00 2000 00 4000 00	$2100 00	$1672 11 258 25 628 00	80 81 82
M. Fernsler, Schaefferstown, Lebanon Co.	Schaefferstown Brickerv'e(St.John's) St. Paul's			1 1		32 15 24	15 3 3	7 12 6		33 9 21		7 15 3	2 10 3		413 152 201	4500 00 3000 00 5000 00	100 00 1700 00 1400 00	443 00 640 00 513 00	83 84 85
M. H. Havice, Shenandoah	Shoop's			1		20				4	4				133			640 00	86
W. L. Heisler, cor. 29th & Kensington sts., Harrisburg (Shoop's charge)	Salem Lingdestown Union Chapel									7		4			88	2700 00		384 00	87
O. H. Melchor, Springtown, Bucks Co.	Durham Springfield Springtown St. John's	1 1 1 1		1 1 1 1	1 1 3	30 15 33 60	8 5 3	4 7 12	1	25 26 8 40		27 26	14 12	4	300 391 102 203	12000 00 8000 00 6000 00 12000 00		1013 18 450 00 200 00 4354 85	88 89 90 91 92
M. P. Hocker, Steelton W. L. Rutherford, 43 N. Front st., Steelton	St. Mark's Stewartsville Luth.	1 1		1 2 1		11 11	5			12	6	21 12	3		64 182	10000 00 9000 00	150 00 75 00	462 40 1072 30 743 00	93 94 95
Wm. E. Fry, Stewartsville, N. J. I. H. McGann, Stone Church, Northampton co.																			
J. M. Deitzler, Union Deposit, Dauphin Co.	St. Paul's, Union Deposit Sand Hill, Sandy Hollow Hoernerstown Bellegrove*	4		4	1	20	10			3	1	21	21		210 186	10000 00 4000 00	800 00	700 00 76 00	96 97

* Now in Palmyra charge.

					CONTRIBUTIONS															
Index Number.	Lutheran.	Union.	Officers and Teachers.	Scholars.	For Support of School and Local Objects.	For Benevolence.	General Synod.	Synodical Treasury.	Home Missions.	Foreign Missions.	Church Extension.	Board of Education.	Beneficiary Education.	Woman's Missionary Society.	Pastors' Fund.	Orphans' Home.	External Objects.	Total Benevolence.	Grand Total.
80	1	..	18	325	$70 00	$134 18	$3 00	$13 00	$52 77	$53 00	$57 00	$15 15	$31 00	$74 50	$3 95	$20 35	$7 73	$331 43	$2003 51
81	..	1	16	82	28 00	3 00	......	7 00	14 60	11 00	16 18	4 00	11 50	....	2 00	....	....	66 28	304 28
82	1	..	14	109	73 00	29 15	1 00	5 00	8 68	9 70	10 50	5 00	7 50	17 00	4 00	6 77	....	75 15	663 40
83	1	1	28	240	148 00	25 68	} 2 00	10 00	25 00	27 00	26 25	....	10 00	25 00	5 21	32 97	... ...	163 43	1284 43
84	1	1	30	170	93 00	8 76		6 00	13 20	12 00	13 50	3 30	9 00	....	2 70	3 90	....	64 50	704 50
85	1	..	23	112	104 00	21 00	90	6 00	13 20	12 00	13 50	3 30	9 00	....	2 70	3 90	....	64 50	704 50
86	..	1	26	100	75 00	3 45	1 40	5 00	20 85	10 57	19 94	4 00	17 24	....	5 00	3 45	3 45	90 90	603 90
87	1	..	21	219	100 00	48 20	1 00	2 50	14 35	13 00	14 42	2 00	6 76	....	2 20	12 00	48 20	116 43	500 43
88	..	1	23	185	23 18	4 64								54 15				54 15	1073 33
89	..	3	45	311	108 55	12 00	} 9 00	10 00	100 00	120 00	60 00	11 00	90 00	16 00	15 00	20 00	......	451 00	901 00
90	..	1	16	66	56 33	12 00	}.	26 00	77 00	52 00	110 00	14 30	223 60	20 00			......	20 00	220 00
91	1	..	60	515	518 53	114 18	3 90	26 00	77 00	52 00	110 00	14 30	223 60	125 00	11 70	20 56	50 00	714 06	5268 91
92	1	..	16	145	112 49	18 50		1 00	6 00	4 00	12 00	1 50	3 00	....	15 71	18 50		61 71	524 20
93	1	..	16	90	69 61	15 30	2 85	19 00	34 96	56 26	30 25	10 45	28 50	12 52	8 55	8 75	30 25	243 34	1315 54
95	1	..	17	162	63 81	27 10	4 00	27 00	52 00	35 00	36 17	12 13	35 00	10 00	12 15	26 55	...	230 00	973 00
96	4	1	30	300	29 00	6 00	3 00	10 00	15 00	15 00	6 00	4 00	10 00	....	41 00	14 00	50 00	168 00	868 00
97	1	..	13	87	25 00	8 00	1 00	6 00	10 00	9 00	6 00	3 00	2 00	....	1 00	8 00	25 00	71 00	147 00

PAROCHIAL REPORT OF THE EAST PENNSYLVANIA SYNOD.—Continued.

Pastor's Name and Address.	Congregations, Names of	Churches.	Stations.	Prayer Meetings.	Students for Ministry.	Catechumens.	Death.	Certificate.	Excommunication and other losses.	Infant Baptisms.	Adult Baptisms.	Confirmations.	Certificate.	Restoration.	Communicant Membership.	Estimated Value of Church Property.	Indebtedness.	Local Expenses for All Objects.	Index No. See line with corresponding No. on page below.
M. Sheeleigh, D. D., Fort Washington	Whitemarsh	1	2										5		316	$15000 00		$1000 00	98
	Upper Dublin	1																		99
J., A. Adams, Williamstown, Dauphin co.	Emmanuel's	1	1			42		7		9	19	1	6	6		147	5750 00		1365 50	100
supplied	Stranstown	1	1													23	2000 00			101
supplied	Port Carbon									17						47	1000 00			102
Disbanded	Templeman's Chapel									6										103
Disbanded	Richland																			104
Totals for 1892		119 9		1	1	2547	389	385	1041	1440	365	1310	702	223	19571	1599450 00	$206108 17	$218872 11	104
Totals for 1891		117 14		1		2942	331	369	476	1173	271	1123	844	202	18766	1603450 00	178858 91	253863 52	105
Excess		2		1	1		58		565	267	94	187		21	865		$27339 26			106
Deficiency		5				565		184					142			$4000 00		$17491 38		107

PAROCHIAL REPORT OF THE EAST PENNSYLVANIA SYNOD.—Concluded.

Index Number.	Lutheran.	Union.	Officers and Teachers.	Scholars.	For Support of School and Local Objects.	For Benevolence.	General Synod.	Synodical Treasury.	Home Missions.	Foreign Missions.	Church Extension.	Board of Education.	Beneficiary Education.	Woman's Missionary Society.	Pastors' Fund.	Orphans' Home.	External Objects.	Total Benevolence.	Grand Total.
98	2	1	35	270	$70 00	$40 00	$1 60	$24 00	$36 45	$34 06	$33 61	$21 39	$25 34		$10 50	$15 60	$120 00	$325 05	$1325 05
99	1	1	24	200	174 64	24 95	90	6 00	13 20	12 00	15 14	3 30	9 00		2 70	3 90	26 45	92 59	1456 09
100	1																		
101	1		12	65															
102																			
103																			
104	5735	1	2119	21377	16091 56	$3888 69	252 14	$1479 00	$3732 10	$1554 31	$3423 53	$921 11	$2341 96	$1181 62	$814 13	$1704 59	$4888 90	$27422 11	$243794 65
105	9434	1	2691	21576	17238 95	6389 63	248 16	793 62	3055 27	4343 21	3702 74	863 11	3271 78	2563 83	682 42	1555 74	5460 25	24354 14	282491 03
106	3	1																	
107			72	199	$1147 39	$500 94	$3 98	$685 37	$638 83	$788 96	$279 21	$57 40	$408 80	$682 21	121 71	$148 85	$565 05	$1205 63	$11687 10

REGISTER OF PASTORS

Who have served Congregations now in connection with the Evangelical Lutheran Synod of East Pennsylvania, or those out of which the present organizations have grown, showing also places and dates of Pastorates within the bounds of Synod, as well as dates of Honorary Degrees and names of Colleges by which the latter were conferred.

ADAMS, JOHN ALEXANDER.
    Williamstown, 1888-date.

AHL, PETER.
    Springfield and Nockamixon, 1789-1797.

ALBERT, JOHN JACOB.
    East Petersburg, 1853-1855.
    Mt. Zion, Martin's Creek, and Christ, Centreville, 1855-1859.

ALBERT, LUTHER ENDRESS. D. D., Penna. College, 1867.
    Trinity, Germantown, 1851-date.
    Whitemarsh (Supply), 1852.

ALLEMAN, BENJAMIN FRANKLIN. D. D., Newberry College, 1885.
    St. John's, Lancaster, 1887-date.

ALLEMAN, HERBERT CHRISTIAN.
    Millersville, 1889.

ANSPACH, FREDERICK REINHARDT. D. D., Franklin and Marshall College, 1857.
    Whitemarsh and Barren Hill, 1841-1850.

ANSPACH, JOHN MELANCHTHON. D. D., Missionary Institute, Selinsgrove, 1890.
    St. Matthew's, Reading, 1872-1877.

ANTHONY, JACOB BACHMAN.
    Minersville, 1874-1875.
    Schuylkill Haven, 1875-1876.

APPLE, BENJAMIN FRANKLIN.
    Maytown, 1862-1864.

AUGHEY, SAMUEL. Ph. D., University of Ohio, 1874: LL.D., Wittenberg
College, 1878.
Pikeland (with Lionville), 1858-1859.
Lionville, 1859-1861.
AULD, EZEKIEL ALEXANDER.
Minersville, 1860-1864.
AURAND, FREDERICK.
Fisherville Charge, 1872-1874.
Millersville and Neffsville, 1883-1884.
AURAND, CHARLES MONROE.
Maytown, 1884-1885.
BAETES, WILLIAM.
Friesburg, 1808-1810.
Brickerville and Schaefferstown, 1810-1836.
Kissel Hill, 1824-1839.
Manheim, 1825-1828 (?).
BAKER, JOHN CHRISTOPHER. D. D., Lafayette College, 1837.
St. Michael's, Germantown, 1812-1828.
Barren Hill and Ardmore, 1812-1828.
Whitemarsh, 1818-1828.
Trinity, Lancaster, 1828-1853.
BARCLAY, JOSEPH HENRY. D. D., Roanoke College, 1876.
Stewartsville, 1859-1863.
St. Paul's, Easton, 1868-1872.
Mission Chapel, College Hill, Easton, 1870-1872.
BARNITZ, JOHN CHARLES.
Ardmore, 1835-1840.
Kissel Hill, 1846-1854.
Manheim (Supply), 1869-1870.
BARNITZ, FREDERICK AUGUSTUS.
St. James', Ashland, 1862-1864.
BAUM, WILLIAM MILLER. D. D., Pennsylvania College, 1867.
Middletown, 1848-1852.
Whitemarsh, 1852-1854.
Barren Hill, 1852-1858.
St. Matthew's, Philadelphia, 1874-date.
BAUM, WILLIAM MILLER, JR.
Phœnixville, 1880-1883.
BECKER, DANIEL RAUSCHER.
Palmyra and Bellegrove, 1892-date.
BECKNER, DANIEL.
Mahanoy City, 1871-1875.

BERKEMEYER, FERDINAND.
    Friesburg, 1855–1857.
BERKINSTOCK, JOHN JUSTUS JACOB.
    St. John's, Easton, 1740–1748.
BERLIN, SOLOMON JESSE.
    Tremont, 1867.
BICKEL, HENRY MILLER. D. D., Western Maryland College, 1892.
    Chalfont, 1874–1875.
    Chalfont, 1889–1890.
    Lutheran Observer Office, 1877–date.
BILLHEIMER, THOMAS CHARLES. D. D., Pennsylvania College, 1886.
    St. Matthew's, Reading, 1877–date.
BOBST, ISAAC WALTON.
    Lititz Charge, 1889–date.
BOYER, SIMON REINHART.
    Kissel Hill, 1862–1864.
BRAAS, ——.
    Greenwich, N. J., 1777–1781.
BREIDENBAUGH, EDWARD.
    Jacob's and St. John's, Pine Grove, 1849–1852.
BREININGER, JOHN GEORGE.
    Fisherville Charge, 1867–1868.
BRICKER, JACOB KISSEL.
    Fisherville Charge, 1877–1879.
BRIDGEMAN, AUGUSTUS L.
    Friesburg, 1852–1854.
BROWN, JAMES ALLEN. D. D., Pennsylvania College, 1859; LL.D.,?Wooster University, 1879.
    St. Matthew's, Reading, 1849–1859.
BROWN, GEORGE GIDEON MALACHI.
    Minersville and Tremont, 1888–1889.
BROWNMILLER, EPHRAIM STEIN.
    Union Deposit, 1874–1881.
BRUNNHOLTZ, PETER.
    Philadelphia, 1745–1757.
    St. Michael's, Germantown, 1745–1751.
    Friesburg, 1749–1756 (?).
BURKHALTER (BURKE), ISRAEL CALVERT.
    Mahanoy City, 1867–1869.
    Columbia, 1875–1877.

BURRELL, JOHN ILGEN.
    Stone Church, 1860–1875.
    Mt. Zion, Martin's Creek, 1860–1864.
    Trinity, Martin's Creek, 1864–1875.

CLARE, RICHARD HENRY.
    Hamilton Charge, 1882–1892.

COLLINS, BENJAMIN BRUBAKER.
    Chalfont, 1877–1881.

COLSON, J.
    Hamilton Charge, 1810–1812.

CONRAD, FREDERICK WILLIAM. D. D., Wittenberg College, 1864; LL.D., Roanoke College, 1889.
    Messiah, Philadelphia, 1866–1872.
    Editor *Lutheran Observer*, 1862–date.

COOK, HERMAN SIDNEY.
    Lionville, 1877–1882.
    Messiah, Harrisburg, 1883–1888.

COOVER, MELANCHTHON.
    Ardmore, 1890–date.

CORNELL, NATHAN HENRY.
    Ardmore, 1844–1848.
    Pikeland, 1863–1874.

CRESSMAN, MARK STETLER.
    Lionville, 1888–date.

CRIST, JACOB BISHOP.
    Maytown, 1852–1855.

CRIST, ISAIAH BENJAMIN.
    Mohrsville, 1883–1885.
    Hummelstown, 1885–1890.

CROLL, ALFRED DELONG.
    Lyons Charge, 1868–1876.

CROLL, PHILIP COLUMBUS.
    Mohrsville, 1879–1882.
    Schuylkill Haven, 1882–1892.
    Seventh Street, Lebanon, 1892–date.

CROUSE, THEODORE LUTHER.
    Christ, Harrisburg, 1890–date.

CRUMBAUGH, JOHN SAMUEL.
    St. John's, Lancaster, 1853–1857.

CRUSE, CHRISTIAN FREDERIC.
    Friesburg, 1819–1824.
    St. Matthew's, Philadelphia, between 1818 and 1827.

CURTIS, SYLVANDER.
    Friesburg, 1866-1868.
    St. James', Ashland, 1868-1870.

CUTTER, WILLIAM ISAAC.
    Brickerville, 1875-1877.
    Lyons Charge, 1877-1878.

DANNER, JOHN A.
    Union Deposit Charge, 1887.

DARON, EDWARD.
    Fisherville Charge, 1869-1872.
    Shoop's Charge, 1872-1878.
    Sandy Hollow, 1872-1875.
    St. John's. Steelton, 1875-1878.
    Lyons Charge, 1878-1880.

DASHER, SOLOMON.
    Memorial, Harrisburg, 1872-date,
    Shoep's Charge, 1881-1885.

DAVIDSON, JOHN HAMPTON.
    Fisherville Charge, 1860-1862.

DEITZLER, JEFFERSON MENNIG.
    St. Peter's, Pine Grove Charge, 1846-47.
    Schaefferstown Charge, including at times Schaefferstown, Strausstown, Mt. Gretna, Womelsdorf, Jonestown, Fredericksburg, Bellegrove, Mt. Zion and Hill Churches, 1850-1865.
    Annville, Hill and Bellegrove, 1865-1890.
    Seventh Street, Lebanon, and Mt. Zion, 1866-1882.
    Union Deposit Charge, 1890-date.

DEITZLER, MARTIN LUTHER.
    St. Paul's, Steelton, and Trinity, Harrisburg, 1890-date.

DELP, WILLIAM SPEECE.
    Chalfont, 1881-1882.

DEMME, CHARLES RUDOLPH. D. D., University of Pennsylvania, 1832.
    Hummelstown, 1819-1822.

DE YOE, LUTHER E.*
    Messiah, Harrisburg, 1891-date.

DIEHL, CASPAR.
    Hamilton Charge, 1805-1810.

DIEHL, GEORGE. D. D., Pennsylvania College, 1856.
    Christ, Easton, 1843-1851.
    Riegelsville, 1850-1851.

* Not a true " Initial," but merely a distinctive letter adopted for convenience

DIEHL, SAMUEL SYLVESTER.
> Kintnersville Charge (Nockamixon and Upper Tinicum), 1892–date.

DIETTERICH, JAMES EUGENE.
> Friesburg, 1887–1891.
> Bridgeton, 1891–date.

DIMM, JONATHAN ROSE. D. D., Pennsylvania College, 1884.
> Barren Hill, 1867–1871.
> Corresponding Secretary Lutheran Publication Society, 1871–1872.
> Messiah, Philadelphia, 1872–1874.
> Pikeland, 1880–1882.

DOMER, SAMUEL. D. D., Roanoke College, 1876.
> St. Matthew's, Reading, 1869–1872.

DORSEY, EDWIN, M. D.
> Columbia, 1860–1863.

DOX, HENRY L.
> Tremont, 1876–1878.

DUNBAR, WILLIAM HENRY. D. D., Pennsylvania College, 1892.
> St. Peter's, Easton, 1874–1880.
> Zion, Lebanon, 1880–date.

DUY, JACOB C.
> Friesburg, 1837–1839.

EARHART, MICHAEL GORDON.
> St. Mark's, Steelton, 1891–1892.

EARLY, JOHN WILLIAM.
> East Petersburg, 1862–1863.
> Maytown, 1865–1867.

ECKERT, JOHN VARNS.
> Maytown, 1876–1880.
> Neffsville and Millersville, 1881–1882.
> Mt. Eden, 1878–date.

EGGERS, LEWIS GUSTAVUS.
> Union Deposit, 1847–1852.

EHREHART, CHARLES JOHN.
> Middletown, 1856–1865.
> Preparatory Department, Pennsylvania College, 1865–1870.

ELLERY, J. FREDERICK.
> Maytown, 1878–1884.

ELLISEN, GEORGE FREDERICK.
> St. Paul's, Allentown, 1793–1796.

EMERY, WILLIAM SADLER.
> Kintnersville Charge, 1865–1879.

ENDERLEIN, JOHN MICHAEL.
    Springfield, 1763-1770(?).
    Nockamixon, 1766-1770(?).
    Maytown, 1770-1778.
    Hummelstown, 1771-1778.
    St. Peter's (Fisherville Charge). 1795-1807.

ENDRESS, CHRISTIAN FREDERICK LUDWIG. D. D., University of Pennsylvania, 1819.
    St. John's, Easton, and St. James', Greenwich, 1801-1815.
    Hamilton, 1803-1805.
    Trinity, Lancaster, 1815-1827.

ENGEL, SAMUEL S.
    Brickerville, East Petersburg and Kissel Hill, 1870-1874.
    Fisherville Charge, 1874-1875.

ENGELLAND, JOHN THEOPHILUS.
    Hummelstown, 1756-(?).
    Middletown, 1767-1773.

ERHARD, AMOS B.*
    Fisherville Charge, 1879-1883.

ERHART, JULIUS.
    Jerusalem, Schuylkill Haven, 1854-1865.
    Salem's, Pine Grove Charge, 1854-1856
    St. Peter's, Pine Grove Charge, 1854-1855.

ERNST, JOHN FREDERICK.
    St. John's, Easton, 1780-1782.
    St. James', Greenwich, 1781-1790.
    Manheim and Maytown, 1802-1805.
    Hummelstown, 1804-1805.

ERNST, WILLIAM GOTTHOLD. D. D., Pennsylvania College, 1839.
    Maytown, 1812-1815.
    Salem, Lebanon, 1815-1836.
    Hill Church, 1815-1836.
    Annville, 1815-1849.

EVANS, WILLIAM PAYSON.
    Friesburg, 1879-1881.
    Columbia, 1881-1888.

EVERETT, THOMAS THOMPSON. D. D., Washington and Lee University, 1881.
    Messiah, Harrisburg, 1888-1890.

EYSTER, DAVID.
    St. Matthew's, Philadelphia (Supply), after 1818, before 1827.

EYSTER, WILLIAM FRANKLIN.
    Trinity, Germantown, 1844-1851.

* Not a true " Initial," but merely a distinctive letter adopted for convenience.

FELTON, EPHRAIM.
>St. James', Ashland, 1887-1889.

FERNSLER, MOSES.
>Fisherville Charge, 1863-1866.
>Berrysburg Charge (including Lykens until 1871), 1866-1878.
>Schaefferstown and Brickerville, 1878-date.

FETZER, CHRISTIAN AUGUSTUS.
>Annville Charge, 1860-1863.
>Berrysburg Charge, 1863-1866.

FICKINGER, CHARLES.
>Minersville, 1869-1870.

FINCKEL, SAMUEL DEVIN. D. D., Irving College, 1859.
>Millersburg, about 1832.
>Middletown, 1837-1840.
>Trinity, Germantown, 1840-1844.
>Ardmore, 1842-1844.

FINKBINER, JOHN WILLIAM.
>Middletown, 1872-1883.

FISCHER, AUGUST HERMANN FRANCKE.
>Barren Hill, 1889-date.
>Conshohocken (Supply), 1889-1890.

FISHBURN, JEREMIAH.
>Berrysburg Charge, 1883-1890.

FISHBURN, WILLIAM HALLER.
>Lykens, 1886-1887.
>Bethlehem, Harrisburg, 1887-date.

FLECK, HENRY RAMEY.
>Stone Church, 1875-1881.

FLECK, CYRUS LEMUEL.
>Riegelsville Charge, (including Upper Tinicum until 1892,) 1887-date.

FOCHT, JOSEPH R.*
>Manheim, East Petersburg and Kissel Hill, 1864-1868.
>Millersville, 1867-1868.
>Hamilton Charge, 1869-1874.

FRANCIS, JACOB MILTON.
>Conshohocken, 1890.

FREDERICK, CHRISTOPHER GOTTLIEB.
>Manheim and Brickerville, 1842-1849.
>Kissel Hill, 1842-1846.

FREDERICK, THOMAS JACKSON.
>Shoop's Charge, 1888-1890.

* Not a true " Initial," but merely a distinctive letter adopted for convenience.

FRIEDERICI, JOHN ANDREAS.
    Hamilton, 1763-1790.
FRIEDERICI, SOLOMON.
    St. John's, Easton, 1782-1798.
FRITSCH, GEORGE WASHINGTON.
    Lyons Charge, 1885-1891.
    Zion's, Ashland, 1891-date.
FRITZ, JOHN HENRY.
    Tannersville (Supply), 1872-1873.
FRY, WILLIAM ENGELBERT.
    Stewartsville, 1801-date.
FUCHS, ANDREAS.
    Mt. Zion, Martin's Creek, 1837-1850.
GEISER, DIXON HOOVER.
    Augsburg, Harrisburg, 1892-date.
GEISSENHAINER, FREDERICK WILLIAM, SR. D. D., University of Pennsylvania, 1826.
    Pikeland, 1818-1822.
GEISSENHAINER, FREDERICK WILLIAM, JR. D. D., University of City of New York, 1863.
    Pikeland, 1817-December, 1826.
GEISSENHAINER, HENRY ANASTASIUS.
    Upper Dublin, 1797-1801.
GEISSENHAINER, AUGUSTUS THEODOSIUS.
    St. Paul's, Allentown 1857-1858.
GERHARDT, LEONARD.
    Maytown, 1838-1847.
    Trinity, Londonderry, between 1838 and 1850.
    Shoop's Charge, 1847-1850.
    Middletown, 1847-1848.
GERHARDT, WILLIAM. D. D., North Carolina College, 1880.
    Maytown, 1847-1850.
GEROCK, JOHN SIEGFRIED.
    Trinity, Lancaster, 1753-1767.
GESCHWIND, LEVI H.*
    Stewartsville, 1884-1885.
GILBERT, DAVID MCCONAUGHY. D. D., Roanoke College, 1880.
    Zion, Harrisburg, 1887-date.
GLADHILL, JOHN TOMS.
    Stone Church, 1889-1891.

* Not a true " Initial," but merely a distinctive letter adopted for convenience.

GEADING, WILLIAM MARQUARD BEETEM.
    St. James', Ashland, 1889–date.

GLAZE, ALFRED RAUP.
    Trinity, Martin's Creek, 1885–1889.
    Gordon, 1892–date.

GLENDTKAMPT, J. A.
    New Amsterdam, S. A., 1777–1779.

GOCKELEN, AUGUSTUS B.
    Pine Grove Charge, 1839–1845.

GOETZ, CARL CHRISTOPH.
    St. Paul's, Allentown, 1785–1788.

GOODLIN, JOHN WALTERS.
    Millersville, 1887–1888.

GOTWALD, LUTHER ALEXANDER. D. D., Pennsylvania College, 1874.
    Zion, Lebanon, 1863–1865.

GOTWALD, WASHINGTON VAN BUREN.
    St. John's, Lancaster, 1866–1869.

GRAVES, URIEL.
    Schaefferstown and Strausstown, 1865–1866.
    English, Pottsville, 1866–1868.

GREENWALD, EMANUEL. D. D., Pennsylvania College, 1859.
    Christ, Easton, 1854–1867.

GROSHMER, J. J. M.
    New Amsterdam, S, A., 1756–1760.

GROSS, JOSEPH P.
    Hamilton Charge, (including Tannersville from 1834–1836), 1828–1841.

GROSSMAN, HENRY CLAY.
    Tremont, 1873–1876.
    Phoenixville, 1886–1890.

HACKENBERG, JACOB A.
    St. James', Ashland, 1871–1875.
    Chalfont, 1882–1883.
    Pikeland, 1882–date.

HAESBERT, JOHN F.
    Salem's and St. Peter's (Pine Grove Charge), 1834.

HAINES, GEORGE.
    Hummelstown and Union Deposit, 1854–1856.
    Manheim and East Petersburg, 1857–1858.

HALDERMAN, GEORGE WASHINGTON. D. D., Wittenberg College, 1890.
    Messiah, Harrisburg, 1867–1870.

HAMMA, MICHAEL WOLF. D. D., Wittenberg College, 1876.
  St. Matthew's, Reading, 1866-1869.
HANDSCHUH, JOHN FREDERICK.
  Trinity, Lancaster, 1748-1751.
  St. Michael's, Germantown, 1751-1757.
  Whitemarsh, 1753-1757.
  Philadelphia, 1757-1764.
  Friesburg, 1760.
HARDING, WILLIAM HENRY.
  Maytown, 1891-date.
HARKEY, SIMEON WALCHER. D. D., Wittenberg College, 1851.
  St. Matthew's, Philadelphia (Supply), 1834.
HARPEL, JEREMIAH.
  Ardmore, 1830-1834.
HARPEL, MARK.
  Friesburg, 1833-1835.
  Ardmore, 1834 or 1835.
  St. Peter's, Pine Grove Charge, 1835 (?)-1836 (?).
  Mt. Zion, Martin's Creek, 1850 (?)-1855 (?).
  Brickerville and Trinity, Londonderry, 1859-1870.
HARTMAN, JOSEPH FRANKLIN.
  Pikeland, 1876-1880.
HARTWIG, JOHN CHRISTOPHER.
  Reading, 1757-1758.
HASSLER, JOHN WALDSCHMIDT.
  Chalfont, 1857-1863.
  Chaplain U. S. Army, 1863-(?).
HAUSIHL, BERNARD MICHAEL.
  Trinity, Reading, 1759-1762.
  St. John's, Easton, 1763-1764 (?).
HAVERSTICK, HENRY.
  Ardmore, 1850-1851.
  Ardmore, 1855.
  Whitemarsh (Supply), 1852.
HAVICE, MARCUS HILL.
  Shenandoah, 1891-date.
HAY, CHARLES AUGUSTUS. D. D., Pennsylvania College, 1859.
  Zion, Harrisburg, 1849-1865.
  Professor in Theological Seminary, Gettysburg, 1865-date.
HAY, CHARLES EBERT.
  Fisherville Charge, 1876-1877.
  St. Paul's, Allentown, 1877-1890.
  Fogelsville, 1883-1884.
  St. Matthew's, Allentown, 1890-date.

HAY, EDWARD GRIER.
: English, Pottsville, 1880–date.
HECHT, ANTHONY.
: Upper Dublin, 1785.
HECHT, JOHN PETER.
: St. John's, Easton, 1815–1845.
: St. James', Greenwich, 1815–1837.
HECK, JACOB HENRY.
: Ardmore, 1861–1868.
HEILIG, GEORGE.
: Hamilton Charge, 1841–1857.
HEILIG, THEOPHILUS.
: Riegelsville Charge, 1864–1876.
HEILMAN, LEE MECHLING.
: Messiah, Harrisburg, 1873–1883.
HEINTZELMAN, JOHN DIETRICH MATTHEW.
: Philadelphia, 1753–1756.
HEISLER, WASHINGTON LAFAYETTE.
: St. James', Ashland, 1858–1861.
: Minersville and Tremont, 1883–1887.
: Shoop's Charge, 1891–date.
HEISLER, MARTIN LUTHER.
: Lykens and Williamstown, 1883–1886.
: Dauphin (Supply), 1886–date.
HELD, CYRUS ELMER.
: Hamilton Charge, 1892–date.
HELMUTH, JUSTUS HENRY CHRISTIAN, D. D., University of Pennsylvania 1785.
: Trinity, Lancaster, 1769–1780.
: Brickerville, 1774–1775.
: Brickerville, 1776–1777.
: Philadelphia, 1779–1822.
HEMPING, JOHN ADAM.
: Berrysburg Charge, 1811–1842.
: St. Peter's, Fisherville Charge, 1811–1847.
HENKEL, GERHARD.
: Philadelphia, 1720–1728.
HENKEL, DAVID MELANCHTHON, D. D., Carthage College, 1882.
: Stewartsville, 1855–1859.
HENRY, ELIAS STRICKHOUSER.
: Jacob's and St. John's, Pine Grove Charge, 1852–date.
: St. Peter's, Pine Grove Charge, 1855–date.
: Salem's, Pine Grove Charge, 1856–date.
: Tremont, 1853–1860.

HENRY, SAMUEL.
 Greenwich, 1868-1880.
HENRY, GEORGE CONRAD.
 Berrysburg Charge, 1879-1882.
HESSE, WILLIAM.
 Trinity, Martin's Creek, 1889-date.
HINMAN, WILLIS STUART.
 Columbia, 1888-date.
HIPPEE, LEWIS.
 Trinity, Lancaster (Assistant), 1856-1857.
 Whitemarsh, 1857-1859.
HOCKER, MARTIN PETER.
 St. John's, Steelton, 1883-date.
HOLLOWAY, HENRY CLAY. D. D., Wittenberg College, 1887.
 Middletown 1884-1889.
HOLMAN, SAMUEL AUGUSTUS. D. D., Pennsylvania College, 1884.
 English, Pottsville, 1859-1861.
 Grace, Philadelphia, 1868-1873.
 Calvary, Philadelphia, 1874-date.
HOOPER, PHILIP STANSBURY.
 Stone Church, 1881-1882.
 Phœnixville, 1883-1886.
 Lykens, 1890-date.
HOOVER, FRANCIS TROUT.
 Maytown, 1868-1870.
 St. James', Greenwich, 1880-1883.
HOUSEMAN, JOHN H.*
 Maytown, 1882-1884.
HUBER, ELI. D. D. Pennsylvania College, 1884.
 Schuylkill Haven, 1858-1860.
 Hummelstown and Union Deposit, 1861-1866.
 Messiah, Philadelphia, 1876-1892.
 Professor of English Bible, Pennsylvania College, 1892-date.
HUFFORD, RUFUS WARD. D. D., Wittenberg College, 1891.
 St. John's, Lancaster, 1876-1880.
 Millersville, 1880.
 St. Paul's, Easton, 1880-date.
HUTTER, EDWIN WILSON. D. D., Pennsylvania College, 1866.
 St. Matthew's, Philadelphia, 1850-1873.
ILLIG, T. F.
 Middletown, 1773-1788. (?)

* Not a true " Initial," but merely a distinctive letter adopted for convenience.

JAEGER, JOHN CONRAD.
    St. James', Greenwich, 1792—before 1812.
    Springfield, 1797-1801.
    St. Paul's, Allentown, 1800-1831.

JAEGER, JOSHUA.
    St. Paul's, Allentown (Assistant), 1827-1831.
    St. Paul's, Allentown (Pastor), 1831-1852.

JAEGER, NATHAN.
    Lykens and St. Peter's (Fisherville Charge), 1850-1852.
    Riegelsville Charge, 1863-1864.

JAEGER, THOMAS THEOPHILUS.
    Brickerville, 1850-1852.

JASINSKY, FREDERICK.
    Pikeland, 1811-1815.

JOHNSTON, ELIAS SCHELLHAMMER.
    Messiah, Harrisburg, 1860-1866.

JUNIUS, ———.
    New Amsterdam, S. A., 1832-1840.

KAEMPFER, JACOB.
    Manheim, East Petersburg and Millersville, 1868-1869.

KAST, JACOB KELLER.
    Minersville, 1853-1855.

KAUTZ, BENJAMIN FRANKLIN.
    Berrysburg Charge, 1890-date.

KEEDY, CORNELIUS L.*, M. D.
    Riegelsville Charge, 1861-1862.
    Barren Hill, 1862-1865.

KELLER, BENJAMIN,
    St. Michael's, Germantown, 1828-1835.
    Barren Hill, 1828-1835.
    Ardmore, 1828-1830.
    Whitemarsh, 1829-1835.

KELLER, JACOB B.*
    St. Peter's, Easton, 1886-1888.

KELLY, WILLIAM.
    Stewartsville, 1877-1884.

KINGSLEY, ROBERT F.
    Chalfont, 1874.

KLINE, SAMUEL SNYDER.
    Hamilton, 1858-1860.

* Not a true " Initial," but merely a distinctive letter adopted for convenience.

KLINEFELTER, FREDERICK.
  Tremont, 1868-1872.

KLING, JOHN.
  Phoenixville, 1891-date.

KLOSS, DANIEL.
  Lykens and Williamstown, 1871-1877.

KNOSKE, JOHN.
  Jacob's and Salem, Pine Grove Charge, 1802-1811.

KOONS, EDWARD JACKSON.
  Whitemarsh, 1860-1862.

KOSER, DAVID THEODORE.
  Riegelsville Charge, 1877-1887.

KRAFT, JOHN VALENTINE.
  Philadelphia, 1742.

KRAMER, JOHN PAUL FERDINAND.
  Springfield and Nockamixon, 1801-1803.
  Lykens Valley, 1805-(?).
  Hummelstown and Shoop's, 1807-1808.
  Maytown, 1806-1812.

KRAMLICH, BENJAMIN ELIAS.
  Mohrsville, 1865-1867.

KRAUTH, CHARLES PHILIP. D. D., University of Pennsylvania, 1837.
  St. Matthew's, Philadelphia, 1827-1833.
  Ardmore, 1828-1830.

KROH, HERMAN FREDERICK.
  Lykens, 1887-1889.

KROTEL, GOTTLOB FREDERICK. D. D., University of Pennsylvania, 1865;
  LL. D., Muhlenberg College, 1888.
  Trinity, Lancaster, 1853-1861.
  Annville, 1849-1853.

KRUG, JOHN ANDREW.
  Trinity, Reading, 1764-1771.

KUNZE, JOHN CHRISTOPHER. D. D., University of Pennsylvania, 1783.
  Philadelphia, 1770-1784.

KURTZ, JOHN NICHOLAS.
  Easton (Forks), 1749.
  St. Michael's, Germantown, 1763-1764.
  Upper Dublin and Barren Hill, 1763-1754.
  Middletown (or his son, J. D.), 1788-1793.

KURTZ, WILLIAM.
    Upper Dublin, 1757-1758.
    Salem, Lebanon, 1775-1794.
    Jacob's (Pine Grove Charge), 1780-1798.
    Hummelstown, 1781-1795.

KURTZ, HENRY A.
    Hamilton, 1818-1823.

KUTZ, HENRY DAVID.
    Dauphin, 1868-1869.
    Shoop's Charge (with Sandy Hollow), 1869-1871.

LAITZLE, WILLIAM GOTTLIEB.
    St. Peter's, Armstrong Valley, 1841-1843.
    Millersburg, Werts' and Salem, 1842-1843.
    Union Deposit and Sandy Hollow, 1852-1854.
    Trinity, Londonderry, 1854-1859.
    Maytown, 1855-1862.

LAKE, JOHN WELTER.
    Friesburg, 1871-1874.
    Mahanoy City, 1880-1881.

LANE, PETER PAUL.
    Berrysburg Charge, 1861-1862.

LAZARUS, GEORGE MILLER.
    Chalfont, 1869-1871.

LEESER, JOHN HENRY.
    Trinity, Martin's Creek, 1875-1877.
    Hummelstown, 1877-1885.

LEHMAN, DANIEL.
    Trinity, Reading, 1779-1780.
    Trinity, Reading, 1796-1801.

LENHART, EDWIN.
    Mohrsville (Womelsdorf Charge), 1878-1879.

LENTZ, ALEXANDER WILEY.
    Friesburg, 1882-1886.
    Millersville, 1889-date.

LEOPOLD, OWEN.
    Fogelsville, 1861-1874.

LEPS, JOHN CHRISTIAN.
    St. Paul's, Allentown, between 1778 and 1785.

LETTERMAN, HENRY ALEXANDER.
    Dauphin, 1882-1886.
    Fisherville Charge, 1886-1889.

LEWARS, WILLIAM HENRY.
    Lyons, 1881-1882.
    Mahanoy City, 1882-1886.
    Lititz and Kissel Hill, 1886-1889.
    Neffsville, 1888-1889.
    Palmyra (Supply), 1890-1892.
    Annville and Hill Church, 1890-date.

LINK, ADAM SCHINDLER.
    Hummelstown and Union Deposit, 1858-1861.

LOCHMAN, GEORGE. D. D., Allegheny College, 1819.
    Salem, Lebanon, 1794-1815.
    Hill Church, near Annville, 1794-1815.
    Annville, 1804-1815.
    Zion, Harrisburg, 1815-1826.
    Middletown, 1815-1826(?).
    Shoop's Church, 1816-1826.

LOCHMAN, AUGUSTUS HOFFMAN. D. D., Pennsylvania College, 1856.
    Zion, Harrisburg, 1827-1836.
    Shoop's, 1826-1835.
    Middletown, 1826-1830.
    Dauphin, 1830.

LUCKENBACH, WILLIAM HENRY. D. D., Wittenberg College, 1888.
    English, Pottsville, 1857-1859.

MACK, PETER STAUFFER.
    Hummelstown, 1873-1877.

MAIER, DANIEL.
    Oberlin, 1852-1855.

MAIN, JOHN HARRY.
    Grace, Philadelphia, 1891-date.

MANHART, FRANK PIERCE.
    All Saints', Philadelphia, 1889-date.

MARCLEY, ORLANDO DANIEL STEVENS.
    St. James', Ashland, 1875-1878.
    Gordon, 1876-1878.

MARTIN, JACOB.
    Berrysburg Charge, 1852-1853.

MARTZ, GEORGE JACOB.
    Shoop's, Swatara, Dauphin, Sandy Hollow and Wenrich's, 1855-1868.
    Schaefferstown, Womelsdorf, Strausstown, Myerstown and Richland, 1868-1878.
    Tremont, 1878-1880.
    Union Deposit, Sandy Hollow and Sand Hill, 1882-1883.
    Lyons, Macungie and Salem, 1891-date.

McAFEE, JOHN QUINCY.
    English, Pottsville, 1871-1877.
    Minersville, 1872-1874.
    Minersville, 1875-1877.
    Barren Hill, 1883-1888.

McCRON, JOHN. D. D., Roanoke College, 1857.
    Pikeland, 1843-1847.
    St. James', Greenwich, 1847-1851.
    Stewartsville, N. J., (?)-1851.
    Riegelsville, 1850-1851.
    Pottsville, 1878-1880.

McDOWELL, SAMUEL JAMES.
    Friesburg, 1892-date.

McGANN, ISAAC HENRY.
    Stone Church, 1892-date.

McKNIGHT, HARVEY WASHINGTON. D. D., Monmouth College, Ills., 1883; LL. D., Lafayette College, 1890.
    St. Paul's, Easton, 1872-1880.
    President of Pennsylvania College, 1884-date.

MEALY, STEPHEN A.
    St. Matthew's, Philadelphia, between 1838 and 1841.

MEDTART, JACOB.
    St. Matthew's, Philadelphia, 1834-1838.

MEISTER, EMIL.
    St. Stephen's, Lancaster, 1880-date.

MELCHOR, OLIVER HOFFMAN.
    Springfield, Durham and Springtown, 1879-date.
    Nockamixon, 1880-1892.

MELSHEIMER, FREDERICK THEODORE.
    Maytown, 1784-1801.
    Hill Church, near Annville, 1779-1794.
    Shoop's, 1783-1788.
    Manheim, 1783-1789.

MENGES, JOHN HERSHEY.
    Columbia, 1849-1860.
    Manheim, 1849-1851.
    East Petersburg, 1849-1852.
    East Petersburg, 1855-1857.
    Grace, Philadelphia, 1878-1891.
    Zion's, Manheim, 1891-date.

MENNIG, GEORGE.
    Jacob's and Salem (Pine Grove Charge), 1811-1833.
    St. Peter's (Pine Grove Charge), 1816-1833.
    Jerusalem, Schuylkill Haven, 1821-1836.

MENNIG, WILLIAM GOEPFERT.
    Jacob's and Salem (Pine Grove Charge), 1834-1839.
    St. Peter's, 1837-1839.
    Pottsville, 1834-1859.
    Minersville, 1839-1858.
    Jerusalem, Schuylkill Haven, 1836-1851.
    St. Paul's, Schuylkill Haven, 1837-1859.
    Port Carbon, 1841-1857.
    St. Paul's, Allentown, 1859-1877.
    Fogelsville, 1877-1883.
    Lyons Charge (Supply), 1882.

MENSCH, JOHN NICHOLAS.
    Springfield and Nockamixon, 1803-1823.
    Durham, 1811-1823.

MILLER, S. F.
    New Amsterdam, S. A., 1761-1763.

MILLER, JACOB S.
    Nockamixon, 1773-1789 (?).

MILLER (MOELLER), HENRY.
    Trinity, Reading, 1775.
    Ardmore, 1786-1787.
    Zion, Harrisburg, 1795-1803.
    Middletown, 1795-1803.
    Shoop's, 1796-1803.

MILLER, HENRY SEIPEL.
    Springfield and Durham, 1823-1838.
    Nockamixon, 1823-1838 (?).
    Annville, 1854-1859 (?).

MILLER, JACOB —. D. D., University of Pennsylvania, 183°.
    Trinity, Reading, 1829-1850.

MILLER, CHRISTIAN PHILIP.
    Brickerville and Manheim, 1836-1841.
    Kissel Hill, 1839-1841.

MILLER, CHARLES PETER.
    Springfield and Durham, 1842-1865.
    Nockamixon, 1842-1865 (?).

MILLER, DANIEL.
    Greenwich, 1837-1847.
    Pikeland, 1847-1849.

MILLER, WALTER.
    Shenandoah, 1883-1885.

MITTELHOLZER, JOHN R.
    New Amsterdam, S. A., 1875-date.

MORELL, ELIJAH STEWARD.
    Chalfont, 1883-1888.
    Norwood, 1888-date.

MUHLENBERG, HENRY MELCHIOR. D. D., University of Pennsylvania, 1784.
    Philadelphia and Germantown, 1742-1745.
    Lionville, (Vincent) 1744.
    Easton (Forks), 1749.
    Pikeland, 1751-1770.
    Upper Dublin, 1754-1757.
    Upper Dublin, 1762-1763.
    Barren Hill, 1759-1769.
    Barren Hill, 1776-1786.
    Friesburg, 1760.
    Philadelphia, 1761-1774.
    Brickerville (Warwick), 1770-1773.

MUHLENBERG, JOHN PETER GABRIEL.
    St. James', Greenwich, 1770-1773.

MUHLENBERG, FREDERICK AUGUSTUS CONRAD.
    Manheim, 1771-1778.
    Salem, Lebanon, 1773-1775.

MUHLENBERG, GOTTHILF HENRY ERNST. D. D., Princeton College, 1787.
    Philadelphia, 1771-1779.
    Barren Hill, 1776 (?) -1780 (?).
    Trinity, Lancaster, 1780-1815.

MUHLENBERG, HENRY AUGUSTUS.
    Trinity, Reading, 1803-1829.

NAESMAN, GABRIEL.
    Friesburg, 1743-1745.

NEFF, ISAAC P.,* M. D.
    Minersville and Tremont, 1880-1881.
    Shenandoah, 1881-1883.

NIEMYER, FRANK.
    Hamilton, 1790-1803.

NITTERAUER, CORNELIUS.
    Dauphin, 1851-1853.

PALMER, SAMUEL S.*
    Pikeland, 1874-1875.
    Phoenixville, 1875-1880.

PENTZ, PETER.
    Middletown, 1793-1795.

    * Not a true " Initial," but merely a distinctive letter adopted for convenience.

PETER, JACOB.
    Manheim and Londonderry, 1872–1891.
    East Petersburg, 1874–1891.
    Kissel Hill, 1874–1886.
    Neffsville, 1880–1881.
    Lititz, 1885–1886.
    East Petersburg Charge, 1891–date.

PETERSON, JOHN DIETRICH.
    Zion, Harrisburg and Middletown, 1803–1812.
    St. Peter's (Fisherville Charge), 1807–1811.

PLITT, FREDERICK.
    Pikeland, 1804–1807 (?).

PLITT, JOHN KELLER.
    St. James', Greenwich, 1851–1865.
    Stewartsville, 1851–1855.

PORR, WILLIAM S.*
    Annville, 1859–1860.
    Brickerville, 1874–1875.
    St. Stephen's, Lancaster, 1874–1880.
    Millersville, 1875–1880.
    St. John's, Steelton, 1880–1882.

PRITCHARD, THOMAS CHARLES.
    Barren Hill, 1871–1883.
    St. James', Greenwich, 1883–date.

PROBST, JOHN FREDERICK.
    Hummelstown, 1856–1858.

PYRLAEUS, JOHN CHRISTOPHER.
    Philadelphia, 1742.

RABY, PETER.
    Pikeland and Lionville, 1849–1858.
    Middletown, 1865–1872.
    Grace, Philadelphia, 1874–1876.

REED, DAVID E.*
    Lyons, 1880–1881.

REES, CHARLES.
    Manheim and Brickerville, 1854–1856.
    Kissel Hill, 1855–1856.

REIMENSNYDER, CORNELIUS.
    Pikeland, 1859–1863.
    Columbia, 1863–1865.

REINMUND, JACOB FREDERICK. D. D., Wittenberg College, 1876.
    Zion, Lebanon, 1872–1880.

---

* Not a true " Initial," but merely a distinctive letter adopted for convenience.

RENTZ, WILLIAM FRAZENIUS.
    Lionville, 1882-1888.
REYNOLDS, WILLIAM MORTON. D. D., Jefferson College, 1850.
    Friesburg, 1835-1837.
RHODES, GEORGE MARTIN.
    Columbia, 1870-1874.
RHODES, MOSHEIM. D. D., Wittenberg College. 1878.
    Zion, Lebanon, 1867-1872.
RIACH, ALEXANDER.
    New Amsterdam, S. A., about 1852.
RICHARDS, JOHN WILLIAM. D. D., Jefferson College, 1852.
    St. Michael's, Germantown, 1836-1845.
    St. John's, Easton, 1845-1851.
RICHARDS, MATTHIAS HENRY. D. D., Pennsylvania College, 1889.
    St. James', Greenwich, 1865-1868.
RIGHTMYER, PETER MOSES.
    Chalfont, 1863-1868.
    Friesburg, 1874-1879.
RIZER, PETER.
    Hummelstown and Union Deposit, 1866-1873.
    Stewartsville, 1873-1877.
ROEDEL, WILLIAM DILLER.
    Ardmore, 1851-1855.
ROELLER, ISAAC.
    Fogelsville, 1835-1851.
ROMIG, MOSES S.*
    Williamstown, 1886-1888.
ROSENMILLER, DAVID PORTER.
    Kissel Hill, 1857-1862.
    Manheim, 1858-(?).
    Dauphin, 1870-1880.
ROTH, JOHN JOSEPH.
    St. Paul's, Allentown, 1763-1764.
ROTHS, GEORGE.
    Hamilton Charge, 1874-1882.
ROWENACH, J.
    Pikeland, 1807(?)-1811(?).
RUETER, ADELBERT CHARLES RODERICO.
    East Petersburg, 1852-1853.
RUMPF, ADOLPHUS.
    St. Mark's (Hamilton Charge), 1857-1858.

* Not a true " Initial," but merely a distinctive letter adopted for convenience.

RUPERT, PETER.
    Hamilton Charge, 1812-1818.
    Hamilton Charge, 1823-1828.
RUPLEY, DANIEL E.
    Ashland and Gordon, 1878-1879.
RUTHERFORD, WILLIAM LINCOLN.
    St. Mark's, Steelton, 1892-date.
RUTHRAUFF, JOHN FREDERICK.
    Manheim, before 1825.
RUTHRAUFF, FREDERICK.
    Maytown, 1828-1832.
    Manheim, 1828(?)-1832.
    Pikeland, 1836-1843.
    Lionville, 1838-1843.
RUTHRAUFF, FREDERICK JONATHAN.
    Salem, Lebanon, 1836-1844.
    Zion, Lebanon, 1844-1849.
    Hill Church, near Annville, 1836-1849.
    Schaefferstown, 1837-1849.
RUTHRAUFF, WILLIAM PATTON.
    Christ, Easton, 1867-1870.
SADTLER, J. P., BENJAMIN. D. D., Pennsylvania College, 1867.
    Jacob's and St. John's, Pine Grove Charge, 1845-1849.
    Salem's, Pine Grove Charge, 1846-1848.
    Tremont, 1847-1849.
    Middletown, 1853-1856.
    St. John's, Easton, 1856-1862.
SAHM, PETER. D. D., Pennsylvania College, 1869.
    Manheim, 1833-1835.
    Maytown, 1833-1837.
    Middletown, 1834-1837.
SAMPLE, JAMES REED.
    Mahanoy City, 1887.
SANDT, CHARLES MILTON.
    Gordon, 1888-1891.
    Easton (resident), 1891-date.
SCHAEFFER, FREDERICK DAVID. D. D., University of Pennsylvania, 1813.
    Zion, Harrisburg, 1788-1790.
    Shoop's, 1788-1796.
    St. Michael's, Germantown, 1790-1812.
    Barren Hill, 1790-1812.
    Ardmore, 1790-1800.
    Upper Dublin, 1801-1810.
    Zion's and St. Michael's, Philadelphia, 1812-1834.

SCHAEFFER, FREDERICK CHRISTIAN. D. D., Columbia College, 1830.
    Zion, Harrisburg, Shoop's and Middletown, 1812-1815.
SCHAEFFER, CHARLES FREDERICK. D. D., Pennsylvania College, 1850.
    Ardmore (while student), 1828-1830.
    St. John's, Easton, 1851-1856.
SCHAEFFER, CHARLES WILLIAM. D. D., Pennsylvania College, 1852; LL. D., Thiel College, 1887.
    Whitemarsh and Barren Hill, 1835-1841.
    Zion, Harrisburg, 1841-1849.
SCHAUM, JOHN HELFRICH.
    Upper Dublin, 1758-1762.
SCHEURER, PETER.
    Hummelstown, 1822-before 1830.
SCHINDEL, JEREMIAH.
    St. Peter's (Fisherville Charge), 1843-1845.
    Fogelsville, 1851-1858.
SCHINDLER, DANIEL. D. D., Lebanon Valley College, 1882.
    Zion, Lebanon, 1865-1867.
SCHMIDT, JOHN FREDERICK.
    St. Michael's, Germantown, 1769-1786.
    Upper Dublin and Ardmore, 1769-1785.
    Barren Hill, 1769-(?).
    Philadelphia, 1786-1812.
SCHMIDT, AUGUSTUS HERMAN.
    Springfield, after 1766-before 1789.
    Nockamixon, 1798.
    Easton, 1799-1801.
SCHMUCKER, BEALE MELANCHTHON. D. D., University of Pennsylvania, 1870.
    St. Paul's, Allentown, 1852-1855.
    St. John's, Easton, 1862-1867.
SCHOCK, JAMES L(AWRENCE?). D. D., Pennsylvania College, 1863.
    St. Matthew's, Reading, 1842-1849.
SCHOLL, WILLIAM NACE. D. D., Pennsylvania College, 1866.
    Trinity, Germantown, 1836-1840.
SCHRENK, RUDOLPH.
    St. John's, Easton, 1749-1754.
SCHROEDER, JOHN DANIEL.
    Manheim, 1778-1782.
    Brickerville, 1780-1781.
    Barren Hill, 1776-1782(?).
SCHUHMACHER, DANIEL.
    Reading, 1754-1755.

SCHULTZE, JOHN CHRISTIAN.
Philadelphia, 1732-1733.

SCHULTZE, CHRISTOPHER EMANUEL.
Philadelphia, 1765-1770.
Barren Hill (Assistant), 1765-1769.
Brickerville and Schaefferstown, 1765-1809.

SCHULTZE, JOHN ANDREW MELCHIOR.
Jacob's, Pine Grove Charge, 1798-1802.
Salem's, Pine Grove Charge, 1799-1802.
Lykens Valley, about 1800.

SCHWARBACK, JOHN.
Brickerville, 1775-1776.

SCRIBA, HENRY.
Manheim, 1807.

SECRIST, LEVI KRONE.
Fisherville Charge, 1855-1858.

SEIFERT, HENRY.
Hamilton Charge, 1860-1869.

SELL, DANIEL.
Berrysburg Charge, 1853-1860.

SELL, EDWARD HERMAN MILLER. M. D., 1860.
Fogelsville, 1859-1861.

SENTMAN, SOLOMON.
Barren Hill, 1858-1862.
Lionville, 1863-1870.
Principal Preparatory Department, Pennsylvania College, 1870-1871.

SHANNON, SAMUEL GALBRAITH.
Bethany, Philadelphia, 1889-date.

SHATTO (SHADOW), MARTIN VAN BUREN.
Fisherville Charge, 1884-1885.
Shoop's Charge, 1885-1887.

SHEARER, JACOB FERRELL.
St. Mark's, Conshohocken, 1890-date.

SHEELEIGH, MATTHIAS. D. D., Newberry College, 1885.
Minersville, 1857-1859.
Stewartsville, 1864-1869.
Whitemarsh, 1869-date.

SHERTZ, ALEXANDER HAMILTON.
Maytown, 1885-1890.

SHETLER, DANIEL AUGUSTUS.
Shenandoah, 1886-1888.

SHINDLE, HENRY CLAY.
>   Minersville, 1864-1868.

SHOFFNER, JOHN RUFAN.
>   Lionville, 1871-1876.

SIKES, JAMES ROBERT.
>   St. James', Ashland, 1864-1867.
>   Stewartsville, 1869-1872.

SILL, GEORGE.
>   Whitemarsh, 1863-1869.
>   Chalfont, 1890-date.

SINGMASTER, JOHN ALDEN.
>   Schuylkill Haven, 1876-1882.
>   Lyons Charge, 1882-1885.
>   Macungie Charge, 1885-1886.
>   Mohrsville, 1876-1878.
>   Fogelsville, 1884-1886; 1891-date.
>   St. Paul's, Allentown, 1890-date.

SMITH, CHARLES.
>   Christ, Easton, 1851-1854.

SMITH, WILLIAM H., M. D.
>   Ardmore, 1848-1850.
>   Whitemarsh and Barren Hill, 1850-1852.

SNYDER, HENRY GELWIX.
>   Hummelstown, 1890-date.

SONDHAUS, MARTIN.
>   Trinity, Londonderry, 1854.
>   Maytown, 1855.

SPRECHER, SAMUEL. D. D., Washington College, 1850; LL.D., Pennsylvania College, 1874.
>   Zion, Harrisburg, 1836-1840.

STALEY, FREDERICK WALPOLE.
>   Schuylkill Haven (Supply), 1876.
>   Columbia, 1877-1881.
>   Trinity, Martin's Creek, 1881-1885.
>   Middletown, 1890-date.

STALL, SYLVANUS.
>   Trinity, Martin's Creek, 1877-1880.
>   St. John's, Lancaster, 1881-1887.

STECHER, HENRY GEORGE.
>   Hummelstown, 1830-1854.
>   Shoop's, 1836-1847.

STECK, DANIEL. D. D., Roanoke College, 1874.
    English, Pottsville, 1847–1857.
    English, Pottsville, 1868–1870.
    Schuylkill Haven, 1851–1857.
    Minersville, 1851–1853.
    St. John's, Lancaster, 1858–1862.

STECK, JACOB.
    Minersville, 1855–1857.

STECK, JOHN McLEAN.
    Mahanoy City, 1875–1880.

STECK, WILLIAM HENRY HARRISON.
    Columbia, 1865–1870.
    Ardmore, 1874–1890.
    Coatesville, 1890–date.

STECK, AUGUSTUS REINOEHL,
    Stewartsville, 1886–1891.

STELLING, GEORGE FREDERICK. D. D., Pennsylvania College, 1874.
    Zion, Harrisburg, 1865–1875.

STINE, MILTON HENRY.
    Maytown, 1880–1882.
    Seventh Street, Lebanon, 1883–1892.

STOCK, DANIEL.
    Maytown, 1871–1873.

STOEVER, JOHN CASPAR.
    Brickerville, 1730–1743.
    Philadelphia, 1733.
    Hill Church, near Annville, 1733–1779.
    Near Lebanon, 1733–(?).
    Trinity, Lancaster, 1736–1740.
    Brickerville, 1777–1779.

STOEVER, CHARLES FRANKLIN.
    St. Peter's (Fisherville Charge), 1845–1850.
    Lykens (occasionally), 1845–1850.
    Millersburg and Killinger, 1846–1852.
    Dauphin, before 1849–1852.
    Shoop's, 1850–1854.

STORK, THEOPHILUS. D. D., Pennsylvania College, 1851.
    St. Matthew's, Philadelphia, 1841–1850.

STOVER, JACOB MONROE.
    Fisherville Charge, 1890–date.

STRAUSS, ABRAHAM MILL.
    Tannersville, 1875–1883.

STREIN, JOHN JACOB.
    Maytown, 1815-1825.
STREIT, CHRISTIAN.
    Easton, 1769-1779.
    St. James', Greenwich, 1773-1777.
STREITER, JOHN PHILIP.
    Philadelphia (not ordained), 1737.
STUDEBAKER, ALBERT HEDGES. D. D., Wittenberg College, 1891.
    Zion, Harrisburg, 1881-1886.
SUESSEROTT, BENJAMIN CHRISTIAN.
    Whitemarsh, 1856-1757.
    St. John's, Lancaster, 1870-1876.
    Millersville, 1870-1875.
SWARTZ, JOEL. D. D., Wittenberg College, 1868.
    Messiah, Philadelphia, 1874-1875.
    Zion, Harrisburg, 1875-1880.
SWOPE, DAVID.
    Whitemarsh, 1855-1856.
TAERKENIUS, JOHN HENDRICK.
    New Amsterdam, S. A., 1752-1754.
THRALL, WILLIAM GARDNER.
    Gordon, 1886-1887.
TITUS, TIMOTHY TILGHMAN.
    Ardmore, 1856-1861.
TOMPKINS, FRANK P.
    Messiah, Harrisburg, 1870-1873.
TOWN, EDWARD.
    Friesburg, 1839.
    Ardmore, 1840-1842.
TRANBERG, PETER.
    Friesburg, 1726-1743.
TRAUGER, JORDAN CALFÉ.
    Minersville and Tremont, 1890-date.
TREIBLEY, DANIEL BENJAMIN.
    Shenandoah, 1889-1891.
TROWBRIDGE, CHARLES REUBEN.
    St. Peter's, Easton, 1888-1892.
TRUMP, CHARLES SAMUEL.
    Stone Church, 1883-1888.
ULERY, CHRISTIAN DETRICH.
    Lionville, 1861-1862.

UNRUH, JOHN NICHOLAS.
> Friesburg, 1858-1866.

VALENTINE, MILTON. D. D., Pennsylvania College, 1866; LL.D., Wittenburg College, 1886.
> St. Matthew's, Reading, 1859-1866.

VALENTINE, MILTON HENRY.
> Messiah, Philadelphia, 1892-date.

VAN BUSKERK, JACOB.
> St. Michael's, Germantown, 1766-1769.
> Ardmore, Upper Dublin and Barren Hill, 1765-1769.
> St. Paul's, Allentown, 1769-1778.
> Upper Dublin, 1785-1795.

VANHOFF, JOHN HENRY.
> Hummelstown, 1811-(?).
> Middletown, 1830-1834.

VOGELBACH, JACOB TRAUGOTT.
> Middletown, 1844-1847.
> Oberlin, 1845-1847.
> Oberlin, 1850-1852.
> St. Paul's, Allentown, 1852-1857.

VOIGT, JOHN LUDWIG.
> St. Michael's, Germantown, 1764-1765.
> Upper Dublin and Barren Hill, 1764-1765.
> Pikeland, 1779-1793.

WAGNER, REUBEN SCHULER.
> East Petersburg, 1847-1849.

WALTER, CLINTON ELMER.
> Trinity, Germantown, (Assistant), 1892-date.

WALTZ, FREDERICK.
> Jerusalem, Schuylkill Haven, 1852-1854.
> St. Peter's, (Fisherville Charge), 1855-1869.

WAMBOLE, JACOB.
> Pikeland, 1827-1830.
> Lionville, 1833-1836.

WARNER, ADAM NICHOLAS.
> Minersville, 1878-1879.

WATERS, JAMES QUIGLEY.
> Barren Hill, 1865-1867.

WATKINS, HORATIO JAMES.
> Ardmore, 1869-1874.

WEAVER, GEORGE PETER.
    Berrysburg Charge, 1862-1863.
    Annville and Hill Church, 1863-1864.
    Schuylkill Haven, 1864-1866.
    Maytown, 1873-1875.

WEBER, JOHN JACOB.
    Zion's, Ashland, 1857-1891.

WEBER, JAMES HENRY. D. D., Wittenberg College, 1891.
    St. James', Ashland, 1879-1887.
    Gordon, 1879-1886.

WEDEKIND, AUGUSTUS CHARLES. D. D., Pennsylvania College, 1867.
    Zion, Lebanon, 1850-1863.
    Hill Church, near Annville, 1850-1853.
    Bellegrove, 1850-(?).
    St. John's, Lancaster, 1863-1865.

WEINLAND, JOHN FREDERICK.
    St. Michael's, Germantown, 1786-1789.
    Barren Hill, 1786-1789.
    Ardmore, 1787-1789.
    Pikeland, 1790-1800.

WEISER, REUBEN BENJAMIN. D. D., Pennsylvania College, 1876.
    Mahanoy City, 1869-1871.
    Minersville, 1870-1872.

WELDEN, CHRISTIAN FREDERICK. D. D., Muhlenburg College, 1889.
    Springfield, Durham and Nockamixon, 1838-1842.

WHETSTONE, AMOS MOSER.
    Millersville and Neffsville, 1884-1885.

WHITECAR, CHARLES PITMAN.
    Chalfont, 1871-1872.

WICHTERMAN, JOSEPH.
    St. Paul's, Allentown, 1793.

WIETING, ARCHIBALD.
    Sandy Hollow, 1844-1853.
    Middletown (resident), 1852-1862.

WILDBAHN, CHARLES FREDERICK.
    Trinity, Reading, 1782-1796.

WILE, HARRY BARR.
    St. Peter's, Easton, 1880-1885.

WILLARD, PHILIP.
    Schuylkill Haven, 1861-1864.
    Pottsville (Supply), 1862.
    Financial Agent Lutheran Board of Publication, 1863-1868.
    Superintendent Tressler Orphans' Home, Loysville, 1869-1889.

WILLIAMS, JOHN RENTZLE.
    Bethany, Philadelphia, 1883-1888.
    Chalfont, 1888.

WILLOX, JOHN ROBERT.
    Friesburg, 1842-1851.
    Riegelsville Charge, 1851-1861.

WIRT, JOHN ADAM.
    Lykens and Williamstown, 1877-1883.

WORDMAN, HENRY BURCHARD GABRIEL.
    Trinity, Reading, 1752-1753.

YEAGER—See JAEGER.

YEISER, ALFRED.
    Schuylkill Haven, 1866-1876.

YINGLING, SAMUEL.
    St. John's, Steelton, 1878-1880.
    Shoop's Charge, 1878-1881.

YOUNG, JOHN DAVID.
    Manheim, 1789-1790.

ZIMMERMAN, AMOS K.*
    Union Deposit Charge, 1885-1887.

ZIMMERMAN, ISAAC PETER.
    Mahanoy City, 1887-date.

* Not a true " Initial," but merely a distinctive letter adopted for convenience.

INDEX

OF

CHURCHES AND PASTORAL CHARGES.

	PAGE
Ackermanville	238
Allentown, St. Matthew's	291
Allentown, St. Paul's	78
Allowaystown, N. J.	49
All Saints', Philadelphia	289
Annville Charge	58
Annville Church	60
Ardmore	90
Ashland, St. James'	215
Ashland, Zion's	211
Augsburg, Harrisburg	130, 308
Barren Hill	95
Bartonsville	89
Bellegrove	182
Berbice, S. A.	309
Berrysburg Charge	136
Berrysburg Church	137
Bethany, Millersville	245
Bethany, Philadelphia	279
Bethel, Berbice, S. A.	322
Bethesda, Berbice, S. A.	322
Bethlehem, Harrisburg	130, 284
Bowerman's	135
Brickerville	52
Bridgeton, N. J.	304
Brodheadsville	90
Calvary, Philadelphia	259
Carsonville	136
Centennial, Kimberton	116, 117

	PAGE
Central, Phœnixville	116, 271
Centreville	228
Chalfont	214
Christ, Bellegrove	182
Christ, Easton	249
Christ, Harrisburg	295
Christ's, Bridgeton, N. J.	304
Christ's, Hamilton	86
Christ's, Springtown	64
Christ's, Stone Church	228
Coatesville	299
Cohansey	49
Columbia, Salem	179
Columbia, Second Street	179
Conshohocken	296
Dauphin	175
Dublin, Upper	69
Durham	63
Easton, Christ	249
Easton, St. John's	248
Easton, St. Paul's	248, 262
Easton, St. Peter's	262
East Petersburg Charge	144
East Petersburg Church	144
Ebenezer, Berbice, S. A.	309
Emanuel, Friesburg, N. J.	49
Emanuel's, Pottsville	171
Emanuel's, Williamstown	253
English, Minersville	191

(369)

	PAGE
English, Pottsville	171
Fetterhoff's	133
First, Annville	60
First, Shenandoah	278
First, Stewartsville, N. J.	197
Fisherville Charge	132
Fisherville Church	135
Fogelsville	154
Forster Street, Harrisburg	130, 224
Friesburg, N. J.	49
Germantown, St. Michael's	155
Germantown, Trinity	155, 156
Gordon	272
Grace, Manheim	145
Grace, Philadelphia	247
Greenwich, N. J.	104
Hamilton Charge	86
Hamilton Church	86
Harrisburg, Augsburg	130, 308
Harrisburg, Bethlehem	130, 284
Harrisburg, Christ	130, 295
Harrisburg, Memorial	130, 256
Harrisburg, Messiah (Forster st)	130, 224
Harrisburg, Trinity	131, 306
Harrisburg, Zion	127, 224, 256, 284, 306
Harrisburg and Steelton Ch'ge	131, 306
Hill, Annville	58
Hill, Kissel	146
Hill, Sand	76
Hoernerstown	77
Hummelstown	72
Huntersville	213
Immanuel, Norwood	287
Jacksonville	136
Jacob's, Pine Grove Charge	118
Jerusalem, Schuylkill Haven	220
Killinger	136
Kimberton	116, 117
Kintnersville Charge	65
Kissel Hill	146
Lafayette Hill	95

	PAGE
Lancaster, St. John's	201
Lancaster, St. Stephen's	260
Lancaster, Trinity	201
Lebanon, Salem	165
Lebanon, Seventh Street	207
Lebanon, Zion	165, 207
Lionville Charge	148
Lionville Church	116, 149, 150
Lititz Charge	146
Lititz Church	147
Londonderry	144
Lower Merion	90
Lower Mt. Bethel	236
Lykens	195
Lyons Charge	231
Lyons Church	232
Macungie	233
Mahanoy City	241
Manheim, Grace	145
Manheim, Zion's	110
Martin's Creek Charge	236
Martin's Creek, Mt. Zion	236
Martin's Creek, Trinity	236
Maytown	105
Memorial, Harrisburg	130, 256
Memorial (Bethany), Philadelphia	279
Messiah, Fisherville	135
Messiah, Harrisburg	130, 224
Messiah, Philadelphia	238
Middletown	99
Milford, Upper	234
Millersburg	138
Millersville	245
Minersville	191
Minersville and Tremont Charge	191
Mohrsville	234
Mount Bethel, Lower	236
Mount Bethel, Upper	228
Mount Carmel, Berbice, S. A.	322
Mount Eden	276
Mount Eton	90
Mt. Hermon, Berbice, S. A.	322
Mt. Lebanon, Berbice, S. A.	322

INDEX OF CHURCHES AND PASTORAL CHARGES.

	PAGE
Mt. Zion, near Lebanon	209
Mt. Zion, Martin's Creek	236
Neffsville	147
New Amsterdam, S. A.	309
Nockamixon	65
Northampton (Allentown)	78
Norwood	287
Oberlin	126
Palmyra Charge	182
Palmyra Church	182
Philadelphia, All Saints'	289
Philadelphia, Bethany	279
Philadelphia, Calvary	259
Philadelphia, Grace	247
Philadelphia, Memorial	279
Philadelphia, Messiah	238
Philadelphia, St. John's	141
Philadelphia, St. Matthew's	140, 141, 238
Philadelphia, St. Michael's	140
Philadelphia, Zion's	141
Phillipsburg, N. J.	104
Phœnixville	271
Pikeland Charge	114
Pikeland Church	114
Pine Grove Charge	118
Pine Grove, St. John's	120
Pine Grove, St. Peter's	119
Pleasantville	233
Pottsville, Emanuel's	171
Pottsville, English	171
Puff's	69
Raubsville	189
Reading, St. Matthew's	159
Reading, Trinity	159
Rexmont	57
Richland	57
Riegelsville Charge	184
Riegelsville Church	184
St. James', Ashland	215
St. James', Carsonville	136
St. James', Chalfont	214
St. James', Greenwich, N. J.	104

	PAGE
St. John's, Bartonsville	89
St. John's, Brickerville	52
St. John's, Easton	248
St. John's, Fogelsville	154
St. John's, Hoernerstown	77
St. John's, Lancaster	201
St. John's, Mahanoy City	241
St. John's, Maytown	105
St. John's, Palmyra	182
St. John's, Philadelphia	141
St. John's, Pine Grove	120
St. John's, Pleasantville	233
St. John's, Steelton	266
St. John's, Tremont	192
St. John's, Union Deposit	77
St. Mark's, Conshohocken	296
St. Mark's, Hamilton Charge	88
St. Mark's, Steelton	301
St. Matthew's, Allentown	291
St. Matthew's, Lionville Charge	116, 149
St. Matthew's, Macungie	233
St. Matthew's, Philadelphia	140, 141, 238
St. Matthew's, Reading	159
St. Matthew's, Schuylkill Haven	220
St. Michael's, Germantown	155
St. Michael's, Philadelphia	140
St. Paul's, Allentown	78
St. Paul's, Ardmore	90
St. Paul's, Easton	248, 262
St. Paul's, Fisherville Charge	135
St. Paul's, Gordon	272
St. Paul's, Lionville Charge	116, 149, 150
St. Paul's, Lititz	147
St. Paul's, Lyons Station	232
St. Paul's, Millersburg	138
St. Paul's, Raubsville	189
St. Paul's, Schuylkill Haven	220
St. Paul's, Steelton	307
St. Paul's, Stone Church	228
St. Paul's, Strausstown	235
St. Paul's, Tannersville	88
St. Peter's, Easton	262
St. Peter's, Fisherville Charge	133
St. Peter's, Lafayette Hill	95

	PAGE		PAGE
St. Peter's, Middletown	99	Trinity, Coatesville	299
St. Peter's, Neffsville	147	Trinity, Germantown	155, 156
St. Peter's, Pikeland	114	Trinity, Harrisburg	131, 306
St. Peter's, Pine Grove	119	Trinity, Lancaster	201
St. Peter's, Riegelsville	184	Trinity, Londonderry	144
St. Stephen's, Lancaster	260	Trinity, Martin's Creek	236
Salem, Berrysburg	137	Trinity, Reading	159
Salem, Columbia	179	Trinity, Springfield	62
Salem, Killinger	136		
Salem, Kissel Hill	146	Uhlersville	189
Salem, Lebanon	165	Union, Durham	63
Salem, Lyons Charge	234	Union, Mohrsville	234
Salem's, Oberlin	126	Union, Nockamixon	65
Salem's, Pine Grove Charge	118	Union, Whitemarsh	66
Sand Hill	76	Union Deposit Charge	76
Sandy Hollow	76	Union Deposit Church	77
Schaefferstown Charge	52	Upper Dublin	69
Schaefferstown Church	55	Upper Milford	234
Schuylkill Haven, Jerusalem	220	Upper Mount Bethel	228
Schuylkill Haven, St. Matthew's	220	Upper Tinicum	65
Schuylkill Haven, St. Paul's	220	Upper Uwchlan	149
Schuylkill Haven, White Church	220	Uwchlan	150
Second Street, Columbia	179	Uwchlan, Upper	116, 149
Seventh Street, Lebanon	207	Vincent, Zion	148
Shenandoah	278	Vincent, West	116, 149
Shoop's Charge	122	Warwick	52
Shoop's Church	122	Wert's	136
Springfield	62	White Church, n'r Schuylkill Haven	220
Springtown Charge	62	Whitemarsh Charge	66
Springtown Church	64	Whitemarsh Church	66
Star of Bethlehem	136	Williamstown	253
Steelton, St. John's	266		
Steelton, St. Mark's	301	Zion, Dauphin	175
Steelton, St. Paul's	307	Zion, Harrisburg	127
Stewartsville, N. J.	197	Zion, Lebanon	165, 207
Stone Church, Christ's	228	Zion, Lykens	195
Stone Church, St. Paul's	228	Zion, Lionville	148
Strausstown	235	Zion, Mount, near Lebanon	209
Straw's, Fisherville Charge	135	Zion's, Ackermanville	238
Straw's, Greenwich, N. J.	104	Zion's, Ashland	211
		Zion's, East Petersburg	144
Tannersville	88	Zion's Hummelstown	72
Tinicum, Upper	65	Zion's, Manheim	110
Templeman Chapel	57	Zion's, Philadelphia	141
Tremont	192	Zion's, Vincent	148

CONSTITUTION

OF THE

EVANGELICAL LUTHERAN SYNOD

OF

EAST PENNSYLVANIA.

(Adopted at Lancaster, September, 1892.)

ARTICLE I.

NAME, ORGANIZATION AND MEETINGS.

SECTION 1. *Name.* The Name, Style and Title of this Synod shall be, "The Evangelical Lutheran Synod of East Pennsylvania." This Synod shall always be in connection with the General Synod of the Evangelical Lutheran Church in the United States.

SEC. 2. *Territory.* The territory of this Synod shall be defined in general terms as that part of South-eastern Pennsylvania between the Delaware and Susquehanna rivers.

SEC. 3. *Members.* This Synod shall consist of all the ordained ministers and licentiates submitting to this Constitution, together with the lay delegates from the pastorates within its bounds. Ministers in the general service of the church may likewise become members.

SEC. 4. *Congregations.* Any Evangelical Lutheran congregation may become connected with the Synod, if within its bounds, by acceding to the provisions of this Constitution. Isolated congregations outside of its territory may also be admitted by special action of the Synod.

SEC. 5. *Lay Delegates.* Each pastorate shall have the right to send one lay delegate to Synod. Any congregation or congregations not properly organized into a pastorate, or any congregation of a pastorate having any matter to present, may send a commissioner, who may be heard in behalf of said congregation, but shall have no vote.

SEC. 6. *Meetings.* The Synod shall meet annually at such time and place as may be determined, official notice thereof being given at least four weeks previous to the time appointed. Special meetings shall be called, when requested by one-fourth of the ordained ministers, at such time and place as the President may designate, notice thereof being given in the church papers at least three weeks previous, stating the object; and the business shall be confined to what is stated in the call.

SEC. 7. *Other Ministers.* Ministers from other Lutheran Synods may be invited to seats, but they shall have no vote. Their names, when thus invited, shall be entered on the Minutes. Ministers in good standing in other orthodox denominations may be introduced to Synod.

SEC. 8. *Quorum.* Two-fifths of the members of Synod shall constitute a quorum, provided that one-third of the ordained ministers of Synod be present.

SEC. 9. *Elections.* All elections shall be by ballot.

ARTICLE II.

DOCTRINAL BASIS.

The Doctrinal Basis shall be "the Word of God, as contained in the Canonical Scriptures of the Old and New Testaments, as the only infallible rule of faith and practice, and the Augsburg Confession as a correct exhibition of the fundamental doctrines of the Divine Word, and of the faith of our Church founded upon that Word."

ARTICLE III.

JURISDICTION.

SECTION 1. *Maintaining Order.* It shall be the duty of Synod to maintain order and good government among the churches within its bounds, and to this end it shall see that the rules of government and discipline prescribed in this Constitution and in the Formula of the General Synod are properly observed by the pastors and churches under its care.

SEC. 2. *Promotion of Piety.* It shall be the duty of Synod to devise and execute all suitable measures for the promotion of piety and the general prosperity of the Church, and to provide supplies for destitute congregations.

SEC. 3. *Forming Pastorates.* It shall have power to form and change pastorates, paying due regard to the rights and wishes of congregations. (See Art. VI.)

SEC. 4. *Exclusion.* It shall have power to exclude from Synodical fellowship any congregation obstinately refusing to comply with the regulations and decisions of Synod, and no congregation thus excluded shall be served by any minister belonging to Synod, except by special permission of Synod or of the President.

SEC. 5. *Appeals.* It shall receive appeals from the decisions of Church Councils and Conferences, when regularly brought before it, and shall review the proceedings and decisions to which they refer, and shall have full power to affirm or reverse the same, or to determine the questions presented thereby. Notice of such appeals must be given to the Council or Conference by the appellant, with the reasons in full, within three weeks after the time when the decision was rendered, and a full record of the case must be furnished the Synod by the Council or Conference. Upon the filing of such notice by the appellant, as above provided for, it shall be the duty of the Clerk or Secretary of such Church Council or Conference, within ten days thereafter, to make out a complete record of the case, with the findings thereon, and transmit it with the original papers to the Clerk or Secretary of the body to which such appeal may be taken.

SEC. 6. *Citing Witnesses.* It may cite church members to appear and give testimony, and may endeavor to obtain other witnesses if the case require it.

SEC. 7. *Charges against Ministers.* It shall have power to examine and decide all charges against ministers and licentiates, except such as may be otherwise specially provided for by this Constitution.

ARTICLE IV.

OFFICERS OF SYNOD.

SECTION 1. *Officers.* The officers of Synod shall be a President, Secretary and Treasurer, who shall be elected annually from among the ordained ministers, and who shall also be the officers of the Ministerium. The same persons shall not be eligible for more than three successive years.

SEC. 2. *President.* [1] He shall preside at all meetings of the Synod, decide questions of order, subject to an appeal, and discharge all the duties usually devolving on the presiding officer of such a body.

[2] He shall appoint all committees not specially named or elected by Synod.

[3] He shall, after the Synod is duly constituted by enrolling the names of the members, present a written report of all his official acts during the Synodical year, and may present such additional statements and recommendations, as in his judgment should claim the attention of Synod. The report shall be dealt with as other papers belonging to Synod.

[4] He shall deliver a discourse at the opening of each annual meeting of Synod, or appoint a substitute; and shall, in connection with the pastor of the church, have direction of the religious services during Synod, and the appointment of persons to preach; unless Synod shall appoint a special committee on religious services, of which he and the pastor shall be members.

[5] He shall give advice to members of Synod and congregations when requested, or when in his judgment such advice is needed.

[6] Should he become disqualified for the discharge of his duties, by removal from the Synodical bounds, resignation, sickness, death, or any cause, the Secretary shall succeed him and discharge the duties of the office until the next meeting of Synod.

[7] He shall, with the Secretary, subscribe all official documents of the Synod, and sign all orders on the Treasury.

[8] He shall perform the ceremony of ordination, assisted by the Secretary and Treasurer, and give to approved candidates letters of license, which, as well as certificates of ordination, he is to subscribe with his official signature.

[9] He has authority to refer the adjustment of all matters requiring his decision in congregations to their respective Conferences, or in their interim to the Presidents thereof. A report of the proceedings shall be made to him.

[10] He has authority to summon a meeting of the Church Council of any congregation or a congregational meeting, at the request of at least one-fourth of its electors, when the proper officers refuse to call it.

SEC. 3. *Secretary.* [1] He shall keep an accurate and faithful record of all the proceedings of Synod, carefully preserve all the papers, seal, etc., of the Synod, subject to its direction, and shall do all the official writing not otherwise provided for.

[2] He shall give notice (either by circular or in the church papers) of the time and place of the Synodical meeting, at least four weeks previous to the time appointed.

[3] He shall keep a register of the names of all the ministers and licentiates, arranged according to their age in office, and also of all the congregations.

[4] He shall receive all moneys, keep an account thereof and give receipts, pay over the same semi-monthly to the Treasurer and take his receipt therefor. He shall give a bond for the faithful performance of his duties, the cost of the same to be paid by the Synod.

[5] If the business should render it necessary, the President may appoint an Assistant Secretary, whose office shall expire at the close of the meeting of Synod.

[6] Should he become disqualified for the discharge of his duties, the President shall require all the property of Synod in his possession, to be delivered to him, and shall appoint a Secretary to act until the meeting of Synod.

SEC. 4. *Treasurer.* [1] He shall receive from the Secretary all moneys, and hold them, together with all bonds, certificates and documents, subject to the order of the Synod.

[2] He shall keep, and present at each annual meeting of Synod, a detailed and faithful account of the state of the Treasury. He shall give a bond for the faithful performance of the duties of his office, the cost of the same to be paid by the Synod.

[3] Should he become disqualified for the discharge of his duties, the President shall take charge of all the moneys, certificates, bonds, etc., belonging to Synod, and retain them until a Treasurer is elected at the next meeting of Synod.

SEC. 5. In the interim of the meetings of Synod, the administration of its affairs shall be entrusted to its officers, whose action shall be authoritative and binding upon all parties owing allegiance thereto, subject, however, to appeal at the next ensuing meeting of Synod.

ARTICLE V.

MINISTERS.

SECTION 1. *Pastoral Interference.* No minister or licentiate shall preach or perform other ministerial acts in the pastorate of another except by his consent, or, in his absence, by that of the Church Council.

SEC. 2. *Dismission.* Any minister or licentiate, in good standing, who removes into the bounds of another Synod, shall, on application to the President, receive a certificate of honorable dismission, and such a certificate shall be required by the Synod of those applying for admission into it.

SEC. 3. *Admission.* Any minister or licentiate of any Synod belonging to the General Synod, called to any of our churches, shall present to our President a letter of honorable dismission within one month from the date of taking charge: and upon so doing shall be regarded as a member of this body and under its jurisdiction. In the case of a licentiate, his ordination shall be performed by this Synod, unless for satisfactory reasons the President shall determine otherwise.

SEC. 4. *Reception of Ministers from other Ecclesiastical Bodies.* Ministers from other ecclesiastical bodies can only be received by a two-thirds vote of the Ministerium, upon recommendation of the Examining Committee, and by publicly subscribing to the doctrinal basis of the Synod.

SEC. 5. *Notice to the President.* Any minister resigning or accepting a pastorate shall give due notice thereof to the President.

ARTICLE VI.

CONGREGATIONS AND PASTORATES.

SECTION 1. The Council of a congregation, or the Joint Council of a charge, may consider and act on the resignation of a pastor.

SEC. 2. A pastor cannot resign a portion of his pastorate and continue to serve the remaining part, without consent of the Joint Council and the approval of the President of Synod.

SEC. 3. No congregation or congregations shall withdraw from the pastorate with which it is connected, without the consent of the Joint Council and the approval of the President of Synod.

SEC. 4. If any members of the congregation desire for good cause to organize themselves into a new congregation, they must first be dismissed for that purpose, and any organization formed without such dismission shall be regarded irregular, and any minister of the General Synod participating in such organization shall make himself liable to charges.

SEC. 5. No congregation shall make any enactments in conflict with this Constitution or with the Formula of Government.

SEC. 6. Any vacant congregation in arrears to a former pastor shall be required to make satisfactory adjustment thereof before calling a successor.

SEC. 7. Vacant congregations shall report to the President of Synod at once, and are requested to confer with him with a view to being supplied with a pastor as soon as possible.

ARTICLE VII.
EDUCATION.

SECTION. 1. *Education Committee.* There shall be an Education Committee of five, at least three of whom shall be ordained ministers, to which all applications for beneficiary aid shall be made, and who shall obtain from the instructors of beneficiaries the official report annually of their scholarship and deportment, and who shall make a detailed statement to the Synod annually.

SEC. 2. *Qualifications of Applicants.* The applicant shall have been a member of the Lutheran Church for at least one year, and must be qualified to enter the Freshman class in Pennsylvania College. He shall, if deemed necessary, submit to a physical examination, and give evidence of industry, intellectual endowment, piety, and a call to the ministry.

SEC. 3. *Obligations.* Every beneficiary shall be required to take a full course in college and seminary, unless otherwise permitted by Synod, or by consent of the Committee. He shall be required to give promissory notes to the Treasurer of Synod for the amounts received by him, which notes shall be canceled when he shall have been in the ministry three years, provided he is in connection with some Synod belonging to the General Synod.

ARTICLE VIII.
DELEGATES.

SECTION 1. *Delegates to General Synod.* In the election of delegates to the General Synod, principals shall be first balloted for, and afterward alternates; and after the second ballot the persons having the lowest number of votes shall be dropped. No clerical member shall be eligible more than twice in succession, unless he be President or Secretary of the General Synod. When a delegate-elect shall remove beyond the bounds of the Synod, before the meeting of the General Synod, he shall not be entitled to represent the Synod, provided always, that ministers in the general service of the Church shall be exempt from this rule.

SEC. 2. *Directors of the Theological Seminary.* This Synod shall elect the required number of Directors of the Theological Seminary at Gettysburg, for a term of five years, who are expected to be constant and faithful in attendance upon the meetings of the Board.

ARTICLE IX.
CONFERENCES.

SECTION 1. The Synod shall divide itself into Conference Districts for the purpose of holding Conference meetings.

SEC. 2. The chief object of such meetings shall be the preaching of the Word, mutual consultation and encouragement in the work of the Lord, the promotion of the cause of religion among the churches represented, and the fuller development of the possibilities of the district.

SEC. 3. Conferences shall be entrusted with the organization of new churches, the supply of vacant congregations with preaching, the formation and maintenance of pastorates.

SEC. 4. The records of the proceedings of Conferences shall be submitted to Synod for examination and review, and an abstract thereof read by their Secretaries at the meeting of Synod.

ARTICLE X.
PROCESS AGAINST A MINISTER.

SECTION 1. As the honor and success of the Gospel depend very much on the character of its ministers, Synod ought to guard with the utmost care and impartiality the conduct of its members.

SEC. 2. All Christians should be very cautious in giving credit or circulation to an evil report of any member of the church, and especially of a minister of the Gospel. If any member knows a minister to be guilty of a private censurable fault, he should warn him in private; if this prove fruitless, he should apply to the Church Council, who shall proceed as specified in Chap. III., Sec. 5, of Formula of Government.

SEC. 3. If accusation be lodged, according to Chap. III., Sec. 5, with the President within two months of the next Synodical meeting, he shall defer the matter to said meeting; yet, if the charge be one of gross immorality, or circulating fundamental error in doctrine, he shall immediately direct the accused to suspend all his ministerial duties until his case is decided. If such accusation be lodged with the President at an earlier date, he shall, if the charge be one of gross immorality, or circulating fundamental error in doctrine, immediately appoint a committee of five ordained ministers of the Synod, to meet without unnecessary delay at a suitable place, and institute a formal investigation of the case, according to the principles of the Formula. The chairman of the committee shall give at least ten days' notice of the time and place of meeting to all parties concerned.

SEC. 4. The President may, at his discretion, intrust the matter to Conference, and notify the members to meet and proceed as above.

SEC. 5. Any three members of the committee, or a majority of the Conference thus meeting, shall have power to proceed and hold a fair and impartial investigation of the case, and to take all such necessary measures as may be just and proper to determine the guilt or innocence of the accused.

SEC. 6. If the accused confess, and the matter be such as gross immorality, or circulating fundamental error, he shall be immediately suspended from the exercise of the office until the meeting of Synod.

SEC. 7. If a minister accused of gross offences, being duly notified, refuses to attend the investigation, he shall be immediately suspended from office.

SEC. 8. If the accused deny the charge, and yet, on examination of the evidence, be found guilty, the committee or Conference shall nevertheless proceed to pass sentence on him.

SEC. 9. The highest punishment which can be inflicted by a committee or special Conference, appointed as above specified, is suspension from clerical functions; and this sentence is to be reported at the next meeting of the Synod, and remain in force until reversed by the Synod.

SEC. 10. Any minister intending to appeal from the decision of a committee or Conference, shall give notice to the chairman of the committee or Conference, within three weeks after the decision was made, that both parties may be prepared for a new trial.

SEC. 11. Conferences, not specially convened for the purpose, may attend to any charges of importance against a minister within their bounds, if all the parties concerned are prepared and willing to proceed.

SEC. 12. If at any time the accusation be lodged with the President, according to Chap. III., Sec. 5, for a less offence than those specified in Sec. 3 of this Article, he shall take no other steps in the case than to exhort accused and accusers to mutual forbearance, and to refer them to the next Synod.

SEC. 13. If accusation against a minister, present or absent, be made immediately to the Synod, and the Synod believe itself in possession of all the evidence necessary to a just decision, the case may be immediately examined and sentence passed, provided the accused shall have had fifteen days' notice, together with a written specification of the charges brought against him. But if the necessary evidence be not before Synod, and the offense be such as specified in Sec. 3, it shall be intrusted to a committee or Conference, to proceed as above specified.

SEC. 14. If a minister be found guilty of gross immorality or circulating fundamental error in doctrine, his sentence of suspension shall not be removed until he shall give satisfactory evidence of penitence and reformation, and his restoration shall be by the same judicatory which suspended him, or at its recommendation.

SEC. 15. If the common report of a minister's guilt of any of the charges above specified be such as seriously to injure the cause of religion, and his own church do not proceed against him, it shall be the duty of any other minister or layman, having obtained signatures of two other credible men, to report the case to the President.

ARTICLE XI.

MINISTERIUM.

SECTION 1. The Ministerium is composed of the ordained ministers of Synod.

SEC. 2. Licensed candidates may be present, unless requested to withdraw, and may take part in the discussions, but have no vote.

SEC. 3. The Ministerium shall be the proper body, by whom all charges of heresy against a minister are to be examined and decided; as also all appeals from the decision of a church council on a charge of heresy against a layman, or from the decision of a special Conference on a similar charge against a minister.

Sec. 4. When ordained ministers of other religious denominations make application for admission into connection with the Synod, the Ministerium shall be the body to decide on the case.

Sec. 5. A two-thirds vote of the ordained ministers present shall be required for the licensure of an applicant, the renewal of his license, the ordination of a licensed candidate, or for the admission of an ordained minister of another denomination.

Sec. 6. All business not specifically entrusted to the Ministerium in this Constitution, shall belong to the Synod.

Sec. 7. The order of business of the Ministerium may be as follows:
  (1) Opening with prayer.
  (2) Communication by the President of any business he may have to report.
  (3) Presentation of names of applicants for Licensure.
  (4) Presentation of applications for Ordination.
  (5) Presentation of applications for admission of ministers from other denominations.
  (6) Reports of Examining or other Committees appointed by the Ministerium.
  (7) Promiscuous business relating to the ministry.
  (8) Closing with prayer.

ARTICLE XII.

LICENSURE AND LICENTIATES.

Section 1. All applications for licensure must be made to the President of Synod.

Sec. 2. Applicants must appear before the Examining Committee, which must always be composed of ordained ministers, and, upon satisfactory evidence of fitness by testimonials from the Faculty of a Lutheran Theological Seminary of the General Synod, may be recommended to the Ministerium for licensure without further examination. Cases not covered by the foregoing rule must be referred by the President to the Ministerium for special action.

Sec. 3. A licentiate shall have power to perform all ministerial acts during the time specified in his license.

Sec. 4. A licentiate shall have the same rights and privileges in Synod as ordained ministers, except to hold office.

Sec. 5. A licentiate before accepting a call must obtain the consent of the President of Synod.

SEC. 6. A licentiate, after he has taken a charge, shall not leave it without the sanction of the Synod, or of the President.

SEC. 7. All licenses shall extend to the time of the next annual meeting of the Ministerium.

SEC. 8. Every licentiate must keep a journal of his ministerial acts, which, with a few sermons and his certificate of licensure, he must deliver to the President annually at the opening of Synod for the inspection of the Ministerium.

ARTICLE XIII.

ORDINATION.

SECTION 1. All applicants for ordination must appear before the Examining Committee and submit to a thorough examination in at least the following subjects: Personal Piety, and the motives of the applicant for seeking the holy office, Hebrew, New Testament Greek, English Bible, the Evidences of Christianity, Natural and Revealed Theology, Church History, the Augsburg Confession, Pastoral Theology, Homiletics and Church Government, and shall be recommended to the Synod for ordination upon favorable report of the Committee and by a two-thirds vote of the Ministerium.

SEC. 2. Whenever the Synod has decided that an individual shall be ordained, the ceremony may be performed either at the meeting of Synod, or, if preferred, in the church by which he has been called, by the special Conference, or by a Committee appointed for the purpose by the President of Synod.

ARTICLE XIV.

INSTALLATION.

SECTION 1. When a minister is ordained in his own church, his installation, according to the usual form, should take place at the same service.

SEC. 2. Any minister called to labor in any of the congregations of this Synod, and duly accredited according to Sec. 3, Art. V., may at any time after the presentation and acceptance of his credentials be installed as pastor by a committee appointed by the President.

ARTICLE XV.

AMENDMENTS.

This Constitution may be altered or amended by a two-thirds vote of the Synod, provided notice has been given one year previous.

ARTICLE XVI.

ORDER OF BUSINESS.

I. General Order.

1. Opening Prayer.
2. Calling of the Roll.
3. Reading of the Minutes.
4. Unfinished Business.

5. Reports.
6. New Business.
7. Closing Prayer.

II. Special Order.

1. Wednesday evening—Opening Sermon and Synodical Communion.
2. Thursday, 9 a. m.—Opening of Synod, with Singing, Reading of Scriptures and Prayer. Calling the Roll. Presentation of Certificates by Lay Delegates. Presentation of Credentials by Commissioners. Reception of New Members. President's Report. Election of Officers. Rules of Order. Annual Reports of Conference Secretaries.
3. Thursday, p. m.—Appointment of Committees. Admission of Applicants for Licensure and Ordination. Vacant for Committee Work.
4. Thursday evening—Sermon. Church Extension.
5. Friday, a. m.—Report of Treasurer. Education.
6. Friday, p. m.—Theological and Literary Institutions. Vacant for Committee Work after 3.30.
7. Friday evening—Sermon. Education.
8. Saturday, a. m.—Parochial Reports.
9. Saturday, p. m.—Publication. Systematic Benevolence. Meeting of Ministerium.
10. Saturday evening—Religious Services.
11. Sunday, a. m.—Preaching.
12. Sunday, p. m.—Sunday-school Service.
13. Sunday evening—Sermon.
14. Monday, a. m.—Home Missions. Church Extension. Vacant Congregations.
15. Monday, p. m.—Foreign Missions. Orphans' Home.
16. Monday evening—Sermons. Missions.
17. Tuesday, a. m.—Sunday-schools.
18. Tuesday, p. m.—Ministerium. Appointment of Speakers.
19. Tuesday evening—Licensure and Ordination.